D0745062

CQ GUIDE TO

CURRENT AMERICAN GOVERNMENT

Fall 2001

CQ PRESS

A Division of Congressional Quarterly Inc.

Washington, D.C.

Congressional Quarterly Inc.

Congressional Quarterly Inc., an editorial research service and publishing company, serves clients in the fields of news, education, business, and government. It combines the specific coverage of Congress, government, and politics contained in the *CQ Weekly* with the more general subject range of an affiliated service, the *CQ Researcher*.

Under the CQ Press imprint, Congressional Quarterly also publishes college political science textbooks and public affairs paperbacks on developing issues and events, information directories and reference books on the federal government, national elections and politics. Titles include the *Guide to the Presidency*, the *Guide to Congress*, the *Guide to the U.S. Supreme Court*, the *Guide to U.S. Elections* and *Politics in America*. CQ's A-Z collection is a reference series that provides essential information about American government and the electoral process. The *CQ Almanac*, a compendium of legislation for one session of Congress, is published each year. *Congress and the Nation*, a record of government for a presidential term, is published every four years.

CQ publishes the *Daily Monitor*, a report on the current and future activities of congressional committees. An online information system, CQ.com on Congress, provides immediate access to CQ's databases of legislative action, votes, schedules, profiles and analyses. Visit www.cq.com for more information.

CQ Press
A Division of Congressional Quarterly Inc.
1255 22nd St. N.W., Suite 400
Washington, DC 20037
(202) 822-1475; (800) 638-1710

www.cqpress.com

Printed in the United States of America
05 04 03 02 01   5 4 3 2 1

♾ The paper used in this publication meets the minimum requirements of the American National Standard for Information Sciences—Permanence of Paper for Printed Library Materials, ANSI Z39.48-1992.

ISSN 0196-612-X
ISBN 1-56802-607-2

Contents

Contents

Introduction

Congressional Quarterly's *Guide to Current American Government* is a collection of articles selected from the *CQ Weekly* magazine, a trusted source for in-depth, nonpartisan reporting and analyses of congressional action, presidential activities, policy debates and other news and developments in Washington. The articles in this book, which have been chosen and arranged to complement American government textbooks, are organized into four sections: Foundations of American Government, Political Participation, Government Institutions and Politics and Public Policy.

Foundations of American Government. This section examines issues and events that involve interpretation of the U.S. Constitution. Its focus in this edition of the *Guide* is the 2000 presidential election crisis—specifically, the controversial December 12 Supreme Court ruling that decided the election in favor of George W. Bush.

Political Participation. This section explores current issues in electoral and party politics. It includes reports on the election reform movement spawned by the Florida punch card debacle, the campaign finance reform debate, Sen. James M. Jeffords' decision to leave the Republican Party and the preparations by the national parties for the decennial redistricting process.

Government Institutions. This portion of the *Guide* looks at the inner workings of the major institutions of American government. Aspects of the Congress, the judiciary, the presidency and the bureaucracy are discussed in turn. Particular emphasis is given to the Jeffords party switch and the consequent leadership upheaval in the Senate.

Politics and Public Policy. This section provides in-depth coverage of major social policy issues, including tax cuts, education overhaul, the next wave of welfare reform, the energy crisis and consumer privacy online and in medical and financial record keeping.

Guide to Current American Government reprints articles largely unchanged from their original appearance in the *CQ Weekly*. The date of original publication is provided with each article to give readers a time frame for the events described. Page number references to related and background articles in the *CQ Weekly* and the *CQ Almanac* (available at many school and public libraries) are provided to facilitate additional research.

Foundations of American Government

This section focuses on the unprecedented involvement of the U.S. Supreme Court in the presidential election of 2000. Voting problems and ballot irregularities in the state of Florida—where George W. Bush led Al Gore by the narrowest of vote margins—triggered weeks of confusion over who had won that state's 25 electoral votes to capture the presidency. In the end, after five weeks of vote recounts and legal challenges, the Supreme Court ruled that the manual recounts of disputed ballots in certain Florida counties violated voters' constitutional right to equal protection and due process. The controversial December 12 decision, handed down by a sharply divided Court, effectively decided the election in George W. Bush's favor and provoked heated debate over whether the Court had done the right thing.

The first article in this section examines the reaction to the Court's ruling in *Bush v. Gore*. Also discussed are the election reform proposals that emerged in the wake of election 2000. The second selection is the text of the Court's December 12 order.

Facing the Judgment of History

Supreme Court takes a rare and controversial hand in the electoral process

When the Supreme Court made its historic decision to hear the case of a disputed presidential election, many thought the high court would play a mostly symbolic role.

Traditionally, the court has viewed political contests as a thicket best left to the elected branches of government.

But with its Dec. 12 opinion, the Supreme Court's involvement was anything but symbolic. The ruling essentially decided the 2000 presidential election in favor of Texas Gov. George W. Bush, and in doing so split the court along ideological lines while possibly opening a Pandora's box in election law.

The court found that Florida's hand counting of votes violated the Constitution because it did not treat all votes equally. This was the first time the court applied the constitutional right to equal protection to an election contest, and many observers believe it will lead the court to be more involved in elections.

"Once let loose, it's not easily cabined," said A.E. Dick Howard, a University of Virginia law professor. "Lawyers love to imitate a successful theory, and they will look at this and say, 'Aha!'"

The decision also seems likely to justify a flurry of new bills aimed at improving, and imposing uniformity on, methods of voting across the country. Already, several bipartisan measures have been introduced in Congress, and the issue could be something the two parties can agree to address early in the 107th Congress. *(Bills, p. 3)*

The court's holding that the recount violated the Constitution was 7-2, but a narrow 5-4 majority also found that it was too late to improve the hand counting and stopped any further action in Florida. That decision cemented the vote total certified on Nov. 26,

Demonstrators outside the U.S. Supreme Court building await the Court's decision in *Bush v. Gore.*

which had the Republican Bush beating Democrat Vice President Al Gore by 537 votes.

Gore acknowledged the finality of the decision and the authority of the court by formally conceding the election to Bush on Dec. 13.

Scathing Dissents

The court's decision, which was unsigned, came less than two days after lawyers for Bush and Gore pleaded their case to the justices. Six opinions were issued as part of the ruling, including four scathing dissents that warned of the damage the court may suffer by getting so involved in choosing the winner of a presidential election.

Justice John Paul Stevens feared that the vitriolic attacks on judges by the Bush campaign, which came after adverse opinions in lower courts, could undermine confidence in the justice system.

"It is confidence in the men and women who administer the judicial sys-

tem that is the true backbone of the rule of law," he wrote. "Time will one day heal the wound to that confidence that will be inflicted by today's decision. . . . Although we may never know with complete certainty the identity of the winner of this year's Presidential election, the identity of the loser is perfectly clear. It is the Nation's confidence in the judge as an impartial guardian of the rule of law."

Early reaction from court watchers seemed to agree.

"I think that this court will go down in history as the Supreme Court that stopped the counting of votes in a presidential election," said DePaul University law professor Jeffrey Shaman.

"The court did tremendous damage to itself," added Drake University government professor Dennis J. Goldford. "A lot of people will see this as an attempt to stretch and cover Bush's case."

Others said the court did what was necessary in a difficult situation. "The U.S. Supreme Court's decision reflects a proper and prudent enforcement of the Constitution," said House Majority Whip Tom DeLay, R-Texas.

Howard, the Virginia law professor, said the decision was a "reminder of how self-confident the court is."

He said the decision also shows the increasing weakness of what legal scholars call the political question doctrine — an unwritten maxim of the last 170 years that courts don't answer questions political institutions can resolve. "The notion of judicial restraint seems a bit quaint," he said.

A significant majority of the court, seven justices, found that the Dec. 8 plan ordered by the Florida Supreme Court requiring the hand count of all the state's "undervotes" violated the 14th Amendment.

The court ruled that because different standards were being applied to evaluating ballots for which machines could not discern a vote, the

Election Overhaul Proposals Spring Up

The voting problems in Florida that triggered weeks of confusion over the winner of the presidential election also led some members of Congress to propose legislation that would change election systems or initiate studies on ways to improve them.

Those efforts may have received a boost from the Supreme Court decision Dec. 12 that finally ended the recount dispute in Florida. Though the court is typically loath to tell Congress what to do, it suggested that better voting systems may reduce election lawsuits in the future.

"This case has shown that punch-card balloting machines can produce an unfortunate number of ballots which are not punched in a clean, complete way by the voter. After the current counting, it is likely legislative bodies nationwide will examine ways to improve the mechanisms and machinery for voting," the majority opinion said.

Members began introducing bills in both the House and the Senate just after the Nov. 7 election.

On Dec. 14, Speaker J. Dennis Hastert, R-Ill., told reporters Congress should explore ways to improve the electoral process, though he gave no specifics.

Senate Judiciary Committee Chairman Orrin G. Hatch, R-Utah, has said his panel will hold hearings on the topic. Sens. Mitch McConnell, R-Ky., chairman of the Senate Rules and Administration Committee, and panel member Robert G. Torricelli, D-N.J., plan to offer legislation to address a wide variety of election concerns.

Bills already introduced include:
- **S 3273**. By Sen. Charles E. Schumer, D-N.Y., who is a member of the Rules Committee and Judiciary Committee, the bill would require the Federal Election Commission to study electoral changes and award grants to states to improve voting

procedures.
- **HR 5653**. By Rep. Asa Hutchinson, R-Ark., the measure would authorize $325 million in grants through the U.S. Department of Justice to state and local governments for voting process improvements.
- **HR 5631**. By Rep. Peter A. DeFazio, D-Ore., the bill would establish a Federal Elections Review Commission. Nick Lampson, D-Texas, has introduced a similar bill (HR 5647).
- **S 3269**. By Sen. Arlen Specter, R-Pa., a senior member of the Judiciary Committee, the measure would create a Commission on the Comprehensive Study of Voting Procedures. Marcy Kaptur, D-Ohio, introduced the companion bill (HR 5645) in the House.
- **HR 5643**. By Rep. Spencer Bachus, R-Ala., the bill would clarify the authority of the General Services Administration to assist presidents-elect.

plan violated the portion of the amendment which prohibits states from denying "to any person within its jurisdiction the equal protection of the laws."

At issue was how election officials counted ballots where the hole for the candidate was not completely punched through and the machine did not detect a vote for president. Sometimes, part of the paper came out, other times, there was just an indent or "dimple."

The Florida Supreme Court had instructed the county canvassing boards to try to discern the "intent" of the voters on those ballots, but the state court offered no uniform standard by which the county boards should evaluate each ballot.

"The formulation of uniform rules to determine intent based on these re-occurring circumstances is practicable, and, we conclude, necessary," the Supreme Court said. "The search for intent can be confined by specific rules designed to ensure uniform treatment. The want of those rules here has led to unequal evaluation of ballots in various respects."

That led the court majority to the conclusion that, practically speaking, a recount was impossible. "Upon due consideration of the difficulties identified to this point, it is obvious that the recount cannot be conducted in compliance with the requirements of equal protection and due process without substantial additional work."

It was the first time the equal protection clause, which has largely been used to defend the rights of minorities in civil rights cases, had been applied by the high court to an election outcome.

"What the court has done here is constitutionalized an area," said Shaman.

The court, knowing it opened a new area of the law for election challenges, tried in its opinion to minimize the impact of the decision.

"Our consideration is limited to the present circumstances, for the problem of equal protection in election processes generally presents many complexities," the majority opinion said.

"It's like they took a walk on the wild side and are now going to go back

to a safe tea room," Goldford said.

Scholars disagree on whether the court can actually make that retreat.

Additional Opinions

In a separate, concurring opinion, the court's three most conservative members said they also thought the Florida Court had gone beyond the bounds of judicial interpretation and rewritten Florida law.

Chief Justice William H. Rehnquist wrote the brief, which also was signed by Justices Antonin Scalia and Clarence Thomas. Justices Sandra Day O'Connor and Anthony M. Kennedy had joined the three in the majority opinion, but not in the conclusions of the Rehnquist decision.

Rehnquist concluded that "the Florida Supreme Court's interpretation of the Florida election laws impermissibly distorted them beyond what a fair reading required, in violation of Article II." Article II of the Constitution grants to state legislatures the authority to set up the process to pick electors for the presidential election.

Each of the four justices who

3

Five Weeks of Challenges

Nov. 7, Election Day
• Television networks project Al Gore the victor in Florida, then retract and, early on the morning of Nov. 8, project a George W. Bush victory.

Nov. 11
• Bush's attorneys file lawsuit in U.S. District Court to block Gore's request for manual recounts.

Nov. 13
• Miami federal judge rejects Bush's request to bar hand recounts.

Nov. 17
• Florida Supreme Court prohibits Secretary of State Katherine Harris from certifying results, as she had planned to do on Nov. 18, until further notice.
• Federal appeals court in Atlanta refuses Bush's appeal of the Miami judge's decision not to block manual recounts in Broward and Palm Beach counties.

Nov. 21
• Florida Supreme Court rules manual recounts may continue and that those votes must be included in the state's final tally. The court sets a deadline for certifying the election on Nov. 26, a Sunday, or early Nov. 27.

Nov. 24
• U.S. Supreme Court agrees to hear Bush's appeal on constitutionality of Florida Supreme Court decision to allow recounts and extend the state deadline for certification.

Nov. 26
• Palm Beach misses 5 p.m. deadline by 90 minutes. Harris refuses to accept additional votes, certifies Bush the winner of Florida by 537 votes.

Nov. 27
• Gore contests results from Miami-Dade, Nassau and Palm Beach counties in Leon County Circuit Court, where Florida's capital is located.

Nov. 28
• Gore and Bush file briefs with U.S. Supreme Court.

Dec. 1
• U.S. Supreme Court hears arguments on Bush's appeal regarding recount deadline.
• Florida Supreme Court refuses Gore's appeal to immediately begin recount in his election challenge.

Dec. 2-3
• Trial is held on Gore's election challenge before Leon County Circuit Judge N. Sanders Sauls.

Dec. 4
• Unanimous U.S. Supreme Court sends case back to Florida Supreme Court, requesting a better explanation for decision to extend recount deadlines.
• Sauls rejects Gore's election challenge.

Dec. 5
• 11th Circuit U.S. Court of Appeals in Atlanta holds hearing on Bush's request to stop manual recounts, which earlier was rejected by U.S. District Court.

Dec. 7
• Florida Supreme Court hears Gore appeal of Sauls' decision to reject the election challenge.

Dec. 8
• By 4-3, Florida Supreme Court orders manual counts of undervotes in all Florida counties and adds 383 votes to Gore's total.
• Bush campaign appeals to 11th U.S. Circuit Court of Appeals and U.S. Supreme Court to halt manual recounts.

Dec. 9
• Hand counts resume in morning.
• Federal appeals court refuses to take up case.
• U.S. Supreme Court rules 5-4 to halt recounts and sets Dec. 11 for arguments. Hand counts cease.

Dec. 11
• Lawyers for Bush and Gore argue before U.S. Supreme Court.

Dec. 12
• At 10 p.m., U.S. Supreme Court rules 5-4 that Florida Supreme Court violated Constitution, and overturns its Dec. 8 order. High court determines there is not enough time for state to set a standard for counting questionable ballots, resume hand count, and complete it because federal law says Dec. 12 is last day state electors can be chosen and still be safe from challenge in Congress.

dissented from the majority decision that ended the election by declaring that time had expired on efforts to find a uniform standard on recounts, penned an opinion in bitter opposition.

Stevens, the oldest member of the Supreme Court, said the equal protection concerns were lessened because a district court judge oversaw the process.

He implied that the majority's decision could open a flood of legal action in political contests because about 33 states use the same kind of subjective standard as Florida's intent of the voter when evaluating disputed ballots.

Justice David H. Souter and Justice Stephen G. Breyer joined the court's majority in finding that the hand recount posed equal protection problems. But, they said, that did not mean Gore's challenge should be thrown out.

"To recount those [votes] manually would be a tall order, but before this Court stayed the effort to do that, the courts of Florida were ready to do their best to get their job done. There is no justification for denying the State the opportunity to try to count all the disputed ballots now," wrote Souter, who was appointed to the court by President George Bush in 1990.

Justice Ruth Bader Ginsburg focused on the deference usually granted to state court interpretations of state law. "I would have thought the 'cautious approach' we counsel when federal courts address matters of state law. . . and our commitment to 'build[ing] cooperative judicial federalism' . . . demanded greater restraint."

Breyer argued that the decision would set the court down the path of facing more such troubling political questions. "Of course, the selection of the president is of fundamental national importance. But that importance is political, not legal. And this court should resist the temptation unnecessarily to resolve tangential legal disputes, where doing so threatens to determine the outcome of the election." ◆

High Court Ends Presidential Vote Recount, Citing Equal Protection, Due Process

Following is the text of the U.S. Supreme Court's Dec. 12 order in the case contesting Florida's recount of disputed ballots for president.

SUPREME COURT OF THE UNITED STATES
No. 00-949
GEORGE W. BUSH, ET AL., PETITIONERS v. ALBERT GORE JR., ET AL.
ON WRIT OF CERTIORARI TO THE FLORIDA SUPREME COURT
[December 12, 2000]
PER CURIAM.

I

On December 8, 2000, the Supreme Court of Florida ordered that the Circuit Court of Leon County tabulate by hand 9,000 ballots in Miami-Dade County. It also ordered the inclusion in the certified vote totals of 215 votes identified in Palm Beach County and 168 votes identified in Miami-Dade County for Vice President Albert Gore Jr., and Senator Joseph Lieberman, Democratic candidates for President and Vice President. The Supreme Court noted that petitioner, Governor George W. Bush asserted that the net gain for Vice President Gore in Palm Beach County was 176 votes, and directed the Circuit Court to resolve that dispute on remand. The court further held that relief would require manual recounts in all Florida counties where so-called "undervotes" had not been subject to manual tabulation. The court ordered all manual recounts to begin at once. Governor Bush and Richard Cheney, Republican candidates for the Presidency and Vice Presidency, filed an emergency application for a stay of this mandate. On December 9, we granted the application, treated the application as a petition for a writ of certiorari, and granted certiorari.

The proceedings leading to the present controversy are discussed in some detail in our opinion in *Bush v. Palm Beach County Canvassing Bd. (Bush I).* On November 8, 2000, the day following the Presidential election, the Florida Division of Elections reported that

petitioner, Governor Bush, had received 2,909,135 votes, and respondent, Vice President Gore, had received 2,907,351 votes, a margin of 1,784 for Governor Bush. Because Governor Bush's margin of victory was less than "one-half of a percent . . . of the votes cast," an automatic machine recount was conducted under §102.141(4) of the election code, the results of which showed Governor Bush still winning the race but by a diminished margin. Vice President Gore then sought manual recounts in Volusia, Palm Beach, Broward, and Miami-Dade Counties, pursuant to Florida's election protest provisions. Fla. Stat. §102.166 (2000). A dispute arose concerning the deadline for local county canvassing boards to submit their returns to the Secretary of State. The Secretary declined to waive the November 14 deadline imposed by statute. §§102.111, 102.112. The Florida Supreme Court, however, set the deadline at November 26. We granted certiorari and vacated the Florida Supreme Court's decision, finding considerable uncertainty as to the grounds on which it was based. On December 11, the Florida Supreme Court issued a decision on remand reinstating that date.

On November 26, the Florida Elections Canvassing Commission certified the results of the election and declared Governor Bush the winner of Florida's 25 electoral votes. On November 27, Vice President Gore, pursuant to Florida's contest provisions, filed a complaint in Leon County Circuit Court contesting the certification. Fla. Stat. §102.168 (2000). He sought relief pursuant to §102.168(3)(c), which provides that "[r]eceipt of a number of illegal votes or rejection of a number of legal votes sufficient to change or place in doubt the result of the election" shall be grounds for a contest. The Circuit Court denied relief, stating that Vice President Gore failed to meet his burden of proof. He appealed to the First District Court of Appeal, which certified the matter to the Florida Supreme Court.

Accepting jurisdiction, the Florida Supreme Court affirmed in part and reversed in part. *Gore v. Harris* (2000). The court held that the Circuit Court

had been correct to reject Vice President Gore's challenge to the results certified in Nassau County and his challenge to the Palm Beach County Canvassing Board's determination that 3,300 ballots cast in that county were not, in the statutory phrase, "legal votes."

The Supreme Court held that Vice President Gore had satisfied his burden of proof under §102.168(3)(c) with respect to his challenge to Miami-Dade County's failure to tabulate, by manual count, 9,000 ballots on which the machines had failed to detect a vote for President ("undervotes"). Noting the closeness of the election, the Court explained that "[o]n this record, there can be no question that there are legal votes within the 9,000 uncounted votes sufficient to place the results of this election in doubt." A "legal vote," as determined by the Supreme Court, is "one in which there is a 'clear indication of the intent of the voter.' " The court therefore ordered a hand recount of the 9,000 ballots in Miami-Dade County. Observing that the contest provisions vest broad discretion in the circuit judge to "provide any relief appropriate under such circumstances," Fla. Stat. §102.168(8) (2000), the Supreme Court further held that the Circuit Court could order "the Supervisor of Elections and the Canvassing Boards, as well as the necessary public officials, in all counties that have not conducted a manual recount or tabulation of the undervotes . . . to do so forthwith, said tabulation to take place in the individual counties where the ballots are located."

The Supreme Court also determined that both Palm Beach County and Miami-Dade County, in their earlier manual recounts, had identified a net gain of 215 and 168 legal votes for Vice President Gore. Rejecting the Circuit Court's conclusion that Palm Beach County lacked the authority to include the 215 net votes submitted past the November 26 deadline, the Supreme Court explained that the deadline was not intended to exclude votes identified after that date through ongoing manual recounts. As to Miami-Dade County, the Court concluded

5

that although the 168 votes identified were the result of a partial recount, they were "legal votes [that] could change the outcome of the election." The Supreme Court therefore directed the Circuit Court to include those totals in the certified results, subject to resolution of the actual vote total from the Miami-Dade partial recount.

The petition presents the following questions: whether the Florida Supreme Court established new standards for resolving Presidential election contests, thereby violating Art. II, §1, cl. 2, of the United States Constitution and failing to comply with 3 U.S.C. §5, and whether the use of standardless manual recounts violates the Equal Protection and Due Process Clauses. With respect to the equal protection question, we find a violation of the Equal Protection Clause.

II

A. The closeness of this election, and the multitude of legal challenges which have followed in its wake, have brought into sharp focus a common, if heretofore unnoticed, phenomenon. Nationwide statistics reveal that an estimated 2 percent of ballots cast do not register a vote for President for whatever reason, including deliberately choosing no candidate at all or some voter error, such as voting for two candidates or insufficiently marking a ballot. See Ho, More Than 2M Ballots Uncounted, AP Online (Nov. 28, 2000); Kelley, Balloting Problems Not Rare But Only In A Very Close Election Do Mistakes And Mismarking Make A Difference, Omaha World-Herald (Nov. 15, 2000). In certifying election results, the votes eligible for inclusion in the certification are the votes meeting the properly established legal requirements.

This case has shown that punch card balloting machines can produce an unfortunate number of ballots which are not punched in a clean, complete way by the voter. After the current counting, it is likely legislative bodies nationwide will examine ways to improve the mechanisms and machinery for voting.

B. The individual citizen has no federal constitutional right to vote for electors for the President of the United States unless and until the state legislature chooses a statewide election as the means to implement its power to appoint members of the Electoral College. U. S. Const., Art. II, §1. This is

the source for the statement in *McPherson v. Blacker*, 146 U. S. 1, 35 (1892), that the State legislature's power to select the manner for appointing electors is plenary; it may, if it so chooses, select the electors itself, which indeed was the manner used by State legislatures in several States for many years after the Framing of our Constitution. History has now favored the voter, and in each of the several States the citizens themselves vote for Presidential electors. When the state legislature vests the right to vote for President in its people, the right to vote as the legislature has prescribed is fundamental; and one source of its fundamental nature lies in the equal weight accorded to each vote and the equal dignity owed to each voter. The State, of course, after granting the franchise in the special context of Article II, can take back the power to appoint electors. ("[T]here is no doubt of the right of the legislature to resume the power at any time, for it can neither be taken away nor abdicated") (quoting S. Rep. No. 395, 43d Cong., 1st Sess.).

The right to vote is protected in more than the initial allocation of the franchise. Equal protection applies as well to the manner of its exercise. Having once granted the right to vote on equal terms, the State may not, by later arbitrary and disparate treatment, value one person's vote over that of another. See, e.g., *Harper v. Virginia Bd. of Elections*, 383 U. S. 663, 665 (1966) ("[O]nce the franchise is granted to the electorate, lines may not be drawn which are inconsistent with the Equal Protection Clause of the Fourteenth Amendment"). It must be remembered that "the right of suffrage can be denied by a debasement or dilution of the weight of a citizen's vote just as effectively as by wholly prohibiting the free exercise of the franchise." *Reynolds v. Sims*, 377 U. S. 533, 555 (1964).

There is no difference between the two sides of the present controversy on these basic propositions. Respondents say that the very purpose of vindicating the right to vote justifies the recount procedures now at issue. The question before us, however, is whether the recount procedures the Florida Supreme Court has adopted are consistent with its obligation to avoid arbitrary and disparate treatment of the members of its electorate.

Much of the controversy seems to revolve around ballot cards designed to

be perforated by a stylus but which, either through error or deliberate omission, have not been perforated with sufficient precision for a machine to count them. In some cases a piece of the card — a chad — is hanging, say by two corners. In other cases there is no separation at all, just an indentation.

The Florida Supreme Court has ordered that the intent of the voter be discerned from such ballots. For purposes of resolving the equal protection challenge, it is not necessary to decide whether the Florida Supreme Court had the authority under the legislative scheme for resolving election disputes to define what a legal vote is and to mandate a manual recount implementing that definition. The recount mechanisms implemented in response to the decisions of the Florida Supreme Court do not satisfy the minimum requirement for non-arbitrary treatment of voters necessary to secure the fundamental right. Florida's basic command for the count of legally cast votes is to consider the "intent of the voter." This is unobjectionable as an abstract proposition and a starting principle. The problem inheres in the absence of specific standards to ensure its equal application. The formulation of uniform rules to determine intent based on these recurring circumstances is practicable and, we conclude, necessary.

The law does not refrain from searching for the intent of the actor in a multitude of circumstances; and in some cases the general command to ascertain intent is not susceptible to much further refinement. In this instance, however, the question is not whether to believe a witness but how to interpret the marks or holes or scratches on an inanimate object, a piece of cardboard or paper which, it is said, might not have registered as a vote during the machine count. The factfinder confronts a thing, not a person. The search for intent can be confined by specific rules designed to ensure uniform treatment.

The want of those rules here has led to unequal evaluation of ballots in various respects. See *Gore v. Harris*. ("Should a county canvassing board count or not count a 'dimpled chad' where the voter is able to successfully dislodge the chad in every other contest on that ballot? Here, the county canvassing boards disagree"). As seems to have been acknowledged at oral argument, the standards for accepting or rejecting contested ballots might vary not only from county to county but indeed within a single county from one recount team to another.

The record provides some examples. A monitor in Miami-Dade County testified at trial that he observed that three members of the county canvassing board applied different standards in defining a legal vote. And testimony at trial also revealed that at least one county changed its evaluative standards during the counting process. Palm Beach County, for example, began the process with a 1990 guideline which precluded counting completely attached chads, switched to a rule that considered a vote to be legal if any light could be seen through a chad, changed back to the 1990 rule, and then abandoned any pretense of a per se rule, only to have a court order that the county consider dimpled chads legal. This is not a process with sufficient guarantees of equal treatment.

An early case in our one person, one vote jurisprudence arose when a State accorded arbitrary and disparate treatment to voters in its different counties. *Gray v. Sanders*, 372 U.S. 368 (1963). The Court found a constitutional violation. We relied on these principles in the context of the Presidential selection process in *Moore v. Ogilvie*, 394 U.S. 814 (1969), where we invalidated a county-based procedure that diluted the influence of citizens in larger counties in the nominating process. There we observed that "[t]he idea that one group can be granted greater voting strength than another is hostile to the one man, one vote basis of our representative government."

The State Supreme Court ratified this uneven treatment. It mandated that the recount totals from two counties, Miami-Dade and Palm Beach, be included in the certified total. The court also appeared to hold *sub silentio* that the recount totals from Broward County, which were not completed until after the original November 14 certification by the Secretary of State, were to be considered part of the new certified vote totals even though the county certification was not contested by Vice President Gore. Yet each of the counties used varying standards to determine what was a legal vote. Broward County used a more forgiving standard than Palm Beach County, and uncovered almost three times as many new votes, a result markedly disproportion-

ate to the difference in population between the counties.

In addition, the recounts in these three counties were not limited to so-called undervotes but extended to all of the ballots. The distinction has real consequences. A manual recount of all ballots identifies not only those ballots which show no vote but also those which contain more than one, the so-called overvotes. Neither category will be counted by the machine. This is not a trivial concern. At oral argument, respondents estimated there are as many as 110,000 overvotes statewide. As a result, the citizen whose ballot was not read by a machine because he failed to vote for a candidate in a way readable by a machine may still have his vote counted in a manual recount; on the other hand, the citizen who marks two candidates in a way discernable by the machine will not have the same opportunity to have his vote count, even if a manual examination of the ballot would reveal the requisite indicia of intent. Furthermore, the citizen who marks two candidates, only one of which is discernable by the machine, will have his vote counted even though it should have been read as an invalid ballot. The State Supreme Court's inclusion of vote counts based on these variant standards exemplifies concerns with the remedial processes that were under way.

That brings the analysis to yet a further equal protection problem. The votes certified by the court included a partial total from one county, Miami-Dade. The Florida Supreme Court's decision thus gives no assurance that the recounts included in a final certification must be complete. Indeed, it is respondent's submission that it would be consistent with the rules of the recount procedures to include whatever partial counts are done by the time of final certification, and we interpret the Florida Supreme Court's decision to permit this. . . . This accommodation no doubt results from the truncated contest period established by the Florida Supreme Court in *Bush I,* at respondents' own urging. The press of time does not diminish the constitutional concern. A desire for speed is not a general excuse for ignoring equal protection guarantees.

In addition to these difficulties the actual process by which the votes were to be counted under the Florida Supreme Court' s decision raises fur-

ther concerns. That order did not specify who would recount the ballots. The county canvassing boards were forced to pull together ad hoc teams comprised of judges from various Circuits who had no previous training in handling and interpreting ballots. Furthermore, while others were permitted to observe, they were prohibited from objecting during the recount.

The recount process, in its features here described, is inconsistent with the minimum procedures necessary to protect the fundamental right of each voter in the special instance of a statewide recount under the authority of a single state judicial officer. Our consideration is limited to the present circumstances, for the problem of equal protection in election processes generally presents many complexities.

The question before the Court is not whether local entities, in the exercise of their expertise, may develop different systems for implementing elections. Instead, we are presented with a situation where a state court with the power to assure uniformity has ordered a statewide recount with minimal procedural safeguards. When a court orders a statewide remedy, there must be at least some assurance that the rudimentary requirements of equal treatment and fundamental fairness are satisfied.

Given the Court's assessment that the recount process underway was probably being conducted in an unconstitutional manner, the Court stayed the order directing the recount so it could hear this case and render an expedited decision. The contest provision, as it was mandated by the State Supreme Court, is not well calculated to sustain the confidence that all citizens must have in the outcome of elections. The State has not shown that its procedures include the necessary safeguards. The problem, for instance, of the estimated 110,000 overvotes has not been addressed. . . .

Upon due consideration of the difficulties identified to this point, it is obvious that the recount cannot be conducted in compliance with the requirements of equal protection and due process without substantial additional work. It would require not only the adoption (after opportunity for argument) of adequate statewide standards for determining what is a legal vote, and practicable procedures to implement them, but also orderly judicial review of any disputed matters that might arise. In addition, the Secretary of State has advised that the recount of only a portion of the ballots requires that the vote tabulation equipment be used to screen out undervotes, a function for which the machines were not designed. If a recount of overvotes were also required, perhaps even a second screening would be necessary. Use of the equipment for this purpose, and any new software developed for it, would have to be evaluated for accuracy by the Secretary of State, as required by Fla. Stat. §101.015 (2000).

The Supreme Court of Florida has said that the legislature intended the State's electors to "participat[e] fully in the federal electoral process," as provided in 3 U. S. C. §5.; see also *Palm Beach Canvassing Bd. v. Harris* (Fla. 2000). That statute, in turn, requires that any controversy or contest that is designed to lead to a conclusive selection of electors be completed by De-

cember 12. That date is upon us, and there is no recount procedure in place under the State Supreme Court's order that comports with minimal constitutional standards. Because it is evident that any recount seeking to meet the December 12 date will be unconstitutional for the reasons we have discussed, we reverse the judgment of the Supreme Court of Florida ordering a recount to proceed.

Seven Justices of the Court agree that there are constitutional problems with the recount ordered by the Florida Supreme Court that demand a remedy. . . . The only disagreement is as to the remedy. Because the Florida Supreme Court has said that the Florida Legislature intended to obtain the safe-harbor benefits of 3 U.S.C. §5, Justice Breyer's proposed remedy — remanding to the Florida Supreme Court for its ordering of a constitutionally proper contest until December 18 — contemplates action in violation of

the Florida election code, and hence could not be part of an "appropriate" order authorized by Fla. Stat. §102.168(8) (2000).

None are more conscious of the vital limits on judicial authority than are the members of this Court, and none stand more in admiration of the Constitution's design to leave the selection of the President to the people, through their legislatures, and to the political sphere. When contending parties invoke the process of the courts, however, it becomes our unsought responsibility to resolve the federal and constitutional issues the judicial system has been forced to confront. The judgment of the Supreme Court of Florida is reversed, and the case is remanded for further proceedings not inconsistent with this opinion. Pursuant to this Court's Rule 45.2, the Clerk is directed to issue the mandate in this case forthwith.

It is so ordered. ◆

Political Participation

This section presents a range of articles on key components of electoral and party politics: campaigns, elections, voters and political parties.

The 2000 presidential election devolved into a protracted court fight and exposed the nation's election system as an unreliable hodgepodge of local standards, inconsistent procedures and old equipment. Congress rushed to devise remedies. But as the first article in this section reveals, lawmakers are discovering the need to proceed with caution on election reform because it raises fundamental questions about what the federal involvement should be in election matters that have long been the province of states.

The second article in this section examines the results of the 2000 elections and the voting patterns that emerged around the country to produce a virtual dead heat in the presidential and congressional elections.

The next selection turns to the topic of campaign finance reform and the role of money in politics. The five key arguments against and in favor of reform are examined in turn.

In a stunning development with far-reaching consequences for a Senate divided 50-50 along party lines, Vermont senator James M. Jeffords announced on May 24, 2001, that he was leaving the Republican party to become an Independent. The fourth article in this section examines Jeffords' role—predefection—as one of the few remaining moderate Republicans in the Senate and his growing uneasiness over the conservative orientation of the Republican Party.

The decennial redistricting process, which began the week of March 5, 2001, with the release of census data, will significantly influence who controls Congress for the next 10 years. The Republican and Democratic parties have launched redistricting programs in which they are studying state voting laws, giving members of Congress advice on how to protect their voting bases, and raising money for the lawsuits that will likely be filed to challenge the new district lines. This mobilization of the parties is the subject of the final article in this section.

Election 'Reform' Movement Gives Way to Caution

Parties agree that states should get federal aid but differ on mandating standards

It was an embarrassing revelation for the world's most prosperous and enduring democracy: lost ballots, candidates in court, election workers haggling over the meaning of a dimple on a punch card.

The 2000 presidential election had devolved into a protracted court fight and exposed the nation's election system as an unreliable hodgepodge of local standards, inconsistent procedures and old equipment, running in many cases on meager budgets and the kindness of volunteers.

Congress responded to the Florida debacle, and the street protests it spawned, with a rush to devise remedies. Members of both parties called news conferences, introduced bills and declared that the nation needed sweeping changes in the way it elected its leaders.

"The experience of the last election must never, ever be repeated," Sen. Robert G. Torricelli, D-N.J., said in a January news conference with Mitch McConnell, R-Ky.

But six months after the November election drew to a controversial conclusion in the Supreme Court, lawmakers are confronting fundamental questions about federal involvement in what has long been the province of states. Congress still faces pressure to fix the system, but the pressures to preserve the status quo may be even greater.

The Constitution grants Congress wide authority to regulate the election of federal candidates; the question is whether Congress will choose to use it.

The groups most affected and most angered by the problems that came to light in 2000 were blacks and other minorities, who have historically been at the margins of political power. They say their treatment was reminiscent of the systematic abuses minorities suffered before the federal government stepped in to secure the franchise with the 1965 Voting Rights Act.

"The outcome of election 2000 was to dissipate, deteriorate and undermine the fundamental right to vote," said Rep. Sheila Jackson-Lee, D-Texas.

Still, lawmakers in both parties remain leery of mandating national standards for state-run systems. State and local officials are united in their opposition to edicts out of Washington. And companies that manufacture voting machines also favor the wide-open competition of locally run systems.

Unless the mood on Capitol Hill shifts, the business of running elections is likely to remain in the hands of local governments, where it has been since the nation's founding.

"We want to ensure that the elections in America continue to be run at the state and local level," said Bob Ney, R-Ohio, chairman of the House Administration Committee, which is drafting a bill on election system changes. "I think it's important to make clear that we don't want to federalize or nationalize the election process. Our decentralized system of government has served us well."

Some say Congress should forcefully mandate changes, and that position gained new influence in the debate when the Senate flipped to Democratic control. The primary bill promoting national standards for voting machines, access to polling places and the upkeep of voter rolls (S 565) is sponsored by the incoming chairman of the Senate Rules and Administration Committee, Christopher J. Dodd, D-Conn.

The Senate's incoming majority leader, Democrat Tom Daschle of South Dakota, supports the bill, which would order states to adopt "uniform and non-discriminatory" statewide standards for voting machines and election procedures by 2004. Daschle also is backing a competing measure from McConnell, Torricelli and others that would create standards and offer federal money to encourage states to comply, but would not require states to follow the standards.

Congress almost surely will act, even if it stops short of mandates. Members of both parties agree that Congress should provide, perhaps for the first time ever, federal money to pay for improving elections. It remains to be seen how much money will be provided — one bill proposes $2.5 billion over five years — and whether it would be in the form of an annual appropriation or a one-time infusion of cash.

"It's going to cost some money if you're going to get confidence back in our system," Ney said.

Many members also support attaching strings to those dollars, requiring that states provide guarantees of accuracy and establish safeguards against accidentally tossing qualified voters off the rolls or turning them away from the polls.

State officials want the cash to buy new machines, educate voters and train election workers, but they do not want federal mandates. They say they are working on the problems exposed by the 2000 election. According to the National Conference of State Legislatures, more than 1,600 election "reform" bills have been introduced in state legislatures and 167 have passed. More than 20 bills are awaiting signatures from governors. Florida, notably, has already put the finishing touches on its own revamp.

Bush v. Gore

But federal aid will not satisfy those calling for national standards for elections, and they promise a fight.

Some see new leverage for their cause in the Supreme Court ruling in *Bush v. Gore*, which stopped recounts of Florida's presidential ballots and effectively handed the presidency to Republican George W. Bush over Democrat Al Gore. In a 5-4 decision, the majority said the recount should be halted because standards for determining voter intent on partially punched ballots varied by county and therefore violated constitutional rights to equal protection. Proponents of national standards say the logic for a uniform system is inescapable in that decision.

Mechanical voting machines, like this one from the 1960s, are being replaced in some states with electronic systems. The disputed 2000 election focused attention on voting.

Stewart said. "Even if things go just as they usually go, there will be Palm Beach counties all over this country."

Larry Sabato, a University of Virginia political scientist, said the public expects some response from Washington, but probably not sweeping changes.

"Congress will have to do something," Sabato said. "What is that something? Probably it will be enough, as far as the public is concerned, to give money to states."

He said the widespread concern stirred by the five-week post-election standoff in Florida seems to have cooled. The public's attention has wandered to other things.

"I give lots of presentations about the November elections, and I almost never get questions about this," Sabato said. "It was so 'yesterday.' "

Emotional Stakes

Members of Congress have a personal stake in the nitty-gritty of election administration, especially at a time when the balance of power between the two major parties is so close. Their political future, not to mention their legitimacy as lawmakers, hangs on how elections are run and how votes are counted back home.

Some proponents of federal "election reform" talk of even higher stakes. Members of the black caucus and other advocates of mandates, including Dodd, say it is a civil rights issue, and they draw emotional parallels to the struggles of the 1960s to end segregation and secure equal rights for African-Americans. Many of the problems with voting machines and confusion over voter rolls, which caused poll workers to keep some properly registered voters from casting ballots, occurred in precincts dominated by minorities, immigrants and the elderly. The U.S. Commission on Civil Rights is investigating and is expected to issue a report this month.

In the ensuing debate about the fairness of the system, the black caucus and others have talked about the importance of federal intervention to protect minority voting rights.

When they talk about upgrading voting machines and securing voter rolls, they refer to past marches and slain activists. They pointedly cite a high-water mark of federal involvement in assuring the franchise for minorities: the Voting Rights Act that ended literacy tests and other discriminatory tactics aimed at keeping blacks from voting. (*1965 Almanac, p. 533*)

"So many people have fought and died for the right to vote," said Rep. Barbara Lee, D-Calif., at a press conference May 16. "Medgar Evers. Martin Luther King . . . "

Lee and other members of the black caucus have rallied behind the legislation sponsored by Dodd and Rep. John Conyers Jr., D-Mich., (HR 1170) that would order states to change the way they run elections. They have even discussed making their votes on campaign finance legislation now pending in the House contingent upon action on election overhaul.

Under the Dodd-Conyers measure, voting systems, for ex-

"I think *Bush v. Gore* opens the door," said Jackson-Lee, vice chairwoman of the Congressional Black Caucus. "And the reason is that the Supreme Court said there must be uniform standards. Now, obviously you would like to think that the 50 states could collaborate together and uniform standards all of a sudden would be there at the end of the day. Frankly, I don't think that will occur."

What voters want Congress to do — and how much they care about the issue — is anyone's guess. Polls taken immediately after the 2000 election showed an appetite for change, although pollsters have not asked the question since.

However, fears that 2002 will bring a repeat of last fall's mess may prompt Congress to help states upgrade their voting machines. In pressing for broad action, Jackson-Lee and other members of the black caucus predict widespread outrage if the problems seen in the 2000 elections crop up again in 2002. Time to act is running short, they say.

Charles Stewart, a political scientist at the Massachusetts Institute of Technology, said the public and the press will be watching next year for a repeat of election problems found in such places as Florida's Palm Beach County.

And unless the system improves, problems should be easy to find, he said. "Then the Jell-O will really hit the fan,"

ample, would have to be designed to notify voters when they had made a mistake on their ballots, such as voting twice for a single office, and give them a chance to fix their errors. States would have to mail sample ballots and voting instructions 10 days before Election Day and offer provisional ballots, which permit people whose names do not appear on registration rolls to cast a vote on Election Day while election officials verify that the person was omitted from registration lists improperly. After the 2000 election, officials in Florida and elsewhere faced accusations that they had improperly turned people away from the polls because of sloppy voter registration records. (*2001 CQ Weekly*, p. 1150)

"In federal elections, national elections, there must be basic, minimum standards," Dodd said. "In the 1960s, we said there was no compromising on access to public accommodations — restrooms and restaurants. We think a voting booth deserves no less a status than a restroom or a restaurant."

'All Votes Compromised'

A Democratic "special committee on election reform," created in the House after efforts to establish a bipartisan panel collapsed, says Congress should consider uniform national standards for maintaining registration lists, identifying voters at the polls and handling other aspects of elections.

Conyers, who is on the election committee and a member of the Congressional Black Caucus, sees a clear national interest at play. When ballot recounts and lawsuits in Florida held up the presidential election last year, the nation learned that America's election system is a patchwork affair, spread across 50 states and more than 3,000 counties. It also learned that problems in one state can affect voters everywhere, he said.

"All our votes were compromised by the election procedures and problems in Florida," Conyers said. "You really have to have tunnel vision not to see that voting is a national problem. It's not a state-by-state problem."

Some in Congress have questioned whether they have the authority to dictate election rules to states. But Conyers dismisses any questions about congressional power. On that point, he says, the Constitution is clear.

Article 1, Section 4, leaves it to each state to set the "time, place and manner" of House and Senate elections, but it says Congress may "by law make or alter such regulations" at any time. (*Legal provisions, p. 13*)

"What we want to do is set basic minimum federal standards," Conyers said. "For those who are worried about questions of authority and jurisdiction, rest your little hearts and minds. It's written into the Constitution."

Conyers points out that as a practical matter, if Congress sets regulations for federal elections, all others would fall into line because no state is likely to bear the expense of maintaining one voting system for federal elections and another for state and local races.

Many legal scholars agree with Conyers' interpretation of the Constitution.

"When it comes to federal elections, Congress has considerable power if it chooses to exercise it," said Richard Pildes of New York University Law School.

Congress also can force changes in state laws by attaching conditions to federal money, much as it has used highway dollars to force states to set speed limits on interstates, Pildes and others said. That authority, which the courts have upheld, is rooted in Article 1, Section 8, of the Constitution.

In addition, there is the Constitution's 14th Amendment, guaranteeing all citizens equal protection under the law, and the 15th Amendment, forbidding states from denying anyone the right to vote on the basis of race. If there is evidence that minority voters or others are being treated unfairly, Congress has the power to step in.

It was the 14th Amendment's guarantee of "equal protection" that formed the basis for the Supreme Court ruling in *Bush v. Gore*. The court's majority concluded that Florida's recounts violated the Equal Protection Clause because different counties used different standards to determine which votes to count.

But the court also took pains to limit its ruling to the standoff in Florida, writing that "the problem of equal protection in election processes generally presents many complexities."

That qualifier has muddied the waters for analysts and scholars. The wider implications of *Bush v. Gore*, if any, are still unclear, said Nate Persily, a professor at the University of Pennsylvania Law School.

"The reach of the ruling could be anything from insignificant to transformative," Persily told a study panel from the National Conference of State Legislatures on May 9. "We're only at the beginning of analyzing it."

Pildes says *Bush v. Gore* seems at least to provide an opening for requiring some internal uniformity in the way states and counties run elections. Congress would have the power to pass laws enforcing such uniformity in both state and federal races, Pildes said.

But Pam Karlan, a Stanford University law professor, said she doubts *Bush v. Gore* gives Congress any more power than it already has.

"A lot of it depends on whether lower courts take it and run with it," Karlan said. "But I don't read *Bush v. Gore* and say, 'Whoa, there's a new equal-protection argument here.'

"This case I look at and say, 'There's going to be a lot of litigation here, but I don't know that it's going anywhere.' "

Bruce Cain, director of the Institute of Governmental Studies at the University of California Berkeley thinks state and local control of elections is secure, unless Congress wants to "underwrite this whole enterprise."

Elections are like education, he said: The tradition of local control is so long, the costs so varied and the bureaucracies so entrenched that Congress would have trouble meddling with the status quo even if it wanted to.

The real power of the *Bush v. Gore* decision may lie in the fear of lawsuits, which could prod states to act. The American Civil Liberties Union already has filed four lawsuits based on the ruling, demanding that California, Georgia, Florida and Illinois get rid of voting systems it says are flawed and discriminatory.

Partnerships, Not Mandates

In the House Administration Committee, now the center of the House debate on the issue, Ney and top Democrat Steny H. Hoyer of Maryland have crossed party lines to strike an agreement in principle on "election reform." They will work to define the federal role in overhauling the nation's election system, but they have agreed to avoid mandates on states.

In the Senate, McConnell and Torricelli have been joined by Sam Brownback, R-Kan., and Charles E. Schumer, D-N.Y., to produce a bill that steers clear of mandates.

Their bill (S 953) is a synthesis of two competing pieces of legislation that would make the grant money it offers

The Power of Congress

States and counties have operated — and paid for — the elections of federal officeholders since the nation's founding. But legal scholars say Congress has several sources of authority within the Constitution to determine how federal elections are run.

■ **Article 1, Section 4:** "THE TIMES, PLACES AND MANNER OF HOLDING ELECTIONS FOR SENATORS AND REPRESENTATIVES, SHALL BE PRESCRIBED IN EACH STATE BY THE LEGISLATURE THEREOF; BUT THE CONGRESS MAY AT ANY TIME BY LAW MAKE OR ALTER SUCH REGULATIONS, EXCEPT AS TO THE PLACES OF CHOOSING SENATORS."

Analysis: This section gives Congress power to regulate congressional elections. In practice, that means Congress can affect how all elections are run, since states are unlikely to maintain separate voting systems for federal candidates.

In 1842, Congress used its authority under this section to require states to elect their congressional delegations from single-member districts. At the time, some states elected more than one House member from a single district.

In February, the Supreme Court reaffirmed Congress' power over congressional elections in a case called *Cook v. Gralike*, striking down a Missouri law that required a ballot label for candidates opposing term limits. The court stressed that any authority states have over congressional elections is delegated from Congress. *(2001 CQ Weekly, p. 489)*

■ **Article 1, Section 8:** "THE CONGRESS SHALL HAVE POWER TO LAY AND COLLECT TAXES, DUTIES, IMPOSTS AND EXCISES, TO PAY THE DEBTS AND PROVIDE FOR THE COMMON DEFENSE AND GENERAL WELFARE OF THE UNITED STATES . . ."

Analysis: Using the taxing and spending authority granted by this section, Congress has attached strings to federal money to compel states to change or adopt laws. It could do the same with money sent to states for modernizing voting equipment and training election workers.

In the 1980s, South Dakota officials challenged the power of Congress to withhold federal highway money to force them to raise the legal drinking age. In 1987, the Supreme Court upheld Congress' authority in *South Dakota v. Dole*.

■ **The 14th Amendment, Section 1:** "ALL PERSONS BORN OR NATURALIZED IN THE UNITED STATES, AND SUBJECT TO THE JURISDICTION THEREOF, ARE CITIZENS OF THE UNITED STATES AND OF THE STATE WHEREIN THEY RESIDE. NO STATE SHALL MAKE OR ENFORCE ANY LAW WHICH SHALL ABRIDGE THE PRIVILEGES OR IMMUNITIES OF CITIZENS OF THE UNITED STATES; NOR SHALL ANY STATE DEPRIVE ANY PERSON OF LIFE, LIBERTY, OR PROPERTY, WITHOUT DUE PROCESS OF LAW; NOR DENY TO ANY PERSON WITHIN ITS JURISDICTION THE EQUAL PROTECTION OF THE LAWS."

Analysis: This amendment forbids states from applying their laws in a discriminatory or arbitrary way; it could be construed to apply to election procedures that treat ballots differently. Section 5 of the amendment expressly gives Congress the power to pass legislation to enforce its provisions.

■ **The 15th Amendment, Section 1:** "THE RIGHT OF CITIZENS OF THE UNITED STATES TO VOTE SHALL NOT BE DENIED OR ABRIDGED BY THE UNITED STATES OR BY ANY STATE ON ACCOUNT OF RACE, COLOR, OR PREVIOUS CONDITION OF SERVITUDE."

Analysis: This amendment protects the voting rights of minorities. Section 2 of the amendment expressly gives Congress the power to pass legislation to enforce its provisions.

■ ***Bush v. Gore:*** Legal scholars and public officials are still debating the broader implications of the Supreme Court's ruling in *Bush v. Gore*, which stopped ballot recounts in Florida last December and allowed Republican George W. Bush to claim that state's 25 electoral votes and thus the presidency. Much attention has focused on two paragraphs.

In the first, the court relies on the Equal Protection Clause of the 14th Amendment to stop the recounts because counties used different standards to determine the intent of voters: "THE RIGHT TO VOTE IS PROTECTED IN MORE THAN THE INITIAL ALLOCATION OF THE FRANCHISE. EQUAL PROTECTION APPLIES AS WELL TO THE MANNER OF ITS EXERCISE. HAVING ONCE GRANTED THE RIGHT TO VOTE ON EQUAL TERMS, THE STATE MAY NOT, BY LATER ARBITRARY AND DISPARATE TREATMENT, VALUE ONE PERSON'S VOTE OVER THAT OF ANOTHER."

But the court also sought to confine the ruling's impact: "OUR CONSIDERATION IS LIMITED TO THE PRESENT CIRCUMSTANCES, FOR THE PROBLEM OF EQUAL PROTECTION IN ELECTION PROCESSES GENERALLY PRESENTS MANY COMPLEXITIES."

---

contingent on states adopting provisional balloting and meeting standards for accuracy, accessibility and accountability. A new Election Administration Commission would set the standards.

Schumer said that approach would help encourage changes while respecting the long tradition of local control.

"A carrot is much better than a stick," he said. "I've talked with many secretaries of state. They'd be on the warpath if we mandated something."

Local control works, Brownback said. Some counties in his home state of Kansas, for example, are content with hand-counted paper ballots. Their populations are so small that anything more sophisticated — and expensive — makes no sense, he said. *(Technology, p.14)*

At recent hearings on Capitol Hill, state and county officials have been quite clear: They want the federal government to be a partner in the effort to improve elections, not a dictator.

"I want something that debunks the myth that we have federal elections," Ohio Secretary of State J. Kenneth Blackwell told the House Administration Committee on April 25. "We don't. We have 50 state elections where the president and other federal officeholders are elected. I want to make sure we don't go down the slippery slope of federalizing elections."

Blackwell and others want federal guidance in setting standards and identifying the best practices in election administration. They also want federal money to help pay for new equipment and the training of election workers.

But ultimately, state and local officials say they know best what kinds of equipment and procedures work for their constituents.

"We're not asking you to solve the problems," Arkansas Secretary of State Sharon Priest told the House Administration Committee. "We need some help. But states and localities are working to address the problems. "

Companies that make the equipment argue that innovation in voting technology will be stifled if a single voting system is imposed upon states and counties.

"That's not good for us," said Travis Harrell of Austin-based Hart Inter-Civic Inc., which makes the eSlate Electronic Voting System, "that's not good for the government, that's not good for the country."

Florida has acted decisively. On May 9, Republican Gov. Jeb Bush signed the most sweeping election overhaul passed by any state so far.

The bill bans error-prone punch-card voting machines and orders counties to replace them by 2002 with electronic or "optical-scan" machines. It sets aside state money for the new equipment, a computerized statewide voter-registration database and education for both voters and poll workers.

Other states also have acted:

• Georgia has passed a law requiring a uniform statewide system by 2004. The state will conduct a pilot project to test electronic "touch-screen" voting in municipal elections this year.

• Maryland's Democratic Gov. Parris N. Glendening has signed a bill requiring the state to work with counties to adopt a uniform voting system. The state will cover half the costs of modernizing voting machines statewide.

• Indiana's governor has signed a bill that could eliminate punch-card and lever voting machines by 2005. The state will establish a fund to help counties pay for updating machines.

Some states, including Kansas, Virginia and South Dakota, have passed measures aimed at improving the maintenance of voter rolls, according to the National Conference of State Legislatures. Others, including Montana and Pennsylvania, have launched studies of their election procedures.

"Some critics have recently suggested that states are dragging their feet on enacting necessary reforms, that we are waiting for federal money to address this problem," said Democrat John A. Hurson, majority leader of the Maryland House of Delegates. "Nothing could be further from the truth." ◆

Varied Needs, Varied Systems

The 1,900 registered voters of Chase County, Kan., still vote with pencil and paper. And odd as it may seem in this computerized age, County Clerk Sharon Pittman says the system works just fine.

"Check a box," Pittman says. "No hanging chads."

Now consider Los Angeles County, home to 4.1 million registered voters. Ballots are printed in seven languages, including Korean and Tagalog. Last November, the county's voters cast nearly 2.8 million ballots — more than statewide totals in 41 of the 50 states.

"Can you imagine us with paper ballots on election night?" said County Clerk Conny B. McCormack. "It's only funny in the most macabre sense."

McCormack wants to get her county into the computer age by replacing the 1968-vintage punch-card machines with electronic "touch-screen" voting. But when that will happen, no one can say. The estimated cost is $100 million.

As Congress and state lawmakers look to improve the fairness and accuracy of the nation's election system, few disagree that part of the answer is new technology. But the needs are so diverse that a national solution is likely to remain elusive.

What is more, early results from one ongoing study suggest new technology is not always an improvement over the old standbys.

Researchers at the Massachusetts Institute of Technology and the California Institute of Technology found that polling places using electronic voting machines saw a higher percentage of spoiled or unmarked ballots than those using "lever machines," technology introduced in the 19th century.

After the spectacle of Florida's recounts, some in Congress have focused on eliminating punch cards. Those machines, used widely in Florida, taught the nation about "hanging" chads, the little bits of paper left when voters do not punch completely through a punch-card ballot.

But in Utah, 23 of the state's 29 counties use punch cards, and Republican state House Speaker Martin R. Stephens told a House committee recently that the system works fine. Meanwhile, Florida, Georgia and other states are scrambling to get rid of punch cards. Florida plans to lease optical scanners, like the machines used to grade standardized student tests, for the 2002 elections. Georgia plans to test touch-screen machines in this year's municipal elections.

Which system is best?

The MIT/Caltech study looked at data from more than 2,700 counties and municipalities, and found that overall, 2 percent of presidential ballots cast in the past four elections were spoiled or unmarked. Problems were fewest in counties using lever machines, paper ballots and optical scanners.

Counties using punch cards and electronic machines saw the most problems.

The results from new electronic machines indicate that makers may still be struggling to make the ballot designs user-friendly, said one of the researchers, Stephen Ansolabehere of MIT. Or, he says, voters are still getting used to the new technology. Or both.

Everyone seems to agree that whatever system a county uses, the ballots should be tallied as they are cast in each precinct, not later at a central location. That is the surest way to catch ballot errors before voters leave the polling place, officials and researchers say.

Most agree that technology is not the only answer. Voter education is important. So is training for poll workers.

Larry Sabato, a University of Virginia political scientist, worries that all the talk about voting machines might distract from the need for education and training.

"This is so American," Sabato said. "We have a tendency to blame inanimate objections for our shortcomings."

Breaking the Tie: Parties Seek Formula for Majority Status

Sharp regional differences in voting patterns underlie near-deadlock in 2000 elections

Behind the bare statistics of the virtual dead heat in last year's presidential and congressional elections is a more complex reality: a nation riven into three distinct parts by ideology, geography and demographics.

One side of this political triangle is rural, white, located in the Rocky Mountain and Great Plains states and the conservative South — and is overwhelmingly Republican.

The opposite side is intensely urban and has a large contingent of minorities. It dominates much of the mid-Atlantic and Northeastern states and the Pacific Coast — and is just as overwhelmingly Democratic.

Making up the third leg is a geographically and demographically diverse group that has a common trait: residence in the suburbs. Shifting away from its historically Republican roots, it split pretty much down the middle in 2000 — helping ensure that the election would end in a virtual tie.

These three starkly different segments of the nation have emerged from the smoke and fog of the 2000 race for the presidency. And as each national party now tries to chart a course for the milestone battles coming up in 2002 and 2004, Republican and Democratic strategists are groping for a battle plan that might break the deadlock.

The problem is, each party is so firmly attached to its base constituencies that it is difficult for either to reach far enough into the political center to gain a clear majority — despite each party's declaration that it embodies the moderate view and that the other side really represents the extreme.

A county-by-county analysis of the 2000 election results, based on Congressional Quarterly's compilation of official returns, shows that the nation's current partisan balance is the sum of regional and demographic divisions that the parties will be hard-pressed to overcome.

With many suburbs that once were GOP strongholds now trending Democratic, both parties will be focusing on gaining the initiative in these areas. But it is not clear how either one would be able to grab a decisive advantage.

Many suburban voters, according to political analysts, feel the pull of Republicans' calls for tax cuts, increased parental choice in educational options and private investment of Social Security funds. But just as many seem to favor Democratic liberalism over Republican social conservatism on issues such as abortion, gay rights and gun control.

So as they bid to establish "majority party" status, both Democratic and Republican strategists face the double bind of attracting new voters without alienating their core supporters: social liberals, minorities and organized labor for the Democrats; social and business-oriented fiscal conservatives for the Republicans.

Rep. Adam Smith, D-Wash., a prominent member of the centrist New Democrat Coalition, summed up the problem for party strategists. "The key in any of these elections is the swing voters, those folks who will vote for one party or the other in a given election...," Smith said. "The question is, who are they and how do you get them?"

As Clear as Gray and White

Each party's strengths and weaknesses are as clear as the colors used on CQ's map to denote the counties carried by Republican George W. Bush (white) and those carried by Democrat Al Gore (gray). *(Map, pp. 16–17)*

The most reliable Republican areas still form an "L" — a pattern first described by Congressional Quarterly after three consecutive GOP presidential victories in the 1980s. It takes in the Rocky Mountain and Plains states and sweeps south and east to envelop the Old South.

Some of these states are longtime GOP strongholds; others have swung Republican over recent years in response to the perceived liberalism of the national Democratic Party.

Even more than usual, the rural regions that define many of these states rejected the Democratic nominee in 2000. In many counties, Gore finished 20 percentage points or more behind the 1996 rate of his predecessor on the Democratic ticket, Bill Clinton, whose Southern charm won over some white working-class voters who had wandered away from the party. *(1996 election analysis, 1997 CQ Almanac, p. 10-3)*

Bush's rural gains put him over the top in several states that Clinton had carried, including Clinton's home state of Arkansas, Gore's home of Tennessee, and the usual Democratic dominion of West Virginia. *(Chart, p. 22)*

But the once-dominant GOP showing in the suburbs has slipped. While Bush improved slightly on 1996 GOP nominee Bob Dole's performance in suburban counties, he still finished well below the percentages that Republican presidential candidates were accustomed to receiving before Clinton's first win in 1992. *(Chart, p. 21)*

The Democrats' power base, meanwhile, lies along the Pacific Coast, where many residents are more culturally liberal than the Republican Party as a whole, and in states in the Northeast and Midwest, where social liberalism and labor unions tend to be strong.

California, which gave the nation GOP Presidents Richard M. Nixon and Ronald Reagan, has swung especially hard to the Democrats. The nation's most populous state — it will have 53 of the 435 House seats after the 2002 election and 55 of the 535 electoral votes in 2004 — is now a basic building block for the Democrats' election strategy.

In each of these regions, the Democrats' advantages are built on a foundation of complete and unshakable domi-

2000 Presidential Vote, by County

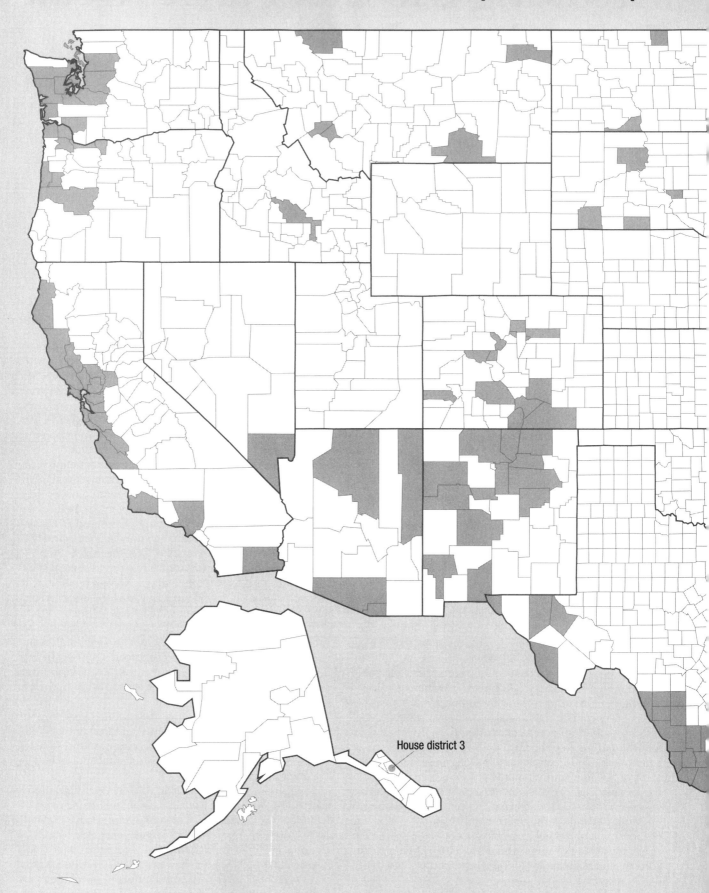

House district 3

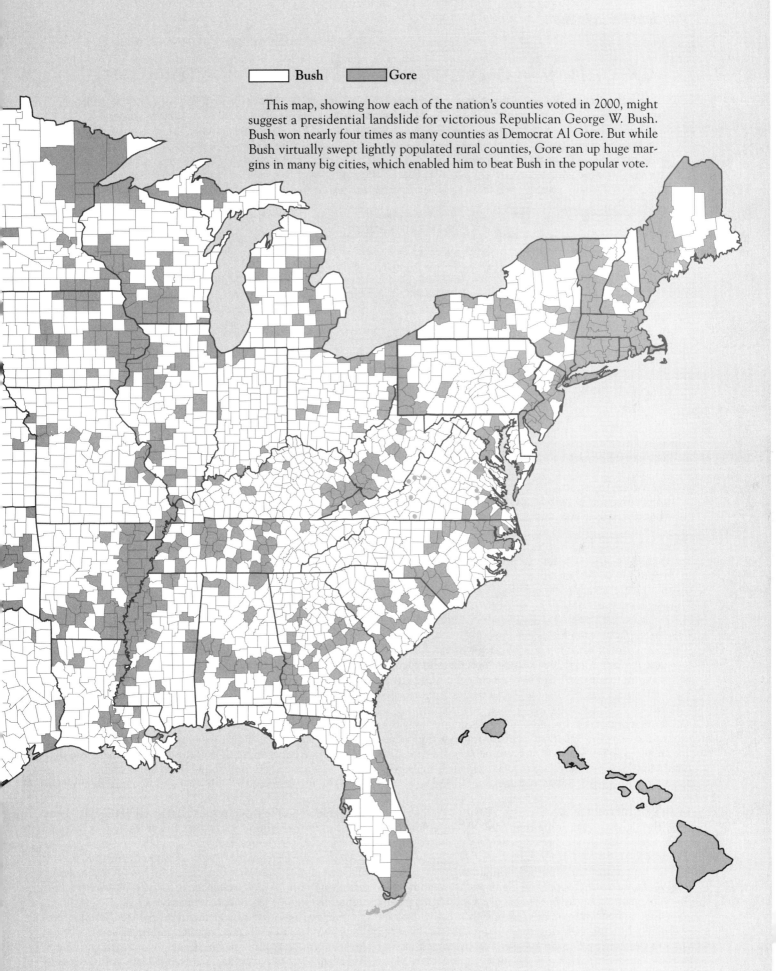

Bush **Gore**

This map, showing how each of the nation's counties voted in 2000, might suggest a presidential landslide for victorious Republican George W. Bush. Bush won nearly four times as many counties as Democrat Al Gore. But while Bush virtually swept lightly populated rural counties, Gore ran up huge margins in many big cities, which enabled him to beat Bush in the popular vote.

Urban Vote Remains Strongly Democratic

The Democratic Party has politically dominated most of the nation's major cities since the 19th century, when the party's appeal to immigrants fueled the growth of urban Democratic "machines." This strength was supplemented by the alliance between the Democrats and organized labor in industrial cities. And over the past few decades, increasing populations of loyally Democratic minority voters have stretched the party's advantage to overwhelming levels. In the sample of cities below, Democrat Al Gore outran Republican George W. Bush in 2000 by ratios ranging from 2-to-1 (in Denver) to nearly 19-to-1 (in Detroit). But even the urban vote is subject to regional variation, with Bush doing much better in some cities of the conservative South. For example, Bush's edge in Jacksonville — a city that has a large military-related population and incorporates much of its own suburbia — was crucial to his narrow and controversial election-clinching victory in the state of Florida.

CITY	2000 Total Vote	2000 Winner	1996 Winner	1984 Winner
San Francisco	319,771	Gore, 76%-16%	Clinton, 72%-16%	Mondale, 67%-31%
Denver	198,347	Gore, 62-31	Clinton, 62-30	Mondale, 50-48
Jacksonville [1]	265,181	Bush, 57-41	Dole, 50-44	Reagan, 62-38
Chicago	961,059	Gore, 80-17	Clinton, 80-15	Mondale, 65-34
Baltimore	192,404	Gore, 83-14	Clinton, 79-16	Mondale, 71-28
Boston	184,603	Gore, 72-20	Clinton, 74-20	Mondale, 63-36
Detroit	300,478	Gore, 94-5	Clinton, 92-5	Mondale, 80-19
St. Louis	124,752	Gore, 77-20	Clinton, 75-18	Mondale, 65-35
New York	2,186,436	Gore, 78-18	Clinton, 77-17	Mondale, 61-39
Philadelphia	561,180	Gore, 80-18	Clinton, 77-16	Mondale, 65-35

[1] Totals shown are for Duval County, Fla. Jacksonville encompasses all of Duval County except the communities of Atlantic Beach, Jacksonville Beach, Neptune Beach and Baldwin.

Sources: State election offices; CQ's America Votes books.

nance in the big cities. (*Chart, above*)

The political power behind that grip is the party's long-lasting hold on the loyalties of minority group voters, especially African-Americans.

Despite an effort at outreach to black voters — including high-profile speakers and performers at last summer's Republican National Convention in Philadelphia — exit polls showed Bush received just 9 percent of that group's votes, less even than other recent GOP presidential candidates.

Republican leaders say, though, that they have not given up on a breakthrough that could help get them back in the hunt for the urban vote.

"By and large, I think that Bush has an opportunity with a large megaphone to talk to some constituencies that agree with us on a lot of issues but aren't voting with us — Hispanics, some African-Americans, techies — people who ought to be voting more with us," said Rep. Thomas M. Davis III, R-Va., chairman of the National Republican Congressional Committee (NRCC), the party's House campaign arm.

For the purposes of this story, "urban" is defined as within the borders of a city; "suburban" applies to areas within a standard metropolitan statistical area but outside the core city's limits; and "rural" is equivalent to areas defined as "non-metropolitan" by the Office of Management and Budget.

Bush's Rural Rule

Although Gore ran more than 500,000 votes ahead of Bush nationally, Bush carried nearly four times as many counties: 2,472 to 675 for Gore.

This fact underscores Bush's dominance in the nation's rural areas. Bush swept sprawling Plains and Mountain states that have many counties but few people. Gore's strength, by contrast, was concentrated in a few heavily urbanized states.

Bush's showing in Montana was typical. He defeated Gore in the state by 25 percentage points, the largest victory margin for any Republican presidential candidate in Montana since Warren G. Harding in 1920. Bush's performance

in Montana was all the more impressive in that Clinton carried the state for the Democrats by 3 percentage points in 1992 and only lost it by 3 percentage points in 1996.

Bush did not lose a single county in Nebraska, Utah and Wyoming. He lost just one county each in Idaho and Nevada; two each in Kansas and North Dakota; and five each in Montana and South Dakota.

Strong rural support also enabled Bush to come close in Minnesota, Iowa and Wisconsin, which Gore had viewed as locked into his electoral vote base: These states voted for Democrat Michael S. Dukakis in 1988 and for Clinton twice.

Why did Bush thrive and Gore fail in rural America?

For one thing, analysts say that cultural issues helped Bush and hurt Gore. Rural residents are more likely than their suburban and urban counterparts to be opposed to abortion rights and gay rights and supportive of gun owners' rights. Analysts say rural residents are more likely to attend church services, and issues of character and trust resonate more strongly with these voters.

Marty Wiseman, a political scientist at Mississippi State University, said the "lines are being more clearly drawn than ever before between rural, traditional values and those that would be more commonly found in urban settings."

"The further you got from the city, the more Republican it got," said NRCC head Davis.

"That's because this election, despite all of the talk about tax cuts and reforming Social Security, was largely a cultural election," Davis contended.

There are Democratic observers who concur that the atmosphere of scandal that shadowed Clinton — especially in the years after his 1996 re-election — was a burden to Gore, especially in more socially conservative areas.

Surveys conducted by Democratic pollster Stan Greenberg found that Democrats had their largest advantages on issues such as protecting the environment and passing a health care "patients' bill of rights." But Republicans polled strongly on tackling moral problems facing the country.

Virginia, New Jersey Races May Serve As Referendums on GOP Rule

While most major election contests are a year away, there are a handful of states in which there is no vacation from politics.

Most prominent this year are Virginia and New Jersey, which will hold contests for governor. These races will be watched as early tests of public opinion about the direction of the new Bush administration and Republican-controlled Congress.

In both Virginia and New Jersey, Republicans will be defending their hold on the governorship, while Democrats plan to mount vigorous takeover efforts.

But there is a big difference between the states: Virginia Republicans are seeking to stay on a roll that has brought them to political dominance in the state, while the New Jersey GOP will be trying to break a losing trend in major statewide races.

Needing a 'V' in Virginia

The election for governor of Virginia is important for Republicans, who are trying to extend their winning streak for that office to three consecutive elections.

But for Virginia Democrats, the contest has an even higher level of urgency: They need a win this year to rescue them from the partisan oblivion to which they have been exiled in statewide politics.

Like most Southern states, Virginia had a longstanding tradition of Democratic dominance. Just a decade ago, Democrats held all three statewide constitutional offices — governor, lieutenant governor and attorney general — and held majorities by wide margins in both chambers of the state legislature. Democrats also made up a majority of the state's congressional delegation.

But they have suffered a string of losses since then. Republican Gov. George F. Allen was elected in a landslide in 1993, and the GOP swept the statewide offices four years later, led by Republican gubernatorial victor James S. Gilmore III. Republicans won control of both legislative chambers in 1999.

And in 2000, the GOP scored a crowning victory, when Allen ousted two-term Democratic Sen. Charles S. Robb and gave Virginia two Republican senators. Four-term GOP incumbent John W. Warner is the state's senior senator.

Despite their setbacks, Democrats have two things going for them.

One is that Virginia politics allows frequent opportunities for comebacks. It is the only state in which governors cannot succeed themselves after serving a single four-year term.

As a result, Gilmore — who in January was elected by the Republican National Committee as its chairman — is ineligible to seek re-election as governor, as was Allen in 1997.

Democrats also have their strongest possible candidate this year in high-tech tycoon Mark Warner.

Warner, who made a fortune in the cellular telephone business, made a splash in his first bid for political office. In 1996, Warner — then a political unknown — took a surprising 47 percent of the vote in a two-man race with Republican incumbent Sen. Warner (no relation).

Mark Warner is expected to spend heavily on his 2001 campaign from his own pockets, as he did in his Senate bid. But this time, he already has brought in substantial campaign donations from other sources.

His strong ties to the technology sector, a major factor in the politics of the populous Northern Virginia suburbs of Washington, are viewed as a big asset.

And while Warner is running unopposed for the Democratic nomination, the Republicans face the prospect of a two-candidate brawl for their nod.

Vying to succeed Gilmore are the other two Republican state elected officials: Lt. Gov. John Hager, a retired tobacco company executive, and Attorney General Mark Earley.

Earley is a prodigious vote-getter. He outperformed Gilmore and Hager in 1997 when he beat Democrat Bill Dolan for attorney general with 57 percent of the vote. Earley has also sought to reach out to black

(Box continues on page 20)

Greenberg wrote that the "conservative cultural rebellion against Clintonism" contributed to Gore's defeat. He said Gore "ran behind expectations, not among upscale voters, but among the downscale — the non-college white electorate where values concerns were most pronounced."

Greenberg found a "pattern of anti-Clinton feeling in Midwest states with significant rural and small-town populations." He said that anti-Clintonism was "particularly pronounced" in Missouri, Wisconsin, Iowa, Kentucky and Ohio. Clinton carried all five states in 1992 and 1996; Bush won three of the five — Missouri, Kentucky and Ohio — and only narrowly lost Wisconsin and Iowa, which had not voted Republican for president since 1984.

"Bill Clinton's personal ratings were particularly low and the trust issue particularly pronounced in the battleground states central to an Electoral College majority," Greenberg wrote.

Democratic Rep. Ted Strickland, who represents a number of poor rural counties in southern Ohio's 6th Congressional District, saw another problem for Gore: rural voters who were dissatisfied with the economy.

The Clinton presidency was associated with strong national economic growth, but, Strickland noted, the upswing was not felt in many rural areas.

"Unless the economy turns around in some of these areas, Mr. Bush could be feeling some of the same dissatisfaction four years from now that Mr. Gore experienced this year," Strickland said.

Historically, when the farm economy goes sour, the party occupying the

(Continued)

voters, a sizable constituency in Virginia that generally votes strongly Democratic.

But Hager's 1997 defeat of former Democratic Rep. L.F. Payne Jr. — who began the campaign a heavy favorite — was as impressive as Earley's victory.

The GOP nominee will be picked at the party's state convention in Richmond on June 2. The state Republican Party last year chose this nominating method over a primary.

A convention made up of party activists is seen by many Virginia political analysts as benefiting Earley over Hager. Though both men have close ties to social conservatives, Earley is regarded as having stronger rapport with this key Republican constituency.

Gilmore, never shy about wading into party nomination fights, asked Hager late last month to run for re-election as lieutenant governor in the interest of party unity.

But Hager refused, saying that he would "keep on trucking."

The general election outcome appears too close to call at this early stage of the race. Warner is expected to run well in Northern Virginia, his home base and the state's most reliably Democratic territory.

Either of the Republicans would likely have an advantage elsewhere in the state. Hager is from the Richmond region, and Earley is from the Chesapeake area in southeast Virginia.

Mainly rural western Virginia may be up for grabs. Though the region is conservative-leaning, Warner performed respectably there in his 1996 Senate race. But he may have to mute or calibrate his position in favor of some gun control measures when campaigning in this area. Opposition to Democratic presidential nominee Al Gore's support for gun control was one reason this region swung so strongly to Republican George W. Bush last November.

New Jersey: An Early Exit

State law barred two-term Republican Gov. Christine Todd Whitman from running this year for a third term. So both major parties have long been gearing up for the race to succeed her.

The post-Whitman era began nearly a year earlier than scheduled, though. The governor was confirmed by the Senate Jan. 30 as President Bush's choice to head the federal Environmental Protection Agency.

While there may be state pride in Whitman's appointment to the high-profile post, her ties to Bush may not be an unalloyed blessing for Republicans seeking to regain footing in a state that has been trending Democratic in big races. Bush lost New Jersey to Democratic presidential nominee Al Gore by 56-40 percent.

"Democrats want to figure out how to translate Gore's win in the state to the gubernatorial race," said Rider University political scientist David P. Rebovich.

Rebovich said Democrats will try to tie the GOP nominee for governor to parts of Bush's conservative agenda that are unpopular in the state. "The trick here for New Jersey Republicans is to maintain their independence."

But Somerset County Republican Chairman Dale Florio contended, on one hand, that Bush will be more popular in New Jersey as president than he was as a candidate, and on the other hand, that national issues will have limited relevance in the state-level race. "There are a lot of issues that will interest the people of New Jersey . . . but people will really be looking at the [governor's] race based on the candidates," Florio said.

Yet Bush's poor New Jersey showing was symptomatic of the GOP's recent problems. Also in 2000, Democrat Jon Corzine held off Republican Rep. Bob Franks (1993-2001) for the seat left open by retired Democratic Sen. Frank R. Lautenberg (1983-2001). And Whitman won re-election in 1997 by just 1 percentage point over Democrat Jim McGreevey.

McGreevey, now the mayor of the New York City suburb of Woodbridge, is likely to again be the Democratic nominee for governor this year. Citing his strong 1997 performance, Democratic officials are trying to clear the field for McGreevey in the June 5 primary.

Republicans, on the other hand, appear headed for a primary fight.

Holding the inside track is Donald DiFrancesco, the state Senate president who became acting governor when Whitman left for the EPA job. DiFrancesco, like Whitman, is regarded as a moderate on social issues.

But he could face a stiff challenge from Jersey City Mayor Bret Schundler, a darling of conservative activists who is a strong advocate of school choice and opponent of abortion rights.

White House often takes the lion's share of the blame.

The situation in 2000 had a parallel in 1986, during the Republican administration of Ronald Reagan. The national economy had been booming, but the farm economy was not doing well.

The result then was a voter backlash in several farm states. The defeats of two one-term GOP senators from usually Republican states — James Abdnor of South Dakota (by Democrat Tom Daschle) and Mark Andrews of North Dakota (by Democrat Kent Conrad) — helped the Democrats reclaim the control of the Senate they had lost in the 1980 elections.

Gore's positioning on other issues, such as his strong connection to environmental groups, vexed some rural voters.

Republican Rep. Jo Ann Emerson said this was the case in her district, southeastern Missouri's 8th.

The 8th, which abuts Arkansas, voted for Clinton in 1992 and 1996, yet backed Bush by a 20 percentage-point margin last November.

Clinton "was never perceived as a liberal or as an environmental extremist," said Emerson. "He never had to speak about environmental issues as clearly and as loudly as Vice President Gore."

Emerson said that her district, along with being "very pro-life" and "very pro-gun," is "very conservative when it comes to over-regulation."

Straw in Their Hair

Presidential candidates often cite their rural upbringings to help cultivate

GOP's Suburban Slippage Aided Gore

The suburbs of most U.S. cities, with their overwhelmingly white and wealthy populations, once were Republican strongholds. But over the past few decades, many suburbs became more racially, ethnically, economically — and politically — diverse, even as the Republicans' affiliation with religious conservatives raised qualms among some suburban voters. The results are illustrated in the chart below. Democratic presidential nominee Al Gore carried each of the states listed — California, Illinois,

Michigan, New Jersey, New York and Pennsylvania — in 2000, aided by greater suburban support than was typical for Democratic candidates through the 1980s. The last column shows how much better George Bush ran in these suburban counties in his 1988 victory than did George W. Bush in 2000. Figures in that column are rounded based on exact percentages and may vary slightly from the difference between Republican votes in the 1988 column and Republican votes in the 2000 column.

STATE	COUNTY	LOCATION	2000	1996	1992	1988	Bush 1988-Bush 2000 (%)
CALIFORNIA	Orange	southeast of L.A.	Bush, 56-40	Dole, 52-38	Bush, 44-32	Bush, 68-31	12
	Riverside	southeast of L.A.	Bush, 51-45	Dole, 46-43	Clinton, 39-37	Bush, 60-40	8
	Santa Barbara	northwest of L.A.	Gore, 47-46	Clinton, 47-42	Clinton, 43-35	Bush, 54-45	8
	Ventura	west of L.A.	Bush, 48-47	Clinton, 44-43	Clinton, 37-36	Bush, 62-37	14
	STATEWIDE		**Gore, 53-42**	**Clinton, 51-38**	**Clinton, 46-33**	**Bush, 51-48**	**9**
ILLINOIS	Cook	parts outside Chicago	Gore, 57-41	Clinton, 54-38	Clinton, 44-39	Bush, 58-41	18
	Lake	north of Chicago	Bush, 50-48	Clinton, 45.6-45.5	Bush, 44-37	Bush, 64-36	14
	DuPage	west of Chicago	Bush, 55-42	Dole, 51-40	Bush, 48-31	Bush, 69-30	14
	STATEWIDE		**Gore, 55-43**	**Clinton, 54-37**	**Clinton, 49-34**	**Bush, 51-49**	**8**
MICHIGAN	Macomb	northeast of Detroit	Gore, 50-48	Clinton, 49-39	Bush, 42-37	Bush, 60-39	12
	Oakland	north of Detroit	Gore, 49-48	Clinton, 48-44	Bush, 44-39	Bush, 61-38	13
	Wayne	parts outside Detroit	Gore, 53-44	Clinton, 53-37	Clinton, 42-40	Bush, 56-43	12
	STATEWIDE		**Gore, 51-46**	**Clinton, 52-39**	**Clinton, 44-36**	**Bush, 54-46**	**7**
NEW JERSEY	Bergen	NYC suburbs	Gore, 55-42	Clinton, 53-39	Bush, 44-42	Bush, 58-41	16
	Monmouth	NYC suburbs	Gore, 50-46	Clinton, 48-40	Bush, 44-38	Bush, 61-38	15
	Morris	NYC suburbs	Bush, 54-43	Dole, 49-41	Bush, 52-32	Bush, 68-31	14
	STATEWIDE		**Gore, 56-40**	**Clinton, 54-36**	**Clinton, 43-41**	**Bush, 56-43**	**16**
NEW YORK	Nassau	Long Island	Gore, 58-38	Clinton, 56-36	Clinton, 46-41	Bush, 57-42	19
	Rockland	NYC suburbs	Gore, 57-40	Clinton, 56-36	Clinton, 47-41	Bush, 57-42	17
	Suffolk	Long Island	Gore, 53-42	Clinton, 52-36	Bush, 40-39	Bush, 61-39	19
	Westchester	NYC suburbs	Gore, 59-37	Clinton, 57-36	Clinton, 49-40	Bush, 53-46	16
	STATEWIDE		**Gore, 60-35**	**Clinton, 60-31**	**Clinton, 50-34**	**Dukakis, 52-48**	**12**
PENNSYLVANIA	Bucks	north of Philadelphia	Gore, 50-46	Clinton, 45-42	Clinton, 39-38	Bush, 60-39	14
	Chester	west of Philadelphia	Bush, 53-44	Dole, 49-41	Bush, 44-35	Bush, 67-32	14
	Delaware	southwest of Philadelphia	Gore, 54-43	Clinton, 49-40	Clinton, 42-41	Bush, 60-39	17
	Montgomery	northwest of Philadelphia	Gore, 54-44	Clinton, 49-41	Clinton, 43-40	Bush, 60-39	16
	STATEWIDE		**Gore, 51-46**	**Clinton, 49-40**	**Clinton, 45-36**	**Bush, 51-48**	**4**

Sources: State election offices; CQ's America Votes books

a common-man image. Clinton emphasized his childhood in Hope, Ark., and Dole mentioned growing up in Russell, Kan.

Though it is well known that Bush and Gore are children of privilege, each tried to strike a homespun pose in their outreach to rural voters.

Gore often spoke of working summers on his family's farm in Carthage, Tenn. When Gore moved his campaign headquarters from Washington, D.C., to Nashville in September 1999, it was viewed as a symbolic effort to get more in touch with the everyday lives of ordinary Americans.

Bush made frequent visits to his

ranch in Crawford, Texas, two hours away from the state capital of Austin where he presided as governor. He was often seen during the campaign wearing jeans and cowboy boots.

But Bush also frequently spoke of "restoring honor and dignity" to the White House, a not-so-subtle reference to Clinton's personal scandals. It was a message that resonated with socially conservative rural voters.

Some Democrats complained that the Gore campaign compounded its problems by making little or no effort to attract rural voters. Strickland said Clinton came to his district four times during his presidency, but Gore did not

come to the district once during the 2000 campaign.

"It was as if my part of Ohio did not exist in this campaign," Strickland said.

It can hardly be said that there was a great "coattails" effect in Bush's victory for House Republicans. The GOP lost a net of two House seats nationally.

Yet the GOP's issue advantage in rural areas helped the party capture four contests for seats formerly held by Democrats that were crucial to the Republicans' continued, if narrow, control of the House:

• Republican Sam Graves won the seat in northwestern Missouri's 6th

Big Rural Gains Helped Bush Clinch White House Win

A huge advantage in rural areas enabled Republican George W. Bush to win his razor-thin Electoral College victory in 2000. The eight states in this chart — Arkansas, Kentucky, Louisiana, Missouri, Nevada, Ohio, Tennessee and West Virginia — have large rural populations, and all backed Bush after giving their electoral votes in 1996 to the Democratic ticket of President Bill Clinton and Vice President Al Gore. The rural jurisdictions listed within each state were those in which Bush showed the most improvement over 1996 GOP nominee Bob Dole. Figures in the far-right column are rounded based on exact percentages and may vary slightly from the difference between GOP votes in the 1996 column and in 2000.

STATE	COUNTY/PARISH	LOCATION	Congressional District	2000 Winner and Percentage	1996 Winner and Percentage	Bush Improvement over Dole 1996 (%)
ARKANSAS	Scott	far west; Oklahoma border	3	Bush, 60-36	Clinton, 53-33	27
	Pike	southwest	4	Bush, 57-40	Clinton, 55-33	24
	Prairie	east-central	1	Bush, 53-45	Clinton, 62-29	24
	Arkansas	east	1	Bush, 53-45	Clinton, 63-29	24
	Montgomery	west	4	Bush, 57-38	Clinton, 53-33	24
	STATEWIDE			**Bush, 51-46**	**Clinton, 54-37**	**14**
KENTUCKY	Owsley	east	5	Bush, 80-19	Dole, 53-37	27
	Hickman	far west; Missouri border	1	Bush, 54-44	Clinton, 56-32	22
	Trimble	north; Indiana border	4	Bush, 60-38	Clinton, 49-39	21
	Union	far west; Illinois/Indiana border	1	Bush, 51-47	Clinton, 57-31	21
	Carlisle	far west; Missouri border	1	Bush, 54-44	Clinton, 56-34	21
	STATEWIDE			**Bush, 57-41**	**Clinton, 46-45**	**12**
LOUISIANA	La Salle	central	5	Bush, 75-23	Dole, 45-39	30
	Cameron	southwest; Texas border	7	Bush, 62-34	Clinton, 51-33	29
	Catahoula	central	5	Bush, 61-36	Clinton, 52-34	27
	Winn	north-central	5	Bush, 63-34	Clinton, 51-38	26
	Sabine	west; Texas border	4	Bush, 65-32	Clinton, 47-39	26
	STATEWIDE			**Bush, 53-45**	**Clinton, 52-40**	**13**
MISSOURI	Mercer	far north; Iowa border	6	Bush, 68-30	Clinton, 44-42	26
	Reynolds	southeast	8	Bush, 56-42	Clinton, 55-31	26
	Scotland	far northeast; Iowa border	9	Bush, 61-36	Clinton, 47-37	25
	Shannon	southeast	8	Bush, 59-38	Clinton, 50-35	24
	Grundy	northwest	6	Bush, 63-33	Clinton, 44-40	23
	STATEWIDE			**Bush, 50-47**	**Clinton, 48-41**	**9**
NEVADA	Lander	central	2	Bush, 77-19	Dole, 50-30	27
	White Pine	east; Utah border	2	Bush, 64-31	Dole, 40.03-39.97	24
	Elko	northeast; Idaho/Utah borders	2	Bush, 78-18	Dole, 55-27	23
	Humboldt	north; Oregon border	2	Bush, 73-23	Dole, 51-32	22
	Pershing	northwest	2	Bush, 69-27	Dole, 47-36	21
	STATEWIDE			**Bush, 50-46**	**Clinton, 44-43**	**7**
OHIO	Meigs	southeast; West Virginia border	6	Bush, 59-38	Clinton, 45-38	20
	Vinton	southeast	6	Bush, 55-41	Clinton, 49-35	20
	Mercer	west; Indiana border	8	Bush, 68-28	Dole, 50-36	18
	Noble	east	18	Bush, 57-38	Clinton, 43-40	18
	Gallia	southeast; West Virginia border	6	Bush, 59-38	Clinton, 43-41	18
	STATEWIDE			**Bush, 50-46**	**Clinton, 47-41**	**9**
TENNESSEE	Sequatchie	southeast	3	Bush, 56-42	Clinton, 49-42	14
	Obion	northwest; Kentucky border	8	Bush, 50-49	Clinton, 54-37	13
	Morgan	east-central	3	Bush, 51-47	Clinton, 52-39	12
	Polk	southeast	3	Bush, 52-46	Clinton, 51-40	12
	Rhea	east-central	4	Bush, 60-38	Dole, 49-43	12
	STATEWIDE			**Bush, 51-47**	**Clinton, 48-46**	**5**
WEST VIRGINIA	Tyler	northwest; Ohio border	1	Bush, 66-31	Clinton, 53-26	39
	Webster	central	3	Gore, 53-45	Clinton, 69-20	25
	Preston	north	1	Bush, 63-34	Dole, 41.3-41.1	22
	Randolph	east-central	2	Bush, 55-42	Clinton, 54-33	22
	Lewis	central	2	Bush, 59-38	Clinton, 47-37	22
	STATEWIDE			**Bush, 52-46**	**Clinton, 52-37**	**15**

Sources: State election offices; CQ's America Votes books

District left open by retired Democratic Rep. Pat Danner (1993-2001).

• Melissa Hart won western Pennsylvania's 4th District, which Democratic Rep. Ron Klink (1993-2001) had left open to run for the Senate.

• Shelley Moore Capito won in West Virginia's 2nd District to succeed nine-term Democrat Bob Wise (1983-2001), who was making a successful bid for governor.

• Mark Kennedy won narrowly in southwestern Minnesota's 2nd District, ousting Democratic Rep. David Minge (1993-2001).

All four districts voted for Clinton in 1992 and 1996 and Bush in 2000.

"Rural America believes in freedom," Kennedy said. "Bush did a good job of enunciating how in many, many ways he was for freedom, and I think that people had a sense of Gore . . . that he was more for having the government having more control over your life."

Capito is regarded as a moderate on some social issues, including abortion. But her campaign's emphasis on conservative values was evident in an Oct. 25 news release attacking House Democratic leader Richard A. Gephardt of Missouri, who campaigned for her Democratic opponent, Jim Humphreys.

The release said Gephardt was "anti-West Virginia" for voting against parental notification for a minor's abortion and against a constitutional amendment that would bar desecration of the U.S. flag.

Davis of the NRCC referred to Hart's district, a blue-collar area in the Pittsburgh region, as "culturally conservative," adding that Hart "won it on guns and abortion."

Sticking to Their Guns

A political reversal on the issue of firearms regulation was one of the biggest setbacks endured by the Democrats in Campaign 2000.

After two students used high-powered weapons in a massacre at Columbine High School in Littleton, Colo., in April 1999, Democrats sought to gain the initiative on the gun control issue by demonstrating that gun violence is not confined to urban centers.

But a 1999 House vote aimed at requiring background checks on purchases at gun shows — what Clinton and most Democrats called "closing the gun show loophole" and described as common-sense regulation — was highly unpopular in rural areas. So was Gore's call for licensing of all handguns. (*Gun control debate, 1999 CQ Almanac, p. 18-3*)

According to Greenberg, 48 percent of people who voted in last November's presidential election owned guns, up from 37 percent in 1996. He attributed that to a strong groundswell of political activism among supporters of gun owners' rights.

"That 11-point rise in the gun-owning electorate was not produced by massive gun sales; it was produced by the increased engagement and mobilization of pro-gun voters," Greenberg said.

Strickland recalled campaigning at an event last year and speaking to several older men who were selling guns.

"One of them said, 'You know, I don't want Al Gore taking my guns, but I don't want George Bush taking my Social Security either,' " Strickland said. "I suspect the gun issue won out over Social Security."

William Galston, a professor at the University of Maryland and centrist Democrat who was a domestic policy adviser to President Clinton, said Gore's strong support for gun control did more to fire up the other side than his own.

"I say that with some chagrin, as someone who believes strongly in reasonable gun safety legislation, as I think most Democrats do, but it's clear that there is a lot of intensity on the other side of that issue that we have to think through," Galston said.

The issue also played out to the Democrats' detriment in several congressional races.

For example, the Democrats had high hopes of recapturing the House seat in east-central Kentucky's 6th District: Democratic former Rep. Scotty Baesler (1993-99), who had left the seat open for a 1998 Senate bid that failed, was challenging his freshman Republican successor, Ernie Fletcher.

But the 6th District's constituency is mainly conservative and pro-gun, and Baesler's past support for gun control measures drew him the vocal opposition of the National Rifle Association (NRA). This was a major factor in his unexpectedly lopsided loss: Fletcher defeated Baesler by 18 percentage points.

Yet even as this issue helped Bush swamp Gore in many rural areas, it aided Gore's ability to hold his own in many of the nation's suburban regions. This — combined with his dominance in the core cities — put Gore over the top in a number of key battleground states of the Northeast, Midwest and Far West.

A New Age

During their long histories as exclusive provinces of wealthy white Protestants, suburbs were identified with Republican politics. As late as 1988, when the elder George Bush ran successfully for president, the GOP still dominated in many traditionally Republican bedroom communities.

But the Republicans' continued edge then masked evolutionary changes that would alter the suburbs' political dynamic.

Many suburbanites — even a large number of affluent professionals who might have been sympathetic to Republican economic stances — hold moderate or liberal views on social issues such as abortion rights and gun control. Thus developed a suburban wariness of the national Republican Party's conservatism on social issues and its alliance with religious conservative activists.

According to centrist Democratic groups such as the Democratic Leadership Council (DLC) and New Democrat Network, suburban gains for their party were ensured by its tendency — since Clinton's overtly centrist first presidential campaign in 1992 — to speak the suburbanites' language of the technology-driven "new economy."

"This is the bottom line: The New Economy is creating a new electorate that demands a new politics," DLC president Al From wrote in a special "Why Gore Lost" issue of Blueprint, the organization's policy magazine.

"The sharp class differences of the Industrial Age are becoming less distinct as more and more Americans move into the middle and upper-middle classes. . . ," From wrote. "The new electorate is affluent, educated, diverse, suburban, 'wired' and moderate. And it responds more favorably to the New Democrat political philosophy than to any other."

Also, increased economic opportunity and laws barring housing discrimination have made the suburbs dramatically more diverse in ethnicity and race, drawing in large numbers of traditionally Democratic-voting urbanites.

NRCC head Davis argues that these changes have played a definitive role in the Democrats' suburban gains.

He even suggests that the definition of suburbs needs to be adapted to include the outer counties of metropolitan areas — now typically described as "exurban" — which are increasingly being enveloped in suburban sprawl and which also tend to vote more conservatively and Republican than the older inner suburbs.

Davis said counties that lie immediately outside central cities, which political analysts refer to as suburbs, have

Adam Schiff was one of four California Democrats to win GOP-held seats in 2000. Schiff beat incumbent James E. Rogan in suburban Los Angeles' 27th District, once a GOP bastion.

"actually turned into cities."

Davis cited Arlington County, Va., which is located across the Potomac River from Washington, D.C., as an example of a county that was once largely suburban but which has adopted urban qualities.

Arlington has large Latino and Asian-American populations and numerous ethnic restaurants and shops.

"Arlington was a suburban county when I grew up," said Davis, whose own district, Virginia's 11th, abuts Arlington. "The people who move into Arlington today aren't moving to be away from the city, they're moving to be in the city, near the action."

In the 1950s, when Davis was a boy, Arlington County gave Republican presidential candidates about the same vote percentages as they received statewide. But the gap has significantly widened since then.

In 1984, Reagan received 62 percent of Virginia's presidential vote and 48 percent of the Arlington County vote — a 14 percentage-point difference. By 2000, the gap had increased to 18 percentage points, as Bush received 52 percent of the statewide vote but just 34 percent of the vote in Arlington County .

There are exceptions to the GOP suburban slide. Republican candidates continue to do quite well in suburban areas of states regarded as conservative bastions, especially in the South. For example, most counties outside Charlotte, N.C., Columbia, S.C., and Atlanta voted strongly Republican.

Sport-Utility Voting

Gore's relative success in key suburban areas was essential to his victories in crucial states.

In Michigan, which Gore won narrowly, the Democrat carried Oakland and Macomb counties outside of Detroit. Both voted Republican for president as recently as 1992.

In Illinois, which Gore carried decisively, Bush lost by 56-41 percent in the Cook County suburbs of Chicago — where his father won by 58-41 percent in 1988.

Bush narrowly carried Lake County, north of Chicago — which in 1984 gave 68 percent to the Republican ticket headed by Reagan.

Pennsylvania went narrowly for Gore. But Bush would have won the

state had he achieved a stronger showing in the suburbs of Philadelphia — the city that held the Republican National Convention that nominated Bush for president.

Bush lost Montgomery County, located northwest of Philadelphia, by 10 percentage points — the largest margin of defeat for a Republican presidential candidate in the county since conservative Barry M. Goldwater lost it by 14 percentage points in his landslide defeat by Democrat Lyndon B. Johnson in 1964. Mainly affluent Montgomery is home to Philadelphia's famed "Main Line" suburbs.

Bush also lost Bucks County, north of Philadelphia, and Delaware County, southwest of the city, by the largest vote margins for a Republican candidate since Goldwater.

Back in Virginia, Davis' home district gave Gore a 2 percentage-point edge last November, about the same as Clinton's 1996 victory margin. Four-term Republican Davis has been able to politically dominate the district, which cuts across the Northern Virginia suburbs of Washington, D.C., largely because he is widely viewed as a centrist Republican.

Elsewhere, Democrats have been consolidating gains in suburban House districts long known as Republican strongholds.

Democratic Rep. Rush D. Holt — who captured New Jersey's 12th District in a major 1998 upset over Republican incumbent Mike Pappas — again surprised a number of observers in 2000, as he fended off a fierce challenge by Republican former Rep. Dick Zimmer (1991-97) in one of the year's closest races.

Democratic Reps. Joseph M. Hoeffel of Pennsylvania's 13th District and Dennis Moore of Kansas' 3rd District fended off determined Republican opposition to win second terms in suburban seats.

Democrats also added another trophy last year in New York's 2nd District. Their nominee, Steve Israel, easily beat Republican Joan B. Johnson for the seat left open by Republican Rep. Rick A. Lazio for his ultimately failed Senate bid against Democrat Hillary Rodham Clinton.

Republican registrants outnumber Democrats in the 2nd, located in Long Island's Suffolk County suburbs. Though Democrat Thomas J. Downey previously had a long tenure in the seat

(1975-93), Republican Lazio subsequently dominated it for eight years.

Political Power Crisis

One of the most troubling developments for GOP election strategists is the party's backslide in suburban areas in California, which has contributed to a series of Democratic gains in the nation's mega-state.

In the presidential contest, the Bush campaign spent heavily in California. But Bush lost the state by 12 percentage points, only a marginal gain over Dole in 1996.

Three Southern California Republican incumbents were ousted in the same election.

Two of them had represented areas of suburban Los Angeles: James E. Rogan (1997-2001), who lost a historically expensive contest to Democrat Adam Schiff in the 27th District that broke campaign spending records; and Steven T. Kuykendall (1999-2001), who was overtaken by the comeback victory of Democratic former Rep. Jane Harman (1993-99) in the 36th District.

The other, Brian P. Bilbray (1995-2001), lost to Democrat Susan Davis in the 49th District, which reaches from downtown San Diego to the city's affluent northern suburbs.

Democrats also made a pickup in California's 15th District, which Republican Rep. Tom Campbell left open in 2000 for a Senate bid that failed.

Republicans recruited state Rep. Jim Cunneen, a fiscally conservative, socially moderate candidate in the mold of the popular incumbent, for whom he once worked as a top district aide. Republican strategists touted Cunneen as the perfect fit for the Silicon Valley district. Yet he lost to Democratic state Rep. Mike Honda by a whopping 13 percentage points.

Democrats now hold a 32-20 advantage in the House delegation, assuming their expected victory in this spring's 32nd District special election to replace the late Democratic Rep. Julian Dixon (1979-2000), who died Dec. 8. (*2000 CQ Weekly, p. 2810*).

With Democratic Gov. Gray Davis and a Democratic-dominated state Legislature in place, California alone accounts for more than a third of the districts in which Democrats have complete control over the redistricting process. (*Redistricting outlook, 2001 CQ Weekly, p. 114*)

One big problem for Republicans in California is that the suburbs tend to lean toward moderation on social issues — while the state party organization is dominated, as it has been for many years, by activists who hold strongly conservative views on those issues.

GOP Rep. Davis, who as NRCC head encouraged Republican candidates in 2000 to run as moderates if that would help them get elected, acknowledged his party's California quandary.

"Until the state party comes to grips and looks in the mirror and decides it wants to start winning elections again, instead of being right, we're just not going to be competitive out there," Davis said.

Democrats' Urban Renewal

As in most of the nation's populous states, the Democrats' greatest numbers are found in California's metropolitan cities. For example, Gore defeated Bush in San Francisco 76 percent to 16 percent, a 60 point edge that bettered Clinton's 1996 vote performance by 4 points.

Strength in the cities has been a foundation of the Democratic base going back to the 19th century, when the party attracted the nation's burgeoning population of immigrants who felt excluded by a Republican Party then dominated by nativist sentiment.

The Democrats' urban dominance was enhanced and cemented during the administration of President Franklin D. Roosevelt, whose New Deal policies appealed directly to industrial workers, liberal city-dwellers (including many Jewish voters) and blacks (many of whom had stayed loyal to the GOP, the "Party of Lincoln").

The Democratic percentages have only become larger as the cities have become increasingly populated by African-Americans — now the party's most loyal voters — and Hispanics. Many city-dwelling whites also are Democrats, including "limousine liberals" who reside in more upscale areas, or working-class laborers who belong to unions.

As a result, Democrats represent an overwhelming percentage of urban congressional districts. The small handful of Republicans who represent urban districts tend to agree with the positions of labor unions on issues such as increasing the minimum wage and opposing trade measures.

If Republican candidates have nowhere to go but up in the cities, they have shown no signs of significant improvement.

As recently as 1988, the elder Bush won 30 percent of the presidential vote in the city of Chicago; George W. Bush took just 17 percent of the Chicago vote last year as the Republican nominee. Reagan took 46 percent in the New York City borough of Queens in his 1984 landslide; Bush took just 22 percent of the Queens vote last year.

The cities provide Democrats with a valuable cache of votes to offset their deficits in some suburbs and most rural areas. Democratic presidential candidates rely on strong showings in cities such as Detroit and Philadelphia to carry critical "swing" states.

In last year's Senate race in New York, Democrat Hillary Rodham Clinton won New York City by more than 1.1 million votes, while she lost the rest of the state by about 275,000 votes. In Michigan, then-Rep. Debbie Stabenow's wide Democratic victory margin in Wayne County, which includes Detroit, enabled her to unseat Republican Sen. Spencer Abraham (1995-2001).

The problem for Democrats is that the urban vote does not have the clout that it used to. The populations of many cities have been static or even declined over the past few decades, while suburban and exurban populations have boomed. As a result, cities now make up a much smaller percentage of the total vote than in the past.

In 1952, New York City cast 48 percent of the statewide presidential vote. In the 2000 race, New York City voters accounted for just 32 percent of the statewide electorate. In 1952, Chicago voters cast 41 percent of the statewide vote in the presidential election, compared to 20 percent in 2000.

And Republicans, looking for a silver lining, point to local victories in Democratic strongholds such as New York City, where Republican Rudolph W. Giuliani is mayor, and Los Angeles, which is headed by Republican Richard Riordan.

But most GOP successes in cities have come despite — and not because of — their candidates' partisan label.

Giuliani backed New York Democratic Gov. Mario M. Cuomo in his unsuccessful 1994 re-election bid and opposes national GOP platform positions on most social issues. Riordan endorsed California Democratic Sen. Dianne Feinstein for re-election last year. ◆

Debating McCain-Feingold

A preview of arguments likely to be heard from both sides on the role of money in politics

"The purification of politics is an iridescent dream," Kansas Republican Sen. John James Ingalls wrote more than a century ago. In a week's time and down the hall from Ingalls' straight-backed statue in the Capitol, his political descendants will open debate on legislation intended to further curb the power of money in political campaigns.

After nearly six years of footwork and filibuster, the Senate will spend two weeks on the merits of a campaign finance bill written, revised and probably memorized by two unlikely allies and political renegades: Republican John McCain of Arizona and Democrat Russell D. Feingold of Wisconsin.

The centerpiece of their legislation (S 27) has been the same since the 1996 elections: a ban on "soft money" contributions to national political parties, unregulated cash that is redefining campaigns.

The bill would for the first time restrict "issue ads" typically bought by interest groups, corporations and labor unions to express their views on an issue that might figure in a campaign. Issue ads that identify a particular candidate would be banned within 60 days of a general election; corporations and unions could not use their treasuries to pay for them.

Anyone who spent more than $10,000 a year on broadcast ads would have to disclose who paid for them, and coordination between candidates and interest groups would be considered a political contribution subject to financial limits and reporting requirements.

On March 19, the 38-page bill goes before the full Senate for two weeks of debate, with no limit on the number of potential amendments. Every senator will want to have a say, a chance to perhaps capture public attention or persuade a reluctant colleague. In the end, the arguments may be boiled down to five reasons to support the bill and five reasons to oppose it:

ARGUMENTS FOR

'Soft' Money Is Corrupting Politics

For McCain and Feingold, the 1996 and 2000 elections were case studies in the corrosive effect of unregulated "soft" contributions to political parties, distinguished from "hard" money given directly to campaigns and both regulated and reported.

Former Vice President Al Gore's 2000 campaign was haunted by allegations that he had used his White House phone to help the Democratic Party raise "soft" money in 1996 and even canvassed a Buddhist temple on a trip to California. Contributions approaching a half-million dollars to his library may have helped persuade former President Bill

Clinton to pardon fugitive financier Marc Rich in the closing hours of his administration. Already, President Bush has rewarded major Republican Party contributors with ambassadorships in Europe.

While individuals are limited to $1,000 contributions per candidate per election and political action committees are held to $5,000, anyone can donate as much as he or she wishes to a national party committee. Under the vague definition of "party building" activities, the committee is free to use the cash on advertising that can benefit or harm particular candidates.

Corporations, industrialists, unions, professional associations and interest groups of all persuasions were not long in exploiting this gap in campaign finance law that had been created by a combination of a 1978 ruling by the Federal Election Commission (FEC) and a 1979 revision (PL 96-187) of the Federal Election Campaign Act. *(FEC, p. 28)*

Soft money that amounted to only about $22 million in the 1984 national campaigns had risen to $260 million in the 1995-96 election cycle, then nearly doubled to more than $480 million in 1999-2000. In the 1996 presidential campaign, 20 people made contributions of at least a quarter-million dollars; in 2000, the number was up to 78.

"The extraordinary spending in the 2000 election gives monied interests more influence on the Congress and the President than ever before," Feingold said during the bill's January unveiling.

Banning such donations, supporters of the bill say, would bring government closer to average Americans.

Mindful that the Supreme Court considers campaign contributions protected free speech, McCain-Feingold supporters say their soft money ban could survive a legal challenge. They cite a Supreme Court comment in last year's *Nixon v. Shrink Missouri Government PAC* decision recognizing "a concern not confined to bribery of public officials, but extending to the broader threat from politicians too compliant with the wishes of large contributors. "

Special Interests Hide Behind 'Issue' Ads

A rising tide of campaign ads masquerading as issue advocacy and often paid for anonymously or by generically named organizations threatens to overwhelm political finance controls and disclosure.

"Most of the time we don't know where these ads come from or who pays for them," Sen. Dianne Feinstein, D-Calif., complained during a 1998 debate. "All we see are vicious personal attack ads which pop up on television during a campaign and, occasionally, a follow-up newspaper article or report claiming credit and detailing the particulars of the attack."

The Annenberg Public Policy Center at the University of Pennsylvania estimates that $509 million was spent on issue ads during the 2000 election cycle, about a third of it by Republican and Democratic parties.

The Growth of Soft Money (millions of dollars)

Although hard money contributions given directly to candidates still provide the bulk of money spent on political campaigns, soft money donations to political party committees have grown in volume in recent years.

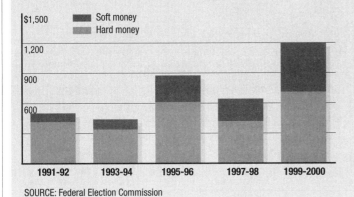

	1991-92	1993-94	1995-96	1997-98	1999-2000
DEMOCRATS					
Hard money	$155.5	$121.1	$210.0	$153.4	$269.9
Soft money	36.3	49.1	122.3	91.5	243.1
REPUBLICANS					
Hard money	266.3	223.7	407.5	273.6	447.4
Soft money	49.8	52.5	141.2	131.0	244.4
TOTAL	**$507.9**	**$446.4**	**$881.0**	**$649.5**	**$1,204.8**

SOURCE: Federal Election Commission

This flood of ads helped shift Sen. Thad Cochran, R-Miss., to support the McCain-Feingold bill. "We're defenseless against the juggernaut of huge, unregulated, undisclosed expenditures by groups," he said.

According to a memo by the political watchdog group Common Cause, "Particularly where such ads are run right before an election, it is overwhelmingly clear that they are intended by their sponsors to be campaign ads, and they have the same effect on the voters as campaign ads. As a matter of common sense and political reality, such ads should be treated by law the same as any other campaign ads."

A provision in the bill, offered by Republican Sens. Olympia J. Snowe of Maine and James M. Jeffords of Vermont, would regulate issue ads that attack or praise a candidate.

Supporters argue that the bill is needed to shed light on thinly veiled campaign advertising paid for by corporate and labor groups. For example, it would prevent the pharmaceutical industry from putting money into Citizens for Better Medicare, which aired television ads in congressional races last year. The Snowe-Jeffords proposal would ban corporate and labor-funded broadcast ads that refer to a federal candidate within 30 days of a primary or 60 days of a general election. It does not cover direct mail, voter guides, telephone banks or Internet communications.

The bill would permit corporate and labor PACs to air such ads, but money for those efforts would be subject to standard contribution limits and disclosure. Nonprofit groups could pay for such issue ads if they raised the money solely from individual contributors, thus preventing labor unions and corporations from funneling money through shell groups.

Campaign Finance Laws Are Antiquated

The current campaign finance system has been changed little since it was enacted in 1974, in the wake of Watergate. When Congress last revised the fundraising law in 1979, the distinction between hard and soft money did not exist, and therefore was never addressed. No significant campaign finance legislation has been signed into law since that time, and current practices have evolved around the laws. The Federal Election Commission, evenly divided between Republicans and Democrats, has been able to make only minor adjustments.

"The laws are less and less relevant to what is happening," said Trevor Potter, a former member of the commission and general counsel to McCain's presidential campaign. "This is something Congress will have to do, not the FEC."

For instance, recent campaigns saw an explosion of "527 groups" or "stealth PACs" — political action committees that used a loophole in the finance laws to raise and spend unlimited amounts of unreported money before Congress passed a law (PL 106-230) requiring disclosure. (2000 CQ Weekly, p. 2898)

Even then, several of the high-profile 527s said they would reorganize in order to continue their activities without disclosure.

After the 2000 elections, FEC commissioner Karl J. Sandstrom said the episode was a "poster child for an enfeebled FEC."

Another outdated concept in campaign finance law is the "magic words" test, which describes advertisements that use specific language to advocate the election or defeat of a candidate. A study by the Brennan Center for Justice at New York University School of Law found that in the 1998 congressional elections, just 4 percent of candidate ads used the "magic words."

Not changing the laws to keep up with current practices, supporters argue, will only lead to greater influence of money in politics and further scandals.

Fundraising Distracts From Governing

From the day they reach the Capitol, members of Congress must start frantically raising money for their next campaigns. Many lawmakers become almost consumed by the hunt, racing from reception to dinner to the telephone. Some quit Congress because of it.

Even those relatively safe from political challenge must set aside a certain amount of time each week or month to raise money — time they cannot spend on legislation or constituent service.

During a 1997 Senate debate on an earlier version of the McCain-Feingold bill, Democrat Harry Reid of Nevada spoke his frustration: "We must bring attention back to what the real issues are in campaign finance — that is, the fact that senators and representatives spend large amounts of their time and their efforts simply raising money in order to pay for escalating media costs."

"Take a small state like the State of Nevada or . . . the State of Arizona: $4 million, which has a relatively small campaign fund in this modern era, sadly. To raise that much money, you have to raise about $13,000 or $14,000 a week every year. You don't take a week off for Christmas. If you do, you have to raise more money. If you do that 52 weeks a year for six years, you can raise enough to be competitive in a race. . . . In some states it takes a lot more money. In those states, you have to raise twice that much or three times or four times that much. Instead of raising $13,000 or $14,000 a week, people have to raise $50,000 a week."

Candidates Must Be Divorced From Interest Groups

Once a corporate executive, a union, lawyer or political action committee has contributed the maximum amount of money to a candidate, there are other ways they can help. The McCain-Feingold bill defines the relationship between organizations and candidates during a campaign and seeks to restrict the kind of activities they can undertake together.

For example, an interest group that has already contributed the maximum to a candidate could not pay for an advertisement, purchase supplies or lease a car at that candidate's request. Issue ads coordinated with a federal candidate would be considered contributions and thus subject to hard money limits.

Supporters argue that this would limit a candidate's ability to call upon a friendly industry or trade association to spend additional money on his or her behalf. The same restriction would apply to political parties, removing party committees as conduits for interest groups seeking to provide additional support for a preferred candidate. PACs would still be allowed to make unlimited independent expenditures against a candidate.

ARGUMENTS AGAINST

The First Amendment Protects Political Activity

The bedrock argument against campaign finance laws in general and the McCain-Feingold bill in particular is the constitutional protection of free speech. In its 1976 *Buckley v. Valeo* decision, the Supreme Court ruled that political contributions are akin to speech. Contributions to influence a particular federal election can be limited in the interest of removing "corruption and appearance of corruption," the court said, but spending by a candidate in pursuit of office cannot. The decision has largely framed the campaign finance debate ever since.

Opponents say a ban on soft money would deny contributors a voice in politics. "In order to do what McCain-Feingold would like to do, you do have to amend the First Amendment for the first time in history," said Mitch McConnell, R-Ky., the Senate's most implacable enemy of campaign finance legislation.

Though Republicans like McConnell bridle at restrictions on soft money, since their party raises more of it, some Democrats have grown edgy about the limits since they have

Regulatory Agency Struggles With Torrent of Money

The Federal Election Commission, created by Congress in 1975, is charged with administering and enforcing the Federal Election Campaign Act (PL 93-443), which sets the rules governing financing of congressional and presidential races.

The FEC collects campaign filings, audits and administers the public funding of presidential campaigns and assesses fines against violators. It also provides statistics and data to the press and research groups.

Because Congress seldom passes campaign finance legislation, the agency has had to interpret the 1975 law through advisory opinions issued case by case. The agency has sought legal guidance as a litigant in federal court cases, including a Supreme Court case in February involving the constitutionality of limiting parties' spending in coordination with candidates.

To assure that no political party controls the commission, its six members are split between Republicans and Democrats. Commissioners are nominated by the president and confirmed by the Senate. The chairmanship rotates and currently is held by Danny L. McDonald, a Democrat nominated by President Ronald Reagan. Vice Chairman David Mason, a Republican, was nominated in 1998 by President Bill Clinton.

Critics long have derided the FEC as "toothless" in the face of the ever-growing flow of money into federal campaigns. Part of the problem, they say, is that election law violations are handled in lawsuits that are not settled until elections are over. In response, the FEC instituted a program that favors mediation over legal action. At least six cases have been resolved through arbitration.

been closing the fundraising gap.

Interest groups, such as the anti-abortion National Right to Life Committee, said that restrictions on "issue" ads would unfairly limit the right of corporations, unions and trade associations to be involved in elections and legislative activity. The committee contends that a corporation could not buy a radio or television ad within 30 days of a primary election that said, "Urge [Congressman X] to vote against the McCain-Feingold bill."

Douglas Johnson, the group's legislative director, said March 1 that the rules on issue ads would "disrupt our ability to inform like-minded citizens regarding what their elected officials are doing, and two, greatly impede our ability to effectively communicate with elected representatives on our members' behalf."

The bill's reporting requirements for independent expenditures also raise constitutional questions. Under McCain-Feingold, for example, an organization buying air time for an independent expenditure of more than $10,000 would have to report the purchase to the Federal Election Commission within 48 hours of the time it is made. The Right to Life Committee maintains that Congress "lacks the authority to demand that [we] declare in advance when and where we intend to utter a politician's name to the public."

Soft Money Strengthens Political Parties

Soft money has put political parties — which some feared were becoming irrelevant to modern campaigns — back in the game, providing much-needed cash for party activities, including training candidates and running "get out the vote" phone banks.

Opponents of the McCain-Feingold bill argue not only that banning soft money is unconstitutional, but that it would hamstring the ability of parties to raise money and support their candidates.

Last year, when McConnell organized hearings on the role of parties, Duke University political scientist Michael C. Munger testified that banning soft money would make special interest groups even more powerful by "crippling" party organizations. While the bill would ban soft money gifts to parties, it would not prevent lobbying or membership groups from collecting similar donations from individuals as long as they were spent on "issue" advertisements.

Political parties now use soft money to help pay for many things beyond ads, including consultants, office space, salaries and equipment. That way, they have more "hard" money to give candidates. Taking soft money away from parties, opponents of the bill say, would leave them weaker against special interests and would especially hurt their ability to finance challengers to incumbents. Since incumbents tend to attract the bulk of PAC money, challengers often rely on party funds.

Contribution Limits Are Too Strict

The debate over soft money has generated new interest in loosening limits on direct contributions to candidates that have not been changed since 1974 — $1,000 per person and $5,000 for each PAC for each election.

The McCain-Feingold bill "does not seriously address the reality that hard-money contribution limits have been deteriorated by 30 years of inflation," said Don Thoren, president of the National Association of Business Political Action Committees.

McConnell said in a March 1 debate, "There's no question that at the very least they should be indexed for inflation. It's utterly absurd to be operating in 2001 with 1974 dollars."

In its current form, the McCain-Feingold bill would increase the amount of hard money that could be given to state parties — from $5,000 to $10,000 — but not other limits. Many Republicans and at least one Democrat in the Senate say the limits on contributions to candidates need to be increased.

Tennessee Republican Sen. Fred Thompson plans to offer an amendment that would approximately triple the hard money limits and index them for inflation. Sen. Chuck Hagel, R-Neb., has again introduced a campaign finance bill (S 22) that also would triple hard-money limits and index them.

Hagel's proposal has drawn support from at least three Democrats who also support McCain-Feingold, evidence that a hard money increase could attract a bipartisan majority in the Senate.

The high cost of buying time on television for campaign commercials, a chief use of hard money by political candidates, is another reason to increase the current limits. A study released March 6 by the Alliance for Better Campaigns puts the cost of political television ads in 2000 between $771 million and $1 billion. In addition, Republican fundraisers support raising the limits, saying it will improve fundraising by campaigns at a time when many donors have been drawn to soft money.

Republican Party committees raised 10 percent more hard money during the 1999-2000 election cycle than they did during the 1995-96 period, while soft-money receipts went up 73 percent.

Unions Would Have an Unfair Advantage

As long as labor unions can spend their members' dues for political purposes without consulting them, Democrats will enjoy an unfair advantage, according to opponents of the McCain-Feingold bill.

Many Republicans, including President Bush, say that union members should be able to request that their dues not pay for political activities if they do not agree with the position or candidate the union is backing.

Such a provision, which Republicans call "paycheck protection," is not in the bill and is considered a "poison pill" that would alienate Democrats if it were included.

In making the case against paycheck protection, McCain has said that if it were enacted, then shareholders in public corporations also should be given the chance to vote on whether corporate funds are used for contributions to political groups or issue advertisements.

Instead, the bill codifies the Supreme Court's decision in the 1988 case of *Communications Workers of America v. Beck*, which requires unions to give non-union members the right to object to their fees being used for political purposes. The provision does not apply to dues-paying members.

The Right of Association Would Be Limited

The McCain-Feingold bill's effort to keep candidates and interest groups at arm's length would restrict the ability of organizations, including non-profits, to discuss legislative goals or strategy with members of Congress, opponents say. The restrictions even worry some Democrats.

The AFL-CIO argues that the coordination limitations are so broad that they "could outlaw virtually any union activity," including lobbying visits and candidate appearances before union audiences. The bill defines coordinated activity as "anything of value" provided to a candidate who previously has had discussions with a group on campaign activity.

The Alliance for Justice, a collection of liberal public-interest groups, said that the coordination provisions would prevent nonprofits from discussing an issue with a candidate and then running their own ads on that issue later in the election.

"In an attempt to go after the truly bad actors, the bill unfortunately slips into areas that are protected," said alliance spokesman Tim Mooney.

For example, the bill would prevent an organization from hiring a consultant or other staffer who previously had worked in a similar capacity for a political candidate. ◆

Anguished Transformation From Maverick to Outcast

Vermont moderate foresaw little comfort in the aggressively conservative GOP

The morning after Sen. John H. Chafee of Rhode Island died in the autumn of 1999, James M. Jeffords of Vermont took the floor in a silent Senate to eulogize his colleague of 10 years. The two New Englanders were moderate Republicans, a minority in their party, and it had drawn them close. They would have lunch together each Wednesday and sometimes dinner at the Metropolitan Club downtown, when the talk would drift from their families to issues of state.

When Jeffords had to hurry to the Senate floor to vote on an unfamiliar issue, he would look first to see how Chafee had voted and follow suit, knowing that if nothing else, he would not get in trouble.

"When you have that kind of an individual whom you can count on to give you the right direction, it is very important here," Jeffords said, "especially on some of the tough issues we have where those of us who are called moderates have to cast votes at times where we don't get friends on either side of the aisle."

There were nine moderate Republicans in the Senate when Jeffords came over from the House in 1989. Chafee's death made it six. With Jeffords' decision to become an Independent, he leaves behind only four.

They have been barely tolerated by the conservative majority of Republicans, who put a high price on party loyalty and discipline. Chafee's stubborn independence, along with his support for clean air and civil rights legislation, cost him the job of Senate GOP Conference chairman in 1990, the No. 3 leadership position. Some colleagues wanted to take away his chairmanship of the Environment and Public Works Committee.

In 1993, when Jeffords and Republican David F. Durenberger of Minnesota (1975-95) voted for a Democratic campaign finance reform bill, conservative Texas Republican Phil Gramm went to the offices of the party's senatorial campaign committee and tore their photographs off the wall. "They're not Republicans anymore," he fumed.

But as both parties have become more doctrinaire in recent decades, Republican and Democratic leaders have generally found their moderates useful in building compromise.

In a 1990 speech to a Republican fundraising breakfast on

Chafee, left, and Jeffords at a 1998 news conference. "It is not often we get to be close to someone in this body," Jeffords said. "This was a personal one to me."

a soggy October morning in Vermont, then-President George Bush said of Jeffords: "He knows how to work with the leadership on both sides of the aisle. He wants to make something happen, not just give a little rhetoric out there. He wants to reach a solution. And he understands bipartisanship, because he's made it happen.

"We need more of that spirit on Capitol Hill," Bush said.

Last year, Jeffords himself told the Burlington Free Press, "If you didn't have the people like me in the middle, Congress would never accomplish anything."

With the disputed election of Bush's son as president last November and a Senate evenly divided between the two parties, moderates were seen as gaining influence. Jeffords saw an opportunity to help the new chief executive put into practice what he expected to be a bipartisan approach, particularly on issues such as education, the environment and health care.

Instead, the new administration and Republican leaders in the House and Senate adopted an aggressively conservative agenda that left Jeffords feeling increasingly alienated.

When he balked at Bush's proposed $1.6 trillion tax cut, bargaining instead for more resources for a program he had helped pass in 1975 to educate the disabled, he was met with retribution. The White House left him off the guest list when a Vermont educator was honored as teacher of the year, and rumors spread that dairy price supports vital to Vermont would not get reauthorized. (2001 CQ Weekly, p. 1247)

"I think he probably looked in the mirror and saw five more years of total misery, in addition to being completely ignored," a top aide to a senator close to Jeffords said. "And that's really what drove him."

"Looking ahead," Jeffords told a crowded hotel room in Burlington on May 24, "I can see more and more instances where I will disagree with the president on very fundamental issues — the issues of choice [abortion], the direction of the judiciary, tax and spending decisions, missile defense, energy and the environment, and a host of other issues, large and small."

"In order to best represent my state of Vermont, my own conscience and principles I have stood for my whole life, I will leave the Republican Party and become an Independent," Jeffords said. Later, he added, "I was not elected to this office to be something that I am not."

Uneasy Deadlock

Politics does not remain long in perfect balance, and the advent of an evenly divided Senate in January set off speculation in Washington's hyperactive political community on how long it would remain that way.

Even as Majority Leader Trent Lott, R-Miss., and Minority Leader Tom Daschle, D-S.D., negotiated an uneasy power-sharing arrangement, everyone from lawmakers to cab drivers speculated on the chances that a senator in the political borderlands of age or ideology might die or defect and so tip the balance.

Georgian Zell Miller, a conservative Democrat in the Senate for less than a year, set tongues wagging in late January when he announced support for former Sen. John Ashcroft, R-Mo. (1995-2001) as attorney general — anathema to most Democrats — and then appeared at a news conference beside Gramm to support Bush's $1.6 trillion tax-cut proposal.

Miller professed to be mystified by the speculation. "That shows how weird this place is up here," he said. But the question of which party they really belong in has dogged conservative Southern Democrats for years, and some, such as Gramm, Alabama Sen. Richard C. Shelby and Georgia Rep. Nathan Deal, have become Republicans. Most of the others have retired or been defeated.

In April, the spotlight shifted to moderate Republicans Jeffords and Lincoln Chafee of Rhode Island, who is John Chafee's son and, if anything, more of a maverick. Both Chafee and Jeffords had voted against Bush's tax package, forcing the Senate to pass a more modest, $1.35 trillion alternative.

Chafee was seen as closer to Democrats on the issue, exerting leverage on Bush. Brown University political scientist Darrell West told The Wall Street Journal, "He's become one of the most powerful people in Washington, the Republican most likely to defect."

But it was Jeffords who had begun to reconsider his position within the party.

In April, during a local television show in Vermont, he said administration officials would not try to punish him for his tax cut vote because they knew "it's a short walk across the aisle." A Jeffords spokesman later told the newspaper Roll Call, "Sen. Jeffords is a Republican, and he expects to be a Republican the rest of his life."

His roots, indeed, are deep. His family immigrated to Vermont's Green Mountains in 1794 and have been Congregationalists and, eventually, Republicans ever since. The family

home is near the Cold River between Rutland and Shrewsbury in south-central Vermont. His father, Olin Jeffords, was chief justice of the Vermont supreme court. Jeffords himself took a law degree from Harvard before entering politics.

Vermont has long stood for an individualist brand of Republicanism — fiscally conservative as a rule, yet moderate, even liberal, on social issues. The political predecessors Jeffords invoked in his farewell address on May 24 were often mavericks within their own party. George Aiken (1941-75), a senator for 34 years, was a champion of farmers but considered a radical by many in the GOP. Sen. Ralph Flanders (1946-59) introduced a resolution to censure flamboyant fellow Republican Joseph McCarthy (1947-57) in 1954.

Most also economized on words and cash. Aiken spent $17.09 on his last re-election campaign, in 1968. Jeffords, who rarely holds news conferences and speaks sparingly on the Senate floor, lived in a camper when he first came to Washington in 1975 because he had a $40,000 campaign debt from his House race.

He now lives in a town house in the Eastern Market neighborhood of Capitol Hill and walks to work. He practices the martial art of Tae Kwon-Do for meditation and discipline.

"I think it's very important to be self-sufficient," Jeffords told an Associated Press reporter when he was running for the Senate in 1988. "I think people who know how to take care of themselves feel a lot more secure in our society."

Making of a Moderate

Almost from his arrival 26 years ago, Jeffords steered his own course, unsettling and sometimes infuriating his party elders. In some years, he was apt to vote with Democrats as often as with Republicans, many of whom considered him a Democrat in everything but name. *(Story, p. 32)*

He was the only Republican who voted against President Ronald Reagan's signature tax cut in 1981, and one of only two who voted against Clarence Thomas' confirmation to the Supreme Court. He sided with President Bill Clinton on family and medical leave, motor-voter registration and the Brady handgun control bill. An enthusiastic supporter of the arts, he strongly backed the National Endowment for the Arts, although it was a favorite target of conservatives who thought the agency wasted money and financed lewd or anti-religious works.

Jeffords was one of five Republicans who voted against convicting Clinton after his impeachment trial in 1999, preferring a Democratic plan to censure him instead.

In a generally pro-business party wary of environmental activists, Jeffords was one of only 10 Republicans endorsed by the Sierra Club in 2000.

Jeffords served on the Environment and Public Works Committee during his first four years in the Senate, when his friend John Chafee was the ranking Republican, but he left in 1992 for the Foreign Relations Committee.

In January, Jeffords asked for a seat on Environment and Public Works, in addition to his other assignments, in order to have a say when the Clean Air Act came up for reauthorization. Vermont has a continuing problem with acid rain pollution from Midwestern power plants and industries.

Party leaders turned him down.

"I think that the general feeling of the Republicans are that they would rather not see the environmental side strengthened on that committee," Jeffords told a Gannett

Jeffords' Switch Unlikely to Mean A Change in Voting Habits

Long before he decided to declare himself an Independent, Vermont Sen. James M. Jeffords carved out a voting record that defies easy categories. He sometimes staked out positions that few other Republicans occupied — like refusing to endorse President Bush's tax cut, insisting instead on increased spending for one of his favorite causes, special education. But he has not always sided with Democrats on crucial votes or typically Democratic issues.

So what can Democrats expect from the man who is about to hand them control of the Senate?

Colleagues and other observers say that Jeffords' voting behavior is unlikely to change much on issues he cares about, such as education, managed health care, environmental preservation and protecting Vermont's dairy industry.

"The votes haven't changed. One person has changed his label," said Sen. John Kerry, D-Mass., following Jeffords' May 24 announcement that he would leave the GOP and become an Independent.

In the 12 years since he came to the Senate, and even during his earlier House career, Jeffords has routinely crossed party lines to join Democrats on some issues, while staying close enough to Republicans on procedural votes to help ensure that a narrow GOP majority kept control of the Senate.

Observers describe Jeffords as a social liberal and fiscal conservative. He not only opposed Bush's $1.6 trillion tax cut; he also voted against President Ronald Reagan's 1981 tax cut plan (PL 97-34), which drew the support of conservative Democrats.

Jeffords cosponsored President Bill Clinton's health care plan in 1994. Five years later, he was one of five Republican senators who voted to acquit Clinton on both articles of impeachment before the Senate. Those positions kept him popular in his home state.

His independent streak will probably continue even while he caucuses with Democrats, experts say. "He's been very consistent in his beliefs," said Garrison Nelson, a University of Vermont political science professor who has known Jeffords for years. "Jim Jeffords cannot be bullied, bribed or flattered into doing what he doesn't want to do."

Nelson said Jeffords should not be expected to begin voting like Bernard Sanders, an Independent and Vermont's only member of the House, who votes with Democrats on nearly every issue. Even some of his former colleagues agree that Jeffords' voting patterns won't change much.

"He'll probably vote with us as much now as he did last week," said Senate Majority Whip Don Nickles, R-Okla.

The biggest impact of Jeffords' switch could be on Bush's judicial nominations. Jeffords was one of two Republicans to vote against the nomination of Clarence Thomas to the Supreme Court in 1991. (Former Sen. Bob Packwood, R-Ore., 1969-95, was the other.)

In the past, Jeffords has sided with Republicans on procedural votes involving nominees, even some that he supported against the wishes of his party. In 1999, he voted with most Republicans to delay consideration of two nominations submitted by Clinton, those of Richard A. Paez and Marsha L. Berzon to the 9th Circuit Court of Appeals.

Jeffords eventually voted to confirm Paez and Berzon, opposing a majority of Republican senators.

"Now he won't have to worry about that pressure," Nelson said.

Party-Line Votes

Since coming to the Senate in 1989, Jeffords has never ranked below third among Republicans in terms of opposition to a majority of his colleagues on party-line votes. (CQ defines party-line votes as those in which a majority of one party votes against a majority of the other.)

Jeffords was the leading Republican in opposing his own party on such votes for eight years in a row (1989-96) and shared the top spot with Arlen Specter, R-Pa., in 1998. In the following two years, Jeffords was surpassed in opposing a majority of Republicans only by Specter (1999) and Lincoln Chafee of Rhode Island (2000).

But when it mattered most — when Republicans needed his vote to maintain control in the Senate — Jeffords tended to side with his party.

During his House service, Jeffords consistently agreed with a majority of his own party on party-line tallies less than 50 percent of the time.

That pattern continued in the Senate until 1995, when Republicans regained a majority. From then on, with the exception of 1998, Jeffords voted with Republicans on a majority of party unity votes.

For example, he has voted with Republicans on 59 of 74 party-line cloture votes since 1994. Of the 15 votes he cast against his party, eight were on campaign finance legislation that he strongly supported.

His highest level of agreement with the GOP came in 1999, when he agreed on two-thirds of the votes identified by CQ as party unity votes.

On party-line votes this year, Jeffords has sided with a majority of voting Republicans 60 percent of the time, which is in line with his past voting patterns in a Republican-led Senate. Many of those votes came on on the tax cut package (HR 1836) and the fiscal year 2002 budget resolution (H Con Res 83) — despite his disagreements with portions of both measures.

Democratic leaders expect Jeffords to join them on procedural votes as he did with the GOP when he was a Republican, despite Jeffords' identification as an Independent. Asked if Jeffords would bolster Democrats on cloture and other votes, Harry Reid, D-Nev., replied: "No question."

But on substantive issues, he is likely to chart his own path, as he has throughout his career. In 1996, for example, his was one of three Republicans to vote against a bill that would have granted the president line-item veto authority, but he also voted for a balanced-budget amendment later that year, disagreeing with most Democrats.

The group AIDS Action in 1999 called Jeffords "the leading voice of moderation on health care issues in the Republican Party." But Jeffords has consistently supported a GOP-backed plan on managed care that would place limits on the right to sue health plans, something many Democrats oppose.

When Patty Murray, D-Wash., tried to add $11.4 billion to an education bill in 1999 for the purpose of hiring 100,000 new teachers, it was Jeffords who led his 54 GOP colleagues in turning back one of Clinton's signature initiatives on a party-line vote.

But last year Jeffords provided one of 13 GOP votes crucial to broadening the federal hate crimes law, an amendment offered by Sen. Edward M. Kennedy, D-Mass., and backed by all but one Senate Democrat.

"Yes, he's a moderate and to the left of Republicans," said Sarah Binder, a political science professor at George Washington University who has written extensively about moderates. "But for Democrats, he's actually pretty conservative."

Binder sees Jeffords as being more in line with Senate Democrats like John B. Breaux of Louisiana and Zell Miller of Georgia than with more liberal members of the caucus. Both Breaux and Miller have caused headaches at times this year for Democratic leaders by siding with Republicans.

Miller was the first Democrat to come out in support of Bush's tax plan, for example, and Breaux was pivotal in gaining acceptance of a $1.25 trillion tax cut — much higher than most Democrats wanted at the time but very close to the final number in the tax bill.

In the end, the surest guide to Jeffords' voting may be his Vermont roots. Jeffords and his Vermont colleague, Democrat Patrick J. Leahy, have had a record of agreeing on issues large and small.

Beginning in 1995, the two have matched positions on 63 percent of all votes, while on CQ-selected key votes they have been in harmony 56 percent of the time. The two disagreed on several high-profile votes lately, including passage of the bill granting permanent normal trade relations with China.

Jeffords was one of eight senators opposed, while Leahy voted for the measure. Jeffords also voted for the GOP's managed care bill in 1999, which all Democrats opposed. ◆

Always a maverick: Jeffords, right, with Sen. Robert Stafford, R-Vt., in 1985.

Portrait of an Independent

Vermont Sen. James M. Jeffords has sided with fellow Republicans on party-line votes less than half the time, except when his party controlled the Senate. The graph shows the percentage of the time that Jeffords supported or opposed his party on votes that pitted a majority of Republicans against a majority of Democrats.

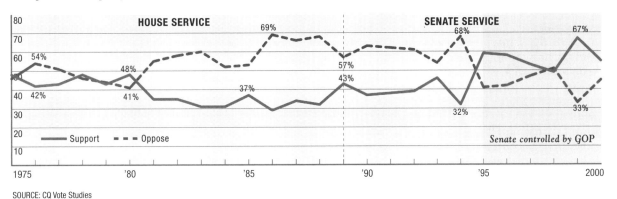

SOURCE: CQ Vote Studies

News Service reporter at the time. "And I am an environmentalist."

His passion, however, is education, in particular legislation (PL 94-142) he helped write and pass his freshman year in the House in 1975 that requires states to provide special education programs for children with disabilities and also authorizes the federal government to shoulder 40 percent of the cost.

Neither Congress nor the White House has come anywhere close to that level of support — it is closer to 15 percent — leaving states and local school boards with the sort of "unfunded federal mandate" that many conservatives complain about. (*1975 CQ Almanac, p. 651*)

Jeffords has been chairman of the Health, Education, Labor and Pensions Committee since 1997. Conservatives had tried to block his promotion but were overruled by Lott in a gesture of party unity. Despite their ideological differences, the two men sang together in an informal quartet called the Singing Senators.

His tenure as chairman has been difficult at times. Last year, conservatives essentially hijacked an education bill and left Jeffords a bystander. His amendment to fully fund the federal share of the Individuals with Disabilities Education Act (IDEA) was defeated 53-47. (*2000 CQ Weekly, p. 1048*)

Going to School

By Jeffords' own account, however, he was optimistic that his fortunes would change with George W. Bush's election, that the new president would make education a priority and try to compromise with Democrats and Republican moderates.

At a March 6 news conference, Jeffords laid down his personal marker with legislation to fully fund the special education legislation.

"I have said before, and I will say it again, this issue will not go away and neither will I," he said.

While the Senate took up a budget resolution incorporating Bush's tax cut plan in late March, Jeffords told the White House he had reservations. He believed in cutting taxes, but only when other federal priorities, such as education, were taken care of. Bush was trying to pass the plan counting only on Republican votes, and Jeffords used his leverage to bargain for full funding of the special education program.

White House officials subsequently said Jeffords had shaken hands on a deal to fund the program from discretionary funds — subject to annual appropriation — then reneged and demanded more money for the program. Jeffords said he wanted mandatory spending, essentially making IDEA an entitlement.

Meanwhile, the White House was trying to put pressure on Jeffords to bring him into line. White House Chief of Staff Andrew H. Card Jr. gave interviews to reporters in Vermont, saying Jeffords should give the new president's agenda a chance. (*2001 CQ Weekly, p. 773*)

By April 4, the talks had collapsed, and Jeffords appeared with John B. Breaux, D-La., at a news conference for Breaux's $1.25 trillion alternative tax plan. "I feel very comfortable here," Jeffords said.

Afterward, he joined fellow moderates Chafee and Arlen Specter of Pennsylvania in voting for an amendment by Tom Harkin, D-Iowa, to reduce the tax cut by $448 billion.

It was during the tax debate that Daschle and Minority Whip Harry Reid, D-Nev., opened conversations with Jeffords. According to Christopher J. Dodd, D-Conn., Jeffords had come to realize he would have to oppose Bush on many issues in the future. Reid held open the possibility of the chairmanship of the Environment and Public Works Committee, where Reid is ranking Democrat.

On April 16, Roll Call published a story speculating that Jeffords might change parties. Among the evidence were his recent television comment in Vermont about being a "short walk" away from Democrats and his tenuous position in the party on education issues.

Judd Gregg, a conservative from neighboring New Hampshire and the second-ranking Republican on Jeffords' committee, had sent out a news release that he would be "spearheading" this year's reauthorization of the Elementary and Secondary Education Act.

When Bush on April 23 honored a Middlebury, Vt., high school social studies teacher named Michele Forman as the nation's teacher of the year, Jeffords was not invited to the Rose Garden ceremony. Administration officials said the slight was not intentional.

In a potentially more serious development, rumors began that Senate Republican leaders would try to eliminate the Northeast Interstate Dairy Compact, a price support program that benefits Vermont dairy farmers.

The pace was moving fast enough for political consultant Norman J. Ornstein to warn Republican leaders in a May 14 newspaper column: "Push Jeffords far enough and he can use the nuclear weapon he has in his arsenal" — defection to the Democrats. The snubs and rumors appear to have played a minor role in Jeffords' decision, if at all. In his farewell speech, he said they had "nothing to do with it. Nothing at all."

Caught by Surprise

Republicans appear to have had no warning that Jeffords was drifting away until he told Lott on Monday evening, May 21. They tried to throw the levers in reverse. The White House contacted influential Republicans in Vermont, including campaign contributors, and asked them to help, while Lott rounded up Jeffords' friends in the Senate.

Fellow moderate Republican Olympia J. Snowe of Maine met privately with Jeffords on Tuesday morning, May 22. "I asked him what exactly had transpired, and it was, obviously, the things that happened at the White House," she later told CNN. "You know, the teacher of the year, judgeships and so on. And then, of course, in the education bill, and not being included in the kinds of decisions that he thought he should have been included in when it came to being a chairman."

Jeffords met with Cheney on Tuesday morning, then separately with Bush at the White House. Neither meeting went well.

On Wednesday, May 23, before heading back to Vermont to make his announcement, Jeffords met with the moderates as a group. "It was the most emotional time that I have ever had in my life," he said later, "with my closest friends urging me not to do what I was going to do because it affected their lives very substantially."

It was on the plane back to the Green Mountains that Jeffords said he made his final decision, but if anything it was just a final check. The path had long since been cleared. ◆

National Parties Mobilize For Battle Over Lines

GOP talks softly while Democrats opt for a big stick

In 1991, as the Georgia legislature redrew its congressional districts in accordance with new census numbers that gave the state an additional House seat, the national Democratic Party stayed out of the way.

State Democrats seemed to have the matter well in hand with wide majorities in both houses of the state legislature and Zell Miller in the governor's office. But state House Speaker Thomas B. Murphy had his own agenda: to get Republican Newt Gingrich, Murphy's representative in Congress, out of his back yard.

The map Murphy helped draw succeeded in moving Gingrich into another district, but it splintered surrounding Democratic strongholds and left several Democratic incumbents in less-secure seats.

Democrats went from holding nine of the state's 10 congressional seats before redistricting, to holding just four of 11 by 1995 — the year Gingrich became Speaker of the House.

"I don't think the General Assembly fully understood what was at risk with Congress," said former Rep. George "Buddy" Darden, a Georgia Democrat who had been in Congress 10 years before losing his redrawn seat in 1994. "They [national Democrats] should study the Georgia example as the perfect way not to do it."

Today, as states prepare to go through the decennial redistricting process again, national Democrats say they will not make the same mistake. Both parties in Washington are bracing for a battle over drawing the lines that will determine who holds control of Congress for the next 10 years.

The Democratic National Committee and the Republican National Committee have launched redistricting programs in which they are busily studying state voting laws, giving members of Congress advice on how to protect their voting bases and raising money for what probably will be a slew of lawsuits filed against the final state lines.

DNC chairman Terry McAuliffe already has pledged to raise $10 million for the Democratic effort.

"This is a top priority for the chairman," said DNC spokesperson Jenny Backus. "This is critical for winning back the House."

Among the main goals of the Democratic Party is to persuade its members to put party unity above personal agendas in order to avoid a fiasco similar to the one that occurred in Georgia.

Martin Frost, D-Texas, who is leading the House Democrats' redistricting strategy this year, has met with the Democratic congressional delegations of every state in recent months to pass along his message of unity.

"We're urging that they work together as a delegation," said Frost.

As head of IMPAC 2000 — a political committee formed to provide resources and raise money for the Democrat's re-

districting strategy — Frost also is helping the delegations hire lawyers to study state and national election law that will come into play during the redistricting process.

Following the 1991 map drawing, more than 40 states ended up in court battling over their congressional lines.

Democrats believe the courts again will have the final say in determining the fate of many state lines. They want lawyers prepared with their own maps and legal arguments to push for scenarios that will best help their cause.

National Republicans are less forthcoming about their budget and strategy. They say Washington can have only a small impact on the redistricting process.

"The governors and the state legislatures do this," said Rep. John Linder, R-Ga., who is head of the task force on redistricting at the National Republican Congressional Committee. "It would be overreaching for us to tell them how to do it."

Changing Times

With so much at stake, national Republicans are making their views felt in state capitols. No place better exemplifies that than Texas, where Rep. Joe L. Barton has revived the Texans Against Gerrymandering political action committee (TAGPAC) to raise money to cover the cost of hiring lawyers and lobbyists to influence how the lines in Texas will be drawn.

Barton formed the PAC in 1990 for that year's redistricting and now has the combined muscle of fellow Texans Majority Leader Dick Armey and Majority Whip Tom DeLay behind the effort.

"We think Texas is very critical in redistricting," Armey said. "Everybody expects California to be a disaster, and Texas historically has been a badly gerrymandered state."

If national Republicans do play the smaller role Linder

Jigsaw Politics

This is the first installment in a yearlong series in the CQ Weekly on how the decennial redistricting process will play out in key states. Reapportionment of the 435 seats in the House, as required every 10 years by the Constitution, must be accomplished by the complex process of redrawing congressional districts in the 43 states that have more than one member in the House. That process, which began the week of March 5 with the release of census data, must be completed before the primary election season next year, and has the potential to determine the balance of power in Congress for the next decade.

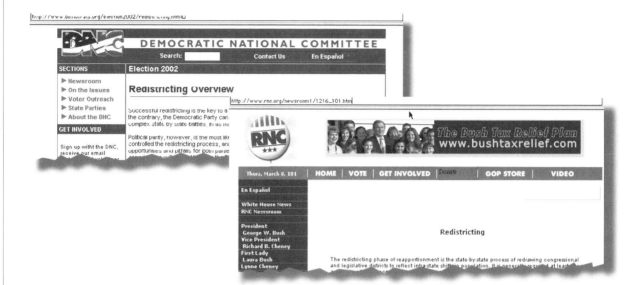

says he envisions, it would be a shift from what the party did 10 years ago. Back then, because Republicans were considered an entrenched minority in the House and controlled only a handful of state legislatures, the national party formulated one broad strategy to help their party in every state.

At the same time, state Republicans, because of their paltry numbers, were much more dependent on national money and therefore were much more easily influenced by the national organization.

Times have changed.

"Republicans today have many more seats at the table in different states, and the individual Republicans in individual states are much more in control this time," said Benjamin Ginsberg, a lawyer with the firm Patton Boggs, who has worked with Republicans on redistricting for more than a decade and joined President Bush's legal team in last year's Florida recount battle.

Going into the last round, Democrats had complete control (the legislatures and governorships) over redistricting in states encompassing 172 districts. Republicans had complete control of just five, with the remaining districts drawn under split party control or by independent redistricting commissions.

This year, the Democrats' control has shrunk to 144 districts, while the Republicans' control has soared to 98 districts. (*2001 CQ Weekly, p. 39*)

Parties Differ in Defining Roles

Ginsberg said the Republican Party will be able to serve an important role as a clearinghouse of information and advice for state lawmakers, but the ultimate decisions on remapping will be in the hands of the states.

Linder agreed. "Democrats are overreaching their role," he said of his rival party's redistricting plan. "I can't imagine state legislators in Georgia turning around [to Congress] and saying, 'How do you want us to draw the maps?' "

But just as Republican gains over the past decade have led the national party to change its game plan, Democratic losses have forced that party to rethink its strategy.

Ten years ago, Democrats were convinced they would always hold the House majority — having been in control without interruption since 1955 — and did little to work as a team for the broader good of the party. Most House Democrats at that time had never experienced the bitter taste

of being in the minority.

But Republicans gained a majority in the House in 1995 and have held it since. Today, nearly half the Democratic caucus has never served in the majority.

Democrats admit they fell victim to their own arrogance.

"It's much better now than 10 years ago," Frost said. "We had senior members who wanted to strike side deals and work on their own. Now we have younger members willing to work together."

Learning From the Last Time

One of the first things Democrats are doing as a team is hiring lawyers to represent their state delegations during the upcoming redistricting battles.

So far, about half a dozen Democratic congressional delegations have hired lawyers, and many more are making plans to do so.

"The [Michigan] delegation is preparing to address the challenges of redistricting and will be fully prepared with legal counsel for the battles that loom before the state legislature and the courts," said Rep. John D. Dingell, D-Mich., who is heading up his delegation's redistricting program.

Michigan is slated to lose one seat in 2002. Republicans, who control the state House, state Senate, governorship and state Supreme Court, are expected to target a Democratic seat for elimination.

Delegations' lawyers are studying the history of voting rights laws in various states, developing map outlines, analyzing demographic shifts, and preparing legal arguments to defend Democratic maps before the courts.

"A lot of the law has not been totally settled in the courts," said Sam Hirsch, with the law firm Jenner & Block, which has been hired by several Democratic delegations, including Texas and Ohio. "We're getting a good and thorough understanding of the relevant law. We want to make sure whatever we propose is, in fact, legal."

The lawyers are being paid by a combination of money raised by the state delegations and money from Frost's IMPAC 2000 committee. Aides say IMPAC 2000 will be a "multimillion-dollar" operation to assist with redistricting over the next two years.

A number of lawsuits already have been filed by various state party activists in preparation for the upcoming battles. In Ohio last December, state Democrats filed two suits — one state, one federal — to force the courts to set strict deadlines for finalizing new district lines. The party hopes to ensure that disputes are settled before primary elections begin.

Two similar suits were filed in Texas, and others have been filed on various grounds in Minnesota, Utah, Virginia and Wisconsin, according to the National Conference of State Legislatures.

Members Hire Lobbyists

While Frost and other national Democrats are working to keep House members unified and working as a team, several lawmakers are taking matters into their own hands.

Along with lawyers hired to represent state delegations, several House members have independently hired lobbyists to track the redistricting activity surrounding their home bases.

Often, state lawmakers will look beyond party loyalty or even legal precedent, and instead place personal relationships and political ambition above all else in drawing congressional lines.

Because members of Congress cannot always spend quality time with their state-level colleagues, lobbyists can help forge positive relationships.

In New York, a state that will lose two seats, Democratic Reps. Gary L. Ackerman and Maurice D. Hinchey have hired lobbyists.

Because the state legislature is split — Democrats hold the House and Republicans control the Senate — it is likely that one Republican seat in upstate New York and one Democratic seat in the New York City area will be eliminated.

"I hired her to ensure that the people of the 26th congressional district are represented in the reapportionment discussions," Hinchey said of his $3,000-a-month lobbyist. "I'm here [in Washington], and that person is in New York."

Hinchey predicted other members may soon get into the act. He said the lobbyist he hired has been contacted by several other members expressing an interest in her services.

Tim Storey, redistricting coordinator with the National Conference of State Legislatures, said he has not heard of any other members hiring lobbyists during the reapportionment process.

"I think that is relatively unique," Storey said. "Now, that's paid lobbying. There will be all other manners of lobbying going on in all its varieties."

Storey said state legislators become exceptionally popular at the start of each decade. Or, as one Republican close to the redistricting effort said: "It's the one time when state legislators can get their calls returned immediately."

Storey said he began to see representatives of the national parties dropping in at redistricting meetings of the National Conference of State Legislatures about a year and a half ago.

As much as politics and the law play into remapping, Storey said it also comes down to personal relationships. Congressmen "better pay attention or you'll be at a greater disadvantage in 2002," he warned. "It's very personal. You don't want to anger the guy who can draw you into oblivion."

Along with personal connections, the parties are hoping money will make a difference in the way state lines are drawn.

Individual members of Congress and the national parties actively raised and contributed money for state lawmakers across the country to help them win election last year.

In Texas, the national parties poured millions of dollars into a state Senate race that was key in determining who would control the chamber. Republicans won the race and held onto their 16-15 seat majority. The state House is controlled by Democrats. Texas will pick up two congressional seats in redistricting.

The National Republican Congressional Committee contributed $50,000 to GOP state lawmaker Todd Staples in his bid for the seat. The NRCC gave an additional $468,000 to the Texas State GOP.

The Democratic Congressional Campaign Committee gave Staples' opponent, lawyer David Fisher, $1,000 and sent nearly $2.4 million to the state Democratic party.

In the end, total spending in that state Senate contest set a record for a state legislative race.

Many members of Congress today are still hosting fundraisers for their local officials in hopes of currying favor with them.

Personal Politics

There is no preventing self-interest from working its way into the map-drawing process. Frequently, state lawmakers draw redistricting lines with the intent of creating new congressional seats in which they themselves could run.

Darden, the Georgia Democrat who was an inadvertent victim of his own party's control of redistricting, pointed out that of the seven Georgians who first won seats in Congress during the 1992 elections that followed the last redistricting cycle, all but one came directly out of the state legislature.

"The way it works in reapportionment is, you look out for yourself," Darden said. "The [state] House and Senate members were looking out for themselves."

That may be even more true this time around.

Since 1990, term limits have been enacted for state lawmakers in 13 states, according to the advocacy group U.S. Term Limits. Hundreds of state representatives and senators, including 75 in Florida, 42 in Ohio and almost 100 in Michigan, will be forced to leave their jobs at the end of the year. Many political observers believe that will prompt more state lines to be drawn out of political self-promotion.

"That's the wild card," Storey said. "Some of these state lawmakers are thinking about that."

National Republicans say there is little they can do to prevent such personal agendas from leading the redistricting process. Linder admitted House members and congressional candidates with the closest ties to the state legislatures will "have the inside track."

"There will be an awful lot of internal politicking going on," Linder admitted, "and I'm not the least bit interested in getting involved."

But ex-congressman Darden said the confluence of personal and political agendas should push national Democrats to take as large a role as possible over the next two years.

"The DNC didn't pay much attention to Georgia last time because they thought there was no way Georgia could blow it," Darden said.

"Don't assume because you have control of the state legislature that it will necessarily translate into a favorable plan. . . . In my view, Democrats in 2001 will pay a lot more attention to drawing congressional lines because they know, having experienced what took place in 1991, that disaster can occur." ◆

Government Institutions

The articles in this section provide insight into the workings of the major institutions of American government, looking in turn at Congress, the judiciary, the presidency and the bureaucracy.

In late May 2001 Sen. James M. Jeffords, who represents the small Northeastern state of Vermont, decided that he no longer identified with the Republican party and changed his political affiliation to Independent. As a consequence of his decision, control of the Senate and its agenda switched to the Democrats, who now outnumber the Republicans 50 to 49, with Jeffords supporting the Democrats in organizing the chamber. The first three articles in this section look at the political and legislative implications of Jeffords' surprising defection and the leadership upheaval that followed. In a fourth article on the legislative branch, the focus shifts to one of the defining characteristics of the 107th Congress—that it is a body of relative newcomers. The 107th Congress is also notable for the increase in the number of female senators. This gain is discussed, as is the fact that ethnic minorities made no significant electoral progress in 2000.

Shifting to the judiciary, the next article covers the battle over the handling of judicial nominations, which must be confirmed by the Senate. During much of Bill Clinton's presidency, Democrats had fumed as Senate Republicans turned many of his judicial nominees into political hostages. So when Republican George W. Bush ascended to the presidency, the question was whether the Democrats—who at first were at parity in the Senate and then claimed majority control—would retaliate. The prospects for judicial nominees are examined in this report.

The next two articles shift the focus to the presidency and the outlook for the young administration of George W. Bush. Vice President Dick Cheney's likely role in the Bush presidency is examined, along with the skills and experiences he brings to his office. Stock is taken of George Bush's first 100 days in office and the pragmatic streak that emerged as Bush's legislative agenda moved from the playbook to the playing field of Congress.

Finally, the section turns to the bureaucracy. An article on the U.S. Postal Service, an agency suffering from deepening debts in this era of electronic communications, reports on the new urgency on Capitol Hill for an overhaul of postal laws. An article related to the regulatory powers of government examines the new form of regulatory activism that appears to be taking hold in Washington, one that has industries sidestepping Congress and enlisting the executive branch to ease regulatory burdens. A final brief report covers outgoing FBI director Louis J. Freeh's contrite visit to Capitol Hill, during which he was asked to explain the FBI blunders that delayed the execution of Oklahoma City bomber Timothy J. McVeigh.

Speaking in Burlington, Vt., Jeffords said the Republican Party's direction under Bush has not been what he had expected and he could not support it.

Government Institutions

Shakeup In the Senate

One man's move ends GOP's six-year reign

All along, the 50-50 Senate was understood to be fragile and unforgiving. And a change in control because of a single, untimely departure might set off a shock wave of extraordinary consequences.

Yet no one expected this. One Republican, feeling increasingly uncomfortable with his party and his president, decided to change his political identity and in doing so changed the world around him, too.

When Vermont Sen. James M. Jeffords announced May 24 that he would leave the Republican Party and turn control of the Senate over to the Democrats, he did precisely that. Not only will Majority Leader-to-be Tom Daschle, D-S.D., assume power in this new Senate, but so too will old hands like Edward M. Kennedy, D-Mass., Robert C. Byrd, D-W.Va., and Patrick J. Leahy, D-Vt.

Jeffords' stunning decision has remarkable consequences for George W. Bush's agenda and his presidency. Jeffords' impact on the Senate as an institution in the tripartite U.S. democracy promises to be even more profound.

Republicans had hoped to spend much of the rest of the year passing piecemeal tax bills to complement Bush's landmark cuts in tax rates. Now, the summer will feature liberal icon Kennedy leading the charge, first to pass a patients' bill of rights, later to raise the minimum wage.

CQ Weekly May 26, 2001

It now will be up to the crafty Byrd, who returns to the post of Appropriations Committee chairman, to shepherd the fiscal 2002 spending bills through a Senate composed of 50 Democrats, 49 Republicans and an Independent Jeffords, who will caucus with the Democrats.

All-important nominations of federal judges will have to pass through a Judiciary Committee likely chaired by the liberal Leahy. Bush's designs for a multibillion-dollar missile defense system will face renewed skepticism, as will his plans to permit drilling for oil in the Arctic National Wildlife Refuge in Alaska.

Democratic chairmen will have the power to hold hearings on legislation, schedule bills for committee votes and launch investigations into administration policies — as well as to delve into possible future scandals.

A Senate controlled by Democrats offers the party a national megaphone and gives them power to proactively offer an agenda to counter Bush's, rather than having to use the guerrilla tactics available to the minority.

But it also carries responsibilities for Democrats. Now that they will control the Senate, they will have a far greater ability to counter Bush's agenda with their own. In short, Democrats will share the accountability for making democracy work — and share the blame for gridlock.

"When you're in the minority you can sit back and watch government self-destruct," said Paul C. Light, director of governmental studies at the Brookings Institution. "Now Democrats will have a stake in governing."

An Old-Fashioned Senate?

The Senate traditionally runs on unanimous agreements, and the potential for filibusters makes 60 votes the practical threshold for most bills. Split evenly between the parties, it was always seen as the ultimate test for Bush's legislative agenda. Now the dynamics of this crucible will change dramatically.

Now, it will be Democrats bringing legislation to the floor and Republicans lobbing the hand grenades, perhaps in the form of popular amendments to cut taxes.

Daschle has for years chafed at the way Trent Lott, R-Miss., ran the Senate, using parliamentary tactics to deny Democrats for weeks at a time the opportunity to offer popular amendments on issues such as a patients' bill of rights, campaign fi-nance overhaul or an increase in the minimum wage.

Daschle promises to run the Senate the old-fashioned way: throw a bill on the floor, let all sides take a whack at it for a week or two — hopefully not three — and wrap it up late on a Thursday. This strategy requires the majority, particularly one with a 51-49 edge, to take tough votes and to stick together. But being able to establish the terms of the debate is a key advantage.

"We may lose some of the things we put on the table, but we set the table," said Sen. Charles E. Schumer, D-N.Y.

For Republicans, who had nominal control under the 50-50 Senate but often lost votes, the return to the minority does not mean they will lose opportunities to push Bush's agenda.

"Under Senate rules, as we've learned from the Democrats when they were in the minority, you can offer amendments and issues that are important to you as an individual senator or as a party," said Lott, who will step aside for Daschle as soon as Congress returns from the Memorial Day recess.

Republicans and Democrats were quick to point out that although majority control of the Senate will change, the composition of the membership will not. And that the key to winning a majority is to win the center.

Can Daschle hold Democratic moderates such as Zell Miller of Georgia, Ben Nelson of Nebraska, and John B. Breaux of Louisiana? Or can they be lured away by Bush, who holds the power to sign their legislative priorities into law?

For Republican moderates, such as Olympia J. Snowe and Susan Collins of Maine, the most important question may well be whether to cast their lot with a center-left coalition comprised mostly of Democrats or to try pulling their party and their president toward the center.

Snowe said Jeffords' defection "should be a wake-up call for our party's leaders that the voices of moderate Republicans must be welcomed and respected. It demonstrates that,

---

Lott, left, did not realize the rumors of Jeffords' departure from the GOP were true and did not begin lobbying to keep him until it was too late. Daschle, center, quietly courted the Vermont Republican after learning he might be receptive. Daschle and Reid, right, will become the Senate's top two leaders.

CQ PHOTOS / SCOTT J. FERRELL

quite literally, the Republican Party can be the majority party only as long as it is big enough to accommodate the divergent views of the broad spectrum of Republicans throughout the country."

The week of May 21 was among the most surreal in recent memory inside the capitol. It opened with a scattering of rumors that Jeffords might defect, mentioned during the Sunday morning talk shows.

But the talk failed to stir the White House or Senate Republican leaders, who had been unhappy with Jeffords' stand against Bush's budget. They did not know, it became clear, that this was no idle threat by a grumpy party loyalist. They did not know Jeffords had been mulling the idea for weeks.

By Tuesday, the talk-show gossip had become menacingly real. Jeffords met with Vice President Dick Cheney at the Capitol around noon that day, and the news spread at the weekly GOP policy luncheon shortly thereafter. Jeffords was ferried to the White House for a mid-afternoon one-on-one with Bush in the Oval Office.

By most accounts, the meeting did not go well. Bush asked Jeffords if his administration had treated him poorly, and Jeffords responded that the problems were over policy.

But, Jeffords made clear, they also were intractable. He would later tell Vermont reporters that he used his time alone with Bush to say "very frankly that I think he'll be a one-term president if he doesn't listen to his moderates."

There was little Bush could do but ask Jeffords to hold off until the tax bill was finished so Democrats would not suddenly control the conference committee on a piece of legislation that had traveled so far. "It was clear the senator's mind had already been made up," White House spokesman Ari Fleischer said May 24.

A Brief Delay, a GOP Offer

By late Tuesday, the Senate was in a frenzy, and Jeffords began informing his colleagues. He pulled Lincoln Chafee, R-R.I., off the Senate floor to speak privately on the top of the steps to the Capitol. He told Larry E. Craig of Idaho, a fellow member of the now-defunct "singing senators" quartet. He promised an announcement the next day.

On Wednesday, however, Jeffords said he would delay his decision and make an announcement in Vermont 24 hours later, prompting a last-ditch efforts by Republicans to keep him. Speculation bloomed about a leadership post for the Vermont iconoclast. Just before he got on the plane to Burlington, Jeffords met with about 10 of his colleagues in a heartfelt meeting just off the Senate floor.

"It was the most emotional time that I have ever had in my life, with my closest friends urging me not to do what I

The Transfer Of Leadership

Sen. James M. Jeffords of Vermont has announced that he will leave the Republican Party and become an Independent. He will do so no sooner than June 5, but when he changes his party affiliation, Tom Daschle, D-S.D., will automatically become the Senate Majority Leader.

Trent Lott, R-Miss., will become the minority leader, and all the chairmen of the Senate's 20 committees will switch from Republicans to Democrats. The special 50-50 power-sharing agreement that Lott and Daschle previously struck will dissolve.

A new organizational resolution will have to be approved by the Senate, finalizing committee rosters and giving freshmen, who without the 50-50 plan will have no assignments, seats on committees. The resolution, which must be negotiated and is subject to a filibuster, will give Democrats one-seat majorities. It is expected to leave unchanged the even split of staff and resources that had been agreed to under the 50-50 deal.

---

was going to do because it affected their lives very substantially," Jeffords recalled in his announcement.

By leaving the GOP, Jeffords will strip his colleagues — including some close friends — of their chairmanships. Charles E. Grassley of Iowa, who along with Jeffords was among the handful of GOP freshmen in the 1974 post-Watergate class, saw his long-sought dream of running the Finance Committee dissipate after a maddeningly short few months in control.

As for Democrats, most were careful not to say anything impolitic before the announcement was final. Daschle, who along with Democratic Whip Harry Reid of Nevada quietly worked to cement Jeffords' decision to join their caucus, secluded himself with colleagues and aides.

Reid, who promises to be a major player in helping Daschle run the Senate, would be in line to head the Environment and Public Works Committee. But he opted to step aside, several senators confirmed, to focus on the whip post and to offer Jeffords the chairmanship of the committee.

"He's a team player par excellence," said Joseph I. Lieberman, D-Conn.

Adding to the tumult was renewed speculation that Georgia Democrat Miller might leave his party and preserve a 50-50 Senate run by Republicans. "This might be a short-lived [Democratic] majority," said a Democratic lobbyist roaming the halls of the Senate on Wednesday.

But Miller, who later acknowledged in a televised interview that he had toyed with the idea of making some sort of switch, quickly settled the rumors: "I will not switch to the Republican Party and have no need to proclaim myself an independent," Miller said in a statement. "But a word of warning to my fellow Democrats at this time," Miller added ominously: "What is sorely needed around here is much more getting along and much less getting even."

Jeffords gave his speech at a hotel in Burlington. Around Washington, he is known as an uninspiring orator, and in hallway conversations he can be halting. But in Vermont, Jeffords was forceful and direct.

He said today's national Republican Party had lurched too far to the right to accommodate the moderate-to-progressive traditions of the party in Vermont.

"It is only natural to expect that people like myself, who have been honored with positions of leadership, will largely support the president's agenda. And yet, more and more, I find I cannot," Jeffords said. "Looking ahead, I can see more and more instances where I'll disagree with the president on very fundamental issues — the issues of choice, the direction of the judiciary, tax and spending decisions, missile defense, energy and the environment." (*Text, 2001 CQ Weekly, p. 1280*)

The switch in control comes as the Senate agenda was

sure to turn to issues Democrats would have forced onto the agenda anyway. They were poised to take advantage of Senate rules that permit any senator to offer unrelated legislation to most bills that come to the floor.

The looming shift in power will focus much attention on Daschle, a soft-spoken but steely protégé of former Majority Leader George J. Mitchell, D-Maine (1980-95). Mitchell skillfully ran the Senate from 1989 to 1995, and many insiders believe he inflicted extraordinary damage to the presidency of the elder Bush. *(Daschle, 2001 CQ Weekly, p. 1212)*

It also gives such legends as Byrd and Kennedy their gavels back. In fact, the re-emergence of Byrd, whose penchant for home-state projects is legendary, gives Republicans a bogeyman to help paper over their own internal divisions on federal spending.

House and Senate Republicans faced the prospect of an internal holy war this summer on appropriations, as conservatives insisted on meeting Bush's demand for a 4 percent spending increase while more moderate appropriators argued that was not realistic.

Byrd could become a convenient scapegoat for higher spending, but he signaled May 24 that he would endeavor to live within the spending limits set by the fiscal 2002 budget resolution (H Con Res 83). "The change in the Senate majority does not change the fundamental dynamics of the . . . appropriations process," he said.

House Republicans are free to continue passing Bush's agenda untrammeled. In fact, some lawmakers and aides suggested a renewed emphasis on Republican purity in the House because many concessions to the Senate would no longer be made in advance. "It lets us be a little more conservative than we would have been," said a GOP leadership aide. *(House, 2001 CQ Weekly, p. 1238)*

Republicans had always worried the Senate might switch hands, but most people focused on the possibility that an elderly member such as 98-year-old Strom Thurmond, R-S.C., might die and be replaced by a Democrat.

It is to Democrats' advantage that they did not take over the Senate by any default or fluke. It is difficult to imagine the triumphant entrance of Daschle onto the national stage had he become majority leader through no effort of his own.

"We know that we have a divided government — Republicans in the White House and now Democrats leading the Senate," Daschle said in remarks carried live on cable networks. "The only way we can accomplish our agenda, the only way that the administration will be able to accomplish their agenda, is if we truly work together."

Aftermath

As Republicans met after Jeffords' announcement to discuss their next steps, Snowe urged them to give moderates a position in the leadership, which was awarded to Arlen Specter, R-Pa., the next day.

"This should never have happened," Snowe told reporters after what was said to be a difficult party meeting. "For the first time in history, we had all three branches of government, and now we've lost it. Hopefully, we're going to learn something from that."

Bush spoke in Cleveland after Jeffords' announcement, but he rejected suggestions that the party had failed him: "I respect Sen. Jeffords, but respectfully, I couldn't disagree more."

Democrats will have to work together, as well. One potential problem concerns the decision of Joseph R. Biden Jr., D-Del., to waffle on the question of whether he would take the chairmanship of the Foreign Relations Committee, where he is the top Democrat, or return to the helm of Judiciary, where he has seniority.

If Biden were to opt for Judiciary, which could offer a platform for his national political ambitions, it would create a domino effect that would shuffle the leadership of several committees. The loser in this scenario would be Tom Harkin, D-Iowa, who would lose the politically valuable chair of Agriculture just as a difficult re-election bid heats up.

"That's a legitimate concern," Biden said.

Harkin said he has no doubts he will get the Agriculture chair, and aides to other senators who would be affected by a Biden switch dismissed the notion that it might actually occur.

Meanwhile, Republicans used the waning days and hours of their ability to control the floor to win confirmation of several nominations, including the controversial pick of Theodore Olson to be solicitor general. *(Olson, 2001 CQ Weekly, p. 1261)*

On May 23, for example, a total of 19 nominations were confirmed, and during the legislative "wrap-up," six bills were passed by unanimous consent.

"It feels like we're the Polish parliament passing bills and naming government officials as the German tanks come into view outside the walls of Warsaw," quipped a GOP leadership aide.

Nuts and Bolts

The looming transformation of a 50-50 Senate to 50-49-1 unravels the carefully negotiated power-sharing accord reached by Lott and Daschle in January. Under that plan, committee rosters were evenly divided, as were the allocations of staff resources and office space.

The all-important question of the makeup of Senate conference committees was left unresolved, and in a sign of how difficult managing the Senate had become, Lott and Daschle still had not settled that issue even though a bankruptcy bill had passed both chambers and was ready for final negotiations.

Now, Democrats will have an edge in conference talks.

Jeffords' decision to bolt the GOP will take effect once the tax bill conference report is sent to president Bush.

Once Jeffords becomes an independent, Daschle will automatically become majority leader, a post which gives him authority to set the floor schedule.

Among the first tasks will be to establish new committee rosters to give Democrats a one-seat edge in every committee save for the traditionally evenly split Ethics panel.

It takes agreement of both parties in the Senate to name committee rosters, but Republicans are not expected to offer a major struggle. There was an explicit understanding when Daschle and Lott negotiated the 50-50 agreement that if either party won outright control, that party would earn a single-seat edge on committees.

"I have changed my party label, but I have not changed by beliefs," Jeffords said to close his seismic announcement. "Indeed, my decision is about affirming the principles that have shaped my career. I hope that the people of Vermont will understand it. I hope in time that my colleagues will as well. I am confident that it is the right decision." ◆

Senate Democrats' Priorities Drafted With an Eye on 2002

Party may hone 'wedge issues' that cast Republicans as too conservative

Senate Democrats are moving to exploit their newly won advantage in anticipation of what is certain to be a furiously contested battle for control of the chamber in the 2002 midterm elections.

Despite public pledges to find common ground with Republicans, Democrats are expected to frame their "wedge issues" by pushing long-held priorities such as tough protections for patients in health insurance plans, a Medicare prescription drug benefit, a minimum wage increase and environmental initiatives — all of which are popular in polls.

Congressional Republicans already have accomplishments to run on; they have enacted the centerpiece of President Bush's agenda, tax cuts, and are close to passing another, an education overhaul. Those Democrats who had expected to spend the next 18 months in the minority obstructing Bush's policies now concede that they have to figure out how to work with the White House and a more assertive GOP leadership in the House to produce legislation that stands a chance of being signed into law.

"Instead of preventing things we thought were bad for the country from happening, we can try to do some things that are good for the country," said Charles E. Schumer, D-N.Y. He quickly added, "That doesn't mean we'll win them all."

New Senate Majority Leader Tom Daschle, D-S.D., is likely to find himself caught between partisans who want to carve out a platform and those who would rather produce outcomes. In the end, though, both factions want to pad their one-seat majority during an election cycle in which 34 Senate seats — 20 now held by Republicans — are being contested. (*Senate races, 2001 CQ Weekly, p. 1347*)

"The Democratic strategy is contingent on whether Bush and the Republicans have the incentive to compromise," said Sarah Binder, a congressional scholar at George Washington University. "If nothing else, the changeover gives them a platform to define their differences with Republicans, to remind people it was a close presidential election and that public opinion still appears evenly divided between the parties."

The shift in the Senate was brought about by Vermont Sen. James M. Jeffords' June 5 defection from the Republican party to become an Independent. That came as recent polls showed falling public approval for the Bush administration, with particular skepticism over his policies on energy and the environment. An ABC News/Washington Post poll of 1,004 adults conducted from May 31 to June 3 put the president's job approval rating at 55 percent, a decline of 8 percentage points since late April. Democrats were narrowly ahead of the president on the question of who should set the national policy agenda, and 57 percent of those polled believed Democrats were more open to the views of political moderates.

Analysts predict Democrats will quickly try to build an advantage by stressing health-care and environmental issues — two topics on which they continually outpoll Republicans. Daschle has indicated that his early priorities include bringing up legislation to enhance patients' rights and to raise the minimum wage. Other legislative efforts probably will be directed at expanded Medicare drug coverage, overhauling campaign finance rules and retooling the electoral system. And Democrats are almost certain to highlight the looming energy crisis by playing up Bush administration ties to the oil and auto industries. (*Energy, 2001 CQ Weekly, p. 1369*)

"The cauldron is still bubbling, but I think we're seeing a growing gap between how the parties are perceived by the average family," said Democratic strategist Alan Secrest. "It's not too great a leap for voters to see Republicans looking out for [business interests] on energy and environmental policies. Voters already are volunteering it on surveys."

Republicans will continue to try to press their priorities, such as arguing for tax cuts for business as a condition for supporting a Democratic minimum-wage bill. But some analysts say there is little incentive for the GOP to compromise. With Bush's signature on the $1.35 trillion tax cut package (HR 1836 — PL 107-16) and with a Republican-inspired education overhaul package (S 1) headed for likely Senate approval, GOP senators will have two victories to run on. "The biggest parts of the president's agenda, frankly, are done," said Sen. Robert F. Bennett, R-Utah. (*Tax cuts, 2001 CQ Weekly, p. 1364; education, p. 1371*)

Republican strategists say Democrats can easily box themselves in by pushing too hard for initiatives that cannot gain the 60 votes necessary to shut off debate in the chamber. "The danger for Democrats is that if nothing else passes, they appear obstructionist," said GOP strategist Ed Goeas. "If they pick issues that are contentious, nothing gets accomplished and they kind of set themselves up."

Changing Pitches

The Senate flip prompted both parties' fundraising operations to launch new appeals for money. National Republican Senatorial Committee Chairman Bill Frist, R-Tenn., warned of a "Daschle-Clinton-Kennedy-led United States Senate" in appeals to his party's base. Included was an e-mail that Frist sent hours after Jeffords' May 24 announcement, filled with typographical errors and written in lower case, apparently to capture the frantic events of the day. Frist sought donations of $75, $50 or $25.

Lawmakers also stepped up their rhetoric — initially. Senate Minority Leader Trent Lott, R-Miss., sent a strongly worded memorandum to fellow GOP lawmakers over the June 2-3 weekend, declaring that "we must begin to wage the war today for the election of 2002." Lott questioned the

While he pledged to work in a bipartisan way, newly installed Senate Majority Leader Tom Daschle and other Democrats are determined to push issues that will give the party an edge in mid-term elections in 2002. Daschle is shown leaving a June 5 press briefing.

legitimacy of the Democratic majority, though he later backed off that statement.

"We should have a war of ideas, and we should have a full campaign for the Senate in 2002. And I think that's what the people would expect of us," Lott told reporters June 5.

Democratic Senatorial Campaign Committee Chairman Patty Murray, D-Wash., said her party's control of committee chairmanships and the floor will help recruit top candidates to challenge Republican incumbents. Murray said voters will respond if they see popular Democratic initiatives scuttled by filibusters and Republican-led stalling tactics.

"Voters know about the other side," Murray said. "They haven't heard the issues they care about being debated. They're going to see a huge difference and will work to make sure we keep the majority."

Democratic Priorities

Here is a look at some of the key issues the parties will attempt to leverage, with Democratic priorities first:

▶ **Health care.** Daschle said he will bring to the floor a patients' bill of rights to protect individuals in health insurance plans as soon as the chamber concludes action on the education bill. Incoming Finance Committee Chairman Max Baucus, D-Mont., plans to introduce Medicare prescription drug legislation in July, and Daschle has signaled it is a high priority for him as well.

GOP leaders had identified patients' rights and prescription drugs for the elderly as important issues for the 107th Congress, but they had not made clear how they wanted to proceed. Many Republicans expressed concern with liability provisions in both of the competing patients' rights measures and felt they did not want to add an expensive new benefit for the Medicare program, which provides medical coverage to nearly 40 million elderly and disabled Americans.

Democrats will likely remain united behind a patients' rights bill (S 872) sponsored by John McCain, R-Ariz., John Edwards, D-N.C., and Edward M. Kennedy, D-Mass. Kennedy will manage the floor debate and savor every moment. McCain's political star power and Edwards' presidential aspirations virtually guarantee floor fireworks. The alternative (S 889), sponsored by Frist, John B. Breaux, D-La., and Jeffords, I-Vt., will be offered as a substitute but will have a difficult time overcoming the momentum of the McCain-Edwards-Kennedy measure. *(2001 CQ Weekly, p. 1377)*

Democrats also will push for a Medicare drug benefit for all recipients rather than backing a targeted benefit for low-income seniors — an idea many Republicans and Bush have embraced. Republicans will battle back with accusations that both initiatives represent typical big-government strategies. Democrats will argue that Republican resistance proves once again that they are out to protect their allies in the business and employer communities rather than voters.

▶ **Minimum wage.** Democrats want to raise the current $5.15-per-hour rate by $1.50 over three years. Republican leaders have reluctantly countered with proposals to raise the wage by $1 over the same period. The last increase came in the election year of 1996, when moderate Republicans forced their leaders to allow it along with a package of tax breaks to lessen the burden on small businesses (PL 104-188). *(1996 Almanac, p. 7-3)*

Democrats see the minimum wage as a classic way to demonstrate concern for working Americans and perhaps reclaim what analysts call "the compassion issue" from Bush. A coalition of liberal interest groups, including Americans for Democratic Action, the NAACP and the AFL-CIO, is lobbying undecided lawmakers to support the increase.

Republicans insist that any minimum-wage change should again be packaged with tax cuts for small business owners. Some Democrats say targeted tax breaks for small business owners are inevitable, but want to hold down the cost to about $20 billion to $30 billion over 10 years.

Republicans insist on far more generous tax cuts. "We will have an alternative, and it will have more tax breaks," Minority Whip Don Nickles of Oklahoma said June 5.

The likely GOP amendment will include a more generous deduction for business meals and the extension of some tax credits for hiring hard-to-place workers. If it appears that the amendment will win approval, aides from both parties say the Finance Committee is likely to mark up a tax package of its own that could be attached to the wage bill. Baucus and ranking Republican Charles E. Grassley of Iowa, are adamant that all tax legislation should go through their panel.

So far, the White House has offered little guidance. But with increased attention on wages, particularly due to the economic downturn, the administration may feel the need to become more directly involved.

▶ **Campaign finance.** An overhaul (S 27) sponsored by McCain and Russell D. Feingold, D-Wis., passed the Senate on April 2 after an extraordinary two-week debate. The issue has moved to the House, where proponents of a ban on "soft money" and other changes to the campaign finance system face challenges of their own. *(Campaign finance, 2001 CQ Weekly, p. 1365)*

Unless McCain-Feingold passes the House unchanged, which is highly unlikely, it will have to go back to the Senate for approval. The new majority has made passing the legislation a priority, while Lott and other Republican leaders firmly oppose it. Before the power shift, McCain-Feingold supporters faced the prospect of a bill passing the House only to die in a conference committee led by the bill's No. 1 opponent, Mitch McConnell, R-Ky., former chairman of the Senate Rules and Administration Committee. Now bill supporter Christopher J. Dodd, D-Conn., will be the lead Senate conferee.

"It is less of a scary scenario now," Feingold said.

Dodd also is expected to lead a separate Democratic effort to correct flaws in the electoral system that were exposed during last year's presidential election. Democrats have expressed concern over what they believe was the exclusion of minority groups from the process and are championing measures such as expanded voter education initiatives. Republicans also have expressed concern over irregularities, but tended to focus on technical flaws in balloting.

Republican Priorities

▶ **Tax cuts.** While they will fight to pair targeted cuts with the minimum wage increase, Republicans have seen their major political and legislative goal enacted — the $1.35 trillion package of tax cuts for individuals.

Although many conservatives are grousing about the slow rate at which some cuts are phased in and about a provision that would repeal all the cuts in 10 years, they are more than happy to run as members of the party that shepherded to enactment the largest tax cut in 25 years. While Bush is claiming most of the credit for pushing the bill to passage, the final measure was written by two GOP pragmatists — Grassley and House Ways and Means Committee Chairman Bill Thomas of California — and two moderate Democrats, Baucus and Breaux.

Conferees included immediate rebates of up to $300 for individuals and $600 for married couples. Most should be mailed out before the fall. The new law creates a new 10 percent tax rate and cuts all but one of the five higher brackets. It gradually repeals the estate tax, alleviates the major components of the so-called marriage penalty, doubles the per-child tax credit and increases tax incentives for retirement savings.

"A year ago, tax relief was said to be a political impossibility. Six months ago, it was supposed to be a political liability. Today, it becomes reality," Bush crowed June 7.

▶ **Education.** The president's overhaul plan (S 1) is still considered must-pass because it is tied to the reauthorization of the 1965 Elementary and Secondary Education act, the main source of federal aid to public schools. The law's authorization lapsed last year, and Democrats know they cannot be seen as blocking its renewal.

Passage of the education bill would help cement the GOP administration's bona fides on an important social policy issue. The ABC News-Washington Post poll found Bush in a virtual tie with Democrats on who was better suited to lead on education policy — this just six years after House Republicans voted to eliminate the Department of Education.

Senate Democrats have the votes to reshape much of the bill to their liking, especially by boosting funding. Jeffords warned that Bush's plans to improve schools through annual testing are doomed to fail — and punish poor schools unnecessarily — if the money is not there to help them develop high-quality tests and assist underperforming schools.

▶ **Defense.** The details are yet to come on Bush's plans for a national missile defense system and for streamlining Pentagon operations, but congressional Republicans are making a stronger military a rallying cry.

Tossups

▶ **Energy and environment.** Democrats are highlighting what they describe as the Bush administration's overemphasis on increasing oil and gas production at the expense of a balanced approach that stresses conservation. In doing so, they have sought to exploit the advantage their party holds over Republicans on the environment — a key issue to many suburban swing voters. *(2001 CQ Weekly, p. 1370)*

Since the administration's energy strategy was released in May, some Democrats have repeated the charge that GOP stands for "Gas, Oil, Plutonium." Democrats are hoping to tap into deepening skepticism that the plan would help the nation as much as it would benefit the energy industry.

Among the issues Democrats expect will score points on the campaign trail are tightening fuel efficiency standards for sport-utility vehicles and minivans, and, in California and other Western states, imposing price controls on wholesale electricity. As the majority party, Democrats will be able to hold Senate hearings and conduct investigations to try to score political points against the energy industry.

Republicans may be less vulnerable, however, if gas prices level off by year's end and the issue becomes more of an arcane policy debate affecting a handful of states.

Republicans also have moved to play down their interest in oil drilling in Alaska's Arctic National Wildlife Refuge (ANWR). But Senate Democrats have kept their near-unanimous opposition to energy development in ANWR as a weapon in their party's political arsenal, much to the exasperation of some pro-drilling Republicans. ◆

Daschle Promises to Smooth Rough Reality of 50 Plus 1

Democrats weigh their next moves as GOP leaders bone up on minority tactics

Republican negotiators Arlen Specter of Pennsylvania, left, McConnell, at microphone, and Gramm (far right) were less combative than the party rhetoric that began the week. Rick Santorum of Pennsylvania (background) softened his stand, too.

Quick Contents

New Majority Leader Tom Daschle may get a honeymoon in the coming weeks as popular bills, including a patients' bill of rights, are scheduled for floor debate. But Daschle's pledge to allow wide-open debate and free-flowing amendments will be tested when the need to wrap up bills collides with Republicans' desire to exercise their full minority rights.

Tom Daschle promises to run a Senate of freewheeling debate and bipartisan cooperation — and the five-day work weeks required to do so.

But the South Dakota Democrat just named majority leader has inherited a chamber that has been riven by partisanship for years, and one whose traditions have eroded.

As he assumed his place atop the Senate the week of June 4, Daschle was awarded the requisite pledges from Republicans of bipartisan cooperation. Still, there are ample signs that Daschle faces a formidable task as he tries to run a 51-49 institution where 60 votes are the threshold to pass most anything.

Just for starters, the Senate continued its lengthy slog through a rewrite of federal education programs that showed how even a widely supported bill can take weeks to advance under Senate rules.

Daschle faces a Republican conference that is still reeling from the defection of James M. Jeffords, whose switch to Independent cost them control of the chamber. And

while almost half of Senate Republicans have never served that chamber in the minority, the other half is ready to school them on the guerrilla tactics that can vastly complicate life for the majority.

On the other side, Daschle must manage his own caucus, a collection of lawmakers whose divisions were often papered over by the need to remain united, and by the tactics employed by former Majority Leader Trent Lott, R-Miss., who often exerted tight control over the Senate agenda and used heavy handed tactics to limit input from the Democrats.

And finally, Daschle commands a place where any single senator can simply say, "I object," and bring things to a halt.

"I'll be setting 51 place settings in my caucus every week from here on out," Daschle told reporters shortly before becoming majority leader. "But I also recognize it's a very, very slim majority. And just as President Bush, I hope, would recognize that he has a very, very slim majority, that the tenuous nature of our majorities require that we act accordingly. . . . We've got to work together and find common ground."

Still, it is not all bad news for Daschle. The short-term Senate agenda is set, which may give him time to prepare for the challenges ahead. After education, Daschle has cleared room for debate on a patients' bill of rights, then will come a 2001 supplemental appropriations bill and later fiscal 2002 spending bills. With lawmakers across the ideological spectrum — as well as Bush — renewing calls for bipartisanship, chances are that Daschle will have a fairly smooth honeymoon period.

"We're certainly not going to lob any hand grenades at a man who's calm, reasonable, deliberative, even-handed, balanced and fair," said a GOP leadership aide. "Daschle is too smart to make mistakes early."

The administration displayed renewed interest in negotiations on a patients' bill of rights measure that Daschle has assured will come to the floor. Secretary of Health and Human Services Tommy G. Thompson and Deputy White House Chief of Staff Joshua Bolten met with Sen. John McCain, R-Ariz., on June 7 — two days after McCain dined privately with Bush — to discuss McCain's bill (S 872) to give people greater clout in challenging denials of care by their health care plans. (*Managed care, 2001 CQ Weekly, p. 1378*)

After a little more than six years of a GOP majority, lawmakers in both parties are just beginning to sort through the many ramifications, large and small, of the changeover.

"It'll take a while for a minority to get coalesced, just as it does a majority," said Judd Gregg, R-N.H. "Even though it's a very close majority, it still requires different tactical activities, and it'll take a while for us to get comfortable with that as a group."

Guerrilla War

Republicans said there are positives to having minority status — namely greater freedom from the responsibility of governing to express their personal views instead of toeing the party line.

"I have this image of us pushing a covered wagon across the sands and being under attack the whole time — that's what the majority has to do," said Jeff Sessions, R-Ala. "You've got to get the load carried, so you can't particularly fight back a lot of times."

Now that Republicans are in the minority, Sessions said, they are "freer to advocate [their] personal views, and that's very liberating."

Added Phil Gramm, R-Texas: "One of the things about being in the minority is that you're not so focused on trying to get the trains running on time, so you can figure out where you want the train to go."

Meanwhile, Democrats are elated, though they know Republicans can often deny them accomplishments if they

Domenici is one of five Republicans negotiating with Daschle on how to organize the new 50-49-1 Senate.

opt to kill bills with filibusters that require 60 votes to overcome.

"Sixty votes is going to be very hard to do, and if the Republicans dig in their heels, it's going to be very hard on Sen. Daschle," said Agriculture Committee Chairman Tom Harkin, D-Iowa. Harkin said gridlock would also hurt Bush unless the president can "override and overcome the strident, right-wing voices around him. He's going to have to say, 'Look, we can't do it your way.' "

With a Republican in the White House and the GOP in control of the House, however, Senate Republicans — who have come through two disappointing election cycles — may not have much appetite for filibusters of popular legislation heading into another important election year. Democratic legislation can get vetoed or killed by the House. (*Senate issues, p. 44*)

The historic mid-Congress shift in Senate control occurred at 11 a.m. June 6. The desk of James M. Jeffords of Vermont had just been moved to the Democratic side of the aisle, and his decision to leave the GOP and become an Independent aligned with the Democrats had taken effect at the close of business the day before.

Daschle came to the floor 10 minutes early and accepted congratulations from colleagues in both parties — including legendary conservative Jesse Helms, R-N.C., — as he awaited anointment as majority leader.

Promptly at 11 a.m., Harry Reid of Nevada, the Senate's No. 2 Democrat, assumed the chair and recognized Daschle as majority leader.

The first order of business was to pass a series of routine resolutions, including one (S Res 100) naming Robert C. Byrd, D-W.Va., as the president pro tempore, a post that is always given to the most senior member of the majority party. Byrd immediately took the oath of office and then the chair.

Just over a third of the Senate came to the floor to watch the transfer of power and to listen to Daschle's remarks. Among those who stayed away was Jeffords, who said he did not want to distract attention from Daschle's moment.

"This, indeed, is a humbling moment for me. I am honored to serve as majority leader, but I also recognize that the majority is slim," Daschle said. "At the same time Americans are evenly divided about their choice of leaders, they are united in their demand for action. Polarized positions are an indulgence that the Senate cannot afford and our nation will not tolerate."

Lott followed with a speech in which he listed the accomplishments of GOP control, including cutting taxes, overhauling welfare and balancing the budget. Lott vowed that Daschle would receive his "support and cooperation." (*Text of speeches, 2001 CQ Weekly, p. 1395*)

Lott's floor remarks of June 6 stood in stark relief to a bellicose June 2 memorandum he sent to "Republican opinion leaders," in which he said Jeffords' defection was a "coup of one" that "puts at peril the agenda that

Republicans were given a mandate by the American people to deliver."

Many of Lott's GOP colleagues thought the memo churlish, and as the week of June 4 went on, most dropped the confrontational rhetoric.

A New Senate

There was little immediate change as the new Democratic Senate got started, though changes are afoot.

In order to accommodate more open debate and a busy summer, Daschle is promising longer workweeks. Under Lott's leadership, the Senate often voted only Tuesday through Friday. Daschle scheduled votes for Monday, June 11, and promises full workweeks. "My expectation is we're going to work a five-day week," Daschle said.

After complaining bitterly that Lott had abused parliamentary tactics to freeze Democrats out of the ability to offer their agenda on the floor over much of the past Congress, Daschle said he would not employ comparable tactics against Republicans.

"You've heard us . . . criticize the majority when we were in the minority for the lack of fairness," Daschle said. "I think it would be hypocrisy at its worst if we were to take the same tactics. So we're not going to do that."

Lott and others said Republicans will adopt the same guerrilla strategy Senate minority parties have used for years to force consideration of their agendas.

"We will take advantage of our rights in the minority to offer amendments," Lott said, "as certainly the other side has."

When Republicans were last in the minority, for example, they forced votes on issues such as the balanced-budget constitutional amendment in 1994. Later, Democrats took advantage of election-year pressures to push through an increase in the minimum wage in 1996. (*1994 Almanac, p. 85; 1996 Almanac, p. 7-3*)

No matter who controlled the calendar, Democratic-backed bills were likely to be headed to the floor anyway. Democrats and McCain already powered a campaign law overhaul bill (S 27) through the Senate. (*Campaign finance, 2001 CQ Weekly, p. 1365*)

But the key to driving something into law from the minority perch is to have a politically potent issue and a reliable set of allies from the other party. The Republican agenda has few items

that carry the political fear factor that would allow the party to bull its way onto the Democratic-controlled calendar. Outlawing certain late-term abortions is one such item, and popular tax cut leftovers might be another, though in most cases, tax cut-related amendments could be struck by points of order requiring 60 votes to overturn.

Simply put, Republicans have few if any proposals that would change the conversation and put Democrats on the defensive. "If I had any at the tip of my tongue, I wouldn't tell you," said GOP Whip Don Nickles of Oklahoma.

Said Joseph I. Lieberman, D-Conn.: "So far, their agenda has mostly been an old agenda. Tax cuts, what else?"

Daschle hopes he can further complicate the Republican guerrilla strategy by including GOP senators in an open legislative process that leaves them "invested" in a successful outcome. Daschle said that would be far different from the frustration Democrats felt for much of the past few years.

"The reason why you see as much polarization and obstruction on so many occasions is because . . . [Democrats have] not felt invested in the process," Daschle said. "I've heard more than once Democrats saying, 'What do we have to lose if we blow up the place, if we stop everything? There's nothing to lose.' "

Among the steps Democrats hope to take toward this aim is to restore the committee structure, which had become weaker under Lott's leadership. Lott often established Republican-only "task forces" on issues such as patients' rights that usurped the traditional role of committees.

Reorganization Redux

Still to be resolved in the new Senate are questions of reorganization. Without the now-defunct 50-50 power-sharing accord (S Res 8), committee memberships have reverted to the line-ups at the end of the 106th Congress. That means freshmen have no committee seats, and veterans who moved to more prestigious committees are temporarily back to their previous panels.

Initially, some Republicans suggested they were willing to stall the reorganization process in exchange for concessions.

"The first battle will be reorganizing the Senate," Lott wrote in his memo, adding that any reorganization plan must reflect the "reality that the Dem-

ocrats hold a plurality, not a majority, in the Senate, and that their effective control of the Senate lacks the moral authority of a mandate from the voters."

Despite his tough line in the June 2 memo, Lott pointedly excused himself from negotiations on the reorganizing, instead installing a "dream team" of five GOP negotiators: Pete V. Domenici of New Mexico, Gramm of Texas, Orrin G. Hatch of Utah, Mitch McConnell of Kentucky and Arlen Specter of Pennsylvania. The group includes some senators who were highly critical of the 50-50 deal Lott struck with Daschle in January.

Republicans want to influence other issues with the reorganization, such as assurances that Bush nominees will be afforded fair treatment by the Democratic Senate. (*Nominations, p. 55*)

Republicans already won a guarantee that none of their junior members will be bumped from committees. And Daschle said he would support a GOP request to reinstate the 50-50 accord if the Senate were to shift back. Daschle and Republican negotiators both said they expect the resolution to be passed the week of June 11.

For all the attention showered on Daschle and Jeffords, McCain also managed to find the spotlight. He hosted Daschle at his Arizona ranch June 2-3, prompting media speculation that the maverick McCain — whose battles with both Bush and Republican leaders in Congress are legend — might cast his lot with the Democrats. Then on June 2, The Washington Post ran a front-page story saying McCain was mulling a spilt from the GOP to run for president again, as an Independent.

McCain denied plans to quit the party, but his denial seemed carefully worded: "I have no intention of running for president, nor do I have any intention of or cause to leave the Republican Party."

A widely held interpretation is that McCain's intentions could well change if he were given good cause, such as a Bush veto of his signature campaign finance bill.

As for Bush, he spent much of the week reaching out to lawmakers to his left on the political spectrum, including dinner with Daschle.

"I think the president was very candid, and I hope I was equally as candid," Daschle said later. "I think it is fair to say we both hope that we can do it more frequently." ◆

Congress of Relative Newcomers Poses Challenge to Bush, Leadership

Most members have known only an era of sharp divisions, narrow margin of control

Quick Contents

Two-thirds of the House has never legislated in a recession or worked with a president other than Bill Clinton. More senators have a term or less under their belts than at any time in two decades. This shrinking tenure — and the record number of Senate women — are the distinguishing characteristics of the 107th Congress.

A Less Experienced House
Tenure in the House has declined sharply in the past decade. As the 107th Congress begins, 65 percent of the members, or 281 of those represented in the darker, right-hand bars in this graph, have been in office 8 years or less. By contrast, at the start of the 102nd Congress in 1991, the comparable figure was 53 percent, or 229 of the members represented in the lighter, left-hand bars.

Only one in three members of the House of Representatives this year was on Capitol Hill during the Cold War. Just 35 percent were in the House when somebody other than Bill Clinton was president, and only a bare majority have known congressional life under Democratic control.

Although seniority in the Senate remains somewhat constant — the average length of senatorial service at the start of 2001 is a little longer than 11 years, as it has been for the past decade — House tenure is continuing a steep decline that began in the early 1990s. That makes the 107th Congress as remarkable for what its members have not experienced as for what they have.

Almost two-thirds of the members of the House, 65 percent, were first elected in 1992 or since. That means they have never served during a recession, were never called on to debate policies affecting the Soviet Union, did not have a say in authorizing the Persian Gulf War, have known federal surpluses in some cases longer than they have known deficits — and are preparing to do business with a Republican president for the first time. For the 48 percent elected in or since the GOP takeover of Congress in 1994, this year will be their first experience in something other than a divided government.

This is a marked change from a decade ago, before an anti-incumbent sentiment, the last round of redistricting and the GOP sweep ushered in a new generation of lawmakers. Two out of five of the House's members, 38 percent, had been in office for more than 10 years when the 102nd Congress convened in 1991, while only 53 percent had been in office for eight years or less.

In the Senate, while the average length of service has not fluctuated much — and while four of the six longest-serving senators in American history are now in office — there is a parallel wave of relative newcomers. As the 107th Congress began, 45 senators had been in the chamber for six years or less, a figure

CQ Weekly Jan. 20, 2001

not matched since 1981.

This comparative lack of experience among the rank and file — both on a range of issues, and in dealing with different power relationships in Washington — is yet another complicating factor for those in the congressional leadership and the new Bush administration.

All are promising to push for achievements in a Capitol more closely divided along party lines than at any time since the 83rd Congress convened in 1953, the onset of the Eisenhower administration. The House has 221 Republicans, 211 Democrats, two independents and a vacancy almost certain to be filled this spring by another Democrat. The Senate is evenly divided, 50 Republicans and 50 Democrats, so the nominal GOP control of Congress resides in the executive branch — in the tie-breaking vote of Dick Cheney, the new Republican vice president.

History of Division

One result of this razor's edge partisan split is that the House, especially, is an institution in which fewer and fewer members have experience in a Capitol where comity was more regularly apparent. Many say this comity was partly because it was so clear then who was in control and who was not. Only 130 House members are left from the 101st Congress, which adjourned in 1990 and in which the Democrats had an 85-seat advantage.

Of those who have arrived since then, says Norman Ornstein, a political scholar at the American Enterprise Institute, "their entire experience in Congress has been a period of enormous tumult and sharp partisan acrimony, and sharp partisan division, so they don't have much to fall back on in terms of an example of how the institution can function as a cooperative place."

Congress has been slowly but steadily getting older — the average age was 53 years old a decade ago, 54 two years ago and is 55 this year (with 54.4 the average House member's age and 59.8 the average senator's age) —

| 49-50 Years in the House | 47-48 | 45-46 | 43-44 | 41-42 | 39-40 | 37-38 | 35-36 | 33-34 | 31-32 | 29-30 | 27-28 | 25-26 |

but that trend nonetheless reflects this demographic truth: A growing percentage of the membership of the 107th Congress came of age, entered the work force and perhaps got involved in politics in the 1970s and 1980s — during the so-called "me" generation, in which national trends pointed to a resurgence of individual-based, rather than community-oriented, thinking.

Lawmakers now "are less institution-minded," Ornstein said in a Jan. 10 interview. "It just means that you have a challenge for the leaders to get them to think about not just their own ideas or their own party, but the larger institution."

Some "Old Bull" veterans of the Congresses before the 1990s, especially Democrats, see as the turning point in this regard the Republican takeover of six years ago — a victory engineered by Rep. Newt Gingrich of Georgia (1979-99), who rose from the back benches to the Speaker's chair by waging a charismatic campaign against the House as an institution.

"In the Gingrich era, there were no feathers, it was just arrows . . . Everybody became an independent contractor," said former Rep. Dan Rostenkowski, D-Ill. (1959-95), perhaps the best known electoral casualty of the 1994 election.

In a Jan. 16 interview, Rostenkowski said the tone in Congress has changed since his 14-year tenure as chairman of the House Ways and Means Committee, largely because more junior members have never witnessed the atmosphere of cooperation in Washington in which he believes he functioned most effectively. All but two of his years as chairman were during

Republican presidencies. "We cooperated because they wanted to write history, and I wanted to write law," he said. "Everything is one-upsmanship these days."

Beyond the partisan tone that has characterized the past decade, diminished levels of prior political experience also may have diminished Congress' ability and inclination to form bipartisan alliances and issue-based coalitions. A seasoned legislator experienced at cutting deals and reaching out to the other party to grease institutional gears — whether at a local or state level — may be better equipped to do so in Washington than an inexperienced lawmaker.

While the levels of prior service in elective office have stayed relatively constant since the 106th Congress for both House members and senators, the percentage of this year's freshmen in both chambers who can claim prior elective office has shrunk. In the 107th, 73 percent of new House members have held prior

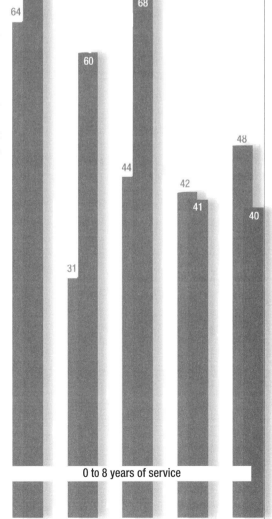

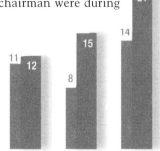

9 to 16 years of service

0 to 8 years of service

23-24 21-22 19-20 17-18 15-16 13-14 11-12 9-10 7-8 5-6 3-4 1-2 Years New
in the House Members

Women and Minorities in the 107th Congress

This is a roster of the women and ethnic minority group members who are representatives and senators in the 107th Congress. It does not include the non-voting delegates from the District of Columbia and the Virgin Islands, both of whom are black women; the delegates from American Samoa and Guam, both of whom are Asian and Pacific Islanders; or the resident commissioner for Puerto Rico, who is Hispanic. All are Democrats.

Blacks
House (36 — 1 R, 35 D)
Alabama: Earl F. Hilliard, D
California: Barbara Lee, D; Juanita Millender-McDonald, D; Maxine Waters, D
Florida: Corrine Brown, D; Alcee L. Hastings, D; Carrie P. Meek, D
Georgia: Sanford D. Bishop Jr., D; John Lewis, D; Cynthia A. McKinney, D
Illinois: Danny K. Davis, D; Jesse L. Jackson Jr., D; Bobby L. Rush, D
Indiana: Julia Carson, D
Louisiana: William J. Jefferson, D
Maryland: Elijah E. Cummings, D; Albert R. Wynn, D
Michigan: Carolyn Cheeks Kilpatrick, D; John Conyers Jr. D
Mississippi: Bennie Thompson, D
Missouri: William Lacy Clay Jr., D
New Jersey: Donald M. Payne, D
New York: Gregory W. Meeks, D; Major R. Owens, D; Charles B. Rangel, D; Edolphus Towns, D
North Carolina: Eva Clayton, D; Melvin Watt, D
Ohio: Stephanie Tubbs Jones, D
Oklahoma: J.C. Watts Jr., R
Pennsylvania: Chaka Fattah, D
South Carolina: James E. Clyburn, D
Tennessee: Harold E. Ford Jr., D
Texas: Sheila Jackson-Lee, D; Eddie Bernice Johnson, D
Virginia: Robert C. Scott, D

Hispanics
House (19 — 3 R, 16 D)
Arizona: Ed Pastor, D
California: Joe Baca, D; Xavier Becerra, D; Grace F. Napolitano, D; Lucille Roybal-Allard, D; Loretta Sanchez, D; Hilda Solis, D
Florida: Lincoln Diaz-Balart, R; Ileana Ros-Lehtinen, R
Illinois: Luis V. Gutierrez, D
New Jersey: Robert Menendez, D
New York: Jose E. Serrano, D; Nydia M. Velázquez, D
Texas: Henry Bonilla, R; Charlie Gonzalez, D; Rubén Hinojosa, D; Solomon P. Ortiz, D; Silvestre Reyes, D; Ciro D. Rodriguez, D

Asians and Pacific Islanders
House (4 — 4 D)
California: Mike Honda, D; Robert T. Matsui, D
Hawaii: Patsy T. Mink, D
Oregon: David Wu, D

Senate (2 — 2 D)
Hawaii: Daniel K. Akaka, D; Daniel K. Inouye, D

American Indians
House (1 — 1 D)
Oklahoma: Brad Carson, D
Senate (1 — 1 R)
Colorado: Ben Nighthorse Campbell, R

Women
House (59 — 18 R, 41 D)
California: Mary Bono, R; Lois Capps, D; Susan A. Davis, D; Anna G. Eshoo, D; Jane Harman, D; Barbara Lee, D; Zoe Lofgren, D; Juanita Millender-McDonald, D; Grace F. Napolitano, D; Nancy Pelosi, D; Lucille Roybal-Allard, D; Loretta Sanchez, D; Hilda Solis, D; Ellen O. Tauscher, D; Maxine Waters, D; Lynn Woolsey, D
Colorado: Diana DeGette, D
Connecticut: Rosa DeLauro, D; Nancy L. Johnson, R
Florida: Corrine Brown, D; Carrie P. Meek, D; Ileana Ros-Lehtinen, R; Karen L. Thurman, D
Georgia: Cynthia A. McKinney, D
Hawaii: Patsy T. Mink, D
Illinois: Judy Biggert, R; Jan Schakowsky, D
Indiana: Julia Carson, D
Kentucky: Anne M. Northup, R
Maryland: Constance A. Morella, R
Michigan: Carolyn Cheeks Kilpatrick, D; Lynn Rivers, D
Minnesota: Betty McCollum, D
Missouri: Jo Ann Emerson, R; Karen McCarthy, D
Nevada: Shelley Berkley, D
New Jersey: Marge Roukema, R
New Mexico: Heather A. Wilson, R
New York: Sue W. Kelly, R; Nita M. Lowey, D; Carolyn B. Maloney, D; Carolyn McCarthy, D; Louise M. Slaughter, D; Nydia M. Velázquez, D
North Carolina: Eva Clayton, D; Sue Myrick, R
Ohio: Marcy Kaptur, D; Deborah Pryce, R; Stephanie Tubbs Jones, D
Oregon: Darlene Hooley, D
Pennsylvania: Melissa Hart, R
Texas: Kay Granger, R; Eddie Bernice Johnson, D; Sheila Jackson-Lee, D
Virginia: Jo Ann Davis, R
Washington: Jennifer Dunn, R
West Virginia : Shelley Moore Capito, R
Wisconsin: Tammy Baldwin, D
Wyoming: Barbara Cubin, R

Senate (13 — 3 R, 10 D)
Arkansas: Blanche Lincoln, D
California: Barbara Boxer, D; Dianne Feinstein, D
Louisiana: Mary L. Landrieu, D
Maine: Susan Collins, R; Olympia J. Snowe, R
Maryland: Barbara A. Mikulski, D
Michigan: Debbie Stabenow, D
Missouri: Jean Carnahan, D
New York: Hillary Rodham Clinton, D
Texas: Kay Bailey Hutchison, R
Washington: Maria Cantwell, D; Patty Murray, D

Members' Occupations
107th Congress

	HOUSE			SENATE			CONGRESS
	DEMOCRAT	REPUBLICAN	TOTAL	DEMOCRAT	REPUBLICAN	TOTAL	TOTAL
Actor/Entertainer		1	1		1	1	2
Aeronautics		1	1	1		1	2
Agriculture	8	17	25	1	5	6	31
Artistic/Creative		1	2*				2*
Business/Banking	56	103	159	8	16	24	183
Clergy	1	1	2		1	1	3
Education	53	38	92*	8	8	16	108*
Engineering	1	8	9				9
Health Care	3	1	4				4
Homemaker/ Domestic	1	1	2	1		1	3
Journalism	1	7	9*	1	6	7	16*
Labor	1	1	2		1	1	3
Law	84	71	156†	28	25	53	210†
Law Enforcement	7	3	10				10
Medicine	6	8	14		3	3	17
Military		2	2		1	1	3
Professional Sports		3	3		1	1	4
Public Service/ Politics	70	56	126	18	10	28	154
Real Estate	2	22	24	2	2	4	28
Secretarial/Clerical		2	2				2
Technical/Trade	1	2	3				3
Miscellaneous	1	5	6				6

* Total includes Independent Bernard Sanders of Vermont; † Total includes Independent Virgil H. Goode Jr. of Virginia.
Note: Some members say they have more than one occupation.

Members' Religious Affiliations
107th Congress

	HOUSE			SENATE			CONGRESS
	DEMOCRAT	REPUBLICAN	TOTAL	DEMOCRAT	REPUBLICAN	TOTAL	TOTAL
African Methodist Episcopal	2		2				2
Baptist	33	30	64†	2	7	9	73†
Christian Church	3		3				3
Christian Reformed Church		2	2				2
Christian Scientist		5	5				5
Disciples of Christ	1		1				1
Eastern Orthodox	1	3	4	1	1	2	6
Episcopalian	7	23	30	3	7	10	40
Jewish	24	2	27*	9	1	10	37*
Lutheran	8	8	16	3	1	4	20
Methodist	16	34	50	10	6	16	66
Mormon	3	8	11	1	4	5	16
Pentecostal		3	3				3
Presbyterian	15	23	38	3	7	10	48
Roman Catholic	76	49	125	14	10	24	149
Seventh-day Adventist	1	2	3				3
Unitarian	1	1	2	1		1	3
United Church of Christ / Congregationalist		3	3	3	2	5	8
Unspecified Protestant	13	25	38		3	3	41
Unspecified, other	7		7		1	1	8

* Total includes Independent Bernard Sanders of Vermont; † Total includes Independent Virgil H. Goode Jr. of Virginia.

office, down from 83 percent two years ago. Only 64 percent of the new senators have held elected office before, down from 78 percent two years ago.

"It may be that the junior members have had less opportunity to learn that their opponents don't have horns, so to speak," said John R. Hibbing, a political science professor at the University of Nebraska at Lincoln. Still, he said, "I think it's going to be a really tough time to foster cooperation. . . . I think it will be tough even for senior members" of the Senate.

'New Blood'

Hibbing and others are more concerned about the effects of an increasingly junior Congress on the institution's legislative agenda. A less senior House and Senate might not be as savvy about the intricacies of the legislative process, they say, and might be less likely to produce substantive bills that can navigate the labyrinth of the legislative process and emerge intact in a Congress with such a tiny working majority.

"There are some fairly dire consequences of having a legislative body that is too junior," Hibbing said. His 1991 book, "Congressional Careers: Contours of Life in the U.S. House of Representatives," maintained that while junior members introduced more legislation and made more speeches, their bills were typically referred to several different committees and ultimately died — clear signals that their policy work was less focused — while senior members' bills more often became law.

"A more selective, successful and focused legislative agenda is something that should be encouraged," he said. "I think we're actually pushing things down to where we get people who are throwing all kinds of things in the legislative hopper and not as many doing focused work."

But the injection of youth and inexperience into Congress has its advocates. While their learning curve may be steep and long, new members can reinvigorate long-stalled debates, some say, and the approaches of political neophytes can change the legislative dynamic.

"It is, in the long term, like hitting the 'refresh' button on your computer — it keeps us in touch," Jack Horner, director of member services for the House Republican Conference, said in a Jan. 11 interview. "It's not that [GOP members are] any less conservative — they're representing the same districts — it's that the way we're approaching the issues as conservatives has matured."

Advocates of term limits for Congress also argue that "career politicians" risk becoming politically entrenched, arrogant and out of touch with constituents as they gain seniority and power. Since losing a pivotal 1995 Supreme Court case, they have been fighting for their cause on individual cases with sporadic success. On Jan. 17, for example, Sen. Paul Wellstone, D-Minn., abrogated a pledge to serve two terms by announcing his candidacy for re-election in 2002. (*Term limits, 2001 CQ Weekly, p. 161; background, 1997 Almanac, p. 1-28*)

For House Democrats, the trend means the number who have known life in the majority is dwindling — to 119, or 56 percent of the caucus this year. (By contrast, 114 Republicans in the 107th, 52 percent of the GOP Conference, have never served in the minority.) And only three chairmen from the 103rd Congress, the most recent one run by the Democrats, remain as the ranking minority members of those committees: Michigan's John D. Dingell of Energy and Commerce, Wisconsin's David R. Obey of Appropriations and Massachusetts' Joe Moakley of Rules.

Operating from the minority, albeit a sizable one, has prompted House Democratic leaders to invite their centrist members to help develop legislative strategy and policy. Likewise, Democrats who have never been in the majority have learned to forge alliances with moderate Republicans in order to have greater influence over what goes on in the House.

"It's a very different caucus for those reasons," Tom Eisenhauer, a spokesman for Democratic Caucus Chairman Martin Frost of Texas, said Jan. 11. "It's a more diverse caucus, it's a more moderate caucus, it's a more pragmatic caucus."

Another Year of the Woman?

The 107th Congress also is notable for the boost in the number of female senators. In 1992, the much-heralded "Year of the Woman," only five of 11 female nominees won Senate seats. In 2000, all six women nominees were elected and a seventh woman — Democrat Jean Carnahan of Missouri — was appointed to the seat to which her late husband was elected. As a result, a record 13 women are in the Senate now, up from nine in the 106th Congress. By contrast, the House gained a

net of three women this year, to 59, or 14 percent of the membership, less than a single percentage point gain from the 106th Congress. (*Background, 2000 CQ Weekly, p. 2642*)

Political experts say the Senate gains and the backgrounds of the new female representatives foretell a bright future for women on Capitol Hill. The vast majority of women in the 107th Congress are professional politicians who have increasingly been able to position themselves to take on and win competitive races. Fifty-three of the 72 women (74 percent) have prior experience in elected office. Nine of the senators (69 percent) and 43 of the representatives (73 percent) used a local or state office to catapult to Congress.

"There are more and more women who are holding positions that have served as springboards in the House, and so more are primed to run," said Irwin Gertzog, an adjunct professor of political science at Rutgers University who is an expert on women in politics.

Recognizing that it is less difficult and less costly to run in an open-seat election contest than to try toppling an incumbent, female politicians have also gotten more savvy. "They were careful, calculating politicians . . . who were able to elbow their way into winning primaries," said Gertzog, who also attributes women's electoral gains to a more progressive political culture in which "more Americans are prepared to not be influenced by gender as they vote."

Few are willing to speculate yet about what effect the arrival of more women on Capitol Hill — most notably in the historically male Senate — might have on the way Congress functions. But few rebut the premise that the increasing number of women will alter an institution that has lagged behind most other venues in reflecting shifts in cultural and workplace norms.

"Very simply, women will always be in the room," Ornstein said. "What we've seen in the past in terms of how the Senate functions, the 'old boy' club . . . they just can't operate in the same way."

Nor will women's influence necessarily be confined to the everyday workings of the Capitol, scholars said. While their gains in the Senate may not be enough to switch the outcome of votes, they may constitute a critical mass of female voices which — if the three Republicans and 10 Democrats band together on an issue — could put a great deal of symbolic

pressure on their male counterparts.

"If you have one after another of the women getting up and taking the same position on one of these issues, it cannot help but penetrate the consciousness of many of these men," Gertzog said. "It's not likely that it will change their minds, but it will have subtle effects."

By the Numbers

Ethnic minorities made no significant electoral gains in 2000, and will again make up about 12 percent of Congress. Racial diversity increased in the 103rd Congress, after House boundaries were redrawn for the 1992 elections because of redistricting, but has since flattened.

The Senate again has only three minority members, none of them black or Hispanic: Hawaii Democrats Daniel K. Akaka, a native Hawaiian, and Daniel K. Inouye, a Japanese-American, and Ben Nighthorse Campbell, R-Colo., an American Indian.

In the House, no parts of the country are newly represented by ethnic minorities this year. Of the 36 black House members (8 percent), only one is a freshman: William Lacy Clay Jr., D-Mo., who succeeded his father. The one freshman among the 19 Hispanics (4 percent) is Hilda Solis, D-Calif., who replaced a Hispanic she defeated in the primary.

The range of backgrounds also has not shifted much since the 106th Congress. The number of members who have served in the military — 133 in the House, 38 in the Senate — continues its decade-long decline. The majority of the 107th Congress has experience in the legal profession, the business world or the public sector. Nearly 40 percent list "law" as an occupation, 34 percent "business" and 29 percent have been public servants. Roman Catholic continues to be the most common religious affiliation, with 149 members claiming it.

The youngest senators, at 40, are Peter G. Fitzgerald, R-Ill., and Blanche Lincoln, D-Ark. The oldest, at 98, is Strom Thurmond, R-S.C., who also holds the record for the longest senatorial service ever, 46 years. Robert C. Byrd, D-W.Va., is second on that list, at 42 years; Edward M. Kennedy, D-Mass., is fifth, at 38 years and two months; Inouye is sixth, at 38 years.

In the House, freshman Adam Putnam, R-Fla., is the youngest member, at 26, while Benjamin A. Gilman, R-N.Y., is the oldest, at 78. ◆

Senate GOP Backs Down From Dispute Over Handling of Nominees

Daschle declares traditional procedures will be followed; organizing resolution unlikely to address confirmation process directly

When Democrats took over the Senate on June 6, some Republicans threatened to go to war to ensure President Bush's judicial nominations would get floor votes, not trusting Democrats to allow them.

After all, Democrats had raised the volume on their rhetoric over the process for judicial confirmations in May when they wanted assurances that the White House would at least consult with them on nominees.

But as happened last month, both sides now appear to be backing down. Republicans retreated from demands for a fail-safe mechanism to get Bush's judicial nominations to the Senate floor and Democrats assured them that nominations would not languish unduly in committee.

New Majority Leader Tom Daschle, D-S.D., is still negotiating with Republicans over a resolution to reorganize the Senate with Democrats in charge, and judicial nominations remain central to the discussion. (*Story, p. 47*)

But it is unlikely the organizing resolution will address the nominations question directly. Instead, it could be part of a side agreement or statement of intent by Daschle.

"Well, we're not going to prescribe any particular way with which to deal with these nominees," Daschle told reporters June 6. "If a nominee fails to be confirmed in the committee . . . we'll consider, as we have in the past when we were in the majority, the option of taking that nomination straight to the floor, regardless of the committee vote."

Few believe Daschle would regularly override the decisions of the Judiciary Committee or its new chairman, Patrick J. Leahy, D-Vt., on Bush nominations. Daschle's words are seen instead as a sign that he would not allow the process to get out of hand.

Even Minority Leader Trent Lott, R-Miss., who had earlier suggested the need for a formal mechanism to guarantee floor votes, said June 7 that Re-

publicans do not want to "fundamentally change" the process.

In an interview June 6, Leahy agreed that a method for moving nominations should not be written into the organizing resolution, saying, "No one wants that." He said such a rule would create a precedent Republicans would come to regret if a Democrat returned to the White House.

He said his desire is to protect the rights of all senators, regardless of party, to participate in the process of selecting judges and be truly consulted by the White House, not simply informed of the choice "two hours before [White House spokesman] Ari Fleischer announces it."

Leahy made it clear that unless he is satisfied that both senators from the home state of a nominee have been consulted by the Bush administration, a nomination will not move.

This had been a matter of deep dispute less than a month ago when Leahy's predecessor at the helm of the Judiciary Committee, Orrin G. Hatch, R-Utah, said opposition from a single home state senator would not necessarily kill a nomination.

Just Starting

The Bush administration has signaled that it intends to give high priority to the nomination and confirmation of federal judges, but even before control of the Senate changed, conservatives already were concerned that the large Democratic minority would slow or stop the process. The battle over the handling of judicial nominees at one point delayed action on other Bush administration nominations. (*2001 CQ Weekly, p. 1071, 1020*)

Now, control of the Senate has shifted to the Democrats before even one of the Bush administration nominees has had a hearing before the Judiciary Committee. As of June 1, there were 103 vacancies on the federal bench: Bush has sent nominations to fill 18 of those seats to the Senate.

Hatch canceled a May 23 hearing

on three of the nominations after Democrats complained they had not had enough time to review the information on the nominees.

Leahy said he expects to begin hearings after the Senate adopts its organization resolution. He cannot act before then because the resolution will determine who sits on his panel.

The Judiciary Committee will not act on a nomination until it has received the report of the American Bar Association (ABA) on each candidate.

The Bush administration decided March 22 to discontinue the ABA's nearly 50-year role of vetting the qualifications of candidates before their nominations were made public. (*2001 CQ Weekly, p. 640*)

Democrats, however, have said they will still rely on reports from the ABA, which has begun reviewing Bush nominations already sent to the Senate. Each nominee is sent a questionnaire, and it usually takes three to four weeks after the questionnaire is returned for the ABA's committee to complete its report. The group evaluates each candidate's integrity, competence and judicial temperament and then rates them as "well qualified," "qualified" or "not qualified."

Meanwhile, liberal interest groups are beginning to mobilize against several of Bush's nominees.

The National Abortion and Reproductive Rights Action League announced it would oppose two of Bush's choices: lawyer John G. Roberts Jr., picked for a seat on the U.S. Court of Appeals for the District of Columbia, which is seen as a stepping-stone to the Supreme Court; and Utah law professor Michael W. McConnell, a nominee for a seat on the U.S. Court of Appeals for the 10th Circuit.

The group believes both men fundamentally disagree with the reasoning in the 1973 landmark Supreme Court decision in *Roe v. Wade*, which made abortion legal across the country, and would work to overturn it.

Jeffrey S. Sutton, Bush's pick for a

The Record on Nominations

The Democratic takeover of the Senate heightened the rhetoric on judicial nominations, as Republicans expressed their fear that President Bush's choices to fill vacancies on appellate and federal district courts would be bottled up in the Judiciary Committee. A key feature of the debate has been the historical treatment of such nominations, especially when the opposing party controls the Senate. The analysis below shows the number of judicial nominees in the entire Clinton, Bush and Reagan administrations who were confirmed, rejected, returned to the White House without final action taken, or withdrawn by the president.

CLINTON (1993-2001)

Appeals Courts
Confirmed	*11 65
Rejected	0
Returned	27
Withdrawn	3

District Courts
Confirmed	*19 307
Rejected	1
Returned	46
Withdrawn	8

BUSH (1989-1993)

Appeals Courts
Confirmed	42
Rejected	0
Returned	12
Withdrawn	0

District Courts
Confirmed	*3 150
Rejected	0
Returned	45
Withdrawn	1

REAGAN (1981-1989)

Appeals Courts
Confirmed	*6 83
Rejected	0
Returned	9
Withdrawn	2

District Courts
Confirmed	*27 292
Rejected	0
Returned	14
Withdrawn	3

*Note: Some nominations that were returned to the White House at the conclusion of a Congress were renominated by the president and, ultimately, confirmed.

SOURCE: Congressional Research Service

seat on the U.S. Court of Appeals for the 6th Circuit, has become the focus of a group called ADA Watch, formed to ensure that provisions of the 1990 Americans With Disabilities Act (PL 101-336) are implemented. The group opposes Sutton in part because he successfully argued a case, *University of Alabama v. Garrett*, before the Supreme Court. The court, by a 5-4 vote announced Feb. 21, threw out the portion of the 1990 law that allowed state employees to sue their employers in federal court. (*2001 CQ Weekly, p. 422*)

Sutton, McConnell and Roberts were among the first batch of 11 appeals court nominees Bush sent to the Senate on May 9.

No Trust

The lack of trust between the two parties on judicial nominations is one of the lingering effects of the Clinton era.

Democrats charge that during the six years the GOP controlled the Senate and the confirmation process, Republicans unfairly denied votes to dozens of Clinton's candidates. Republicans counter that Clinton was able to win confirmation of nearly as many judges as did Ronald Reagan. The Senate did not vote on 73 of Clinton's nominations, compared with 23 of Reagan's. (*Chart above*)

During a nasty fight over two Clinton nominees, an angry Daschle vowed he would not obstruct GOP nominees if Democrats returned to the majority. "There is going to be no payback," he said in 2000. "We are not going to do to Republican nominees, whenever that happens, what they have done to Democratic nominees. . . . [A]re we going to make them wait for years and years to get their fair opportunity to be voted on and considered? Absolutely not. That is not right. I do not care who is in charge. I do not care which president is making the nomination. That is not right."

Republicans initially were not willing to take anyone's word that the process under Democratic control would be fair.

Sen. Rick Santorum, R-Pa., chair-

man of the Senate Republican Conference, raised the possibility of a GOP filibuster of the organizational resolution, on Fox News Sunday on June 3: "I think, if you look at some of the, I think, rather strident language by some of the new committee chairmen, Sen. Leahy in particular, I think we have cause for concern about whether our nominees are going to get through."

Leahy denied any plan to block nominations. "Well, I think my main job is to uphold the Constitution, especially the advice and consent [clause] of the Constitution. I'm not trying to appoint judges. That's the duty of the president of the United States," he said on CBS' Face the Nation on June 3.

"But the advise-and-consent rule has been there from the time of the beginning of this country, and put for a very specific reason, especially when it comes to lifetime appointments to the judiciary," he said. "It's there so that you don't have the federal judiciary lurch either to the right or to the left ideologically, and that you have an independent, highly professional federal judiciary." ◆

Bush's Capitol Course Relies On Cheney's Steadying Hand

Vice president-elect's Washington insider résumé should quickly prove invaluable

Texas Gov. George W. Bush's outsider campaign for the presidency came to rest Dec. 12 on a Supreme Court decision that assures him the White House and a tangle of Washington challenges. Now, President-elect Bush, five weeks late in starting the transition of power, must confront the Capitol Hill reality of partisan divisions and hard-headed ideology.

"It is the challenge of our moment," Bush acknowledged in his Dec. 13 speech after Vice President Al Gore conceded. "After a difficult election, we must put politics behind us and work together to make the promise of America available to every one of our citizens."

To do that, he must overcome the lack of Washington connections he touted in his campaign, and coordinate with the congressional allies he all but ignored. He must keep the peace with conservatives within his own party, and forge new alliances with Democrats of a kind he did not see much in Austin. He must navigate a House that is split almost evenly, and crack the deadlock of a Senate that truly is.

It will be a task of perpetual balancing for the new, "not of Washington" Bush administration. The fulcrum on which much of it is expected to rest is Vice President-elect Dick Cheney.

As Senate president, Cheney will be the tie-breaking vote in the Senate — or perhaps more important, the "101st senator," charged with keeping the chamber from locking up in the first place. As a former House minority whip he will be the administration's point man for dealing with his old colleagues in the other chamber.

A former Defense secretary and White House chief of staff, Cheney will be, by all accounts, the Bush administration's walking, talking reservoir of Washington experience. He is considered calm enough and mature enough to be a soothing presence in a capital that has persisted in shredding itself through years of partisan warfare.

"He will be much more involved in legislation than we've seen in modern times from a vice president," predicted Rep. Rob Portman, R-Ohio, who served in the administration of Bush's father and was Cheney's sparring partner in preparations for the vice presidential debate.

Cheney will not only help set the president's broad leg-

> "We've got a president now. A lot of the work that we will be doing in both houses will be the interpretation of the Bush agenda."
>
> —Rep. Jennifer Dunn

islative agenda, as recent vice presidents have done, he will also carry it down to Capitol Hill. Past and current members predict he will help build coalitions for its passage and weigh in as the details are ironed out.

Anticipating Cheney's role, House Speaker J. Dennis Hastert, R-Ill., has offered to carve out a warren in the Capitol building where he can work. On the day Gore conceded, Cheney spent most of his time on the Hill.

After a meeting with Hastert and House Republican Policy Committee Chairman Christopher Cox, R-Calif., and lunch with five moderate Senate Republicans whose states went for Gore, Cheney said he would always "enjoy very much coming back to Congress" and that "things are going well."

He then turned the lectern over to Senate Majority Leader Trent Lott, R-Miss., who was more than happy to gab with reporters about the day's events.

It was probably a sign of things to come. Though Cheney is widely respected by Republicans and Democrats as a fair and honest person, he is known for playing his cards close to the vest and offering little information to rank-and-file members of Congress and the press. He is a behind-the-scenes workhorse.

In contrast, Lott, who preceded Cheney in the House as minority whip, appears to enjoy public attention and sometimes openly discusses legislative strategies that seem to be in their infancy.

Lott encapsulated the differences between the two men at a Dec. 12 press conference. He said he had given the new administration plenty of suggestions, but "they haven't revealed a whole lot about what they're thinking." He paused and added, "Typical Dick Cheney."

Working With Leadership

Cheney's unflappable temperament, even more than his long legislative experience, is seen as instrumental to paving the way for Bush's agenda. *(Agenda, 2000 CQ Weekly, p. 2846)*

Such diplomatic skills will be called on not only to forge ties with Democrats and others who don't share Cheney's conservative philosophy. He will need to be sensitive about usurping the power of Republicans who head the two chambers.

Despite Lott's reference to Cheney's reserved style, the two are said to be good friends. Former Sen. Alan K. Simpson, R-Wyo. (1979-97), recalls that Lott and his wife, Tricia, once traveled to Wyoming to ski with Cheney and his wife, Lynne. Lott and Cheney served in the House together 10 years, including three in the leadership.

Cheney felt comfortable enough in his relationship with Lott to rib him on television after Lott was seen at a Dec. 2 meeting with Bush at the governor's ranch outside of Waco, Texas, wearing a cowboy hat with several feathers jutting from it. Appearing later on NBC's "Meet the Press," Cheney called Lott a "Mississippi cowboy."

Cheney and Hastert have fewer common experiences to fall back on. Hastert was elected to Congress just three years before Cheney resigned in 1989 to become Defense secretary in the administration of Bush's father, but the two knew each other as part of the Republican Party's vast whip operation.

Few expect that they will need much encouragement to develop a close relationship.

They "have the same kind of style," said John Feehery, Hastert's spokesman. Both are low-key, polite and not prone to being long-winded.

"To have Dick Cheney involved as a vice president on the Hill day to day will be very important to the success of this administration."

—Rep. Rob Portman

Rep. Jennifer Dunn, R-Wash., who campaigned vigorously for the Republican ticket, said it became clear through party meetings that Cheney sees himself as the manager of Bush's legislative agenda.

She said leaders of Congress will have to realize they no longer set the party's agenda. "We all have to remember that now Bush is the leader," she said. "We've got a president now. A lot of the work that we will be doing in both houses will be the interpretation of the Bush agenda."

Though he gets high marks for most of his legislative and executive branch career, Cheney's term as Secretary of Defense was not without controversy. He often rubbed the military brass the wrong way by asserting his civilian authority, but it is unclear if those frictions were the result of an autocratic streak that could cause Cheney trouble in his new role.

Rep. John M. Spratt Jr., D-S.C., served with Cheney in Congress and was a member of the Armed Services Committee when Cheney was secretary. He believes that Cheney's Pentagon decisions, such as canceling construction of the V-22 Osprey aircraft in 1992, showed that he is "a quick study, very bright and very decisive. He will make a tough decision, damn the consequences, and not look back." (*Osprey, 2000 CQ Weekly, p. 2864*)

Working on the Fringes

Perhaps Cheney's toughest task in Congress will be assuring fellow conservatives that he is one of them while he reaches out to Democrats.

Cheney need only show the voting record he built during his House service from 1979 to 1989 to prove he is a dyed-in-the-wool conservative. While in the House, Cheney voted for amending the Constitution to prohibit busing as a method of desegregating schools, but voted against amending it to guarantee equal rights for women.

He was a solid supporter of gun control — going so far as to vote against a bill that would have banned guns that could not be found by metal detectors — and a steadfast opponent of abortion rights. (*2000 CQ Weekly, p. 1871*)

Still, it is unclear if that history will be enough to please conservatives led by House Majority Whip Tom DeLay, R-Texas. DeLay's style is as confronta-

tional as Cheney's is conciliatory. Although Republicans lost seats in the House and Senate, leading nearly everyone to talk earnestly about seeking moderate compromises, DeLay asserts that conservatives are in a stronger position than they have been in the past because Bush will be in the White House and Republicans will control both chambers of Congress. (*Conservatives, 2000 CQ Weekly, p. 2851*)

If push comes to shove, which it

might, former members who worked with Cheney say they expect his conservative beliefs to take a back seat to his pragmatism.

"Dick's a very good conservative," said former Rep. Robert S. Walker, R-Pa. (1977-96), one of the party's firebrands during Cheney's House service. "His working style, having come out of being chief of staff at the White House, was one of understanding that governing requires getting things done. In the end, he was more oriented toward governing than he was to ideological battles."

Simpson predicts that Cheney's willingness to find solutions means conservatives may find "lots of issues that come up where they'll say, 'I can't believe Cheney would be helping do

this.' He won't be bound and shackled by any kind of stiffness or inflexibility or rigidity."

Walker believes Cheney might successfully bridge the divides within and between the two parties. He recalls that as GOP Conference chairman in the 1980s, Cheney often satisfied the wishes of then-Minority Leader Robert H. Michel, R-Ill. (1957-95), and Lott to work with the majority Democrats, while simultaneously putting a sharper edge on legislation that Walker and

Cheney is welcomed to the Senate by Sen. Arlen Specter, R-Pa., left, and Sen. James M. Jeffords, R-Vt., right. As vice president, Cheney is expected to play a big role in relations with Capitol Hill.

former Rep. Newt Gingrich, R-Ga. (1979-99), advocated.

Cheney will also have his work cut out when it comes to forging alliances with Democrats.

While the more moderate members of the party are expected to support many of Bush's initiatives, former Rep. Lee H. Hamilton, D-Ind. (1965-99), said Cheney will have to work to build trust.

"Dick is respected, but he is viewed as a very strong partisan. If he wants their support, he certainly is going to have to reach out to them aggressively," said Hamilton, who chaired a panel that investigated the Reagan administration's Iran-contra dealings in 1987. Cheney was the panel's ranking Republican. (*1987 Almanac, p. 94*)

Cheney won't have to build relations with Democrats from the ground up, either. Cheney's tenure in the House overlapped with that of Minority Leader Richard A. Gephardt, D-Mo., and Senate Minority Leader Tom Daschle, D-S.D., who was in Cheney's freshman class. A House leadership aide said Gephardt agrees with the assessments of others who say Cheney is fair-minded.

However, if Cheney is to truly make headway with Democrats he must address their insistence that they be involved in writing legislation, and not just asked to sign on to bills Republicans have written.

"It is not bipartisan to be presented something as a fait accompli," Spratt said. He believes the first true test for the Bush administration, and therefore for Cheney, will come during the budget process, expected to get under way in February.

"The president will have a choice to make," Spratt said of Bush's budget. "Does he want to ram that through here as quickly as he can . . . or will he say, 'Okay, this is our going-in offer. What will it take for you to come forward and support the package?'"

Republicans involved in the campaign say they believe Democrats will be invited to take part in the closed-door meetings in which legislation is vetted and composed.

They say Cheney has yet to reach out to Gephardt or Daschle because he and Bush did not feel it would have been appropriate while Gore was contesting the election results.

Making Things Work

The 107th Congress will inherit a backload of work from its predecessor. Many of the details of controversial bills to cover prescription drug costs of senior citizens, ensure that patients have more say in their health insurance decisions and cut taxes for various groups have already been hashed and rehashed. But none of the proposals on those issues became law. (*Legislative summary, 2000 CQ Weekly, p. 2883*)

Consensus on the measures, crafted in the heat of the 2000 elections, has been hard to find, however.

Members predict that Bush and Cheney will tackle some of those left-over issues first and attempt to build as much bipartisan support as possible. Many of the issues coincide with planks of Bush's campaign agenda.

Among the issues that could be addressed early in the Bush administration are education, tax cuts and Medicare overhaul.

Cheney's first legislative challenge will probably be a tough one — persuading Sen. John McCain, R-Ariz., to postpone pushing the campaign finance overhaul measure that he has sponsored with Sen. Russell D. Feingold, D-Wis. Republicans have been split on the issue and this measure, making it likely that the GOP would prefer not to consider the bill right away.

> *"The Bush people owe [McCain] big time. If his issue is campaign finance reform, I think it's going to be a done deal. I think John is in the catbird seat over there, more than any other senator."*
>
> —Rep. Ray LaHood, R-Ill.

Transforming McCain, who challenged Bush in the Republican primary, into a team player could not be a more difficult task. Many Senate Republicans are annoyed by McCain's insistence that the bill must be the first measure to come up in the new Congress, and some fear that he will attempt to bring it up in early January, when Democrats temporarily control the chamber. A McCain aide said the senator had not decided on his timing.

But dealing with McCain is likely to be complicated by the fact that Bush's onetime bitter rival for the GOP nomination traversed the country in support of the ticket after he had lost.

"The Bush people owe him big time," said Rep. Ray LaHood, R-Ill. "If his issue is campaign finance reform, I think it's going to be a done deal. I think John is in the catbird seat over there, more than any other senator."

Simpson is confident Cheney can handle the gargantuan task of forcing Congress to function.

"It will be important," Simpson said. "It will work. He won't let it fail."

Cheney will not be left to work entirely alone. The White House will have, as it always does, a legislative staff. David Gribben, a longtime Cheney aide, is expected to play a key role

in that organization, likely serving as the administration's top lobbyist on Capitol Hill. A number of well-connected lobbyists also are being considered for posts in the liaison operation.

Cheney, too, can call on his boss. Bush prides himself in working well with people and bridging differences, having run on a campaign to work with Democrats in Washington the way he did with Democrats in the Texas legislature. And visits from the president have been known to work wonders with ornery members in the past.

Still, it is not clear how Cheney will shoulder the burden of the administration's legislative agenda, while helping choose those who will set the executive branch agenda.

One GOP strategist close to both the Bush campaign and the congressional leadership said that while Cheney's role in Congress will be important, it cannot be all-consuming. "He doesn't have time for two full-time jobs," he said.

'That Great Pool'

Cheney's ability to weather any storm, absorbing the anxiety of those around him, is legendary.

"I've seen him in the toughest of situations with that little half-smile," said Simpson, who employs the Wyoming pronunciation of Cheney's name — chee-ny. Stress "just goes into a great pool down under there."

Some who know Cheney worry that the way he internalizes problems may have contributed to past health problems. Cheney suffered his fourth minor heart attack Nov. 22. He was at work just days later.

Simpson, though, says he suspects the problem is Cheney's penchant for "greasy old ribs with all that barbecue sauce." Simpson said he teases his old friend about losing weight.

Portman said he believes Cheney's natural way of dealing with difficulty will do a lot to help heal partisan divides that were made worse than ever by Gore's loss in the highly contested presidential race. The presidential candidates met in court over Gore's efforts to hand count Florida ballots that had registered no presidential vote through two machine counts.

"There is a lot of healing to be done coming off of Florida," Portman said. "To have Dick Cheney involved as a vice president on the Hill day-to-day will be very important to the success of this administration." ◆

After First Hundred Days, Bush Emerges as Pragmatic Warrior

Dealings on tax cuts and education reveal a president willing to show balance in pursuit of victories

GOP conservatives don't like his landmark education bill. Senate Democrats have bloodied his nose on the budget. Top House and Senate Republicans are duking it out over spending before his very eyes.

So is President Bush stymied in his dealings with Capitol Hill, or what?

The answer is probably "no." After initially staking out what seemed like rigid demands, the most recent moves of this president suggest he will take half- or three-quarter loaves as victories — and that his allies in Congress will willingly, if not always happily, go along.

Bush is going to get a huge tax cut through Congress, even if it falls short of his 10-year, $1.6 trillion goal. His education bill (S 1) will not carry GOP priorities such as taxpayer-funded private school vouchers, but it will offer the opportunity to show the public that he can change the partisan tone in Washington.

"The way I like to describe it is we've come from the ideological to the practical, and I'm a practical man," Bush told the Associated Press on April 25. "I want to get it done."

After his first 100 days in office, Bush is beginning to display a pragmatic streak as his legislative agenda moves from the playbook to the playing field of Congress.

He acknowledged for the first time April 25 that he will have to scale back the size of his tax cuts in the face of resistance in the evenly divided Senate. And his staff was locked in negotiations with liberal icon Sen. Edward M. Kennedy, D-Mass., over the education bill, prompting grumbling — though not open revolt — on Bush's right flank. (*Budget, 2001 CQ Weekly, p. 903; education, p. 917*)

The common thread is that Bush is demonstrating the type of flexibility many predicted would be required after an election that delivered a less-than-resounding mandate and produced a

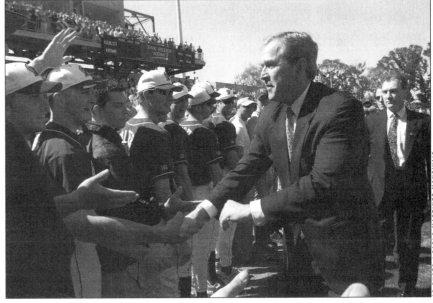

Making another trip to promote his tax cut plan, Bush shakes hands April 25 with members of the Tulane University baseball team before a rally at Zephyr Field in Metairie, La.

50-50 Senate.

And some of Bush's GOP allies seem content to follow the example of master legislators such as Henry A. Waxman, D-Calif., who orchestrated vast expansion of the Medicaid health program for the poor piece by piece, year after year.

"I learned a long time ago . . . the way the Democrats always got things done here is you take a slice at a time," said Sen. Rick Santorum, R-Pa. "The president is taking what's available. Is it everything he wants? No. Can he get a piece of what he wanted? Yes. And he'll come back after that works and get more."

The key to the success of President Ronald Reagan, observes former House Speaker Newt Gingrich, R-Ga. (1979-99), was that any time Reagan could obtain, say, 70 percent of what he desired, he would grab it and declare victory. That is a model that George W. Bush appears to have come to accept.

"Reagan had a much stronger mandate and was able to roll up some pretty significant victories. . . . But Bush is in a little different situation," said Rep.

Michael G. Oxley, R-Ohio. "[Reagan] could make chicken salad out of you-know-what. Whether Bush can do that is still the question. So far, so good."

Flexibility Where It Counts

Bush's flexibility on his twin signature issues of taxes and education is in sync with his promise to try to renew bipartisanship in Washington. But Bush took different paths to the point of compromise on the two issues.

On education, he has worked with Democrats all along. But on the fiscal 2002 budget resolution (H Con Res 83), which will pave the way for his cherished tax bill, Bush took a hard line and relented only after it was apparent that he could not muster enough votes for his $1.6 trillion plan in the Senate.

In both cases, nailing down the details — and negotiating the crosscurrents of his own party — have proven difficult. Conservatives are unimpressed with the direction the education bill is heading, though they have remained relatively restrained in their rhetoric.

"You don't have backbiting. . . . The education bill, some of us are thinking of voting against it because we just don't like it, but I don't think he'll need our votes anyway," said Rep. Paul D. Ryan, R-Wis. "On the tax bill, people are more or less accepting that [Bush] is in an intractable position in the Senate."

At the same time, major disagreements between House and Senate Republicans on fiscal 2002 spending dominated an April 24 White House meeting. Senate Appropriations Committee Chairman Ted Stevens, R-Alaska, favors going above Bush's call for a 4 percent increase in discretionary appropriations, and Stevens and House Majority Whip Tom DeLay, R-Texas, exchanged sharp volleys in front of Bush, giving the new president a first-hand glimpse of the splits in his party.

"It is unclear still in this new Congress and this new administration how much of a restraint there will be on government spending," Bush spokesman Ari Fleischer said in an interview. "It's unclear yet which direction Congress will go. There are big spenders in both parties, unfortunately."

Some conservatives are hopeful that Bush will veto appropriations bills in order to rein in headstrong GOP appropriators, an option that Vice President Dick Cheney has floated.

"He needs to put his foot down early in the process so that people think twice," said Jennifer Larkin, director of House relations for the Heritage Foundation.

Pragmatism Over Conservatism

The upcoming appropriations bills are causing greater rifts than are the fights over paring back the size of Bush's tax cut. For one thing, GOP strategists are plotting to advance tax cuts in several pieces, rather than stuffing them all into one filibuster-proof "reconciliation" tax bill that will be permitted after the final budget resolution is passed.

"If [Congress] decides to pursue vehicles outside reconciliation, alternate means of securing a bigger cut, that's all well and good," Fleischer said.

But on appropriations, any agreement that goes much above Bush's 4 percent is sure to raise the hackles of conservatives.

On the education bill, the White House has consistently displayed a pragmatic streak and a desire to work with Democrats. That led to lengthy negotiations with Kennedy. The bill is shaping up as an excellent chance to burnish Bush's bipartisan credentials.

"Education is a less inherently polarizing issue than is taxes, and there is a big middle ground — and I think an increasing desire among reform-minded Democrats to try some new things," said GOP strategist Ed Gillespie. "He truly does want to change the tone and to put an end to all the bitter partisanship that has dominated this town for the past eight years. And education is an issue that allows you to do that."

Hardball Strikeout

On the budget, Bush's drift to the middle came only after hardball tactics failed. As the Senate debated the budget the week of April 2, the White House lobbied hard for Bush's full $1.6 trillion plan and only grudgingly accepted less. With three moderate Republicans (Lincoln Chafee of Rhode Island, James M. Jeffords of Vermont and Arlen Specter of Pennsylvania) aligned with moderate Democrats, and only one Democrat (Zell Miller of Georgia) solidly in Bush's column, the White House strategy was to try to "pick off" another Democrat. Bush failed, despite a campaign-style tour during which he traveled to 15 states, most represented by moderate Democrats. (*Budget vote, 2001 CQ Weekly, p. 768*)

"It's not working," said one targeted Democrat, who requested anonymity.

"Their strategy, of course, was to peel off a couple of Democrats, and they lost," said Senate Minority Leader Tom Daschle, D-S.D.

After the Senate voted to set the tax cut total at $1.27 trillion, Republicans stepped back and sought to portray the big picture. Republicans pointed out that only last year, Democrats were pushing tax cuts that were paltry compared to what they are willing to support now.

"Last year, [House Minority Leader Richard A.] Gephardt [D-Mo.] at this time was talking $250 [billion] to $300 billion. Now it's $1.2 trillion and rising," said a senior White House official.

"They've got it going in their direction, and I don't know the secret to ungluing their momentum," said Sen. John D. Rockefeller IV, D-W.Va. "I really don't."

Beyond the budget and education, Bush has shown a variety of approaches as he and Congress establish their working relationship.

The Bush team stayed out of the rough-and-tumble almost entirely as the Senate debated and passed the bipartisan proposal to overhaul campaign financing laws (S 27). (*2001 CQ Weekly, p. 776*)

After issuing a set of "principles" that the Senate mostly ignored, the administration signaled that Bush might sign a bill not too far removed from what ultimately passed. One way to view that is as a sign of weakness; on the other hand, the prospect that "reform" of campaign finance laws might actually become law seems to have discombobulated House Democrats.

On the issue of giving patients greater clout in challenging treatment decisions of their health insurers, Bush is mixing a great desire to sign a bill into law with warnings to Congress to not go too far in giving people the ability to claim damages from their health plans. When John McCain, R-Ariz., and Kennedy unveiled a bill (S 283) that would allow patients to claim civil penalties of up to $5 million, Bush said no. (*2001 CQ Weekly, p. 426*)

"He was sending an unmistakable signal: Don't spin your wheels. Don't send me anything that has a $5 million liability cap," Fleischer said.

"Their allies on the Hill . . . all thought that was very useful," said GOP lobbyist Dan Meyer, a former chief of staff to Gingrich. "They felt it was important to send that signal . . . to encourage people to come to the table in a more realistic way."

At the same time, the slipped deadlines on the budget and education serve as a reminder that while Bush has momentum, none of this is going to be easy. Upcoming battles over the specifics on taxes, appropriations, the so-called patients' bill of rights and raising the minimum wage promise to severely test the ingenuity of Bush and his narrow Republican majority in Congress.

"I think it's going to be a blend of models as we go throughout the year. There will be some instances where the president will set clear direction, and we will move heaven and Earth and get there," said Eric Ueland, chief of staff to Majority Whip Don Nickles, R-Okla.

"And there will be some times where all we can do is what the votes will bear." ◆

Faced With Darkening Fiscal Picture, Postal Service Seeks More Autonomy

Most lawmakers agree that a crisis is coming but differ widely on how much rate-setting flexibility to give the troubled agency

Deepening debts at the U.S. Postal Service, generated in part by the explosion in electronic communications, have given new urgency on Capitol Hill to an overhaul of the nation's postal laws.

Electronic payment systems and e-mail provide consumers with quick and inexpensive alternatives to traditional mail, but the rapid growth of those communications is posing a threat to the cornerstone of the nation's 226-year-old mail system — universal service in every corner of the country.

Twin reviews by the Postal Service and the General Accounting Office (GAO) in recent months have concluded with warnings to Congress that financial problems are coming more rapidly than previously expected. The mail service's $9.3 billion debt will probably hit a statutory cap of $15 billion by fiscal 2002, and that prospect has prompted renewed pressure to find cost-cutting measures within the postal system and for passing legislation that would allow the Postal Service to implement them.

Congress has debated the long-term future of the Postal Service since directing it to become a financially independent arm of the government in 1970. That legislation (PL 91-375) came in the aftermath of the first postal strike in history, and was fueled in part by the desire of lawmakers to insulate themselves from difficult decisions on rates and labor disputes. (*1970 Almanac, p. 341*)

Now, the Postal Service says the dream of financial self-sufficiency is dying, and it wants Congress to grant it more power to set its own rates, cut individual deals with big customers, move into new businesses and restructure operations to compete against electronic communications and other courier services.

"It's going to take a cooperative effort between the managers of the postal service . . . and the Congress . . . to

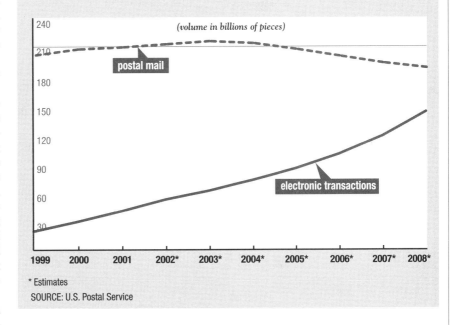

E-mail vs. Regular Mail

The growth of electronic mail as a cheap way for consumers to pay bills and send other communications has contributed to the financial trouble faced by the U.S. Postal Service. In 1999, the GAO worked with congressional oversight committees to develop projections for mail and e-mail volumes in the coming years.

(volume in billions of pieces)

postal mail

electronic transactions

1999 2000 2001 2002* 2003* 2004* 2005* 2006* 2007* 2008*

* Estimates
SOURCE: U.S. Postal Service

come up with a strong bipartisan piece of legislation," Postmaster General William J. Henderson said April 4. "We can't do it by ourselves. We've shown that."

The starting point for the discussions is likely to be a bill introduced in 1999 by Rep. John M. McHugh, R-N.Y., that would have given the Postal Service much of the rate flexibility it is seeking but would have capped rate increases. It drew heated opposition from one major postal labor union and from some Democrats.

The Problem Goes To Congress

This year the debate is expected to be led by bill advocate Dan Burton, R-Ind., who is chairman of the Government Reform Committee. "If we take the necessary steps now to fix the problems," Burton said in a hearing April 4, "maybe we can avoid a full-blown crisis."

The Postal Service has projected a long-term decline in mail volume linked to the growth of the Internet. It currently estimates that the rise of e-mail and electronic payments will cause a drop in mail volume starting in fiscal 2004. Those projections have combined with high gasoline prices and a sluggish economy to produce a financial picture that has drawn the attention of Congress.

The Postal Service's own cost-cutting plans are hindered by a patchwork of laws put in place to protect local post offices. Congress has made closing post offices so cumbersome that the Postal Service declared a voluntary moratorium on the practice to focus internal attention on other possible remedies, even though 26,000 of the nation's 38,000 post offices lose money each year. (*Story, p. 64*)

Lawmakers of both parties fear that

Cost-Cutting Efforts Could Rattle The Cornerstones of Main Street

The Postal Service is challenging a longstanding Washington tradition: Congress' protection of the nation's 38,000 post offices, whether or not they make money.

After projecting a deeper-than-expected deficit of as much as $3 billion for fiscal 2001 this month, the Postal Service's board of governors ordered a study of cost-saving measures, including some that have been politically unpalatable in the past, such as eliminating Saturday mail delivery.

The cuts being reviewed would be commonplace in corporate America, where downsizing is a standard response to losses. But Congress has erected barriers that must now be reconsidered, said Deputy Postmaster General John Nolan.

In an April 17 interview, Nolan said that while the Postal Service is looking into consolidating some post offices, none would close. The Postal Service has had a self-imposed ban on closures since the mid-1990s after decades of battling Congress to execute cost-cutting measures.

Congress toughened restrictions on the Postal Service's ability to close post offices in 1976 by requiring 60 days' notice and a prior review of the impact on the community.

In the 1980s, appropriators added to the burden by beginning an annual ritual of adding language to spending bills requiring the Postal Service to maintain the level of service that existed in 1983 — in other words, six days a week across the country. The language was included again in last year's omnibus spending law (PL 106-554).

"It was taking so much time to close post offices, we decided it was best to have a moratorium," Nolan said.

When Congress directed the Postal Service to become a self-supporting, independent arm of government in 1970 (PL 91-375), it includ-ed language protecting small, unprofitable post offices from being closed purely for economic reasons. The law provided that no small post office be closed "solely for operating at a deficit."

Based on the law, the Postal Service developed rules requiring that closures be justified by emergencies or such things as safety problems.

On Capitol Hill, post offices are considered the cornerstones of Main Street, and lawmakers take pride in naming them. Just three months into the 107th Congress, 18 bills already have been introduced to name post offices in honor of a variety of people ranging from former President Ronald Reagan to late Puerto Rican band leader Tito Puente.

With Congress' history of directing the Postal Service to preserve its post offices, Nolan said the moratorium on closures is likely to remain in effect. Instead, the service may have to scale back services and cut staff at money-losing post offices but not close them down.

For now, there is little sign that Congress would reverse its years of opposition to the closing of post offices or the curtailing of deliveries.

Rep. Bob Barr, R-Ga., said at an April 4 House hearing that the notion of reducing delivery from six to five days a week would be "fundamentally altering what the Postal Service means to many Americans."

Freezing New Projects

While the Postal Service will probably keep existing post offices, it hopes it has found another way to save money: by halting new ones. Last month, the Postal Service announced a plan to temporarily stop construction on 800 post office projects that include new buildings and expansions of existing ones. The move would conserve about $1 billion.

But lawmakers, including Sen. Barbara Boxer, D-Calif., have spoken out in opposition to the plan. Boxer urged the Postal Service to revive California's 47 projects, citing a need to "expand — not halt" post office construction in her state.

"Post office business directly depends on the size of the surrounding population," she said. "And California's population is growing at a rapid rate."

The Top Five Money Losers Among the Nation's Post Offices

The U.S. Postal Service says nearly 70 percent of the nation's 38,000 post office operations lose money because revenues fail to cover operating costs. Here are the five regional post office clusters with the biggest losses in fiscal 1999, the last year for which figures are available.

Post Office	Representative	Fiscal 1999 Loss
Bronx, N.Y.	Jose E. Serrano, D-N.Y.	$36.9 million
Flushing, N.Y.	Jerrold Nadler, D-N.Y.	$25.2 million
New Castle, Pa.	Melissa A. Hart, R-Pa.	$15.0 million
Yonkers, N.Y.	Eliot L. Engel, D-N.Y.	$13.2 million
Silver Spring, Md.	Albert R. Wynn, D-Md.	$12.7 million

SOURCE: Postal Service, House Government Reform Committee

emergency legislation might be required if a broader legislative fix is not developed, including the possibility of providing money for a bailout or for raising the debt limit. The current cap took effect in 1992 under a 1989 law (PL 101-227).

At the core of the discussion over a broader legislative fix is the question of how much leeway lawmakers should give the Postal Service to operate like a business instead of a tightly controlled government monopoly.

The Postal Service has argued that strict rate controls should be applied only to the monopoly part of its business: door-to-door delivery of domestic mail, including stamped envelopes and metered advertising and periodicals. It is this element of the business that faces the greatest threat from a shift in consumer habits toward electronic communications.

The service says rates for the parts of its business where it faces competition — parcel delivery, international mail, air mail and freight — should be determined internally to meet the needs of the competitive market.

Current postal regulations require that all rates be set in one omnibus rate plan. It can take up to two years for such a plan to win approval from the independent Postal Rate Commission.

McHugh's Bill

McHugh's bill would scrap the rate commission and give the Postal Service control of rates for its parcel and air freight businesses, and permit increases in domestic mail based on an adjusted consumer price index. A new Postal Regulatory Commission would be charged with reviewing audits and reports to ensure that the Postal Service did not violate a ban on using proceeds from postage to subsidize new ventures such as courier services and electronic mail.

Burton hopes to shepherd the bill through a tangle of Democratic opposition, in part to remake his reputation from that of a partisan bulldog who staged relentless investigations of President Bill Clinton into that of a bipartisan legislator.

"If he gets a bill passed, he would be the man who saved the Postal Service," said Mark C. Corallo, his spokesman.

In the Senate, Governmental Affairs Committee Chairman Fred Thompson, R-Tenn., plans to hold a hearing on the Postal Service's problems May 15.

Thompson has not yet said whether legislation is needed, but he hails from the home state of delivery giant FedEx Corp. of Memphis.

FedEx recently signed a partnership agreement with the Postal Service and has endorsed the McHugh legislation. In addition, the 1999 bill was strongly supported by Senate Minority Leader Tom Daschle, D-S.D.

McHugh said April 13 that a new draft of his bill has the tacit support of the Postal Service and a number of businesses including FedEx. But the path to easy passage remains blocked by the fervent opposition of the United Parcel Service Inc. (UPS), which fought McHugh's previous bill.

"We ran up against an enormously effective lobbying campaign by UPS," McHugh said. "I am not sure anything will satisfy them."

The split between the two prime rivals of the Postal Service — FedEx and UPS — is expected to continue. UPS competes with the Postal Service in parcel delivery, and recently purchased Mail Boxes Etc., which operates 4,000 outlets that provide services similar to post offices and copy shops. UPS opposes giving the Postal Service greater flexibility to set rates or to pursue new businesses.

Tad Segal, a spokesman for UPS, said his company wanted to continue negotiations with McHugh but he questioned the Postal Service's motives in its recent claims of financial distress.

"The Postal Service is trying to create a climate of fear with all these dire predictions," he said. "The private sector is not going to support giving the Postal Service free rein. . . . The solution lies in more oversight and better management."

UPS and FedEx are influential in Congress. FedEx spent $2.2 million on lobbying last year, while UPS spent $1.4 million. A study by Common Cause found that FedEx gave $1.3 million to both parties last year, with 64 percent going to Republicans. UPS gave $1.2 million, with 82 percent going to the GOP.

Democrats' Concerns

In addition to UPS, McHugh said he expects resistance to continue from pro-union Democrats.

Henry A. Waxman, D-Calif., has been cool to McHugh's efforts, citing the divided views of postal unions and the potential for cuts in service.

McHugh is trying to reach a deal with committee member Danny K. Davis, D-Ill., in an effort to attract more Democratic support. In an interview April 13, Davis said pressure was increasing on both parties to cut a deal, though it will be painful. "We want universal service at a reasonable cost," he added. "You can't get blood out of a turnip. There will be job losses."

McHugh won support in the last Congress from three of the four main postal unions: the National Association of Letter Carriers, the National Rural Letter Carriers Association and the National Postal Mail Handlers Union. The bill was opposed by the 366,000-member American Postal Workers Union (APWU), which represents postal clerks who run post offices and sort mail. Postal clerks face the greatest layoff threat because much of their work can be automated.

Tom Fahey, a spokesman for APWU, said his members fear that the caps on rate increases in McHugh's bill would add pressure on the Postal Service to delete a "no layoffs" provision in the union's contract.

Given the strong opposition from APWU and from the Teamsters union, which represents UPS workers, many Democrats are reluctant to support McHugh's bill. But McHugh and Davis are betting that a deal is possible, and they said they hope the pace of negotiations quickens after a new postmaster general is named to replace Henderson, who is leaving office May 31.

For now, there appears little chance that Congress will move on a proposal from conservative think tanks such as the Cato Institute to simply sell the Postal Service to investors.

Philip M. Crane, R-Ill., sponsored a bill in the 106th Congress that would have turned the Postal Service into a private business. McHugh and Davis said such proposals were unlikely to win strong support this year because many businesses fear competition from a privatized Postal Service.

But Edward L. Hudgins, director of regulatory studies at Cato, said April 18 that the future of the Postal Service is not in the hands of government.

"Now that the Postal Service is faced with losses, politicians are taking a closer look," Hudgins said. "In 10 years, I think it will be a private company. The big government monopoly will be over, and I hope it will be a leaner and meaner operation." ◆

GOP, Businesses Rewrite The Regulatory Playbook

In the drive to reshape federal rules, executive branch is seen as the path of least resistance

Talk about efficiency. Even before tough new air conditioner energy-conservation standards were published by the Clinton administration in January, several major manufacturers began a concerted lobbying campaign to change the rules.

Then George W. Bush became president, and the effort took on greater momentum. The industry won sympathy from important GOP lawmakers such as Senate Majority Leader Trent Lott of Mississippi, Senate Finance Committee Chairman Charles E. Grassley of Iowa and members of the Texas congressional delegation. They petitioned White House aides and officials from the Office of Management and Budget (OMB), which oversees regulations. And they enlisted the support of career Department of Energy officials who, according to industry leaders, had recommended increasing air conditioner and heat pump efficiency by 20 percent instead of the 30 percent that outgoing Secretary Bill Richardson had ordered.

Within weeks, the drive paid off. On April 13, Bush political adviser Karl Rove told reporters that the administration would increase the efficiency standards by 20 percent. The industry was satisfied, but environmentalists were furious.

A new form of regulatory activism appears to be taking hold in the Republican-controlled government. GOP lawmakers, who for years were chafing under President Bill Clinton's regulatory agenda, are moving to undo his policies. And industry lobbyists — aware of the difficulties of trying to shepherd legislation through the evenly divided Senate

CQ Weekly May 5, 2001

— are pushing hard for the administration to use its executive powers to lessen the government burden on business.

In the Reagan years, Republicans complained of the "iron triangle" — an unbreakable alliance among Democratic committee chairmen, agency officials and interest groups that worked in concert to achieve common goals, whether it was funding for special projects or protecting specific constituencies. Reagan OMB directors David Stockman and James C. Miller III made it part of their mission to break the triangle.

Now, it appears, the old iron triangle has been turned on its head. Environmentalists and consumer activists say they fear the formation of a new triad — composed of industry officials, the White House and GOP committee chairmen — that leaves them out of the equation.

"It's fair to say they haven't been seeking us out for advice on how to proceed," said Debbie Sease, legislative director for the Sierra Club.

Today's triangles may not have the permanence or secrecy that characterized the networks of the past. But many regulatory experts predict that the new dynamic will control the rule-making process in more than 50 federal agencies. Corporate lobbyists, mindful of the Republicans' thin margin of control in Congress, are expected to make their case directly to the White House and to political appointees at the agencies, where they are likely to find a sympathetic ear.

"There's a new level of belief that agency regulations are likely to be more helpful than harmful," said Roy Blunt, R-Mo., House chief deputy whip. "For the past eight years, no one ever thought that could be the case. It's mind-boggling to be able to call former House staffers who are now in the White

A Regulatory Timeline

▲ **1970-74:**
President Richard M. Nixon signs an order creating the EPA and legislation establishing the Occupational Safety and Health Administration, the Consumer Product Safety Commission and the National Highway Traffic Safety Administration.

▲ **January 1976:**
President Gerald R. Ford promises in his State of the Union address to cut red tape and address "the petty tyranny of massive government regulation."

▲ **1977-80:**
President Jimmy Carter deregulates the airline, trucking and railroad industries. He also issues an executive order calling for regulatory agencies to be more sensitive to the concerns of those being regulated.

Carter signs the Paperwork Reduction Act (PL 96-511), which directs the Office of Management

and Budget (OMB) to eliminate unnecessary federal paperwork requirements. In addition, the bill creates the Office of Information and Regulatory Affairs within OMB.

Carter also signs the Regulatory Flexibility Act (PL 96-354), which requires federal agencies to consider cost-benefit analysis when writing rules.

House or at an agency to see what they can do to help us."

He and other Republicans say that the administration is simply following the model created by Clinton, who they argue pursued a policy of aggressive regulation, especially in the areas of environment, health and workplace safety.

"I think it's appropriate for this White House to use the administrative side as aggressively as the previous administration," said Sen. Judd Gregg, R-N.H., a member of the Governmental Affairs Committee.

Gregg expects one of the main tools that Republicans will use to change regulatory policy will be OMB's Office of Information and Regulatory Affairs (OIRA), which monitors every major regulation that agencies issue. The nominee to head that office, Harvard professor John D. Graham, is known as an expert on and advocate of risk analysis, a tool researchers use to evaluate the relative harm that can come from various threats to human health and the environment. (*Graham, p. 68*)

Risk analysis is controversial because critics say that it can be used to undermine or undo regulations that society needs. But others say it can be useful to avoid imposing burdensome regulations on business when the risk is not really that great. "There's a distinct possibility that the agency will be used very effectively," said Gregg of New Hampshire.

'Just Wait'

While Republicans often criticized the Clinton administration for changing policy by administrative fiat, that approach is likely to be tempting for the Bush administration given the current balance of power.

"What you'll soon see is that the president will soon go wild with executive orders, even though he complained about it when Clinton did it, because the Senate is such a difficult place for him to navigate," predicted David C. King, professor of public policy at Harvard's John F. Kennedy School of Government. "That's the area in which the president does have an upper hand that he's not likely to lose soon . . . because undoing administrative actions requires consensus, not simply complaint, from Congress."

That sentiment is echoed by Robert E. Litan, director of economic studies at the Brookings Institution. "It's just so

much easier to do things administratively," he said. "The fact that it's a 50-50 Senate makes that even more true."

As the Bush administration has revised or killed Clinton policies, Democrats say they are exploring ways to pressure the administration to back off.

"It's not easy," said Joseph I. Lieberman of Connecticut, ranking Democrat on the Senate Governmental Affairs Committee. "We still have the right to pursue litigation and use the power of investigations and public exposure. The problem is that anything we do legislatively faces a presidential veto."

The Democrats' challenge is likely to become greater as Bush appointees — many of whom come from the private sector, conservative think tanks and trade groups that vigorously opposed Clinton policies — fill agencies and take full control of the regulatory process.

"If you think it's been rough so far, just wait," said William Kovacs, U.S. Chamber of Commerce vice president for technology, environment and regulatory affairs. He predicts big fights over some of the environmental issues, such as clean air standards that were left unresolved in the Clinton years.

Business groups and their congressional allies have a long list of goals. Among them:

• They expect the Occupational Safety and Health Administration to take a cooperative rather than confrontational approach in getting businesses to improve work conditions. Republicans have long argued that this agency is so overbearing and punitive that businesses are afraid to seek its help in addressing problems.

• The health care industry and House Ways and Means Committee Chairman Bill Thomas, R-Calif., have long sought to overhaul procedures used by the Health Care Financing Administration (HCFA), which regulates Medicare and Medicaid, and curtail its power. Now that top hospital lobbyist Thomas A. Scully has been nominated to head the agency, Thomas and the industry are more likely to get what they want.

• The Bush administration is preparing a national energy plan, scheduled to be released in the next few weeks, that is expected to contain a number of proposals that can be accomplished by administrative action, such as allowing in-

▲ FEB. 17, 1981:
President Ronald Reagan issues an executive order barring agencies from issuing a major rule unless OMB decides its benefit outweighs its costs. It also requires OMB approval before a rule can be published.

▲ JANUARY 1985:
Reagan issues an executive order requiring OMB to approve agencies'

annual regulatory agendas.

▲ 1986:
Reacting to complaints that the Office of Information and Regulatory Affairs overruled too many agency decisions and allowed industry groups excessive influence over rulemaking, Congress includes language in the final omnibus continuing resolution (PL 99-591) requiring its administrators to be

confirmed by the Senate. The law also restricts the agency's oversight functions to the "sole purpose" of reviewing information-collection requests contained in proposed regulations.

▲ JANUARY 1992:
President George Bush imposes a moratorium on new regulations and instructs agencies to change existing rules or programs that create regulatory burdens.

Nominee's Faith in Risk Analysis Sharpens Debate on Rulemaking Process

To his supporters, John D. Graham, the soft-spoken Harvard professor nominated to head the Office of Information and Regulatory Affairs, is an academic who will apply common-sense evaluations to the regulations issued by more than 50 federal agencies, ensuring that government resources are applied wisely. They say it makes no sense to spend taxpayers' dollars on problems that may be far less dangerous than perceived.

To his opponents, Graham is someone who will use a patina of science to block government rules needed to protect Americans from health, safety and environmental hazards.

Graham is getting attention because he is one of the foremost proponents of "risk analysis" — which calculates the likelihood of a hazard against the costs and benefits of preventing it. Every major government regulation overturned or created by the Bush administration would go through his agency, which is part of the Office of Management and Budget (OMB).

Robert W. Hahn, director of the American Enterprise Institute-Brookings Institution Joint Center for Regulatory Studies, says Graham will use "the same [criteria] people use every day" to make decisions. "When you think about crossing the street, you [weigh] the increased risk of an accident against the benefit of getting to the other side," he said.

But Joan Claybrook, president of the consumers group Public Citizen, questions the research techniques used by Graham, director of Harvard's Center for Risk Analysis. "The problems with his methodology is that it's garbage in, garbage out," she said. "It's not a neutral evaluation; it's policy-driven toward a predetermined finding."

Sally Katzen, administrator of the Office of Information and Regulatory Affairs under President Bill Clinton, does not believe Graham will drive the agency into a stark anti-regulatory stance.

"Can [risk analysis] be manipulated for ulterior motives? Sure," said Katzen. "Do I suspect that's what the office is going to do? I don't, actually. . . . He's not a madman or an ideologue by a longshot."

Everyone involved in the regulatory debate agrees that Graham will have one of the most politically sensitive jobs in the administration if he is confirmed by the Senate, as most observers expect.

"This executive office is pure hell," said Gary Bass, director of OMB Watch, a public interest group that has been monitoring the agency since the Reagan administration.

"You're hit by the politics of the president. You're hit by demands from industry, public interests, Congress, not to mention the agencies — and almost all of those people have different perspectives. Because of the high stakes, you always end up alienating someone," he said.

Costs and Benefits

Graham argues that risk analysis is a valuable tool in setting budget and policy priorities, and that it makes sense to use systematic methods to figure out whether a perceived threat or hazard is real. He also believes new risks may be created when regulations are issued to fix a problem.

"The basic problem we face as citizens and as policymakers is a distortion of priorities," Graham told the Senate Governmental Affairs Committee in 1995, when he was testifying about regulatory overhaul. "We regulate some often tiny or nonexistent risks too much and ignore larger and better-documented risks."

Critics question the way Graham gauges proposed solutions. Instead of estimating the number of lives that would be saved by a regulation — one commonly used standard — Graham tries to determine how many years of life would be saved.

That means, say critics, that he dismisses problems that might not arise for decades and solutions that might add a few high-quality years to an individual's life.

Wendy Lee Gramm, who headed the Office of Information and Regulatory Affairs in the mid-1980s, defends Graham's methodology. "People say, 'How can you value a life?' But the point is, we're always evaluating tradeoffs," said Gramm, now director of regulatory studies at the Mercatus Center of the George Mason University in Arlington, Va.

"Sometimes it's not life or death; it's just extending a life," said Gramm, who headed a regulatory agency, the Commodity Futures Trading Commission, from 1988 to 1993. "It's not an all-or-nothing decision."

Public Citizen, however, says its criticism of Graham goes beyond his methods. The group claimed in a March report that he has skewed data to supports the claims of corporate donors to the Harvard center such as Merck & Co. Inc., Exxon Mobil Corp., Bethlehem Steel Corp. and the Shell Foundation.

Claybrook takes particular issue with a Harvard center study, released in July, on motorists' use of cell phones. Researchers, including Graham, said they could not clearly document how much the risk of an accident increases if a driver is talking on a cell phone.

"We simply do not have enough reliable information on which to base reasonable policy," the study concluded. "Although there is evidence that using a cellular phone while driving poses risks to both the driver and others, it may be premature to enact substantial restrictions."

Claybrook believes it is obvious that cell phone regulation would save lives and notes that the study was funded by a $300,000 contribution from AT&T Wireless Group.

"It's simplistic and naive to say that the funding automatically corrupts the findings of the study," said David Ropeik, a spokesman for the Harvard Center for Risk Analysis. "We are funded by a number of government agencies, but [critics] don't mention that because it doesn't fit into their thesis."

Ropeik said the cell phone study was reviewed by outside experts and included a disclosure of its funding source.

Public-interest groups say they fear a return to the early days of the Reagan administration, when regulations disappeared down a "black hole" at the Office of Information and Regulatory Affairs. During that time, congressional Democrats charged, regulations would go in for review and disappear for months or years without explanation.

OMB Watch's Bass said he is also concerned the White House may retreat from the more open regulatory processes that evolved under Clinton.

"This nominee has to go on record in terms of what kinds of transparency he would bring to [the agency]," Bass said. "Right now [under Bush], you can't find out anything. You have no idea what criteria is used for upholding some rules and withdrawing others."

Congressional critics worry Graham will be reluctant to allow any rules to go forward. Costs "could lead you always to say no" to regulations, said Henry A. Waxman of California, ranking Democrat on the House Government Reform Committee.

"Not only has the administration acted so far in complete disregard for the views of the public, but they're also putting people in place like Graham, who will continue that pattern," Waxman said.

Some Democrats on the Senate Governmental Afairs Committee are eager to quiz Graham, who joined OMB as a consultant in mid-March and has been visiting Capitol Hill regularly to seek political guidance from his allies and a chance to plead his case before skeptics.

"Based on what I've read about Mr. Graham, we're going to take a very close look at his philosophy, his

Supporters and critics agree that Graham will probably be a cautious regulator.

research [and] the impact of his views about rules and regulations on health and safety," said Sen. Richard J. Durbin, D-Ill.

Still, Graham is expected to be confirmed easily with the support of Democrats such as Carl Levin of Michigan. Three years ago, when Levin and Chairman Fred Thompson, R-Tenn., were pushing for a bill that would require agencies to include risk analysis when writing regulations, Graham testified in favor of their proposal. The measure was reported out of committee but the GOP leadership opted against bringing it to the floor. (*1998 Almanac, p. 15-22*)

Graham's Agenda

Every president since Jimmy Carter has ordered federal agencies to weigh potential costs and benefits when writing a rule. Today, every major regulation with an economic impact of more than $100 million must undergo a formal cost-benefit evaluation. (*Timeline, p.66*)

It is more difficult to evaluate risks, however. Many agencies try to determine the likelihood that a par-

ticular hazard could occur when formulating regulations — but there are no government standards about whether or how to use risk analysis.

Graham would likely change that. Over the past decade, he has repeatedly testified before Congress about problems in the current rule-making process. In 1995 testimony before a House Commerce subcommittee, Graham outlined suggestions to update the system. They included:

• "Broad-based rankings of health, safety and environmental risks that cut across the jurisdictions of existing agencies" and "could help inform the budgetary allocations of Congress and OMB."

• A mechanism "to make sure that the findings of benefit-cost analyses are actually used by federal agencies when making specific rulemaking decisions."

• Stronger White House oversight of federal agencies. "No significant risk assessment should be published by a federal agency without the opportunity for review by an interagency panel of experts under the leadership of the executive office of the president," said Graham.

American Enterprise Institute-Brookings analyst Hahn predicts that Graham's interest in more risk analysis will have two main effects on government policy.

"The administration will be less likely to pass regulations that would be burdensome to the average consumer, and . . . there will be greater attention to achieving the same objectives in less costly ways," Hahn said. "We'll see costs more seriously considered."

A former OMB administrator says Graham's toughest task may be confronting the tension that has always existed between his office and regulatory agencies.

"A lot of agencies have bureaucratic staff with their own agenda and special interests," said James C. Miller III, who headed OMB under Reagan.

"Graham is going to make sure that he has a lot of clout in the White House so that when there's a confrontation with an agency — and there is always some sort of defining showdown — he will win."

creased drilling on public land and easing regulatory restrictions on energy producers. Other agencies are considering low-profile ways to help ease the regulatory burden on businesses. (Energy, 2001 CQ Weekly, p. 1014)

Undoing Clinton's Rules

During his final weeks in office, Clinton issued a number of rules that Republicans say were traps deliberately set to put Bush in politically difficult positions. Clinton signed off on more than 50 regulations after the election, prompting Bush spokesman Ari Fleischer to call him a "busy beaver" in his final days. Republicans note that it is not unusual for incoming presidents to conduct a broad review of last-minute rules signed by their predecessors.

"Some regulations that the Clinton administration put forward were blatantly political," said Rep. Christopher Shays, R-Conn. "And I believe that some of them were done to stiff this administration."

The rules for tighter efficiency standards for air conditioners, issued Jan. 22, were designed to force manufacturers to make their products more energy-efficient by 2006. After intense lobbying by environmentalists and one manufacturer of air conditioners that use less energy, Richardson proposed raising the standard by 30 percent. But that was controversial, especially because the department had considered a 20 percent increase, which the industry had said it could accept.

The companies, arguing that the 30-percent rule would jeopardize profits,

began lobbying. The air conditioning industry hired outside consultants such as Baker, Donelson, Bearman & Caldwell, a Washington lobbying firm headed by former Senate Majority Leader Howard Baker Jr., R-Tenn. (1967-85). The industry's trade group, the Air-Conditioning and Refrigeration Institute, flew company executives to Washington to contact lawmakers representing areas with large factories, such as Texas. And the group found and publicized a Clinton administration Department of Justice memo questioning the wisdom of the regulation.

"We called everyone we could," said David F. Lewis, vice president of government relations for Lennox Industries Inc., a Dallas-based company. "We wore out a lot of shoe leather."

He said industry officials met with Lott and Sen. Thad Cochran, R-Miss., telling them that the rule could hurt air conditioning manufacturing facilities in Mississippi and other states. They also told lawmakers and administration officials that the industry would consider challenging the regulations in court if they were not overturned.

Officials from Lennox as well as Trane Co. and Carrier Corp. also persuaded Grassley, Rep. Joe Knollenberg, R-Mich., and other lawmakers to send letters to the administration urging officials to reverse the rules, saying American jobs were at stake.

Those actions got attention. After Bush took office, his administration called for a new rule that would implement the 20-percent standard.

When the Bush administration De-

partment of Energy announced the change in the Federal Register, it directly cited the trade group's efforts. The department said that it was "of the view that [the association] has raised some substantial questions" about the Clinton standard.

Environmentalists criticized the action, especially because a day earlier they were pleased that the Bush administration had kept in place a Clinton rule, accepted by industry, requiring tighter energy efficiency standards for clothes washers and water heaters.

Bush must still decide on other Clinton policies, including one to control water runoff by farms and loggers. It is on hold until a National Academy of Sciences study is completed this year. Once it is released, the agriculture and forestry industries will lobby for new regulations that would limit costs to comply. (2000 CQ Weekly, p. 585)

Thus far in his term, Bush has already signed legislation (PL 107-5) to kill a Clinton ergonomics rule opposed by many major business groups, who argued that it would cost too much to implement. He has also signaled his intention to reverse or revise Clinton regulations, including one to toughen cleanup standards for hardrock mining operations. (Ergonomics, 2001 CQ Weekly, p. 535; regulations, p. 670)

Bush also stoked public criticism by reneging on a campaign pledge to regulate carbon dioxide and by rejecting the Kyoto Protocol on global warming. (2001 CQ Weekly, pp. 607, 724)

Perhaps the most controversial move was reversing a Clinton rule to reduce

▲ SEPTEMBER 1993:
President Bill Clinton issues an executive order allowing agencies to issue regulations only when benefits "justify" costs. All major rules must be submitted for OMB review, but only those with an annual economic effect of $100 million or more require its approval.

▲ 1996:
Congress passes the Small Business Regulatory Enforcement Fairness Act (PL 104-121), which requires agencies to help small businesses comply with rules and allows for waivers of civil fines. The law includes language establishing the Congressional Review Act,

which requires agencies to submit new rules to Congress and the General Accounting Office and gives lawmakers an expedited way to reject them.

▲ JAN. 20, 2001:
On his first day in office, President George W. Bush orders a 60-day hold on the effective dates of all published Clinton regulations not yet in effect so the new administration can review them.

▲ MARCH 7, 2001:
Congress passes a resolution (S J Res 6) repealing ergonomics rules issued by the Clinton adminstration; Bush later signs it into law (PL 107-5).

the levels of arsenic in drinking water. The rule, issued in December, would have lowered the amount of arsenic permitted in drinking water to 10 parts per billion from 50 parts per billion. EPA Administrator Christine Todd Whitman announced March 20 that the rule would be withdrawn, leading Democrats and some GOP moderates to complain that the administration was out of touch with the public. Some political scientists believe the issue may have tipped the political scales.

Bush's regulatory strategy will be labeled in two categories, "Before arsenic and after arsenic," said Gary Bass, director of OMB Watch, a group that monitors the agency.

George C. Edwards III, professor of political science at Texas A&M University and director of the Center for Presidential Studies in the Bush School of Government and Public Service, said that outcries like the one over arsenic may force the White House to voice more concern about the environment.

"They got a negative reaction to the first regulatory decisions on environmental protection," Edwards said. "It's not what they actually meant . . . and they've been playing catchup ever since. That fact may temper them."

Complaints from environmental activists — and moderate Republicans, who fear a backlash from suburban voters in 2002 — have caused the White House to become more wary about overturning Clinton rules — and more savvy about explaining any changes. Bush announced several pro-environment moves the week of April 16, including decisions to uphold Clinton rules restricting wetlands development and lowering the levels at which factories must report lead emissions.

The White House also has upheld Clinton regulations involving complex medical privacy rules and tougher emission standards for diesel engines. But those actions have not muted criticism. Consumer groups point out that the Bush administration agreed to change the privacy regulations largely because health industry groups protested that the rules would make it tougher to dispense prescriptions and treat patients. (*p. 102*)

The president's decision to uphold Clinton's diesel fuel emission standards pleased automakers as well as environmental groups. According to energy industry lobbyists and environmentalists, however, the administration is quietly

conducting a study that could lead to the rules being relaxed.

Observers predict the administration will always have a strong conservative and pro-business ideology at its core, but they say it is now presenting a more cautious public face to stem concerns.

Graham's Role

GOP lawmakers are encouraging the administration to consider the costs and benefits of any new rules on business, including rules that were proposed during the Clinton years. The focus of that effort will be the OMB's regulatory affairs office.

"This administration will take a responsible, conservative approach," said Sen. Rick Santorum, R-Pa. "We'll do it in a way that's supported by the evidence, and not to appease interest groups."

OMB and Congress have a long history of conflict. During Republican administrations, Democrats charged that OMB officials were delaying, changing or killing regulations ordered by Congress and written by government experts. The agency would write a rule, OMB would put it under "review," sometimes indefinitely, and lawmakers would protest.

Reagan beefed up the agency's oversight power by issuing an executive order in 1981 that required agencies to prove that a regulation's benefits would "outweigh" its costs — a standard Democrats said was often tough to prove. Later, Reagan banned agencies from issuing any regulatory policies that were not approved by OMB at the start of each year. (*1981 Almanac, p. 405*)

Democratic chairmen in the House were outraged by Reagan's actions, and John D. Dingell, D-Mich., then head of the House Energy and Commerce Committee, routinely called officials to Capitol Hill and demanded that they explain regulatory decisions.

"Dingell would beat up on me all the time," said Christopher DeMuth, president of the American Enterprise Institute and an administrator of OMB's regulatory affairs office under Reagan.

In 1986, the Democratic-controlled House forced a showdown by deleting funds for OMB's regulatory division from the fiscal 1987 budget. Lawmakers restored the money after OMB director Miller and Wendy Lee Gramm, head of the regulatory affairs office, agreed to make the rule-making process more transparent by disclosing White

House documents related to regulatory decisions. (*1986 Almanac, p. 325*)

In the first Bush administration, Democrats pushed through a number of bills to strengthen clean air standards. And in each case, the Democratic-controlled Congress, aware of OMB's power, was very specific about how the agencies were to implement the laws such as amendments to the 1990 Clean Air Act (PL 101-549). (*1990 Almanac, p. 229*)

"We had to write a lot of detail in the law because we were afraid to leave it up to EPA," said Henry A. Waxman of California, ranking Democrat on the House Government Reform Committee. "We had to mandate things that otherwise would be [optional] if you had confidence that the people administering it had the same goals in mind as the authors."

After Clinton took office in 1993, he tried to open the regulatory process further when he issued an executive order requiring the White House to document any closed-door meeting between OMB officials and outside groups on a regulation. The order, which also required the cost of a regulation to "justify" its benefit, is still in effect.

With the GOP controlling the White House and Congress, Dingell said he may use discharge petitions — which members may sign if they want to bring a bill from committee directly to the floor — to publicize the issues. But he realizes his options to force real change on a GOP administration are limited.

"I will still do what I can," Dingell said. "But I [could] do a lot more if I were still chairman."

Blocking Regulations

The White House and Congress have several weapons beyond writing a new law that they can use to kill or alter regulations. They include:

• **Reopening a rule.** The 1946 Administrative Procedures Act allows the White House to reopen the rulemaking process by soliciting new public comments, as it did in February with the medical privacy regulation. After considering the comments, the president can either modify a regulation or allow it to take effect without changes.

• **Enforcement.** They can also limit the funds available to agencies to enforce regulations. Bush has proposed cutting the funds of nine agencies and the EPA in his fiscal 2002 budget, which could affect the enforcement of a variety of labor, environmental, health and public safety regulations. (*2001 CQ Weekly, p. 463*)

• **Congressional review.** Congress can reverse a rule through the Congressional Review Act (PL 104-121). Conservative lawmakers successfully used it for the first time ever in March to kill the ergonomics regulation. (*2001 CQ Weekly, p. 312*)

The White House can indirectly reverse a regulation through the courts — either by mounting a weak defense of a rule written by a previous administration or by seeking a settlement with plaintiffs whose arguments it supports. This tactic is a gamble because judges can be unpredictable and their rulings can be appealed. But since the creation of numerous health and safety laws in the 1970s, legal challenges to regulations have become a common tool of both business and public-interest groups.

"One of the best ways to get rid of a regulation is to get a friendly lawsuit," said Jim Tozzi, deputy administrator of the regulatory office under Reagan.

For example, the administration tacitly encouraged a suit brought by the timber industry and western state officials against a Clinton regulation that blocked road building in 58.5 million acres of national forests.

In the suit, the Boise Cascade Corp., a major timber company, argued that the rule was not legal because the Clinton administration did not follow the proper procedures in writing it. Environmentalists had been watching the case to see whether the Bush administration would mount a vigorous defense of the rules. But on May 4, the administration announced a compromise under which the rule would go forward, but could be changed to allow forest plans to be written on a case-by-case basis, with input from local officials.

The judge in the case, U.S. District Court Judge Edward J. Lodge, had indicated that he thought the Clinton process was "grossly inadequate." He must decide by May 12 whether to block the rules.

Environmental groups, which cited the roads issue to attack Bush's environmental record, said the administration's plan was actually an effort to undermine the regulation. The groups had used an advertising campaign that features bucolic images of forests and wildlife, then

Environmental groups, in a demonstration in Lafayette Park across from the White House April 30, protested decisions by the Bush administration to roll back environmental rules issued by Clinton.

shift jarringly to pictures of trees falling to the sound of chainsaws. A narrator says timber companies are trying to destroy the nation's forests, and that Bush may let them. The ad effort, by the Heritage Forests Campaign, released new ads the week of April 30 calling on Bush to strongly defend the rules.

The White House is also said to be considering settlements in several lawsuits that seek to overturn Clinton regulations, including rules to phase out the use of snowmobiles in national parks and to reintroduce grizzly bears to areas in Idaho and Montana. In another suit, business groups are seeking to kill more stringent reporting requirements for lead emissions. In this case, Bush kept the Clinton rule, which required more businesses to report their lead emissions.

Environmental Defense and the Natural Resources Defense Council are joining as many suits as possible in defense of the Clinton rules. The groups say they will fight hard to prevent settlements.

Political Fallout

Democrats say they expect a political backlash from the Bush administration's regulatory decisions.

"We have an election in two years," said Sen. Barbara Boxer, D-Calif. "Let the people decide whether President Bush is being reasonable."

This month, the Sierra Club is running ads criticizing Bush on the environment. A coalition of environmentalists is also issuing daily faxes, e-mails and calls to supporters to generate concern about Bush's energy policy.

Bush's moves on the environment have "invigorated us to try to find ways to stop the administration," said Patty Murray, D-Wash., chairwoman of the Democratic Senatorial Campaign Committee.

A Democratic party television ad released April 29 attacks Bush's arsenic decision and criticizes a proposal by the Department of Agriculture, later scuttled, that would have ended testing of school lunch meat for salmonella.

The ad features a young girl asking, "May I please have some more arsenic in my water, Mommy?" A boy follows with the question, "More salmonella in my cheeseburger, please?"

Administration officials call the ad unfair — Rove called it "laughable" — particularly since the salmonella proposal was never an official position.

"This administration will be judged over the totality of its record," Rove said on NBC's "Meet the Press" April 29.

In the meantime, such ads can be expected to continue as the two parties battle over the role and scope of the regulatory process in getting federal policies changed. And just as industry can effectively mobilize its allies in Congress and the agencies, experts say, so can their adversaries.

"We're seeing a fundamental shift in power," said Harvard's King. "When there are shifts like this, there is always some turmoil. . . . It's natural." ◆

Freeh's Contrite Visit to Hill Fails to Head Off Demands For Stronger Oversight of FBI

The long series of high-profile blunders by the FBI, most recently visible in the delayed execution of convicted Oklahoma City bomber Timothy J. McVeigh, may finally cost the agency some of its prized independence.

Even after soon-to-retire FBI director Louis J. Freeh spent the better part of the week of May 14 apologizing for and explaining the errors that led to the delay of McVeigh's execution, members of both parties suggested that more needs to be done to improve the agency's internal controls.

Arlen Specter, R-Pa., and Richard J. Durbin, D-Ill., both members of the Senate Judiciary Committee, announced May 16 that they plan to introduce legislation to create an inspector general for the FBI. Currently the agency is subject to the Justice Department's inspector general, but Durbin and Specter said the FBI needs its own watchdog.

McVeigh was convicted of the 1995 bombing of a federal building in Oklahoma City, which killed 168 people. He was scheduled to be executed at the federal prison in Terre Haute, Ind., on May 16, but after the FBI disclosed that it had not turned over thousands of pages of evidence to his defense team during the trial, Attorney General John Ashcroft on May 11 postponed the execution for one month.

On May 16 and 17, Freeh testified before the House and Senate appropriations subcommittees with jurisdiction over the FBI on the agency's fiscal 2002 budget request. He said that despite the huge amount of evidence withheld from McVeigh's de-

Freeh spent the week of May 14 enduring harsh criticism over the McVeigh case and other high-profile errors as he sought funding for the FBI's 2002 budget.

fense team — some 3,000 pages covering 700 separate items —none of it would have helped McVeigh. "Nothing in the documents raises any doubt about the guilt of Mr. McVeigh," Freeh insisted on May 16.

But he acknowledged that of the 56 FBI field offices, only 10 followed instructions and sent all of the material they had gathered to Oklahoma City. Freeh said it was not clear why the other offices did not comply with their instructions, but he said the orders had been unambiguous.

"There were 16 communications, two sent from the director's office," Freeh said. "And they are absolutely clear, as far as I can see, that everything and anything was to be retrieved and sent to Oklahoma City."

Posse 'Paranoia'

Traditionally, the FBI is one of the most popular agencies on Capitol Hill. Frank R. Wolf, R-Va., chairman of the House Appropriations Subcommittee on Commerce, Justice, State and Judiciary, noted May 16 that the agency's budget had increased by 65 percent since 1993.

For fiscal 2002, the Bush administration has requested $3.6 billion for the FBI.

But the McVeigh case is only one of several recent problems in the agency. Early this year, a veteran agent was accused of working as a spy. Robert Hanssen was formally charged May 16 with spying for more than a dozen years against the United States for Russia.

After listing a series of other problems with the agency, Rep. David R. Obey, D-Wis., said the incidents fuel the worst fears of those inclined to distrust government.

"I guess I feel so strongly about it because of the district I come from. I come from posse country," Obey said. "I come from militia country. And I've had to fight the paranoia of these people all of my life. I've seen people store up everything from bazookas to you-name-it because they think that their government can't be trusted."

He added that Congress shares the blame for not providing tougher oversight. "I've seen members of Congress more interested in getting an autograph from past directors of the FBI than I've seen them interested in asking tough questions," he said.

Freeh disagreed with that assessment and disputed the need for an inspector general.

"I believe we are the most scrutinized agency in the federal government," Freeh said. "I also believe we should be, because of the enormous power that we have and the potential for abuse that the FBI would have without that scrutiny."

Freeh concluded: "We have had troubles in this agency. We've had failures. We've also had great triumphs. . . ." ◆

73

Politics and Public Policy

The deepest tax cut in 20 years was signed into law on June 7, 2001—the embodiment of President George W. Bush's campaign promise to reduce income tax rates. But committing such a large sum—$1.35 trillion—to tax relief means that both parties will have to keep a close eye on the new bottom line if they are to uphold commitments not to touch Social Security or Medicare surpluses. The first article in this section considers this and other implications of the recently enacted tax cut.

On the education front, the 107th Congress took up reauthorization of the Elementary and Secondary Education Act. The second reading in this section examines that legislation and the key issues in the reauthorization debate.

In 1996 Congress enacted major welfare overhaul legislation that ended welfare as an entitlement and replaced it with a block grant that limits poor families to five years of federal assistance. The questions Congress now faces are important to millions of poor Americans: What comes next? What is to be done for still-unemployed welfare recipients who are about to hit the program's time limits? These are among the concerns explored in this article.

The next selection focuses on patients' rights and legislation designed to give consumers more power with their managed-care health plans. For Sen. Edward M. Kennedy, this issue has long been a signature cause, and the power shift in the Senate—resulting from Sen. James Jeffords' defection from the Republican Party—has placed Kennedy center stage in the battle for managed-care legislation. His role, and the prospects for a patients' rights deal, are examined in this reading.

The section moves next to abortion, a topic over which policy makers struggle each year. Showing clearly that his election has changed the dynamics of the abortion debate, President Bush on January 22, 2001, reinstated Reagan-era restrictions on international family planning aid that President Bill Clinton had abolished. Democrats will try to remove the restrictions with legislation, but with a Congress that is evenly divided on the issue and President Bush holding the veto power, this will be no easy accomplishment.

Americans want the convenience of one-click shopping on the Internet. They want their doctors and pharmacies to have up-to-date and accurate records. They want cutting-edge capabilities on their cell phones. But they also want their privacy, and the difficulty of accommodating both of these demands has made privacy one of the most vexing technology policy concerns facing the government. It is the subject of the next article.

The next report turns to the current energy crisis and one powerful senator's controversial view that the time is right for a comeback of nuclear energy. The history of nuclear power and the economics and safety of atomic energy are among the topics considered in this article.

Moving to environmental concerns, the next selection addresses global warming. Democrats in Congress see President Bush's environmental policies—which include abandoning a pledge to regulate emissions believed to be major contributors to global warming—as a major political liability for the Republicans. Now that the Democrats control the Senate, they are planning a series of steps that they hope will increase pressure on President Bush to deliver proposals for reducing global warming.

President Bush came to office promising to deploy a national anti-missile defense system. Critics of such an initiative fear that Bush's plan would destroy the 1972 Anti-Ballistic Missile (ABM) Treaty—the foundation of the U.S.-Russian nuclear balance—as well as alienate U.S. allies and spark a wide-ranging arms race. As the final article in this section reports, President Bush faces challenges ahead if he is to realize his ambitious missile defense plan.

Tax Debate Assured a Long Life As Bush, GOP Press for New Cuts

The president's unmet requests will be at the center of the next phase, which may see Democrats attempt to rescind some reductions

Enactment of the tax cut reconciliation package the week of June 4 will mark the start of a new fiscal era that will last through the 107th Congress and beyond.

The difference is that $1.35 trillion of the forecast surplus through fiscal 2011 has been swept off the table — money that may no longer be used for spending on defense, education, agriculture or any other priority, including additional tax cuts.

In recent years, lawmakers and the president could rely on increasingly generous surplus estimates to let them break their self-imposed fiscal constraints. But not this time. Even the rosiest forecast this summer would not be enough to countervail what has just been committed for tax relief. And in fact, the next forecast is expected to be no better than the current one, and perhaps a touch worse.

That means both parties will have to keep a close eye on the new bottom line if they hope to uphold one of their few shared commitments: not to touch surpluses in the Social Security or Medicare Hospital Insurance trust funds to pay for anything other than to help reduce the national debt, and to assist in the financial and medical security of the elderly.

The "on budget" surplus remaining after enactment of the tax legislation (HR 1836) — about $1.38 trillion, according to the current Congressional Budget Office forecast — is being eyed for a variety of expensive purposes, from expanding education aid to financing a national missile defense shield to creating a Medicare prescription drug benefit.

The White House and many Republicans have also promised to cut taxes still more. They are being pressured to do so, starting this year, by the business community, which agreed not to lobby

for special provisions in Bush's first tax package with the understanding that their turn would come on the second. The Democrats, especially those emboldened by their party's takeover of the Senate this month, are likely to resist most of those moves and may open a counteroffensive — to stop some of the new tax cuts, especially those benefiting people at the highest income levels..

Shaky Forecasts

They will have plenty of time to gain strength for that effort. Many of the measure's provisions do not take effect until the second half of the decade — after the next two elections for Congress, the next presidential election, and a score of additional revisions to the surplus forecast in light of an evolving economy.

All of this makes current budget forecasts — which historically have been profoundly unreliable even when the revenue outlook is relatively stable — even more uncertain than usual.

"You have to look at revenue flow and income every year," said David C. Colander, a historian of economic

thought at Middlebury College, who predicted that several of the new tax provisions will be altered or repealed in the next decade as economic conditions change. "You can't look at it over long periods of time."

One prime target would be the estate tax, which will be reduced gradually and then repealed nine years from now — at a cost of $53.4 billion in fiscal 2011 alone. "Repeal of the estate tax is not in the cards," said Allen Schick, a professor of public policy at the University of Maryland and an expert on the federal budget process and politics. The reduction in the top income tax rate, now 39.6 percent, will probably also come under assault before it is reduced to 35 percent five years from now, he said. (*Tax cut calendar, p. 78*)

The most dramatic provision in the package is the final one slated to take effect — a repeal of the entire measure at the end of 2010. That sunset was necessary for the legislation to comply with this year's budget resolution (H Con Res 83), which limited the cost to $1.35 trillion through 2011. A vote by 60 senators could have raised that ceiling, but the package's negotiators concluded early on that they could not muster a supermajority. The figure was arrived at after weeks of tortured talks aimed at securing the support of a pivotal group of Senate moderates. (*Background, 2001 CQ Weekly p. 1066*)

Still, the Bush administration said it is confident that the sunset will never happen, because a future Congress and a subsequent president will agree to extend the provisions of the 2001 law. As White House spokesman Ari Fleischer noted May 31, "to do anything other than that is to raise taxes on the American people."

Waiting for Round Two

This year's reconciliation ceiling was too low to accommodate everything the administration wanted, which the White House said totaled $1.64 trillion but which the congressional Joint Committee on Taxation said added up to $1.78 trillion. At least some of President Bush's unmet requests will presumably be at the center of the next tax debate, as will the desires of the business community. Campaigns for some of those wishes — such as a tax break for buying new computer systems — are already under way. *(Box, p. 80)*

The most expensive Bush proposal the bill did not grant, at $48 billion through 2011, was to make permanent the tax credit that businesses may claim on as much as 20 percent of their research and experimentation expenses. That idea is popular in Congress — the Senate included in its version of the reconciliation bill — and it was the only major component of Bush's package that was an explicit tax break for corporate America. But in part because the credit does not expire until 2004, and in part because its extension could be used as a vehicle or sweetener for some future tax package, the urgency of addressing it faded in the final round of negotiations.

Other Bush requests that were left out of the reconciliation measure included proposals to expand the tax benefits of making charitable donations; allow teachers to deduct their out-of-pocket classroom expenses; increase the deductibility of medical and long-term care expenses; and expand tax credits for alternative energy sources.

The bill also did not grant Bush's request for one year extensions of several tax provisions, including a welfare-to-work credit, the "work opportunity" credit and several business-oriented breaks. Renewing such expiring provisions has proved difficult for Congress to resist in recent years.

Another issue that seems certain to be addressed again, although not in this Congress, is the alternative minimum tax (AMT), a parallel tax system that was designed to prevent wealthy taxpayers who use many deductions, exemptions and credits from eliminating their tax liability entirely. The AMT was never indexed for inflation and thus will affect more people in the future — especially after 2004, when a modest adjustment to the AMT included in the reconciliation package will expire. That year, 5.3 million people will be affected by the AMT, about the same as would be without the reconciliation law. The number will jump to 13 million taxpayers the next year and will keep rising to 35.5 million people in 2010, the Joint Tax Committee estimates — twice as many as would be the case if the tax code remained as it is now.

"They're going to have to do a major

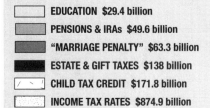

(in billions of dollars by fiscal year)

2001 | 2002 | 2003 | 2004 | 2005 | 2006 | 2007 | 2008 | 2009 | 2010 | 2011

EDUCATION $29.4 billion

PENSIONS & IRAs $49.6 billion

"MARRIAGE PENALTY" $63.3 billion

ESTATE & GIFT TAXES $138 billion

CHILD TAX CREDIT $171.8 billion

INCOME TAX RATES $874.9 billion

NOTES: Figures may not add because of rounding. The totals above are cumulative for fiscal years 2001 through 2011. The columns for each year exclude $13.9 billion in alternative minimum tax relief through 2004 and other miscellaneous provisions that would cost a net $7.6 billion through 2011.

SOURCE: Joint Committee on Taxation

Tax Cut's Cost Will Rise, Then May Fall

Negotiators of the final tax cut reconciliation package (HR 1836) employed several accounting devices to manage the bill's costs. Their overriding goal was to keep the price tag through fiscal 2011 under $1.35 trillion — the ceiling set by the fiscal 2002 budget resolution (H Con Res 83) that may be breached only with the support of 60 or more senators. Many of the tax cuts were phased in slowly, others were limited to certain years, and the payment schedule for some corporate taxes was altered to shift $33 billion in revenue to fiscal 2002 and $7 billion to fiscal 2005, when the projected surplus would not otherwise be robust enough to cover the tax cut. Most importantly, the conference agreement would repeal all the provisions after Dec. 31, 2010 — unless Congress and the president agree otherwise beforehand. If the sunset occurs, the expense of the tax package will begin to shrink dramatically in fiscal 2011, which begins in October 2010 and includes April 15, 2011, when federal income tax returns will be due for the previous calendar year.

Tax Package's Timetable

Following are the main provisions of the tax reconciliation legislation (HR 1836 — conference report: H Rept 107-84) cleared by Congress on May 26 and scheduled to be signed by President Bush the week of June 4. The proposals are organized by the calendar years in which they would take effect, be altered or cease to be effective. The annualized net costs are for fiscal years, as calculated by the Joint Committee on Taxation.

2001 Cost: $73.8 billion

- A 10 percent rate would be created as the new lowest personal income tax bracket and applied — retroactively to Jan. 1 — to the first $6,000 of a single filer's taxable income, the first $10,000 of a single parent's taxable income and the first $12,000 of a married couple's taxable income.
- Taxpayers would receive a rebate of as much as $300 for singles, $500 for single parents and $600 for married couples. Between July 23 and the end of September, about 10 million checks would be mailed out each week, in the order of the last two digits of the lead taxpayer's Social Security number.
- Marginal personal income tax rates would be cut, effective on July 1, when payroll withholding tables would be altered to reflect the changes. The top rate would be cut from 39.6 percent to 38.6 percent; the 36 percent rate would be cut to 35 percent; the 31 percent rate would be cut to 30 percent; and the 28 percent rate would be cut to 27 percent. The 15 percent bracket would not change.
- The credit that may be claimed for a dependent child younger than 17 would be increased from $500 to $600. The current income limits would not change.
- Taxpayers subject to the alternative minimum tax (AMT) could begin claiming the child credit.
- Parents with earned income above $10,000, but with little or no tax liability, could claim as a refundable credit an amount equal to 10 percent of their income above $10,000 — up to the amount of the regular child credit. Those with three or more children could claim a refundable credit using a slightly more generous formula.
- The exemption limit for taxpayers subject to the AMT would increase to $35,750 from $33,750 for singles and to $49,000 from $45,000 for married couples.
- The due date for corporate estimated tax payments would be delayed from Sept. 15 to Oct.1.
- Holocaust survivors or their heirs could exclude from their gross income any Holocaust restitution payments.

2002 Cost: $37.8 billion

- The top tax rate on estates, gifts and generation-skipping bequests would be cut to 50 percent from 55 percent. The 5 percent surtax charged to the wealthiest recipients of such assets would be repealed. The first $1 million in assets, up from $675,000, would be exempt from such taxes.
- The credit for adoption expenses would be increased to $10,000 for all adoptions, including those of children with special needs. The exclusion from income of employer-provided adoption assistance would be extended. The income ceiling for qualifying for the full credit would be doubled, to $150,000.

- The dependent or child care tax credit would be increased from $2,400 to $3,000, annually and from $4,800 to $6,000 for two or more dependents. The maximum share of expenses that could be claimed as a credit would be increased from 30 percent to 35 percent.
- Married couples filing jointly could earn an additional $1,000 and remain eligible for the earned-income tax credit. The income limit varies depending on the number of children in the family.
- The annual limit on tax-free deposits to education savings accounts would increase to $2,000, from $500. Withdrawals could be used to pay elementary and secondary school expenses. The phase-out range for married taxpayers would rise to twice that of singles, making the phase-out range for married taxpayers $190,000 to $220,000 of modified adjusted gross income.
- The definition of "qualified tuition program" would be expanded to include those offered by private institutions.
- The exclusion for employer-provided undergraduate tuition assistance would become permanent and would be extended to graduate study.
- The 60-month limit on the student loan interest deduction would be repealed. The income phase-out range for the deduction would be increased from $50,000 to $65,000 for singles and from $100,000 to $130,000 for married couples.
- Singles with adjusted gross income below $65,000 and married couples with income below $130,000 — whether they itemize or not — would be allowed to deduct as much as $3,000 in higher education expenses.
- Couples with adjusted gross income below $50,000, and singles below $25,000, could claim a credit of up to $2,000 for contributions to Individual Retirement Accounts (IRAs) or other retirement plans.
- Tax-favored contribution limits to both Roth IRAs, in which contributions are taxed but withdrawals are generally tax-free, and traditional IRAs, in which taxes are generally deferred until funds are withdrawn, would increase to $3,000 annually from $2,000; those older than 50 could contribute an additional $500 annually.
- Tax-deferred employee contribution limits to 401(k) and other pension plans would increase to $11,000 annually from $10,500.
- Those changing jobs could keep employer pension plan contributions — or be "vested" — after three years, down from five years. Other restrictions on changing retirement savings plans when switching employers would be eased.

2003 Cost: $90.6 billion

- The top tax rate on estates, gifts and generation-skipping bequests would be cut to 49 percent.
- Tax-deferred employee contribution limits to 401(k) and other pension plans would be increased to $12,000 annually.
- The special-needs adoption credit could be taken in the year such an adoption was finalized regardless of whether the taxpayers had qualified adoption expenses.

2004 Cost: $107.7 billion

- The top marginal tax rate would be cut from 38.6 percent to 37.6 percent; the 35 percent rate would be cut to 34 percent; the 30 percent rate would be cut to 29 percent; and the 27 percent rate would be cut to 26 percent.

• The deduction for higher-education expenses would increase to $4,000 annually. Taxpayers with incomes between $65,000 and $80,000 for singles, and between $130,000 and $160,000 for married couples, could take a deduction of $2,000.

• The top tax rate on estates, gifts and generation-skipping bequests would be cut to 48 percent. The exemption on estates and generation-skipping bequests would be increased to $1.5 million. The separate deduction for the value of an inherited family-owned business would be repealed.

• Tax-deferred employee contribution limits to 401(k) and other pension plans would increase to $13,000 annually.

• The due date for 20 percent of corporate estimated tax payments would be delayed from Sept. 15 to Oct. 1.

2005 Cost: $107.4 billion

• Married couples filing jointly could claim a standard deduction 74 percent greater than that of single filers, up from the current 60 percent. The portion of their income subject to the 15 percent tax rate would increase to 80 percent greater than that of singles, up from approximately 60 percent.

• Married couples filing jointly could earn an additional $1,000 and remain eligible for the earned-income tax credit.

• The child credit would increase to $700.

• Parents with earned income above $10,000, but with no taxable income, could claim as a refundable credit an amount equal to 15 percent of their income above $10,000 — up to the amount of the regular child credit.

• The top tax rate on estates, gifts and generation-skipping bequests would be cut to 47 percent.

• Tax-deferred employee contribution limits to 401(k) and other pension plans would increase to $14,000 annually.

• Tax-favored contribution limits to IRAs would increase to $4,000 annually.

• The increased exemption limit for taxpayers subject to the AMT, created in 2001, would be repealed Jan. 1.

2006 Cost: $135.2 billion

• The top marginal tax rate would be cut from 37.6 percent to 35 percent; the 34 percent rate would be cut to 33 percent; the 29 percent rate would be cut to 28 percent; and the 26 percent rate would be cut to 25 percent.

• Married couples filing jointly could claim a standard deduction 84 percent greater than that of single filers. The portion of their income subject to the 15 percent tax rate would increase to 87 percent greater than that of singles.

• The current limitations on itemized deductions and personal exemptions — which now affect single tax filers with adjusted gross incomes above $132,950 and married couples with incomes above $199,450 — would be reduced by 33 percent.

• The top tax rate on estates, gifts and generation-skipping bequests would be cut to 46 percent. The exemption on estates and generation-skipping bequests would be increased to $2 million.

• Those older than 50 could make an additional $1,000 tax-favored contribution annually to IRAs.

• Tax-deferred employee contribution limits to 401(k) and other pension plans would increase to $15,000 annually and be indexed for inflation thereafter.

• The deduction for higher-education expenses, created in 2002, would be repealed Jan. 1.

2007 Cost: $151.7 billion

• The top tax rate on estates and generation-skipping gifts would be cut to 45 percent.

• The $2,000 credit that low-income taxpayers could claim for IRA and retirement plan contributions, created in 2002, would be repealed Jan. 1.

• Married couples filing jointly could claim a standard deduction 87 percent greater than that of single filers. The portion of their income subject to the 15 percent tax rate would increase to 93 percent greater than that of singles.

2008 Cost: $160.1 billion

• The current limitations on itemized deductions and personal exemptions would be reduced by an additional 33 percent.

• Tax-favored contribution limits to IRAs would increase to $5,000 annually.

• Married couples filing jointly could claim a standard deduction 90 percent greater than that of single filers. The portion of their income subject to the 15 percent tax rate would increase to double that of singles.

• Married couples filing jointly could earn an additional $1,000 and remain eligible for the earned-income tax credit.

2009 Cost: $167.8 billion

• The child credit would increase to $800.

• Married couples filing jointly could claim a standard deduction double that of single filers.

• The exemption on estates and generation-skipping bequests subject to taxation would be increased to $3.5 million.

• The amount that married couples filing jointly could earn and remain eligible for the earned-income tax credit would begin to be indexed annually for inflation.

2010 Cost: $187 billion

• The child credit would increase to $1,000.

• The current limitations on itemized deductions and personal exemptions would be repealed.

• All taxes on estates and generation-skipping bequests would be repealed.

• The top tax rate on gifts would be reduced to be the same as the top personal marginal income tax rate.

• Capital gains taxes on inherited assets would be calculated on the increased value between the time the deceased person acquired the asset and the time of sale. (Now, the taxes are assessed on the appreciation in value since the asset changed hands after death.) The first $1.3 million in an estate's value would be exempt from the new capital gains tax formula, with an additional $3 million exemption for a surviving spouse.

2011 Cost: $129.5 billion

• Unless extended by Congress, virtually all the provisions would be repealed as of Jan. 1, but the provisions would continue to cost the Treasury through fiscal 2011 — in part because that fiscal year would have begun on Oct. 1, 2010.

A Top High-Tech Tax Wish

Silicon Valley is the symbolic headquarters of one of the first and most ambitious campaigns by businesses seeking to be rewarded in the next tax bill.

Hardware and software makers, in concert with other big businesses, are reviving the effort they launched in the 106th Congress to enhance the tax benefits of buying new computers. They want businesses to be allowed to depreciate — or write off — the cost of buying new machines in fewer than the current five years and programs in fewer than the current three. The effect would be to spur more frequent upgrades of business systems and, proponents say, to spur a sluggish economy. (*Background, 2000 CQ Weekly, p. 1660*)

The next opportunity to win that break is likely to be on a bill that would combine a minimum wage increase with tax breaks for the restaurants and other small businesses that are the most frequent users of minimum wage labor. To that end, Silicon Valley lobbyists have won an important ally in the National Federation of Independent Business, which represents 600,000 small-business owners and is a driving force in negotiating the package of tax breaks. Federation officials say they will support inclusion of an accelerated computer depreciation provision.

"We think that quicker depreciation has a good shot at being added to the tax package for the minimum wage bill," said Ken J. Salaets, a lobbyist for the Information Technology Industry Council, which represents 30 high-tech companies. "It's not something that will just help high-tech companies. It will help the entire economy."

One proposal (S 189), by Sen. Christopher S. Bond, R-Mo., would allow companies to depreciate their hardware and software purchases over two years. A more generous proposal (HR 1411) by House Ways and Means Committee member Jerry Weller, R-Ill., would allow businesses to depreciate, in the year of the purchase, the cost of a broad range of office equipment — not only personal computers and their software but also copiers, wireless telecommunications equipment and computer networking systems. Cost estimates have not been made public, but lobbyists say that Bond's proposal would probably cost at least $50 billion over the next decade.

create opportunities for them.

The most prominent is legislation (S 964, formerly S 277) by Edward M. Kennedy, D-Mass., that would increase the minimum wage by $1.50 per hour to $6.65 in 2003. While Democrats would prefer to enact such a proposal on its own, they may have a difficult time without letting Republicans attach some tax provisions, especially if those provisions are designed to help the types of businesses that most often pay the minimum wage and that warn of dire economic consequences whenever an increase is in the offing.

Such a package was being prepared by GOP leaders — who had concluded that raising the wage was politically necessary — before Sen. James M. Jeffords of Vermont decided to become an Independent, thereby giving control of the agenda to the Democrats. (*Senate, p. 1301; minimum wage background, 2001 CQ Weekly, pp. 830, 779*)

The main question for the GOP may be how much it can add to the minimum wage bill before a substantial number of Democrats decide the price is too high.

"Everybody that held their fire in the first tax bill will probably open fire," said Ed Frank, a spokesman for the National Federation of Independent Business. The small-business lobbying group's list of priorities includes AMT relief for small businesses, an increase in the home office deduction and more flexibility to classify their laborers as independent contractors, rather than employees.

Although Bush has at times mentioned a desire to simplify the tax code, enactment of the reconciliation bill will further complicate it. Bruce Josten, an executive vice president of the U.S. Chamber of Commerce, said his organization would prefer that the tax code be simplified, but since Congress is moving in the opposite direction, it is compelled to play the same game. "We have a long list only because we have a longer and longer tax code," Josten said.

Josten said a wage and tax bill "is going to happen," but he predicted it will include no more than $150 billion in business tax breaks during the next decade.

After the Senate voted 58-33 on May 26 to clear the reconciliation measure, Majority Leader Trent Lott, R-Miss., called the tally an "exceptionally sweet victory" but vowed that he would make sure it was not the GOP's last on tax cuts.

tax bill ... to cut the AMT permanently or at least significantly," said Bruce Bartlett, a senior fellow at the National Center for Policy Analysis. "They kind of left themselves a back door to get back at the tax-cutting issue at a future date."

Another provision that sunsets early and appears a likely candidate to be extended would allow up to $3,000 in deductions annually for the cost of higher education — but only from 2002 to 2005, at a cost of $9.9 billion.

Three-fifths of the package's cost, however, comes after 2006. Critics say the measure's back-loaded nature and limited duration have allowed Bush and congressional Republicans to grossly underestimate the true cost. "What they have done is graduated to a whole new level of accounting gimmickry to disguise the full cost of this tax bill," said Kent Conrad of North Dakota, the top Democrat on the Senate Budget Committee.

The Center on Budget and Policy Priorities, a liberal-leaning think tank that is known for the rigor of its budgetary analysis, issued a report May 29 estimating the package's true direct cost at $1.9 trillion through 2011, on the assumption that none of the provisions would be allowed to sunset. Combined with another $400 billion for additional interest payments on the federal debt that would result from the cuts, the group pegged the measure's total cost at $2.3 trillion.

"In terms of budget gimmickry, this exceeds anything we can recall," said the center's executive director, Robert Greenstein.

Democrats to Provide Targets

While the Democratic takeover of the Senate the week of June 4 might end the tax cut debate — at least temporarily — Republicans and business lobbyists say they expect the new majority will

As the new minority leader, he said, he would push to add tax provisions not only to any minimum wage measure but also to the patients' rights bill (S 872, formerly S 283) that the Democrats say they will put before the Senate after it finishes debating the bill (S 1) to revamp federal education policy. (*Health care, 2001 CQ Weekly, p. 1319; education, p. 1313*)

While a dozen Senate Democrats voted for the tax package, two moderate Republicans voted against it: Lincoln Chafee of Rhode Island and John McCain of Arizona, Bush's main opponent for the party's presidential nomination last year.

"I cannot in good conscience support a tax cut in which so many of the benefits go to the most fortunate among us at the expense of middle-class Americans who most need tax relief," McCain said.

No Republicans opposed the deal in the House, which had voted 240-154 earlier in the morning to adopt the report.

At $874.9 billion through 2011, the cuts in income taxes — all the current rates would be lowered except the 15 percent bracket — are by far the most expensive piece of the bill, accounting for 65 percent of its total. The increase in the child tax credit is the next biggest piece, its $171.8 billion cost accounting for 13 percent of the package's value. The $138 billion in reductions in estate and gift taxes account for 10 percent. Because it is being phased in so slowly, the alleviation of the "marriage penalty" will cost just $63.3 billion in the next decade, 5 percent of the total. (*Graphic, p. 77*)

Said Bill Thomas, R-Calif., the chairman of the House Ways and Means Committee: "$1.35 trillion stretched out over 10 years just doesn't get you what it used to."

Thomas and outgoing Senate Finance Committee Chairman Charles E. Grassley, R-Iowa, had unveiled the conference agreement shortly after 9 p.m. on May 25, but it took the rest of the night for aides to overcome several snags — and exhaustion — to put the deal into legislative language. In the interim, bleary-eyed lawmakers descended on the Capitol, hoping they could cast their votes overnight so they might leave Washington as soon as possible for the one-week Memorial Day recess. While some napped on their office couches, others trolled the halls in search of fresh coffee.

Senate leaders initially had set aside several hours to debate the measure, but they scrapped that plan after Paul Wellstone, D-Minn., began suffering severe back pain, the result of an old wrestling injury. Democrats, who had wanted ample time to deliver speeches criticizing the deal, instead pressed for a quick roll call so that Wellstone could head to Bethesda Naval Hospital for outpatient treatment. The period for the vote was then extended for 45 minutes to accommodate Joseph R. Biden Jr., D-Del., who commutes daily from his home in Wilmington and was expecting a later vote.

Republicans lauded the deal as a victory that would not have been possible without Bush's leadership. "Elections have consequences. Leadership makes a difference," said Sen. Phil Gramm, R-Texas.

But some Democrats criticized the measure as a drain on government resources needed to shore up Social Security and Medicare.

"The Republicans have lit the fuse on a time bomb," said Charles B. Rangel of New York, the top Democrat on the House Ways and Means Committee. "Our kids and grandkids are the real losers today, because they will have to dig out of the hole that this tax bill causes." ◆

The Final Tax Votes

The deepest tax cut in 20 years completed its path through Congress on a pair of back-to-back votes May 26, during the first Saturday meetings of the 107th Congress. The House voted 240-154 to adopt the conference report on the reconciliation bill (HR 1836), which would cut taxes $1.35 trillion between fiscal 2001 and fiscal 2011. Just 74 minutes later, the Senate voted 58-33 to clear the bill.

The roster below shows the lawmakers who were not in the mainstream of their parties on these votes. Support was more bipartisan in the Senate, where a dozen Democrats (24 percent of all Democratic senators) voted for the measure while a pair of Republicans (4 percent) voted against it. In the House, the legislation won the backing of just 28 Democrats (13 percent of the chamber's Democratic membership), while every Republican who was present voted for the measure. In both chambers, 9 percent of the membership did not vote.

HOUSE

Democrats YES (28)

Abercrombie	Barcia	Berkley	Capps	Carson	Clement	Condit
Cramer	Dooley	Gordon	Hall *(Texas)*	Hooley	Israel	John
Larsen	Lucas	Matheson	McCarthy *(N.Y.)*	Moore	Peterson	Roemer
Ross	Sandlin	Schiff	Shows	Tauscher	Traficant	Turner

Democrats NOT VOTING (29)

Ackerman	Baca	Becerra
Bentsen	Bishop	Blumenauer
Boyd	Clayton	Coyne
Doggett	Hall *(Ohio)*	Hoeffel
Honda	Kaptur	Lipinski
McCarthy *(Mo.)*	McDermott	Meek
Millender-McDonald	Moakley	Oberstar
Price	Rahall	Rodriguez
Rush	Towns	Waters
Waxman	Wynn	

Independent NO (1)

Sanders

Independent YES (1)

Goode

Republicans NOT VOTING (10)

Cubin	Gillmor	Houghton	
Isakson	Jones *(N.C.)*	King	
Quinn	Scarborough	Spence	Walsh

SENATE

Democrats YES (12)

Baucus	Breaux	Carnahan	Cleland	Feinstein	Johnson
Kohl	Landrieu	Lincoln	Miller	Nelson *(Neb.)*	Torricelli

Democrats NOT VOTING (7)

Akaka	Bingaman	Boxer	
Harkin	Kerry	Leahy	Murray

Republicans NO (2)

Chafee   McCain

Republicans NOT VOTING (2)

Domenici   Enzi

Education Bill Nears Final Hurdle With 'Deal Breakers' Swept Aside

Democrats may try delay measure in conference to push for higher spending

Whatever else happens, the lawmakers who will merge the House and Senate education bills have a powerful reason to succeed: Congress has too much invested in the effort to let it fall apart.

When the Senate passed its bill (HR 1) June 14 to reauthorize the 1965 Elementary and Secondary Education Act (ESEA), the 91-8 vote — a margin even more stunning than the 384-45 vote in the House May 23 — left little room for either side to reject the version that emerges from the House-Senate conference.

The debate consumed six weeks of floor time and was full of temporary flare-ups. But after two of the strongest votes imaginable on such an ambitious overhaul, neither Democrats nor Republicans are likely to decide that the remaining trade-offs are too difficult to make — or that any crisis is truly fatal.

"The reforms in this bill reflect the core principles of my education agenda: accountability, flexibility, local control and more choices for parents," President Bush said in a statement.

"The message is that help is on the way," said Edward M. Kennedy, D-Mass., who took over as the bill's manager this month and parked himself on the Senate floor for almost the entire six weeks to make sure the bill bore a strong Democratic stamp. (*Kennedy, p. 91*)

Even Christopher J. Dodd, D-Conn., who had championed two amendments that Republicans warned would be "deal breakers" if they were approved, simply shrugged off his defeats on both proposals. One, which would have exempted after-school programs from a block grant demonstration program, was rejected, 47-51.

The other, which would have required states to even out the financing disparities between rich and poor school districts, was defeated, 42-58.

"What were they so afraid of?" a grinning Dodd asked after the school financing amendment failed.

That does not mean the conference will be crisis-free. For Democrats and their Senate allies, including James M. Jeffords, I-Vt., the biggest fight will be to persuade Bush to back up the bill's centerpiece — annual test-

ing in reading and math for children in grades 3 through 8 — with more money for poor schools.

To do that, they may keep the education bill holed up in conference until Bush agrees to higher education spending levels in the fiscal 2002 Labor, Health and Human Services, and Education appropriations measure.

That would be a hard strategy to follow, since House appropriators say they are unlikely to start on Labor-HHS until September. Nevertheless, Senate Majority Leader Tom Daschle, D-S.D., raised the possibility of linking the education and spending bills.

"I told the president . . . it was not our desire to complete this work until we have some understanding about the degree of resources that will be made available for all of the issues that we're confronting here," Daschle said.

Daschle is under pressure from Dodd and other Democrats to stall the education bill as leverage to get a better funding deal. If Bush

Quick Contents

The Senate easily passed its education overhaul bill. Now conferees will have to solve several problems, from penalties for low school test scores to targeting Title I funding.

Not to Be Overlooked

These provisions in the Senate education bill (HR 1) have received little attention in the debate but could have a significant impact:

- **Report cards:** Starting in the 2002-03 school year, states and school districts would have to publish "report cards" listing all schools that had been ordered to improve because of poor student performance. State report cards would have to list test scores broken down by race, gender, ethnicity and other subgroups.

- **Dropout prevention:** The bill would authorize $250 million in fiscal 2002 to help states set up dropout prevention programs. The issue is considered important because some critics of President Bush's annual testing program fear it could lead to higher dropout rates, especially among minority students.

- **Rural flexibility:** Rural school districts with fewer than 600 students would be able to combine funds from different federal education programs and spend them on their greatest needs. The provision addresses rural districts' complaints that they receive too little money to make a difference in any particular area because funds for many programs are doled out according to enrollment.

- **Teacher liability:** No teacher could face punitive damages for disciplining a child unless there was "willful or criminal misconduct" or a "conscious, flagrant indifference to the rights or safety of the individual harmed." Supporters say the provision would prevent frivolous lawsuits, but critics believe it is intended to protect the use of corporal punishment.

does not offer one, Senate Democrats who voted for the education bill the first time around might not vote for the conference report, Dodd told reporters.

For Republicans, meanwhile, the Senate bill's price tag itself is an issue. It would authorize approximately $33 billion for ESEA programs in fiscal 2002, compared with the current $18.6 billion. That does not include $8.8 billion the Senate added for special education under the Individuals with Disabilities Education Act (IDEA) — $181 billion over 10 years — even though that law (PL 94-142) is not part of ESEA.

Republicans are also concerned that a "Straight A's" demonstration program that would let seven states and 25 school districts turn most federal education programs into block grants will be dropped under pressure from Senate and House Democrats.

If it is not in the final version of the bill, "you'll lose an awful lot of conservatives in both the Senate and the House" who want to give the states greater flexibility, said Tim Hutchinson, R-Ark.

However, some education groups that have supported "Straight A's" are now signaling that they will not battle to the death for it, especially when other flexibility proposals might pick up greater support in both parties.

One such proposal gaining support is a House provision that would let school districts transfer 50 percent of most program funds from one initiative to another. House Democrats say that is a better flexibility compromise than the "Straight A's" demonstration since it would preserve individual programs while letting local authorities decide where to spend the money.

"We like them both. We're not going to oppose anything that allows local folks to have more control," said Lisa Graham Keegan, chief executive officer of the Education Leaders Council, a group of state education officials that has influenced the Republican education agenda.

Groups that oppose "Straight A's," including teachers' unions and urban school districts, feel more strongly about it and are more likely to cause trouble if it remains in the bill. That squares with House Democrats' insistence that they will not even

consider it.

"Straight A's puts the flexibility in the wrong hands," said Jeff Simering, a lobbyist with the Council of the Great City Schools, which represents large urban districts and has strong ties to the Democrats.

An issue that may unite education and business groups is a mutual dislike of provisions in both the House and the Senate bills for determining how low test scores would have to be before states and schools faced sanctions.

Both bills would cut school funding if students did not make "adequate yearly progress" in reading and math. But education and business groups seem to agree that the House formula is too strict and the Senate formula is so complicated that no school official would ever understand it.

The House bill would require all students to obtain "proficiency" in reading and math in 12 years, a target critics believe most schools could never reach. The Senate version would set a goal of proficiency for every student within 10 years, but the penalties would kick in only if students' scores did not improve by at least 1 percentage point a year, averaged out over three years. That would guard against year-to-year fluctuations, but analysts say it would also make the system too complex.

Some education and business lobbyists want the negotiators to wipe the slate clean and start over. "The House may be too high a standard, but the Senate is too watered down," said Susan L. Traiman, director of the Business Roundtable's education initiative. The

group is composed of corporate chief executives.

Hot-Button Issues

The bill's passage came just as the debate was starting to wander into the kinds of divisive social issues both sides had hoped to avoid.

On the final day of debate, the Senate adopted amendments that would allow schools to expel disabled students for bad behavior and stop school districts from banning the Boy Scouts of America from using school facilities, as several districts are doing to protest the group's refusal to admit homosexuals.

The discipline amendment, by Jeff Sessions, R-Ala., initially failed on a 50-50 tie vote.

However, no one tabled the motion to reconsider the vote — a routine procedure — so Sessions' proposal got new life. The Senate then agreed, 51-47, to reconsider the amendment and adopted it by voice vote.

That all but guarantees that the provision — which would let educators send special-education students to alternative schools if they committed serious offenses such as bringing weapons to class — will end up in the conference report, since the House bill contains similar language.

Sessions said IDEA disciplinary rules have been a source of frustration for many teachers, who believe they undermine their ability to treat special-education students like other students.

But Tom Harkin, D-Iowa, said Sessions' amendment would "turn the clock back and segregate these kids as we did in the past." He proposed an alternative that would have allowed schools to expel students only if their behavior was not related to their disability. It was rejected, 36-64.

The Boy Scouts amendment, by Jesse Helms, R-N.C., would cut off federal aid to districts that refuse to let the organization use school facilities. It was adopted, 51-49.

But Robert C. Byrd, D-W.Va., pointed out that the language — which would have protected the Boy Scouts "or any other youth group . . . that prohibit[s] the acceptance of homosexuals," was so broad that it could have shielded hate groups as well.

So Byrd added language, ap-

proved by voice vote, to narrow protected groups to more than 100 "patriotic societies," including the Boys and Girls Clubs of America and Little League Baseball, Inc.

The Senate then adopted additional language by Barbara Boxer, D-Calif., to give the groups equal access to school facilities regardless of their policies toward homosexuals — without threatening the loss of federal funds if school districts violate the policy. Her amendment was adopted, 52-47.

By the time the Senate voted on vouchers — once a centerpiece of the GOP education agenda — it seemed merely an exercise in proving to conservative groups that the votes were not there.

The Senate rejected, 41-58, an amendment by Judd Gregg, R-N.H., to establish 10 pilot programs to test Bush's idea of allowing parents of children in underperforming public schools to use federal aid for private school tuition.

The Senate did adopt, by voice vote, a public school choice amendment by Gregg and Thomas R. Carper, D-Del., that would authorize $125 million in grants to help communities that allow children in underperforming schools to attend better public schools.

The amendment also would authorize $400 million to help provide facilities and startup costs for charter schools, which are freed from most state and local regulations as long as their academic results improve.

In addition, the Senate revisited a favorite Democratic cause — school construction — adopting an amendment by Dianne Feinstein, D-Calif., that would allow some federal education funds to be used to build small schools.

The proposal, adopted 52-46, succeeded in large part because it did not dedicate specific funds to the initiative.

Targeting Poor Schools

One new conference committee issue emerged when the Senate adopted an amendment by Mary L. Landrieu, D-La., that would require Congress to target any new Title I funds specifically to school districts with the highest concentrations of poor children. The vote was 57-36.

Landrieu used the amendment, which is not in the House version, to call attention to the fact that Title I aid, meant to help poor schools, often

Lieberman, left, Sessions and Jeffords take questions following the education bill vote on June 14. Democrats praised Jeffords' contributions as floor manager before he left the GOP.

does not reach them.

Appropriators have allowed the funds to continue to flow to districts that are no longer poor, according to lawmakers and education groups, because no one wants to give up federal aid.

Since the current $8.6 billion in Title I aid reaches just a third of all eligible poor children, they say, poor schools start off with a small pot of federal funds and then get even less than they should.

According to Landrieu, one in five school districts where 50 percent to 75 percent of students are poor get no Title I funds, while some wealthier districts get a disproportionate share. "The children who need the most help are getting the least money," she said.

Landrieu's amendment is likely to face problems because it is opposed by Harkin, the new chairman of the Labor-HHS Appropriations Subcommittee.

Harkin said he voted against Landrieu's amendment because it would give states an excuse not to do more to equalize their own school financing, which is based on local property taxes and thus leaves huge differences between rich and poor school districts. "They have a totally unequal system based in property taxes, and they want us to come in and bail them out?" Harkin said. "It lets states say, 'Oh well

. . . we don't have to do anything.' "

Harkin, who will write the Senate Labor-HHS bill, was one of four Democrats to vote against the Landrieu amendment. And he vowed to fight the provision in conference. "I'm not going to let that stand," he said.

That is an especially bad sign for Landrieu's amendment, because it basically repeats language Congress approved in 1994, the last time ESEA was reauthorized.

The 1994 law (PL 103-382) established "targeted grants" that required Congress to direct all new Title I money to poor schools while leaving current spending under the old formula — a compromise needed to make sure no district would lose money it already received. Despite that compromise, appropriators never funded the grants. (*1994 Almanac, p. 383*)

Supporters of Landrieu's amendment say appropriators stuck to the old formula because they did not want school districts to forfeit any increases they could have received, let alone take a cut.

Bush supports targeted Title I grants, however, and Landrieu hopes that means the White House will fight for her amendment during conference negotiations. ◆

Welfare Overhaul's Next Wave

Bush proposes other uses for aid money; Democrats call for a focus on reducing poverty

An instructor at Philadelphia's Transitional Work Corporation talks to welfare recipients about the skills they will need to succeed — an issue Congress will face when it reauthorizes the 1996 welfare law.

It was just a sentence buried under a mountain of budget proposals, but that one line in President Bush's first budget may have captured the essence of the coming debate in Congress over the future structure of the welfare system.

In the fiscal 2002 outline he sent to Capitol Hill on Feb. 28, Bush said states should be encouraged to set up tax credits to reward people who give money to private charities. No problem so far; lawmakers from both parties say charities should get more help.

The catch is how Bush proposed paying for the tax credits. He wants to let states dip into a pot of money that used to be politically untouchable: the funds for Temporary Assistance for Needy Families (TANF), the program commonly known as "welfare."

With that proposal, Bush stepped squarely into the heart of the congressional debate over the upcoming reauthorization of the 1996 law (PL 104-193) that wiped out the old welfare system and built a new, time-limited one in its place. (*1996 Almanac, p. 6-3*)

Congress is just starting to turn to the task, but the outlines of the debate are already clear as lawmakers take a good hard look at the biggest social policy change of the 1990s.

Many Republicans will argue that the battle against welfare dependency is essentially over — caseloads have dropped by more than 50 percent, and there are 6.9 million fewer people on the rolls — and that lawmakers should feel free to spend TANF money on other things. Democrats and some moderate Republicans will argue the opposite: The re-

maining welfare recipients have more serious problems that will require just as much federal spending, if not more, to help them leave.

Without saying a word officially, Bush may have picked an early fight with Democrats.

By allowing states to spend welfare funds on other initiatives, the Bush proposal would set "a dangerous precedent," said Benjamin L. Cardin of Maryland, the ranking Democrat on the House Ways and Means Subcommittee on Human Resources. "We should be moving in the opposite direction." Administration officials did not respond to requests for comment on the proposal.

Five years ago, the welfare overhaul produced a flood of emotional and bitter exchanges. Rep. John Lewis, D-Ga., called it "mean" and "downright lowdown." House Majority Whip Tom DeLay, R-Texas, called the criticisms "one last, desperate attempt by the minority to cling to the status quo."

Those kinds of exchanges are unlikely to be repeated this time, because welfare has largely disappeared from the political debate. When Bush first ran for governor of Texas in 1994, "welfare reform" was one of his biggest themes. In his presidential campaign last year, he barely mentioned it.

But the question Congress faces is still important to millions of poor families: What comes next?

Among Republicans, the ideas include toughening work requirements, encouraging marriage and curbing out-of-wedlock births and creating a greater role for faith-based social services. The faith-based proposals are in keeping with the direction Bush has signaled, but they come at a time of growing doubts on Capitol Hill. (*2001 CQ Weekly, Story, p. 609*)

Democrats, meanwhile, will try to ease the program's time limits and shift the emphasis to reducing poverty, not just caseloads.

The reauthorization will be many lawmakers' first look back at the decision to end welfare as an entitlement, available to all families poor enough to qualify, and replace it with a block grant that limits every poor family to five years of federal assistance — after which adults are expected to go to work.

For both parties, the terms of the debate have changed. For Republicans, the task will be to preserve and build upon a welfare overhaul that they consider one of their greatest successes.

"If it ain't broke, don't fix it," said Rep. Wally Herger, R-Calif., the new chairman of the Human Resources Subcommittee, which has jurisdiction over TANF and held its first reauthorization hearing March 15.

"I think it's exceeded everybody's expectations as the most successful legislation in memory," said Rep. E. Clay Shaw Jr., R-Fla., one of the authors of the 1996 law.

For Democrats, the goal is no longer to fight time limits or work requirements, but to make sure poor families are being treated fairly within the boundaries of the new system. They want to call attention to the story they see behind the plummeting caseloads and declining poverty rates: the single mothers who have been unable to leave welfare or thrive in their new jobs.

"The best you can say is that some people are doing as well as can be expected under the circumstances, and others are doing worse," said Sen. Paul Wellstone, D-Minn., who voted against the 1996 overhaul.

Already, some state and local welfare-to-work programs are experimenting with new ways to help "hard-to-serve" welfare recipients — those who have no high school diploma, little or no work history, little knowledge of English, or more serious problems such as mental illness or substance addiction. The lessons of these programs could become important as Congress looks for ways to deal with the changing face of welfare.

They could be particularly important to moderate Republicans, who appreciate the overhaul's successes, but

Sinuon Mel said a transitional work program taught her job skills. Now she is studying for a high school diploma.

are mindful that many poor families have not shared in them.

"We definitely want them to get into the work force. We're not going to go back on that," said Nancy L. Johnson, R-Conn., who chaired the Human Resources Subcommittee in the 106th Congress and remains on the panel. "But we want them to move out of that minimum wage job and up the economic ladder. Not enough states are paying attention to that."

The Other Strands

The TANF reauthorization must be done by October 2002, when the program expires. At the same time, lawmakers will be debating what to do about the other major strands of the safety net for poor families. Food stamps, child-care assistance and transitional Medicaid health insurance coverage for welfare recipients who have gone to work all must be renewed by the same date.

Smaller pieces of the 1996 welfare law, including a contingency fund for states with high unemployment rates and grants to help states with rapid population growth, must be reauthorized by October 2001.

The broad numbers have made the overhaul look like an unqualified suc-

cess. Those numbers, however, do not tell the whole story.

Overall poverty rates are lower than they have been since 1979. In 1996, 13.7 percent of Americans were officially classified as poor, with an income of no more than $13,874 for a family of three; by 1999, that had fallen to 11.8 percent. The trend held up for children and for every major racial and ethnic category. (*Chart, p. 87*)

Most low-income mothers who have left welfare have found jobs, and never-married single mothers — the people most likely to stay on welfare for long periods, according to numerous studies — are moving into the work force in record numbers and earning more than ever.

"The good news is that we have a program that even the critics would admit has worked very well," said Herger.

But some critics say the overhaul left too many people behind. "I think people feel like the problem has been solved — which they shouldn't, because a lot of people have been hurt," said Peter Edelman, one of three Department of Health and Human Services (HHS) officials who resigned in protest in 1996 when President Bill Clinton decided to sign the legislation.

Edelman and other foes of the 1996 law say their greatest fear has been realized: Many families that have left welfare are still struggling. They cite a December study by the Urban Institute, a Washington think tank, that said about a third of former welfare recipients had to skip meals or eat less. About 46 percent said they had been unable to pay rent or utility bills at some point within the previous 12 months.

Many other former recipients have not found jobs. Pamela Loprest, a senior research associate at the Urban Institute and the author of the study, said about a quarter of former welfare recipients had no earnings after leaving the system. Some probably shifted to disability payments, she said, but about 17 percent could not be found.

Those people "are the big concern," said Loprest. "We don't have a good picture of what's happened to these people and how they're surviving."

Even employers who are trying to make the new system work warn Con-

The Changing Face of Welfare

Welfare Rolls Decline

Since the 1996 welfare overhaul, nearly 6.9 million fewer people are on the rolls, a decline of 54 percent.

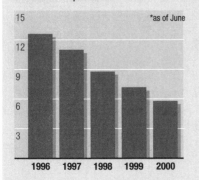

as of June

SOURCE: Department of Health and Human Services, U.S. Census Bureau

Poverty Rates Fall

Supporters of welfare overhaul say it has contributed to a drop in the percentage of people living below the overall poverty level — $13,874 for a family of three in 1999.

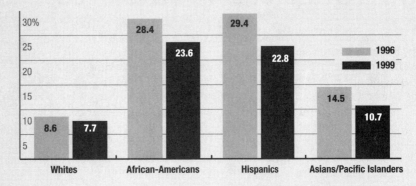

	1996	1999
Whites	8.6	7.7
African-Americans	28.4	23.6
Hispanics	29.4	22.8
Asians/Pacific Islanders	14.5	10.7

Former Recipients Struggle

The Urban Institute interviewed 1,206 adults who stopped receiving welfare between 1997 and 1999. Here are some of its findings from a study released in December 2000.

Employed: 64 percent

Unemployed but worked recently: 10.8 percent

Never employed: 17 percent

Returned to welfare: 21.9 percent

Median hourly wage: $7.15

Median annual earnings*: $16,320

Has to eat less or skip meals: 32.7 percent

Could not pay mortgage, rent or utility bills at some point in last 12 months: 46.1 percent

Adults without health insurance: 37 percent

Children without health insurance: 17 percent

* Assuming 12 months employment

SOURCES: Urban Institute, U.S. Census Bureau

CQ PHOTO/SCOTT J. FERRELL

A counselor at a Philadelphia work program helps clients fill out time cards.

gress not to declare victory too quickly.

"It's easy to gloss over the fact that there are still some major challenges," said Dorian Friedman, vice president of policy at the Welfare to Work Partnership, a national coalition of businesses that promise to hire former recipients. "A lot of the people who have left the rolls and gone to work are still poor."

The biggest unknown is what will happen as more families start running into the time limits on federal TANF benefits. So far, an estimated 60,000 people have hit time limits in 21 states.

No studies have looked specifically at how those people have fared, because the limits have kicked in too recently, but news reports from those states suggest many recipients have

gotten extensions. Some mothers who lost their benefits ended up "broke, sick and depressed," according to a report in The Tampa Tribune in October 1999, a year after Florida's limit on welfare benefits took effect.

Over the next two years, the first time limits will kick in for families in another 27 states and the District of Columbia. States can continue benefits to children and even entire families if the states pick up the tab themselves, but it is not clear how many will do so.

It is also not clear how much of the welfare overhaul's statistical success has been due to the booming economy. Supporters say prosperity alone cannot explain the drops in welfare caseloads or poverty rates, because neither declined in the mid-1980s, when the

economy was also strong.

"This has very little to do with the economy," said Rep. Shaw, "and everything to do with the tremendous success of welfare reform."

Still, "there's a concern that an economic downturn could reverse a lot of the gains that we've achieved," said Elaine M. Ryan, acting executive director of the American Public Human Services Association, which represents state human services administrators.

Moderate Republicans, Democrats and state officials all believe they will have a battle on their hands to prevent conservative Republicans from cutting TANF funds.

Ever since former House Budget Committee Chairman John R. Kasich, R-Ohio (1983-2001), wrote a non-

Private Group Tries to Ease Toughest Welfare-to-Work Cases

PHILADELPHIA — A block from city hall, the Transitional Work Corporation helps "hard-to-serve" welfare recipients, those who are having the toughest time finding work.

The job of this public-private partnership is to reconcile the message of the new system — everyone who can work should — with the reality that many welfare recipients are about to hit the program's five-year time limit and cannot simply be thrown into the job market and expected to succeed.

This is one of the key issues Congress will face when it turns to reauthorization of the 1996 welfare overhaul (PL 104-193): How to make sure people who leave the welfare rolls get the help they need to survive.

The Philadelphia program strikes a balance that, in the eyes of its supporters, shows the solution does not have to be complicated. After participants enroll, they get a part-time job at a city government office or nonprofit organization. They typically work 25 hours a week, aided by mentors in the workplace and job coaches at Transitional Work offices.

That, plus skills training at the program's offices, is supposed to give former recipients the experience they need to move to a permanent job in the private sector six months later. In

the meantime, they receive allowances for such essentials as child care, clothing and transportation.

Since the program began in October 1998, officials say, it has placed more than 3,100 welfare recipients in transitional jobs. Of those, 1,084 have gone on to permanent, unsubsidized jobs; another 521 are currently working in transitional jobs. The remainder dropped out, said officials, either because they did not follow the rules or because late-term pregnancies left them unable to work.

The lesson for Congress, according to those who run the program and those it has helped, is that the nation's remaining welfare recipients need a chance to gain skills before they can move into the work force. Further, subsidies for health insurance, child care and transportation may have to be continued long after former recipients have landed jobs.

"Everybody should go to work," said Richard Greenwald, the corporation's president and chief executive officer. "But you've got to support them."

In other words, the program's counselors say, lawmakers must recognize that many newly working mothers are not earning enough to survive without Medicaid, food stamps and child-care assistance.

"All of the support systems are taken away one by one," said Achée O'Quinn, who steers low-income mothers off welfare and into jobs. "A lot of them are tempted to go back."

Which Comes First?

Before 1996, most welfare recipients were placed in education and training programs to prepare them for the workplace, but critics said those programs dragged on forever.

By the time Congress passed the 1996 overhaul, the consensus had shifted: Welfare offices were told it was best to place recipients in a job — any job — quickly. That approach may have helped shrink welfare rolls, but employers say it also gave them a lot of unprepared workers.

"[Employers] expect to train the workers in the hard skills that are necessary to do the job," said Dorian Friedman, vice president of policy at the Welfare to Work Partnership, a national coalition of businesses that have promised to hire recipients.

But when they get applicants who do not know how to deal with coworkers or customers, she said, "employers don't feel like that is their problem. . . . By the time an applicant comes to them for a job, that stuff should have been taken care of."

The Philadelphia program's solu-

binding budget resolution for fiscal 1999 that called for TANF cuts, the money has been tempting fiscal conservatives. (*1998 Almanac, p. 6-12*)

"I don't think the states are going to get a pass on [TANF cuts]," warned one Senate Republican aide. "Obviously, state budgets have been relatively healthy."

But state officials say they need the funding because the people still on welfare are more likely to have multiple problems, such as mental illness and substance abuse, and thus will be more expensive to move off the rolls.

"The people who are left on the rolls have a lot of problems, and they

need help," said Rep. Johnson, who vowed to fight any TANF budget cuts.

The Players

When welfare legislation begins moving in committee, it will be handled by a cast that is relatively new to welfare policy.

In the House, Herger plans to focus the hearings on "ways to make welfare reform work even better." That could include deciding what to do for welfare recipients who have not been able to find jobs, he said, and ways to "help families stay together and make sure children have two parents."

Herger also brings a longtime pet

cause to the debate: eliminating welfare fraud. He is likely to revive a 1999 proposal to crack down on prison inmates who "illegally receive hundreds of millions of dollars in welfare payments each year."

In the Senate, the Finance Committee has a new chairman, Republican Charles E. Grassley of Iowa, who says the question of how ex-welfare recipients are doing will be critical when the panel starts to write its reauthorization plan.

"We need to know as much as possible about how these former welfare recipients got back in the work force, if they stayed on the job, and how far

"Everybody should go to work," says Richard Greenwald, president and CEO of the Transitional Work Corporation. "But you've got to support them."

tion is to put welfare recipients to work in a transitional job while they receive training in computers, English and math and learn how to deal with customers and co-workers.

Those who have been through the Transitional Work Corporation program say the approach works.

"When they said, 'You've only got five years' [before welfare benefits end], I said, 'Oh my God, what am I going to do?'" said Sinuon Mel, a former welfare recipient. She said she had no work skills and no high school diploma when she joined the program; now she is getting computer skills training and practicing for her general equivalency diploma while doing clerical work in the program's offices.

The nonprofit corporation stretches its budget to rent expensive office space a block from city hall. Program officials say they want to send a message: Everyone in the program is now in the economic mainstream.

The difficulty, however, is not limited to getting that first job. Keeping it, and staying afloat financially, can be just as hard.

For example, when a low-income mother leaves welfare for work, she remains eligible for food stamps if her family's income is low enough. She can also get Medicaid for up to a year and child-care assistance through the Child Care and Development Fund, a federal-state program.

The problem, say caseworkers, is that many people who leave welfare are never informed they can continue to receive temporary Medicaid coverage. As a result, Medicaid enrollment dropped for the first time in years shortly after the welfare overhaul began. (*2000 CQ Weekly, p. 2066*)

Many former welfare recipients also have trouble getting food stamps, say state officials, because federal rules make it tough to keep families on food stamps automatically after they have lost welfare benefits.

For example, when some 3,700 Ohio families hit their welfare time limits in October, the Department of Agriculture told state officials they would have to determine eligibility on a family-by-family basis.

"[Welfare reform has] brought a part of the population out of the house that wouldn't normally be out of the house," said Elmore Johnson, the Transitional Work Corporation's vice president for employer services. "[But] they can't leave them halfway. . . . There should be enough money to support their families."

they've moved to self-sufficiency," Grassley said in a statement.

Johnson and Cardin, who are well-versed in the complexities of welfare policy, and Shaw, who has the institutional knowledge of the debates that shaped the 1996 law, also are expected to play important roles in any discussions of welfare overhaul.

There are also some lawmakers who may not be centrally involved in the committee work but are likely to take an active role in floor debate. They include Sen. Sam Brownback, R-Kan., who believes reauthorization efforts should focus on faith-based organizations that could set up mentoring programs for people who are having the hardest time leaving the rolls.

"This is part of compassionate conservatism," said Brownback. "I would hope we would see more of these steps taken, because we've reduced the welfare rolls a lot."

Lawmakers also will hear from a colleague who has seen welfare firsthand: Rep. Lynn Woolsey, D-Calif., who relied on government aid to supplement her wages when she was a single mother raising three children in the 1970s.

"My fear is that the debate will be about, 'Well, who are these people who are still on welfare? Maybe we should punish them more,'" said Woolsey. "You know what? We're just going to hurt children."

The fact that Bush has not given more clues about his ideas could be a problem for Republicans, who are working with a GOP White House for the first time in eight years and are trying to coordinate their policies with the new administration.

Bush indicated that welfare will not be a back-burner issue when he selected former Wisconsin Gov. Tommy G. Thompson to run HHS, which oversees TANF. As governor, Thompson imposed strict time limits on welfare, but he also argued that states should spend more on services such as child care, health care and transportation that low-income mothers need when they join the work force.

However, in testimony at a March 14 hearing of the Ways and Means Committee, Thompson had little to say about the subject. "We really haven't put that much emphasis on TANF reauthorization yet," he said.

Thompson is not the only one keeping his silence. One House GOP leadership aide said welfare overhaul is "not on our radar screen yet."

Democrats have no shortage of ideas for smoothing the rough edges they see in the new system. Among other things, they want bonuses to states that reduce poverty and exemptions from time limits for welfare recipients who work part time.

They say they are more focused on welfare than Republicans because they expected to take the House back in 2000. "We had to figure out what we were going to do," said Jim McDermott, D-Wash., a member of the Ways and Means Human Resources Subcommittee. House Republicans "can't do anything because they haven't heard what [Bush] wants."

The Issues

Democrats have begun to accept the general idea of time limits, and Republicans have promised to look more closely at people who are not faring well under the new rules. All signs, however, indicate that the two sides will continue to talk past each other on most of the issues. These areas are likely to be the biggest flashpoints:

• **Funding.** The biggest concern of moderate Republicans, Democrats, and state officials will be to maintain the current funding for the TANF block grant, set at $16.5 billion a year through fiscal 2002.

Democrats also are likely to push for more child care funding, a move that is likely to be resisted by both conservative Republicans and moderates such as Johnson. New workers need to be helped with transitional services, Johnson said, but "all of this should be able to be done with the resources we're already providing."

• **Work requirements.** For conservative Republicans, one goal will be to strengthen employment guidelines.

Under the 1996 law, states had to move at least 50 percent of their welfare recipients into jobs or "work activities" such as subsidized employment, on-the-job-training and community service by fiscal 2002. But they could also satisfy the requirement if people simply left the rolls — and so many did so that those who remained did not have to work.

As a matter of principle, however, Republicans believe people should work in exchange for welfare benefits — so they may push for new work requirements for those who have not left.

"Just the threat of a work requirement was moving people off of welfare" even before the 1996 law took effect, said one House Republican aide.

• **Stopping the clock.** One major goal for Democrats will be to change the time limit for people who are working. In 1999, 28 percent of welfare recipients were working but did not earn enough to get by without TANF benefits. Under the 1996 law, that assistance counts against their five-year time limit.

Another likely Democratic objective will be to create more exceptions to the five-year limit for people who have been unable to leave welfare and are about to lose their benefits.

The 1996 law allows states to exempt 20 percent of their caseloads from the time limit because of "hardship." But some Democrats and advocates for the poor believe if the remaining welfare recipients have more serious problems than the ones who left, the 20 percent exemption will not be enough.

"Some people in that other 80 percent are going to be pushed off a cliff," said Wellstone.

• **Faith-based initiatives.** The debate will offer Republicans a chance to expand on Bush's call for more faith-based initiatives. (2001 CQ Weekly, p. 222)

The welfare overhaul already allows federal funds to be used for welfare-to-work programs run by religious groups, a concept Bush wants to expand to a broader range of social services. When Bush outlined his faith-based initiatives proposal during the presidential campaign, he called it "the next bold step of welfare reform."

Brownback sees it the same way. "We need to do more than just say, "Go get a job,'" he said. "But we don't think the old way helped either — just give them a little bit of money and hope everything works out. You've got to work with them on the inside, and then you've got to hold their hand when they get on the outside."

• **Reducing poverty.** Democrats want to do more to reduce poverty. Cardin said the reauthorization proposal he plans to introduce later this year will include bonus payments to states that do the best job of lowering poverty rates.

"Yes, we want people to move off of welfare. Yes, we want two-parent families. Yes, we want families to stay together," said Cardin. "But we also want families out of poverty, and right now that is not an objective of welfare reform."

• **Reducing out-of-wedlock births.** Some conservatives believe the key to trimming welfare dependency further is to keep low-income women off the rolls. They say that means doing a better job of reducing births among unmarried women and promoting marriage.

"What we have is a kind of national neurosis where we don't talk about why child poverty exists or why the welfare state exists," said Robert Rector, a senior research fellow at the Heritage Foundation, a conservative think tank. "Both of them exist because of the erosion of marriage."

Such statements make some conservative Republicans nervous because they fear efforts to encourage marriage could lead to new government programs. Others, however, say there is nothing wrong with the message itself.

"What would be the single biggest thing we could do to reduce child poverty? Maintain intact homes," said Sen. Jeff Sessions, R-Ala. "When you split up a family, there will never be as much money as when families stay together."

• **The needs of Hispanics.** One significant change in the welfare rolls since 1996 has been the growing proportion of Hispanic women receiving aid.

The reason Hispanic women are not leaving the rolls as quickly as white and African-American women is that many lack basic job skills, said Eric Rodriguez, director of the Economic Mobility Project at the National Council of La Raza, an advocacy group. And they are often sent to English classes instead of skills training programs.

To address the issue, La Raza wants Congress to shift away from the 1996 law's "work first" philosophy and put more emphasis on education, training and better access to transitional services.

"The job isn't done," said Friedman of the Welfare to Work Partnership. "There's still a lot more that lawmakers can do." ◆

Kennedy: Pragmatic Gladiator Leads the Managed-Care Fight

Fiery rhetoric, canny negotiating are the liberal senator's hallmark

To an outsider, the Senate debate on overhauling federal education policy would have looked intense and furious. Sen. Edward M. Kennedy was on the floor every minute, his voice at times rising to a shout. His reading glasses came on and off so quickly it seemed they would fly across the Senate chamber.

At one point, the Massachusetts Democrat went into full red-faced, raspy-voiced mode as he fought an amendment to let schools expel students with disabilities who sell drugs or bring guns to school. "We're not going to march backward," Kennedy bellowed at George F. Allen, R-Va., who had just spoken in favor of the amendment.

Behind the scenes, however, the showman disappeared and the dealmaker took over.

Kennedy had spent weeks holed up in the Senate library with Republicans, Democrats and White House officials to defuse longtime disagreements over education proposals such as "Straight A's," which would let states spend money virtually any way they wanted. In the end, the two sides settled on the classic Washington compromise: a demonstration program, with lots of strings attached. The education bill (HR 1) passed 91-8, on June 14. (*Senate action, p. 82*)

"It was a beautiful negotiation," said Sandy Kress, Bush's education adviser. "It was such a high-wire act that if you went just a little farther, the Republicans would have fallen off. And the Democrats had gone as far as they could, too."

It was also classic Ted Kennedy. The rhetoric was impassioned, but negotiations in the background were unemotional and direct. The tone of the message for the crowd was not the same as the one for the cloakroom.

Now, as the Senate prepares to take up the patients' bill of rights, Democrats and Republicans alike will be watching to see if Kennedy will employ that strategy and style on an issue that has for years been a signature cause for him and his party.

There are some big differ-

ences between the two issues. On managed care, Kennedy moves from playing the role of opposition on a Republican bill to leading the floor debate on a topic that both parties view as central to their political fortunes in 2002 and beyond.

It is also one of the highest-profile health care issues Congress has faced in decades — and one that affects millions of consumers in managed-care plans. And Kennedy must manage a multitude of senators with high-profile names and ambitions. His bill (S 1052), for example, is also sponsored by John McCain, R-Ariz. and John Edwards, D-N.C., two potential contenders for the White House in 2004. Its main rival (S 889) is sponsored by Bill Frist, R-Tenn., John B. Breaux, D-La., and James M. Jeffords, I-Vt. — all powerful players in the closely divided Senate.

In addition, consumer groups, business and insurance interests and the medical community are also pushing and pulling lawmakers in both chambers in several directions.

Where the Votes Are

The outcome of the patients' rights debate, which is scheduled to begin June 19 and might run beyond the July 4 recess, is impossible to predict.

The shift in Senate control to the Democrats has given the issue new momentum, as has the recent decision by Rep. Charlie Norwood, R-Ga., to cosponsor a companion bill in the House, which is also expected to take up managed care

Norwood, sponsor of a health bill that passed the House in 1999, announced June 13 that he had abandoned talks with Bush and was endorsing the approach of Kennedy, McCain and Edwards.

Edward M. Kennedy, D-Mass., has built his Senate career around fashioning a stronger safety net for the poor and the elderly while pressing for more labor and environmental protections. Those goals are reflected in nearly 40 years of making laws and speeches, some of which are highlighted below.

LEGISLATIVE RECORD

▶ Cosponsored a provision creating the National Teachers Corps, which recruits and trains teachers to work in poor areas. The program was authorized as part of the Higher Education Act of 1965 (PL 89-329). *(1965 Almanac, p. 294)*

▶ Pushed a provision of the Voting Rights Act of 1970 (PL 91-285) to enfranchise all citizens 18 or older. *(1970 Almanac, p. 713)*

▶ Cosponsored the Senate version of a 1982 bill (PL 97-205) that extended enforcement of the 1965 Voting Rights Act for 25 years and strengthened other areas of the law. *(1982 Almanac, p. 373)*

▶ Was the chief ally of sponsor Tom Harkin, D-Iowa, in pushing the 1990 Americans with Disabilities Act (PL 101-336), which bars discrimination against the disabled in employment, services and accommodations. *(1990 Almanac, p. 447)*

▶ Sponsored legislation (PL 103-259) making it a federal crime to bar access to abortion clinics. *(1994 Almanac, p. 355)*

▶ Helped push legislation (PL 104-188) in 1996 to raise the minimum wage from $4.25 an hour to $5.15. *(1996 Almanac, p. 7-3)*

ON THE RECORD

"For me, a few hours ago, this campaign came to an end. For all those whose cares have been our concern, the work goes on, the cause endures, the hope still lives, and the dream shall never die."
— 1980 Democratic National Convention after bowing out of the presidential race

"Frankly, I don't mind not being president. I just mind that someone else is."
— 1986 Washington Gridiron Club Dinner

"There is little in his record that demonstrates real solicitude for the rights of those who are the weakest and most powerless in our society. . . . We must vote our fears, not our hopes."
— 1990 speech opposing the nomination of David H. Souter to the Supreme Court

"Americans with disabilities deserve more than good intentions. They deserve emancipation from generations of prejudice and discrimination, some of it well-meaning but all of it wrong-minded."
— 1990 speech during debate on the Americans with Disabilities Act

"There is no Democratic or Republican way to heal a sick child. There is no Democratic or Republican way to make the right medical decision; no Democratic or Republican way to fight cancer or ease the pain of HIV and AIDS."
— 2000 speech to the Democratic National Convention

in the coming weeks. Norwood had said he wanted to see if a compromise was possible between the White House and Congress before committing to the measure. Despite meetings between lawmakers and administration officials, including one June 14, the two sides have not come to an agreement.

In the Senate, many members are waiting to see what amendments will emerge. Some liberal Democrats who believe they compromised too much on education may not be willing to move as far on managed care, feeling that their party's current position on patients' rights plays well with voters.

Both sides, however, will be targeting the moderates. Kennedy, for one, knows that Republicans will try to use the same strategy with him that he used with them on education: Peel off enough moderates on important amendments to shape a bill to their liking. (*Moderates, p. 96*)

But he, too, will be targeting the centrists, especially on the early amendments. If undecided GOP moderates see that Kennedy is winning on key provisions, they may feel more comfortable going with him than voting against what could emerge as a victory for consumers. If he wins the support of the moderates, Kennedy along with his allies McCain and Edwards will have significantly more leverage with the White House. Bush has said he "can't live with" the bill as written.

Republicans have indicated that their strategy is to heavily amend the bill. While they have given some indication of their amendments, the list is still evolving, partly because many of the same players on health care have just finished the education debate. Therein lies the risk for Kennedy and the Democrats.

"One of the difficulties is that nobody's got the votes," said Michael B. Enzi, R-Wyo. "There are some people that like all of the versions, some who like none of the versions and some who think changes need to be made. . . . So there will be some testing to see where the votes are, and we'll see what happens."

Some Democrats think Kennedy has a stronger hand on patients' rights than he did on education. "There, he had about 10-15 Democrats who were prepared to cut a deal with the administration," said Sen. Christopher J. Dodd, D-Conn. "I think he had less leverage there than on the patients' bill of rights, where he has far more Democrats who are prepared to support what he wants to do."

Managing the Amendments

During the debate, the Frist-Breaux-Jeffords bill may be offered as a substitute. Its patients' rights provisions are similar to those in the Democratic plan — guaranteed access to specialty and emergency room care, the right to appeal their health plan's decisions on coverage and treatment. But on the most contentious issue, liability, there are key differences. The Frist bill would limit patients' lawsuits against their health plans to federal court. It is similar to Bush's patients' rights principles and has his backing. (*Chart, p. 94*)

The Democrats' bill would permit lawsuits in both state and federal courts. Current law, the 1974 Em-

Employers, Insurers Pull Out Stops To Defeat McCain-Edwards-Kennedy

As the Senate prepares for a floor battle over the patients' bill of rights, business groups are spending millions of dollars to defeat a measure (S 1052) cosponsored by John McCain, R-Ariz., John Edwards, D-N.C., and Edward M. Kennedy, D-Mass.

The groups say the bill would drive up health-insurance premiums and expose employers to lawsuits, which might cause companies to drop health insurance for their workers.

The Health Benefits Coalition, an alliance of business groups that includes the National Federation of Independent Business and the National Association of Manufacturers, began a Washington-based television, radio and print advertising campaign June 12 proclaiming the bill "Bad for the economy. Bad for employees. Bad idea."

While the alliance would not say how much it is spending, its previous campaigns against similar proposals cost $2 million to $3 million, and officials say they are willing to spend that much or more in the current battle.

Employers are stressing that their members provide benefits on a voluntary basis and might change their minds should the bill become law.

Bruce Josten, executive vice president of the U.S. Chamber of Commerce, said many of his members are already struggling with double-digit price increases in insurance premiums, and fear the liability provisions in the measure will drive those costs higher.

Josten and others also say higher health insurance premiums and a softening economy mean that both employees and employers will pay more for health insurance, and that some employers may decide to stop offering coverage.

"Driving employers away from this system makes no sense at all," Josten said.

The Business Roundtable, an association of chief executive officers, meanwhile, has begun a series of ads aimed at Democratic senators the group feels may be open to persuasion — Zell Miller and Max Cleland of Georgia, Ben Nelson of Nebraska, Mary L. Landrieu of Louisiana and Evan Bayh of Indiana.

The ads contend that Kennedy's proposal would increase the number of uninsured people in the lawmakers' states, no small matter for Cleland and Landrieu, who face election campaigns in 2002.

The American Association of Health Plans, which represents managed-care providers, started its own campaign against the measure June 14. Its national television ads feature a small-business owner saying the bill could force her and other small firms to cut health insurance benefits "because of expensive new health care lawsuits."

Karen M. Ignagni, the group's president and chief executive officer, said the measure would "expose the health care system and the working families who rely on it to higher costs and reduced access. It would seriously undermine the ability of many employers to continue to provide health care coverage to their employees. Simply put, new lawsuits could unravel the current system."

The group would prefer legislation that provides prompt and binding independent external reviews of medical decisions as a centerpiece of any patient protection bill, rather than what it views as an invitation to more lawsuits.

The American Medical Association, which supports the McCain-Edwards-Kennedy bill, is battling back with its own ads.

On June 18 the group plans to launch a print and drive-time radio campaign saying that insurers are trying to escape the liability they should bear for any negligence in patient care.

The spots note that 44 states have passed patient protection laws. "Now we need a strong federal law to make sure all of us are protected all the time," the ads state.

ployee Retirement Income Security Act (PL 93-406) generally allows health plans to be sued only in federal court and, in most cases, limits damages to the cost of denied care. The law also exempts large interstate companies from state regulations governing health and pension plans. (*1974 Almanac, p. 244*)

As he did on education, Kennedy can be expected to offer lengthy and loud orations — especially on amendments he opposes and provisions he champions — while pushing to get a bill with the broadest federal reach.

In many ways, the education debate was the perfect warmup for the managed-care showdown. The six weeks of floor debate featured dozens of amendments, with Kennedy steering many Democratic proposals to passage while beating back some Republican amendments.

The debate on patients' rights will likely unfold in much the same way. Don Nickles of Oklahoma, the GOP whip, and Phil Gramm, R-Texas, are expected to offer a series of amendments, including proposals to lower the $5 million liability cap in the Kennedy bill and exempt employers from lawsuits. Democrats contend employers would be shielded under their bill.

Reducing the liability caps might attract moderates in both parties who are worried that allowing more lawsuits would cause employers in their communities to reduce health benefits for workers or drop them altogether. Some moderate Republicans may also look to strip provisions in the bill that would allow lawsuits in state court, preferring to make health plans liable only in federal court.

Other amendments to be offered include provisions requiring patients to exhaust all appeals before heading to

Patients' Rights Plans Compared

The Senate is expected to consider patients' rights legislation (S 1052) sponsored by John McCain, R-Ariz.; John Edwards, D-N.C.; and Edward M. Kennedy, D-Mass., the week of June 18. Republicans are likely to offer amendments to move that measure closer to a competing bill (S 889) offered by Bill Frist, R-Tenn.; John B. Breaux, D-La.; and James M. Jeffords, I-Vt. Principles offered by President Bush may also come into play. The two bills contain a number of similar protections for patients, including guaranteed coverage for clinical trials, specialty care, breast cancer treatment and emergency care, direct access to obstetricians and gynecologists, and visits to out-of-network doctors if the patient pays more. Both bills would also require continuing coverage for serious conditions up to 90 days after a plan drops a doctor or benefit and would bar "gag clauses" that restrict communications between doctors and patients. Major differences among the proposals include:

ISSUE	McCAIN-EDWARDS-KENNEDY	FRIST-BREAUX-JEFFORDS	BUSH PRINCIPLES
Appeals process	Patients would be required to exhaust internal and external appeals before filing suit unless they demonstrated they were irreparably harmed	Patients would be required to exhaust internal and external appeals before filing suit, but could seek a court order to force a health plan to provide care. The plan would contract with reviewers who would select doctors to examine appeals.	Patients would have to go through an internal review and an independent, binding external review before they could sue.
Right to sue	Patients and families could sue their health plans in state court for medically reviewable decisions and in federal court for administrative decisions that resulted in injury or death. Patients could not pursue lawsuits in both forums at the same time.	Patients could sue in federal court over coverage and medically reviewable decisions if their health plan did not follow the external reviewer's decision or was negligent in providing care. Patients could only sue for damages if an external reviewer reversed a plan's decision.	Patients could sue their health plans only in federal court.
Damage cap	Limits on damages in state suits would be set by state law. Punitive damages would be prohibited in federal court, but the court could set a civil penalty of up to $5 million if the plan acted in bad faith. Economic and non-economic damages would not be capped.	Economic damages would be unlimited; non-economic damages would be capped at $500,000. Punitive damages would not be allowed.	Bush has said that any law must include a "reasonable" cap.
Employer liability	Employers would be shielded from liability unless they directly participated in making a decision that resulted in injury or death.	Employers would be shielded from lawsuits if they gave an insurer or other third party authority over medical and administrative health care decisions.	Employers would be shielded from liability unless they "retain responsibility for and make final medical decisions."
States' rights	States could apply to the Health and Human Services secretary for a waiver if their laws were "substantially equivalent to and effective as" federal law.	States could apply to the HHS secretary for a waiver from patient protections of the bill if their own laws were "consistent with" federal law. HHS woould have to approve such requests unless there was "no reasonable basis or evidence for such approval."	Bush would give "deference" to state law and "to the traditional authority of states to regulate insurance."
Scope	Nearly 190 million people would be covered.	Approximately 170 million people would be covered.	"Every person enrolled in a health plan."

court — which backers believe would help curb lawsuits — and specifying the criteria medical reviewers are supposed to consider when they examine a health plan's judgment on coverage and treatment decisions.

Republicans also want what they call "access" provisions aimed at reducing the number of uninsured Americans. These include lifting restrictions on tax-exempt medical savings accounts, which are used to pay for health-care expenses, and accelerating the tax deductibility of health insurance premiums for the self-employed while extending a similar benefit to workers whose companies do not offer coverage.

Moderates in both parties may push for tax credits for the uninsured, and some conservatives may move to exempt companies with 25 or fewer employees from any federal law.

"We'll just start amending it," said Frist. "It will be a good debate on a whole range of issues. It will give us the opportunity to address each of these issues separately."

Frist, a heart and lung transplant surgeon, is expected to be the GOP's point person against Kennedy, but some party members oppose a provision in his bill that would allow judgments against health plans up to $500,000 in federal court.

Frist reiterates that both sides must be willing to move for a deal to emerge. "At the end of the day, I don't think either extreme will win. . . . If people don't care about patients and don't really want a bill, then we won't see any compromise," he said.

Not surprisingly, Kennedy thinks his bill should not be changed. "I don't see the necessity of amendments myself," he said in an interview.

"This bill has been worked and worked and reworked from when it was introduced five years ago. . . . It has been tweaked, adjusted, compromised and changed. I think [we] have a bill that protects consumers, it protects the medical profession and protects families."

Bush has said repeatedly that he opposes several elements of the Kennedy bill, including provisions to allow suits in state court and a $5 million cap on civil damages at the federal level. But Kennedy believes those objections will fade as the Senate debates the bill.

"Once you get started on the floor of the Senate, the climate and atmosphere change. There's always a lot of evaluation and consideration in the committee rooms, the conferences in the back hallways and all the rest. You get out here and get an entirely different reaction. Of course, the administration won't be able to resist," Kennedy said.

Where to Deal?

Kennedy the pragmatist knows that his bill will be changed, as most measures are. On June 14, he and his cosponsors inserted some new language on liability, which has been a critical area of concern for employers and insurers as well as some Democrats and Republicans.

Patients could no longer simply "allege" harm in order to file a lawsuit, but would instead have to demonstrate that they had been harmed before opting out of the review process and heading to court. Individuals could also not sue in state and federal courts at the same time. Insurance agents, hospitals, physicians would not be held liable for decisions made by health insurers.

Kennedy spokesman Jim Manley called the changes "technical corrections" and said he doubted that they would help the bill win any new supporters.

Margaret Camp, a spokeswoman for Frist, said the alterations were "significant concessions" that were made because "they recognized it was a bad bill."

Opponents may also take encouragement from the fact that other liability provisions in the current Kennedy bill are different from earlier drafts. Rather than allow patients to sue for unlimited damages in either state or federal court, his current proposal would send lawsuits for medically reviewable decisions to state courts. Suits involving administrative decisions resulting in injury or death would be sent to federal court. The $5 million cap on federal civil penalties did not exist in earlier versions of Kennedy's legislation.

Such movement suggests that Kennedy may be flexible on liability, although cosponsor McCain said after the June 14 White House meeting that such a scenario is unlikely. "We'll negotiate on most everything, but we feel very strongly" about the bill's liability provisions, he said.

Breaux, who also attended the meeting, said he would be willing to move beyond the $500,000 cap on non-economic damages included in his bill, but stressed that lawsuits must occur in federal court, not at the state level, where juries are likely to award higher damages.

Majority Leader Tom Daschle, D-S.D., also expressed a willingness to negotiate as the Senate debate moved closer, saying "I'm willing to sit down with anybody as long we keep the intent of the bill intact."

John D. Rockefeller IV, D-W.Va., said Kennedy's opponents might be surprised how he deals with them on patients' rights.

"He always has the element of surprise. He has the image that he won't compromise, he can't compromise, he's sort of possessed by the issue. I think he likes that, because then if he has to make an adjustment, it's a bigger deal to those who never thought he would have made it to begin with," Rockefeller said.

Adversaries as Partners

Kennedy allies argue that he has long shown a willingness to compromise in order to achieve a larger legislative goal. In 1996, for example, Kennedy cleared the way for passage of a law (PL 104-191) that allows people to change jobs without losing health coverage when he grudgingly signed off on a demonstration program for medical savings accounts.

The accounts were a centerpiece of the Republican health-care agenda because they allow people to choose where to receive their medical care, rather than be bound by a health plan's list of doctors, hospitals and other providers. (*1996 Almanac*, p. 6-36)

Democrats thought the accounts would skew the health insurance system by attracting mainly wealthy and healthy people, leaving everyone else behind in the traditional health insurance market to face rising premiums.

To minimize that risk, Kennedy talked Republicans into a demonstration program in which only 750,000 accounts would be set up and would be available only to small businesses, the self-employed and the uninsured. He also set a four-year time-limit on the initiative, which was later extended until Dec. 31, 2002 as part of the fiscal 2001 Labor, Education, and Health and Human Services spending bill (PL 106-554).

Kennedy was able to propose and win acceptance for the demonstration program because he has what GOP lawmakers agree is an incredible knack for forming the alliances necessary to pass bills.

Courting the Moderates

Most Senate Democrats are expected to vote with their party to support the patients' rights bill (S 1052) sponsored by John McCain, R-Ariz., John Edwards, D-N.C., and Edward M. Kennedy, D-Mass. The sponsors have also won the support of Republicans Arlen Specter of Pennsylvania and Lincoln Chafee of Rhode Island. But there are several other moderates in both parties whose votes will be needed to pass that bill or a competing proposal (S 889) by Bill Frist, R-Tenn., John B. Breaux, D-La., and James M. Jeffords, I-Vt.

 Susan Collins, R-Maine: As former commissioner of her state's Department of Professional and Financial Regulation, Collins knows first-hand the impact of government regulation on business. Like many of her GOP colleagues, she wants to make sure any new federal law will not cause health care costs to increase or expose employers to new lawsuits, but a tough re-election bid may force her to compromise more on patients' rights than in the past.

 Olympia J. Snowe, R-Maine: The leader of the bipartisan Centrist Coalition, Snowe has consistently searched for middle ground on other health topics, including prescription drug coverage for Medicare recipients. Snowe wants to ensure that increasing liability will not increase health care costs, expose employers to lawsuits or interfere with state laws.

Peter G. Fitzgerald, R-Ill.: He is probably the easiest Republican target for Democrats since he voted with them the past two years when patients' rights legislation reached the Senate floor.

Gordon H. Smith, R-Ore.: He has worked hard to find compromises between Democrats and Republicans, sometimes breaking party ranks on high-profile issues. With a tough re-election race in the offing, Smith may be more eager to push for a deal this year on patients' rights. He is most concerned about liability.

 Tim Hutchinson, R-Ark.: He served on a House-Senate patients' rights conference in 2000 that failed to resolve the two chambers' differences. Being on the winning side this year could help his re-election chances — he won by 5 percent in 1996 and is likely to face a strong Democratic challenger next year. Hutchinson's concerns include making sure any new law will not increase the number of uninsured or lead to a flurry of lawsuits.

 Ben Nelson, D-Neb.: A self-described conservative Democrat, he has not aligned himself with either bill. Issues of concern include scope — how many Americans are covered by any federal law — and whether doctors or health plans have the power to determine medical necessity.

Evan Bayh, D-Ind.: He has not endorsed either bill, but his leadership position in the Senate New Democrats coalition and membership in the Centrist Coalition suggest an openness to the more conservative Frist-Breaux-Jeffords measure.

Mary L. Landrieu, D-La.: Although she has not committed to either bill, Landrieu's voting record indicates a likely tilt toward the McCain-Edwards-Kennedy bill. In 1999 and 2000 she sided with Democrats on patients' rights.

For example, Kennedy and Frist are headed for a floor fight on patients' rights, but they cosponsored legislation in the 106th Congress that would have changed the way hearts, lungs, livers and other organs are allocated to patients awaiting transplants. (*2000 CQ Weekly, p. 2910*)

The two also have teamed up to reduce medical errors and protect the confidentiality of individuals' medical records.

In 1997, Kennedy and Sen. Orrin G. Hatch, R-Utah, worked together to pass legislation that created a state and federal program to help uninsured children get health coverage (PL 105-33). And Kennedy joined Jeffords in 1999 to pass legislation (PL 106-170) allowing disabled Americans to keep their federal health benefits if they return to work. (*1999 Almanac, p. 16-40; 1997 Almanac, p. 6-3*)

Jeffords, who has worked with Kennedy for more than a decade, said he can tell when the Democrat is serious about a deal and when he is not. "I can usually tell when he's playing to the crowd and when he's serious about sitting down and working out things," Jeffords said. "You could listen to him and say, 'Oh my God, there's no hope,' but then you'll get him alone and things are different."

Kennedy has even been receptive to Bush, though he portrayed him during the 2000 presidential campaign as having not just a "credibility gap" but rather "a credibility chasm."

Soon after Bush's inauguration, Kennedy was at the White House, watching a screening of the movie "13 Days," which dealt with the Cuban Missile Crisis that occurred when Kennedy's brother John was president. Kennedy was also invited to the White House for private talks on education.

After one of the meetings, Kennedy told the Boston Sunday Herald that Bush was "personable, he's intelligent, he's sort of feisty and he's engaged. It would be a mistake for Democrats to underestimate George Bush."

Kennedy has other White House alliances as well. Kress, Bush's education adviser, is a Democrat who can talk to Kennedy and Senate Republicans with equal ease. And when Bush Chief of Staff Andrew H. Card Jr. was nominated to be Transportation secretary in the administration of Bush's father, Kennedy praised Card and helped him win an easy confirmation.

These connections may help smooth the way for a patients' rights deal, despite the vast differences that Kennedy has with Bush and Republicans. In the words of one former Senate Democratic aide, Kennedy has "his own 'charm offensive' that outranks President Bush's any day."

But that will probably not be readily apparent during the coming debate on patients' rights.

"He plays two roles," said Susan Collins, R-Maine, who worked with Kennedy on education. "I've found him in private meetings to be very open and easy to deal with. [But] I understand he has another role to play, which is Democratic cheerleader and spokesman for Democratic arguments." ◆

Bush Order Gives GOP an Edge In Annual Struggle Over Abortion

Renewed curbs on family planning assistance overseas are likely to stand up in Congress

Showing clearly that his election has changed the dynamic of the abortion debate, President Bush on Jan. 22 reinstated Reagan-era restrictions on international family planning aid that President Bill Clinton had thrown out in 1993. Democrats vowed to overturn Bush's decision, but in the closely divided Congress they are unlikely to have much luck.

"The White House has the trump card," Sen. Mitch McConnell, R-Ky., chairman of the Foreign Operations Appropriations Subcommittee, said in a Jan. 23 interview. McConnell's panel handles the foreign aid bill that has been, and probably will continue to be, a battleground on the issue.

Bush's directive came against the backdrop of a bitter debate over his nominee to be attorney general — former Sen. John Ashcroft of Missouri, a forceful opponent of abortion. (*Ashcroft, 2001 CQ Weekly, p. 229*)

In the coming months, Congress is expected to debate legislation that would ban certain late-term abortions, and the Bush administration might try to halt sale of the abortion drug RU-486, which was approved by the Food and Drug Administration. (*2001 CQ Weekly, p. 108*)

The family-planning question has become an annual battle. Since Republicans won control of Congress in 1995, Rep. Christopher H. Smith of New Jersey and other anti-abortion Republicans have sought to reimpose the strict "Mexico City" anti-abortion policy first put in place by President Ronald Reagan in 1984 and continued by Bush's father. (*Background, p. 98*)

The Reagan policy, now revived by George W. Bush in a memorandum to the Agency for International Development (AID), bans aid to international organizations that perform or promote abortion as a means of family planning, even if they do so with private funds.

Congress is evenly divided on the issue — the House has a narrow anti-abortion majority; abortion rights supporters have an edge in the Senate.

The House last year rejected, 206-221, an attempt to remove the restrictions from the fiscal 2001 foreign operations bill. The Senate, by voice vote, passed its version of the bill without them. (*2000 CQ Weekly, p. 1743*)

Both abortion rights supporters and their opponents expect the pattern to continue when Congress takes up the fiscal 2002 foreign aid spending bill later this year.

Sen. Barbara Boxer, D-Calif, noted that the 50-50 split in the Senate only makes it more likely that an effort to reverse Bush's decision would win in that chamber.

Future Conference

The change in dynamics this year will be especially evident when House and Senate negotiators seek to work out a compromise version.

In previous years, conference committee members eventually tended to work out a deal that traded symbolic moves to reinstate the abortion restrictions for a continuation of Clinton's policy.

This year, negotiators will be under pressure to agree to Bush's policy if they hope to clear the foreign aid bill, particularly if he threatens to veto the legislation without restrictions.

"Bush's decision will be able to prevail just as Clinton's position was able to prevail for eight years," Republican Jim Kolbe of Arizona, chairman of the House Foreign Operations Appropriations Subcommittee,

Quick Contents

Republicans tried for most of Bill Clinton's presidency to reinstate abortion-related restrictions on international family planning aid, but Clinton blocked them at every turn. Now that President Bush has restored the restrictions by directive, Democrats will try to remove them with legislation. But Bush now holds the veto.

Abortion Issues Ahead

Issue	Description
Mexico City policy	President Bush has reinstated a Reagan-era policy banning aid to foreign organizations that perform or promote abortion as a means of family planning. Democrats will try to overturn it.
"Partial Birth" Abortion	A majority in Congress supports banning this procedure, but constitutional issues remain since the Supreme Court struck down a Nebraska ban for being too vague.
Fetal Protection	Sen. Rick Santorum, R-Pa., a key abortion foe, said a bill expanding the definition of a "person" to include a fetus alive when it leaves the womb would be the first anti-abortion bill of the year.

'Mexico City' Policy's History

The issue of abortion-related restrictions on U.S. aid to international family planning organizations has been debated line by line since it first appeared in 1984. Here is a brief history:

1984 — At the second U.N. International Conference on Population in Mexico City, the Reagan administration announces a new policy of denying assistance to any foreign, non-governmental organization "which performs or actively promotes abortion as a method of family planning," even if that is done with the group's private funds. The directive becomes known as the "Mexico City" policy.

1991 — The House passes a foreign aid authorization bill that would remove the Mexico City restrictions, but the measure ultimately fails. President George Bush had threatened to veto it over the provision.

1993 — In a memorandum to the director of the Agency for International Development, President Bill Clinton rescinds the Mexico City restrictions. "These excessively broad anti-abortion conditions are unwarranted," Clinton writes. "Moreover, they have undermined efforts to promote safe and efficacious family planning programs in foreign nations."

1995 — Blocked in attempts to reinstate the Mexico City policy through legislation, anti-abortion forces in the House resort to cutting appropriations for international family planning programs by 35 percent and blocking payments until July 1996.

1996 — Anti-abortion lawmakers succeed in delaying payment of fiscal 1997 family planning funds until July 1, unless Congress votes separately to release them in March. Congress subsequently approves the early release.

1997 — Negotiators on the fiscal 1998 foreign aid spending bill (PL 105-118) reach a deadlock over a House provision that would essentially reinstate the Mexico City policy. Republican leaders remove the provision but limit spending to the fiscal 1997 level, released at 8 percent a month.

1998 — House leaders keep anti-abortion restrictions off the fiscal 1999 foreign operations spending bill (PL 105-277), but the Mexico City policy is added to a State Department authorization bill, which fails.

1999 — After months of negotiations, Clinton agrees to a one-year deal on the fiscal 2000 foreign aid bill (PL 106-113) that bars aid to family planning groups that perform abortions — except in cases of rape, incest or to save the life of the woman — or that lobby to change abortion laws or government policies in other countries. Clinton can and does waive the restriction, but under the law that triggers a shift of $12.5 million in family planning aid to an account for child survival and disease prevention programs.

2000 — Republicans agree to increase aid for family planning programs, but the fiscal 2001 foreign aid spending bill (PL 106-429) prevents spending the money until Feb. 15, after a new president is inaugurated. Republicans gamble that it will be George W. Bush.

2001 — President Bush reinstates the Mexico City prohibition by directive. "It is my conviction that taxpayer funds should not be used to pay for abortions or advocate or actively promote abortion, either here or abroad," Bush writes.

said in a Jan. 24 interview.

The debate could be awkward for Kolbe, who supports abortion rights and opposes the Mexico City policy. He played down the importance of the restrictions, saying their most substantive effect would be to prevent overseas lobbying on abortion issues.

"I am not going to let this dictate the work that I do as chairman of the subcommittee," Kolbe said. "I've never believed this was worth falling on your sword about."

Bush's announcement came as opponents and supporters of abortion rights rallied in Washington on the 28th anniversary of the 1973 *Roe v. Wade* Supreme Court decision that affirmed a constitutional right to abortion.

"It is my conviction that taxpayer funds should not be used to pay for abortions or advocate or actively promote abortion, here or abroad," Bush wrote.

Nita M. Lowey of New York, ranking Democrat on the House Foreign Operations Appropriations Subcommittee, denounced the move. "The president has abandoned the world's poorest women and families and stands in the way of free speech around the world," she said.

Nancy Pelosi of California, the former ranking Democrat on the subcommittee, said Bush was making a concession to social conservatives. "For the president to toss this as a party favor to the right- wing parade that was here yesterday is frivolous," she told a Jan. 23 news conference.

Bush's action was anticipated when negotiators came to an agreement on the fiscal 2001 foreign operations appropriations bill only weeks before the presidential election.

Clinton had threatened to veto the bill if it included any abortion restrictions on family planning aid. House Republicans had sought to extend a previous, one-year provision that had essentially forced Clinton to accept either some restrictions or a small reduction in family planning funds.

Under pressure from Clinton and hoping for a Bush victory, Smith and other Republicans agreed to a compromise. The measure provided $425 million for family planning but prevented the administration from spending it until Feb. 15, making the fiscal 2001 funds subject to Bush's order. (*2000 CQ Weekly, p. 2552*) ◆

Policing Consumer Privacy: Congress Prepares to Opt In

As concern grows over electronic intrusions, narrowly tailored bills have a chance of passing

Americans want the convenience of one-click shopping on the Internet. They want their physicians and pharmacies to have up-to-date and accurate records. They want cutting-edge 911 capabilities on their cell phones.

They also want their privacy. They want all the new conveniences without making themselves more vulnerable to tracking by criminals, businesses and even the government.

The difficulty of accommodating both these demands has made privacy one of the most vexing technology policy issues facing Congress.

Over the past few years, lawmakers have generally been reluctant to impose potentially burdensome new rules on the booming digital economy for fear of chilling development of the new products that American consumers have so embraced. Instead, Congress has taken a position of non-interference, essentially hoping the technology industry would police itself.

The 107th Congress could well bring a change in that thinking. A growing number of policymakers appear convinced that some government regulation is necessary, especially in the areas of online privacy, electronic surveillance and medical and financial record-keeping. Even some executives in the regulation-averse technology industry are, for the first time, urging Congress to pass limited privacy laws, worried that the lack of federal standards will lead to a confusing patchwork of state regulations.

"The issue has been bubbling up for some time, but in the last Congress we kept asking ourselves, 'What is the appropriate role to take? What are we legislating?' " said Rep. Anna G. Eshoo, D-Calif., who represents most of Silicon Valley and is sponsoring an Internet privacy bill. "It's moving from the back burner to the front burner, and we will probably establish some kind of a

floor [for privacy standards] in this Congress."

Lawmakers are expected to tackle the issue through narrowly focused legislation instead of one or two comprehensive privacy bills. That approach would preserve committees' jurisdictions, although privacy advocates warn it also places the United States at a disadvantage to Europe and Canada, where more sweeping measures have been enacted.

"Congress tends to deal with privacy problems one by one," said Chris Hoofnagle, staff counsel for the Electronic Privacy Information Center (EPIC), a group of privacy advocates. "The problem is, some of the bills don't assure fair information practices and place the burden on the consumer to prevent the information that is being collected from being used. The attitude sometimes is, 'If this isn't a clearly unfair practice, it isn't a problem.' "

Regulating cyberspace has been a humbling exercise to date. Congress could not find a comfortable middle ground when debating whether to tax e-commerce or regulate Internet content. Lawmakers in 1998 deferred on the taxation issue by settling on a three-year moratorium on Internet-specific taxes. And laws passed in 1996 and 1998 to restrict indecent material on the Internet were blocked by courts on the grounds they violated free speech. In the 106th Congress, lawmakers introduced about 200 privacy measures, but failed to agree on any wide-ranging legislation.

A Wish List

A coalition of more than a dozen groups representing consumer, civil liberties, educational, library and labor interests outlined its privacy wish list Feb. 12. The coalition — which includes the American Civil Liberties Union, the Consumer Federation of America and the United Auto Workers — wants Internet companies to both openly disclose their information-gathering practices and to give consumers a handy way to prevent that information from being shared.

The technology industry is not of one mind on the need for legislation, but is signalling it may be receptive to congressional efforts to clarify ground rules for proper conduct in cyberspace. For example, the American Electronics Association (AEA), the nation's largest high-tech trade group, in January suggested a set of minimal privacy standards it could support, but stressed that any Internet privacy bill must preempt state laws.

Major companies such as Hewlett-Packard Co. have taken similar positions. But industry groups such as the Information Technology Industry Council (ITI) are taking a harder line, saying they have yet to see privacy legislation they can support.

"We are not allergic to federal legislation, but we're trying to ask questions: What is the scope of the bill, is it just targeted at the Internet, does it place new burdens on buyers and sellers [in cyberspace]," said ITI President Rhett Dawson.

"It's a very complex and sensitive issue, and members of Congress are looking at it with fresh eyes and getting sobered by the experience."

Legislation in the Works

Lawmakers already have introduced at least 18 privacy bills in the 107th Congress, and the Congressional Privacy Caucus, which includes House and Senate members of both parties, is planning March hearings on one subject of immediate concern — "Web bugs," a variety of tracking software that advertisers can surreptitiously use to monitor consumers' Internet habits.

Separately, Reps. Asa Hutchinson, R-Ark., and James. P. Moran, D-Va., have reintroduced a bill (HR 583) to establish a bipartisan commission to study and make policy recommendations on a wide range of privacy issues. In the last Congress, supporters could not muster the two-thirds majority needed to pass the measure without debate.

Perhaps nowhere is the privacy issue more immediate than in health care. New Department of Health and Human Services rules to safeguard medical records so roiled providers and insurers that they persuaded the Bush administration to delay implementation, which had been set for Feb. 26,

and to reopen them for revision. (*Story, p. 102*)

Consumers' concerns about information security are profound. Polls indicate Americans are increasingly wary of online marketers and believe that information they provide to businesses might be misused.

Surveys of separate groups of 1,200 and 1,000 adults by the consulting firm Wirthlin Worldwide in 2000 and 2001 found many of them were worried about providing personal information over the Internet. When asked to rate their concern on a scale of 1 to 10, with 10 being "extremely worried," nearly half categorized their level of concern a 9 or 10.

Regulators, meanwhile, are urging Congress to take a more activist approach. The Federal Trade Commission (FTC), which polices online commerce, reversed an earlier position and concluded last year that self-regulation by the technology industry has not done enough to protect consumer privacy. In a May 2000 report to Congress, the FTC recommended that lawmakers pass a privacy law that ensures a minimum level of privacy protection and establishes "basic standards of practice for the collection of information online."

The FTC based that recommendation on a survey of heavily visited U.S. commercial Web sites. The study found most of the sites that collected personal information did not notify consumers that the information was being collected and did not offer an "opt-out" feature, which allows customers to explicitly direct site operators not to share the information with third parties.

Some of the consumers' and regulators' concerns may be linked to highly publicized instances of electronic surveillance, such as online marketer DoubleClick Inc.'s in-depth tracking of consumers' online habits and last year's disclosure that the FBI's Carnivore software can "wiretap" e-mail.

Lawmakers say these subjects frequently come up for discussion in town meetings with constituents.

"I represent a lot of people who work for telecommunications companies, and while they salute the technology, the prospect for invasion of privacy online or on the phone is driving them absolutely bananas," said Rep. Rodney Frelinghuysen, R-N.J., a sponsor of four privacy bills.

The range of privacy measures being

Click-and-Tell Policies

According to a May 2000 study by the Federal Trade Commission, Web sites' policies on collecting and sharing personal information vary widely. For instance, only 41 percent of the sites surveyed at random by the agency told visitors what personal information they were collecting and gave them choices as to how it would be used.

Random Sample*

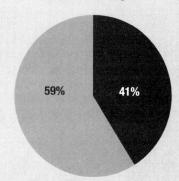

Most Popular Sites**

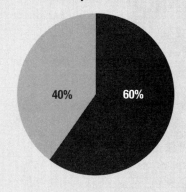

 Informed consumers about information collection policies.

 Did not inform consumers about information collection policies.

* Surveyed 335 sites, selected at random, that had at least 39,000 unique visitors per month.

** Surveyed 91 of the Internet's 100 busiest sites.

SOURCE: Federal Trade Commission

introduced suggests that lawmakers have different perceptions about what to do first. Sen. John Edwards, D-N.C., for example, has proposed legislation (S 197) that would require advertisers to warn consumers when they use Web bugs or other tracking software.

Other lawmakers are focusing on the potential for criminals to steal people's Social Security numbers in order to use their identities to make purchases, take out loans and engage in other financial transactions. Rep. Ron Paul, R-Texas, has proposed a bill (HR 220) that would prevent Social Security numbers from being used for anything other than Social Security or tax purposes.

A related bill (HR 91) by Frelinghuysen would place restrictions on how Internet service providers can use customers' Social Security numbers.

The first stop for most efforts dealing with electronic commerce is likely to be the House Energy and Commerce Committee and the Senate Commerce, Science and Transportation panel, whose chairmen are both receptive to moving privacy measures this year.

House Energy and Commerce Chairman Billy Tauzin, R-La., has indicated he would like to move legislation by this summer that would discourage the extensive collection of personal information. Tauzin's Senate counterpart, John McCain, R-Ariz., unsuccessfully pushed legislation in the last Congress that would have required Web sites to disclose their data collection practices and give consumers a chance to opt out. (*Tauzin, 2001 CQ Weekly, p. 258; McCain, 2000 CQ Weekly, p. 2925*)

The House and Senate Judiciary committees also will weigh in, particularly on electronic surveillance matters that may affect law enforcement and the way the federal government collects personal information.

House Judiciary Committee Chairman F. James Sensenbrenner Jr., R-Wis., warned in January that turf battles could break out on several fronts as the panels jockey for primacy on matters relating to the Internet. (*2001 CQ Weekly, p. 262*)

Tracking the Customer

One area of early consensus may come on the issue of wireless phones and what technology experts call "location privacy."

This is a difficult area for lawmakers because it will require Congress to find a balance between encouraging the use of a new technology and limiting how it is applied for commercial purposes. Enhancements will soon allow many of the nearly 106 million people who use cellular phones or pagers to be located when they dial 911 in an emergency. But some lawmakers say that technology would enable marketers to determine when a person drives past a store or fast-food establishment and send a message urging him to pull over for a special promotion.

Such concerns led Rep. Rush D. Holt, D-N.J., to propose legislation (HR 113) that would prohibit sending unsolicited commercial messages on wireless systems.

A bill (HR 260) by Frelinghuysen would require wireless service providers to disclose how they use location information and require the providers to obtain a customer's written consent before it can be collected and used.

Congress may end up working on parallel tracks with the FTC, which began exploring the issue in December. The Cellular Telecommunications & Internet Association also has asked the Federal Communications Commission (FCC) to issue location privacy rules that could apply to both telecommunications vendors and Internet service providers.

As in the 106th Congress, much attention is expected to be focused on the complicated issue of online profiling and the way marketers track consumers' Web surfing and purchasing habits. Congress will have to decide whether to layer new regulations on the still-evolving business of Internet commerce.

Interest in the subject has been heightened by the advent of Web bugs — nearly invisible pieces of software buried on Web pages that tell online marketers the computer addresses of users visiting their sites.

Privacy advocates also have uncovered instances where a computer code was manipulated to allow the sender of an e-mail message to see what was written when the message was forwarded with comments to other recipients.

Tauzin and John D. Dingell of Michigan, ranking Democrat on the House Energy and Commerce Committee, may collaborate with Robert W. Goodlatte, R-Va., and Rick Boucher, D-Va., on legislation that would require consumers to be given notice that personal information was being collected and also give them the chance to opt out of having it shared with third parties. The legislation also would preempt state Internet privacy laws — a provision widely viewed as a prerequisite for any high-tech industry support.

"Even those of us who are not supportive of massive government regulation of privacy believe there has to be a baseline standard," Goodlatte said. "The public is concerned, and there are always going to be entities that do not comply with self-regulation and go beyond the scope of what is reasonable."

Tauzin spokesman Ken Johnson said it was "very possible" that the Commerce panel chairman would move a bill in the next several months, but that the Louisiana Republican was exploring other options. The panel's Telecommunications, Trade and Consumer Protection Subcommittee will hold privacy hearings in March.

The kind of bill Goodlatte envisions would resemble legislation (HR 237) Eshoo already has introduced with Rep. Christopher B. Cannon, R-Utah. That bill, in turn, mirrors the legislation McCain promoted last year to require disclosure of Web sites' information practices, as well as an opt-out mechanism for consumers.

State vs. Federal Laws

Such proposals remain controversial because they could nullify strong state privacy laws and replace them with weaker federal standards. Privacy groups such as EPIC say these proposals are being prepared at the behest of the technology industry, which they say is really less interested in establishing national privacy standards than in ducking tougher laws that could evolve at the state level.

Such laws could include "opt-in" provisions. These are features that would require consumers to give explicit consent to having their personal information shared, thereby putting the burden on the Web site operator. Many businesses dislike opt-in requirements because they could hinder their ability to compile consumer databases.

"Most in the privacy community will speak against anything that prevents states from passing stronger legislation," said EPIC's Hoofnagle, who rejects the argument that it would be nearly impossible for Internet companies to navigate 50 different state laws. "We want to spur states to do stronger laws. The experience suggests that industry can comply with the strongest

HHS Reopening Medical Privacy Rules To Consider Industry's Objections

In a move that will reopen the partisan debate over sensitive medical privacy regulations, agency officials said Health and Human Services Secretary Tommy G. Thompson has decided to heed industry concerns and consider changes to the final rules published Dec. 28 by the Clinton administration.

Thompson will call, in the Federal Register, for new comments on the first-ever federal medical privacy standards as early as Feb. 26.

Agency officials were drafting a statement Feb. 23 in which Thompson was expected to say the administration "should be open to the concerns of all those who care strongly about health care privacy. After we hear those concerns, our commitment must be to put strong and effective patient privacy protections into effect as quickly as possible."

Thompson's decision, which follows industry demands for a far more business-friendly policy, dramatically changes the debate over the complex regulation. Democrats had hoped the issue would be resolved when the Clinton administration issued the regulations. Instead, years of continued haggling could be in store.

The new comment period, which will last 30 days, gives industry executives a new opportunity to argue for changes that could fundamentally alter several major provisions of the regulations. Thompson said he would assess the comments before determining whether revisions are in order.

The delay "creates an opportunity to ensure that the provisions of this final rule will indeed work as intended," Thompson said.

Although lawmakers declined to comment until official notice to reopen the rules is filed, the decision is certain to enrage Democrats who have been calling for swift implementation of the rules.

The regulations "should be implemented as scheduled to keep our commitment to Americans that their personal medical information is just that — personal," Sens. Edward M. Kennedy of Massachusetts, Patrick J. Leahy of Vermont and four other Democrats had written in a Feb. 15 letter warning President Bush not to delay or revise the regulations .

Health care lobbyists immediately applauded Thompson's move. When she learned of it, American Association of Health Plans President Karen M. Ignagni called the decision a "responsible step."

"This rule, in fact, differed from the guiding principle that was outlined in the original proposed rule in significant ways that may reduce, not improve, consumers' access to quality health care," Ignagni said Feb. 23.

Industry Maneuvers

Thompson's decision came after health care lobbyists had succeeded in delaying the regulations — which had been scheduled to become effective Feb. 26 — for nearly two months by pointing out that the Clinton administration had failed to formally file them with Congress and the General Accounting Office.

The 1996 Congressional Review Act (PL 104-121) requires agencies to file rules at least 60 days before they are set to become effective. After the regulation was formally filed on Feb. 13, a new effective date of April 14 was set, with enforcement to begin in 2003.

The Clinton administration's apparent omission was discovered dur-

law."

Technology industry executives insist that federal standards are necessary because of the myriad possibilities for privacy legislation at the state level.

They point to states including Florida, Illinois, Maine, Maryland and Vermont, which all passed laws governing the release of personal financial information that are more comprehensive than federal standards included in the 1999 financial services overhaul (PL 106-102). That law did not pre-empt tougher state laws. (*1999 Almanac, p. 5-29*)

"Any legislation considered by Congress should be explicitly and solely designed to pre-empt the enactment of a crazy quilt of onerous, contradictory new state laws," said William T. Archey, president and chief executive officer of the AEA.

State officials are anxiously watching the debate over pre-emption, but are being careful not to weigh in too early and antagonize Congress or the high-tech industry. The National Governors Association, for example, has not taken an official position on Internet privacy bills, although it says states have a constructive role to play.

Liability Concerns

Industry officials also worry that federal legislation could include provisions that would give consumers the right to sue Internet companies if their personal information is misused, or that would give the FTC broad power to define what constitutes misconduct in the collection of personal information.

"It's a very worrisome prospect, especially when the legislation only applies to personal information collected on the Internet, but not on phone lines or the mail," said ITI's Dawson.

Financial privacy also will consume lawmakers' attention, driven by concerns about the exchange of sensitive personal information among banks, insurers, brokerages and other institutions. The practice was made easier by the 1999 financial services overhaul, which allowed banks to establish affiliates that sell a wide variety of products.

Legislation (S 30) by Sen. Paul S. Sarbanes, D-Md., would require financial institutions to obtain consumers' consent before they share personal information with affiliates. This would prevent banks from automatically passing information about customers to

ing a series of meetings by industry lobbyists throughout January and early February. Three times a week, health care lobbyists met to pore over the rules, searching for technicalities that would persuade the agency to delay or change the rule. Lobbyists say the regulations are too vague, would cost their industry billions of dollars to implement and do little to protect consumers from prying eyes.

"There are a number of reasons to take another look at this," Alan Mertz, executive vice president of the Healthcare Leadership Council, a coalition of health care interest groups, said Feb. 20. "Our intention is not to rescind the whole rule entirely. We just want it fixed."

Nearly every health care insurer and provider would be affected by the regulations, which for the first time would give patients access to — and some control over — their medical records.

A hospital, for example, would have to obtain a patient's written consent before using information in his or her file to carry out routine treatment. Patients also would be able to make copies of their records and suggest changes, something most state privacy laws do not allow them to do. (*2001 CQ Weekly, p. 332*)

Providers, insurers and others that do not comply would face civil and criminal fines. An individual or company selling confidential medical in-formation could face penalties of up to $250,000 and 10 years in prison.

Patient Care Issues

Several health care trade groups wrote Thompson on Feb. 1 to complain that key provisions in the regulations were "unworkable and could seriously disrupt patient care."

Perhaps the group's greatest concern is a provision that was not in a draft of the regulations issued Oct. 29, 1999. It would require patients to sign specific consent forms before providers could use or disclose personal data for treatment or payment.

Pharmacists, in particular, say the consent requirement would create inconvenient delays. For example, when a physician phoned in a prescription for a sick child, pharmacists fear they would not be able to fill it until a parent came to the pharmacy to sign a consent form.

"Thirty-five to 40 percent of all prescriptions are picked up by someone other than the patient," Carlos R. Ortiz, director of government affairs for CVS Pharmacy, told a Feb. 13 congressional briefing. "There will be chaos at our pharmacy counters, and you will be getting phone calls from constituents about getting their prescriptions filled in a timely manner."

Some health care executives also are frustrated by the structure of the rules, which would provide a floor of federal protections that states could supersede. The result, they say, would be a patchwork of state and federal privacy guidelines.

However, privacy groups are cheering most elements of the new regulations. Advocates say Americans are increasingly concerned about breaches of medical privacy, such as hackers downloading confidential records from databases.

Privacy advocates also are concerned about scientific developments that can now tell patients more details than ever about their genetic makeup. Unless new safeguards are added, consumer groups fear that employers or insurers could use genetic information about patients to discriminate against them.

"We have mapped the human genome, but people are afraid to get tested. The Internet can deliver cutting-edge research and health care services, but people are unwilling to trust their most sensitive information in cyberspace," Janlori Goldman, director of Georgetown University's Health Privacy Project, told a Senate Health, Education, Labor and Pensions Committee hearing Feb. 8.

"We will never fully reap the benefits of these astounding breakthroughs until privacy is woven into the fabric of our nation's health care system," she said.

subsidiaries that sell securities or insurance.

Sen. Richard C. Shelby, R-Ala., wants to expand protections in the 1999 law to prevent banks from selling customers' Social Security numbers. "Looking back, we had a bite at the privacy apple when we did the [financial services] modernization bill. Unfortunately, I think we bit into a worm," Shelby told a housing and finance group Feb. 15.

Sen. Patrick J. Leahy, D-Vt., is likely to trigger this year's first airing of the privacy debate on the Senate floor shortly after the Presidents Day recess. Leahy is expected to offer an amendment to a bankruptcy overhaul bill (S 220) that would prevent companies that file for bankruptcy or go out of business from selling consumer infor-mation they have compiled. (*Bankruptcy, 2001 CQ Weekly, p. 423*)

The measure was prompted by an incident last year in which the Internet toy seller Toysmart.com attempted to sell personal information on the shopping habits of its customers and their children after it filed for bankruptcy. After consumer groups complained, Walt Disney Co., the majority owner of the company, agreed to buy and destroy the information. The fate of Leahy's measure depends less on its merits, however, than on whether Republicans are willing to add it to the bankruptcy bill.

The privacy debate is also moving into other arenas. Some lawmakers believe Congress should enact laws to prevent workplace discrimination or insurance decisions based on health records containing genetic information. Critics say the Americans with Disabilities Act (PL 101-336) already prevents workplace discrimination based on one's genetic profile, and that such measures could prompt a flood of lawsuits.

Such concerns have intensified since the recent publication of the entire sequence of the human genome. Knowing a person's genetic profile could yield clues about current afflictions and whether a person is prone to cancers or other gene-based diseases.

Rep. Louise M. Slaughter, D-N.Y., has put forth legislation (HR 602) that would bar insurers from using genetic information in coverage decisions. A companion bill (S 382) has been offered by Sen. Olympia J. Snowe, R-Maine. ◆

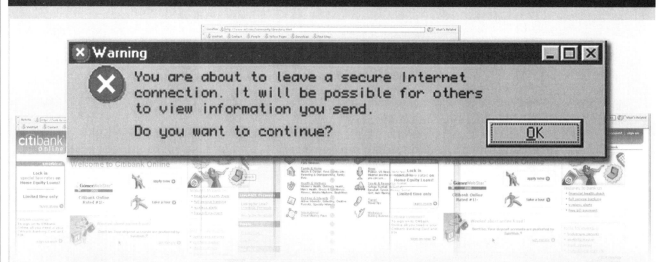

Key Areas for Privacy Legislation

The 107th Congress is expected to consider privacy measures in 2001 that would cover several areas, including Internet tracking technology, wireless-phone ads and the sharing of personal medical records. Some lawmakers, for example, want to curb the use of software that can follow a PC user's Web-surfing habits and trace his e-mail, while others are focusing on protecting consumers' Social Security numbers. Here are the major privacy issues facing Congress and some of the bills that have been offered to address them:

  Online information: Lawmakers are considering a variety of proposals dealing with how Web sites collect personal information. Sen. John McCain, R-Ariz., and Rep. Anna G. Eshoo, D-Calif., have proposed legislation (HR 237) that would require site operators to post their privacy guidelines and give consumers a chance to opt out of sharing information. They also want to establish a federal baseline for privacy protection that could pre-empt stronger state laws. Sen. John Edwards, D-N.C., has introduced a bill (S 197) that would place controls on the use of "Web bugs" and other tracking technology that can give companies detailed information about a person's Internet use.

  Wireless advertising: Reps. Rush D. Holt, D-N.J., far left, and Rodney Frelinghuysen, R-N.J., want to limit the transmission of unsolicited advertising to consumers' cell phones. Holt's bill (HR 113) and Frelinghuysen's measure (HR 260) would limit marketers' ability to track phone users and transmit ads based on their locations.

 Identity theft: Several bills would restrict business use of Social Security numbers. Frelinghuysen has introduced a bill (HR 91) to make it harder for Internet scammers to commit identity theft by stealing Social Security numbers. And Sen. Paul S. Sarbanes, D-Md., left, has introduced a measure (S 30) that would restrict how banks trade customers' personal information with affiliated companies.

 Student Web surfing: Sen. Christopher J. Dodd, D-Conn., and several other lawmakers have proposed a measure (S 290) that would require school districts to notify parents when classroom computers use technology that could collect data on children for commercial purposes. That includes Internet content filters, which are utilized by many schools to block objectionable material but can also track users' surfing habits.

 Medical records: Health and Human Services Secretary Tommy G. Thompson, left, heeding the concerns of GOP lawmakers and health care interest groups, will re-open the rules-making process for medical privacy regulations issued in December by the Clinton administration. The health care industry complained that the rules, as written, could allow medical providers to withhold treatment if patients do not consent to share their medical information.

New Nukes: A Senator's Blueprint for Plentiful Power

Domenici bill revives long-dormant debate on the economics and safety of atomic energy

At the Los Alamos nuclear weapons laboratory in the mountains of New Mexico, they call Sen. Pete V. Domenici "St. Pete" for all the help and money he has brought them over the years.

An intense and influential man who drives the Senate Budget Committee with corporate efficiency, Domenici for years has been the nuclear world's chief apostle in Congress, adding millions to the federal budget for research and development and traveling as far as Russia to evangelize for the industry.

Now, with California facing electricity shortages, natural gas prices soaring and growing concerns over the polluting effects of generating electricity with coal, Domenici and other proponents of nuclear power have seized on the current moment to make their case for a nuclear comeback.

But instead of the jumbo reactors that so inflamed the passions of environmentalists during the nuclear battles of the 1970s and '80s, Domenici and other nuclear advocates envision a landscape studded with a new generation of smaller power plants that are more cost-effective, safer to operate and take months instead of years to build.

"I'm very optimistic that in the next few years we will witness construction of a new reactor, perhaps to

Domenici testifies on nuclear energy before a House subcommittee March 27. "This is the right time," he says. "I will seek any venue I can."

serve as a demonstration test bed for new technologies," he told the National Academy of Engineering in a recent speech. "Not too many years ago, the thought of new reactor construction in the U.S. would have been a pipe dream."

Environmentalists say it is exactly that, and they are incredulous at the thought of reopening a battle they feel they have already won. After the partial meltdown at Three Mile Island more than two decades ago, federal safety regulators imposed regulations that made new nuclear plants uneconomical, and many utilities were forced to abandon partially built power plants. No new reactors have been ordered since 1978.

"Nuclear power is like General Francisco Franco — it's still dead," said Rep. Edward J. Markey, D-Mass., a longtime

anti-nuclear voice in Congress. "I'm sure there's a group of pro-nuclear industry members who seek to advance the issue, but . . . they have a very difficult set of political hurdles to overcome."

But as the Republicans who run the Congress and the White House develop a national energy policy that they say should include a healthy mix of energy sources, Domenici is expected to use his clout with his colleagues and credibility on the issue to push a strong nuclear agenda.

He is currently promoting a bill (S 472) that would authorize $406 million to help develop new types of nuclear reactors, complete work on existing reactors, simplify licensing and create an entire agency within the Energy Department to study management and recycling of nuclear waste.

And as chairman of the Senate Energy and Water Appropriations subcommittee, he is in a position to push through spending for research into new technologies that would answer critics' concerns about the safety of nuclear plants and the disposal of the waste they produce.

"While [emphasizing nuclear energy] may have been the right thing to do for a number of years, it now becomes opportune," Domenici said. "Nuclear power is safe, if not safer than some of the other energy sources, and it is environmentally sound."

Nuclear power proponents cite improvements in the operating performance of the current generation of reactors. Nuclear power plants have become more efficient and less expensive to run. And the number of emergency reactor shutdowns — known as "scrams" — has dropped from 474 at 92 plants in 1985 to 50 at 104 plants in 1998.

Like the debate over whether to allow oil companies to drill in Alaska's remote Arctic National Wildlife Refuge (ANWR), the nuclear issue pits environmentalists against a powerful industry that believes rising energy prices will cause public sentiment to swing its way. Environmentalists think they have the upper hand in both cases.

"If [Domenici's] bill weren't so outrageous, it would just be silly," said Anna Aurilio, legislative director for the U.S. Public Interest Research Group in Washington. "There's a

The Country's Regional Energy Mixes

Most regions of the United States rely on coal-burning plants for the bulk of their electricity. Only New England and the Middle Atlantic region of New York, Pennsylvania and New Jersey depend largely on nuclear power. On the Pacific Coast and in Nevada, hydropower from dams provides most of the electricity. Only in the West South Central region, Alaska and Hawaii does natural gas serve as a major power source.

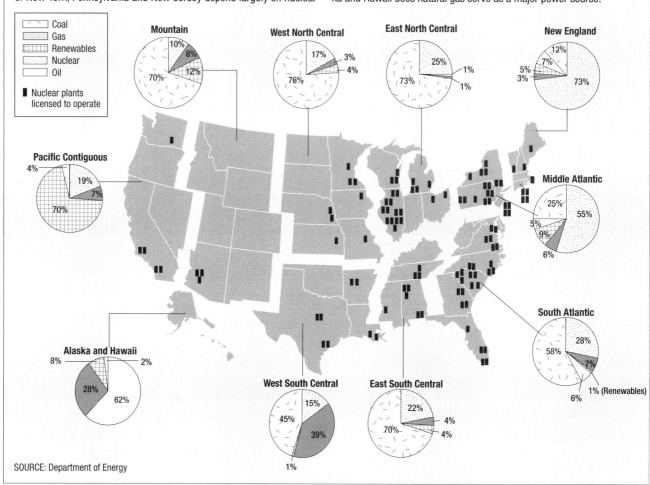

SOURCE: Department of Energy

set of people who want to continue to subsidize the nuclear energy industry and weaken what are already weak public protections. Unfortunately, Sen. Domenici's bill embodies all of these wrongheaded proposals."

While environmentalists are concerned, partly because of Domenici's reputation and influence, it is not clear how far he can push his nuclear agenda.

The Bush administration, with its well-known ties to the oil industry, has not actively promoted nuclear power, saying only that it will have a prominent place in a "balanced approach" to energy policy.

And Domenici's bill could face some competition from a more modest measure (S 242) sponsored by his New Mexico colleague, Democrat Jeff Bingaman, that would authorize $240 million over five years for nuclear-related research. It could attract the support of moderates.

Watts and Waste

Anything seemed possible for nuclear power in its early days. Some predicted that it would run ships, trains and even automobiles by the year 2000. But the industry was unable to produce the cheap electric power it had promised. By 1976, the average cost for electricity from nuclear power plants was about 20 percent higher than from coal-burning plants.

Public utility orders for nuclear plants fell from 34 in 1973 to an average of four a year between 1975 and 1977. In 1978, a year before the Three Mile Island accident near Harrisburg, Pa., only two new plants were ordered and a number were canceled. None have been ordered since.

Meanwhile, the federal government has been unable to decide where to bury for all time more than 40,000 tons of high-level nuclear waste piling up at commercial reactors in 34 states. A federal court had told the government to take control of the waste by 1998. (*1998 Almanac, p. 11-4*)

Congress in 1987 designated Yucca Mountain in desolate central Nevada as the probable burial ground, but no final decision has been made. Yucca Mountain may not be available until at least 2010. (*1987 Almanac, p. 307; 2000 CQ Weekly, p. 2902*)

Domenici's home state of New Mexico is the burial site for waste from nuclear weapons labs. Although it has no commercial nuclear power plants — coal is cheaper there — the first atomic bomb was built at Los Alamos, and there is a second weapons lab, Sandia, in Albuquerque.

It was while talking to scientists at Los Alamos that Domenici decided to "lead a new dialogue," as he puts it, on commercial nuclear energy. He complains that the public's fears have been exacerbated by environmentalists who emphasize nuclear energy's risks while ignoring its advantages.

Domenici first outlined his intentions in an October 1997 address to a scientific conference at Harvard University.

As chairman of the Senate Energy and Water Development Appropriations Subcommittee, Domenici has added millions of dollars for nuclear research and development, including some at Los Alamos. Part of the money has gone for a costly and controversial technology known as transmutation, which seeks to reduce the radioactivity of nuclear waste. (*Byproducts, this page*)

Domenici has worked to fund an investigation of the health effects of low-level radiation — he argues it is not as harmful as the public believes — and ordered the General Accounting Office (GAO) in 2000 to study the scientific basis for what he contends are overly stringent radiation standards for nuclear waste disposal sites. The GAO found no consensus, but said the standards should not be made more strict.

He has extolled the benefits of irradiating food to remove bacteria and other contaminants.

Clearing the Air

Domenici's bill, in addition to authorizing more research and development, would qualify nuclear power for incentives that states receive to meet Clean Air Act requirements. It also would establish nuclear-generated electricity as an "environmentally preferable" product under federal purchasing guidelines, while removing a prohibition against foreign ownership of U.S. nuclear power plants.

Domenici and his bill's cosponsors — 11 Republicans and three Democrats — say they want to keep nuclear energy from falling behind other sources.

One of the cosponsors, Senate Republican Policy Committee Chairman Larry E. Craig of Idaho, said he would like to increase nuclear power's share of the U.S. energy market from 20 percent to at least 30 percent over the next few years. Under current trends, the Energy Department forecasts that nuclear power's share will shrink to 11 percent by 2020 as power plants go out of service and no new ones are built.

Domenici's crusade has helped lift the morale of the nuclear power industry, which has always tried to position itself as a clean and safe source of elec-

Byproducts and Bad Chemistry

The United States is trying to figure out how to safely store highly radioactive waste from nuclear power plants essentially forever. But what if the radioactivity could be reduced so the material would not be a threat after, say, several hundred years?

That is the hope of "transmutation," an experimental process of bombarding spent nuclear fuel with intense neutron beams, converting some long-lived radioactive isotopes into less lethal substances.

The Los Alamos National Laboratory in New Mexico recently began a major research program on transmutation with $34 million allocated in the fiscal 2001 energy and water appropriations law (PL 106-377) by Sen. Pete V. Domenici, R-N.M. The initiative also is studying the future production of tritium for the U.S. weapons stockpile.

"I view our efforts as being part of a bootstrap process, gaining expertise, bringing in new blood and demonstrating the capability of new technology," said Edward Arthur, the program's director.

Domenici and Frank H. Murkowski, R-Alaska, chairman of the Senate Energy and Natural Resources Committee, have introduced bills (S 472, S 389) that would create an agency within the Energy Department to study waste-reduction technologies such as transmutation.

Environmentalists and scientific critics dismiss transmutation as "nuclear alchemy" — prohibitively expensive and technologically questionable. The Energy Department has estimated that a transmutation program could cost as much as $280 billion — $10 billion less than the entire fiscal 2001 defense budget.

A coalition of environmental groups recently singled out transmutation as an example of wasteful spending. Some scientists say it is so technically difficult that it could generate more waste than it is designed to treat.

In 1996, the National Research Council of the National Academy of Sciences, recommended a modest research program on transmutation, but it warned that byproducts of fuel reprocessing, including plutonium, could raise the risk of nuclear proliferation.

But support from Domenici and other lawmakers, including those in Nevada where high-level waste likely will be stored, have kept the concept alive.

"There are so many ill-advised research programs that can't be stamped out because of the political clout they have," said Edwin Lyman, scientific director of the Nuclear Control Institute, a Washington-based nonproliferation group. "This is a perfect example."

In 1999, the Energy Department concluded that the technology could potentially reduce long-term radiation doses from waste to about one-tenth the original levels. It urged Congress to consider spending $281 million over six years to continue research.

That September, the House adopted an amendment by Shelley Berkley, D-Nev., to an energy research bill (HR 1655) that would have authorized an additional $6 million for transmutation research. The bill passed the House but failed to come to a vote in the Senate, though a spokesman said Berkley is considering introducing another bill this year. (*1999 CQ Weekly, p. 2176*)

In the March 1 Bulletin of the Atomic Scientists, Arjun Makhijani, president of the Institute for Energy and Environmental Research and two other scientists wrote that there is "no good solution" to high-level nuclear waste.

"Instead of facing up to the terrible burden that the first half-century of nuclear power will impose on future generations," they wrote, "the votaries of nuclear power technology are trying to persuade the public to cough up billions more in the pursuit of another nuclear chimera — transmutation."

Cheney Indicates Interest

The Bush administration is sending mixed signals on the role nuclear power will play in its forthcoming energy strategy, which is due out later this month.

Vice President Dick Cheney, who is leading the White House effort to develop the energy blueprint, met with several senators March 27 and signaled his interest in giving nuclear power more prominence, according to several of those at the meeting.

"If you're really serious about greenhouse gases, one of the solutions to that problem is to go back and let's take another look at nuclear power . . . to generate electricity without the adverse consequences," Cheney said March 21 on MSNBC's "Hardball."

Energy Secretary Spencer Abraham was less enthusiastic in an April 1 interview on ABC's "This Week," saying nuclear power would be part of a "balanced approach."

"I think there will be a role for nuclear energy," he said, "but we have to also solve the problem of what to do with the waste that's generated from nuclear facilities. We're working on that even as we build our plan."

Congressional aides said the administration's fiscal 2001 budget request due April 9 is expected to recommend less spending for nuclear energy research and development.

The administration already has proposed reducing Energy Department spending $700 million from this year's level. Bush's budget blueprint in February criticized the agency, noting that according to a General Accounting Office study only 10 percent of the agency's programs are finished on time and on budget. (*2001 CQ Weekly*, p. 457)

Abraham indicated, however, that the administration might add to the budget as it shapes its energy plan. "What we're going to have is a budget that's driven by a new policy, not a budget driving the policy," he said.

tricity for a power hungry nation.

Federal energy officials estimate that U.S. electricity demand will rise 45 percent over the next 20 years, which they say will require building more than 1,300 new power plants — about 65 a year.

Domenici said that while he supports more emphasis on renewable energy sources — geothermal, solar and wind — they are not in the same league as nuclear. Renewable sources other than hydro powers now provide just 2 percent of the nation's energy.

"Many of us are willing to double, triple, quadruple the amount of solar and wind," Domenici said. "But America can't solve its energy problems that way."

Nuclear power supporters see hope in recent polls reflecting public discontent with oil and natural gas prices. A Fox News/Opinion Dynamics poll asked 902 registered voters in January whether they favored or opposed building more nuclear power plants as a way to meet the need for more electricity. Forty-four percent said they were in favor, 41 percent said they were opposed and the rest said they were uncertain.

"We need to find ways to encourage the public to assess the relative risks of nuclear power . . . and the government has the bully pulpit," said Paul E. Gray, president emeritus of the Massachusetts Institute of Technology and a longtime advocate of nuclear energy.

Atomic Tours

In an effort to stir up interest and support, the industry's Washington lobbying arm, the Nuclear Energy Institute, has run advertising campaigns and sponsored trips for lawmakers and reporters to Yucca Mountain and countries such as France that rely heavily on nuclear power. The group also has contributed heavily to the political campaigns of lawmakers, most of them Republicans, who support the group's cause. (*Chart, p. 109*)

The industry uses several recent developments to bolster its case:

• The efficiency of nuclear power plants has increased markedly in the past decade — output is up more than 20 percent even though no new plants have been built. At the same time, production costs last year dropped below those of coal-fired plants for the first time since 1987.

• The Nuclear Regulatory Commission (NRC) recently relicensed five nuclear reactors, and the Nuclear Energy Institute estimates that owners of about one-third of the nation's 103 nuclear plants will notify the NRC of their intent to apply for 20-year license extensions.

• In South Africa, Exelon Corp. is developing a new and safer "pebble bed" nuclear reactor that uses graphite-clad uranium spheres the size of tennis balls as fuel. The uranium atoms circulate through the reactor.

Exelon is working with South Africa's electric utility and British Nuclear Fuels Ltd. and plans to build a demonstration plant near Cape Town.

Pebble-bed technology could arrive in the United States within a few years, according to Joe F. Colvin, the Nuclear Energy Institute's president and chief executive officer. (*Colvin, p. 109*)

He said such reactors would have a modular design, making them easier to build, and would generate about 110 megawatts of electricity — far smaller than most current generators. One thousand megawatts is enough to serve about 570,000 people, or a city roughly the size of Washington.

"We need to increase the size of electricity system to almost double what it is today," Colvin said. "It's refreshing that politicians like Sen. Domenici are recognizing this need and bringing some resources to bear on it."

If supporters like Colvin consider Domenici's legislation farsighted, critics of nuclear energy find it misguided. They predict that as more oil and natural gas drilling occurs — and as technological advances make renewable energy more cost-efficient — utilities will turn to those sources instead of trying to build nuclear plants. They say Domenici should just let that happen.

"Sen. Domenici's nuclear energy bill is yet another misguided attempt to subsidize this most dangerous and unforgiving technology," said Wenonah Hauter, director of Public Citizen's Critical Mass Energy and Environment Program.

In particular, Hauter and other environmentalists point to the bill's extension of the 1957 Price-Anderson Act, which limits the liability of the nuclear industry in case of an accident. They say such a measure amounts to a taxpayer-backed insurance policy.

The critics also fault Domenici's bill because it includes several changes in the nuclear licensing system that the NRC has sought in order to streamline the process. The changes would shift from formal hearings, which allow the public to obtain documents through discovery and cross-examine hearing participants, to an informal process in which the public could do neither.

Proliferation Worries

Meanwhile, arms control activists fear that a proposed agency to study how to manage spent fuel would consider converting the plutonium from nuclear weapons into fuel so it could be burned in nuclear power plants. President Jimmy Carter banned such reprocessing, warning it could lead to the proliferation of nuclear weapons in hostile nations. No subsequent president has changed the policy.

Activists say that mixed-oxide fuel from reprocessing is at least four to eight times more expensive than the uranium fuel used in commercial power plants. "If the government became convinced that it has to start another government-subsidized program, that this should be a national priority, that's a concern," said Edwin Lyman, scientific director of the Nuclear Control Institute, a Washington research center focused on halting nuclear proliferation.

Some lawmakers who support nuclear energy do not endorse Domenici's wide-ranging proposals, preferring something closer to Bingaman's bill.

That legislation would authorize funding for nuclear-related research at universities and programs to recruit students into nuclear fields.

"If we lose the university infrastructure that now trains nuclear-capable scientists and engineers, our nation will find it much harder to meet the challenge . . . of maintaining our energy supplies," said Bingaman, the Senate Energy and Natural Resources Committee's ranking Democrat.

Though Bingaman's bill could weaken Domenici's chances, he has a reputation for persistence — and he vowed he would push to make his vision for "new nukes" instead of "no nukes" a reality.

Polishing the Industry's Image

As nuclear energy's chief salesman in Washington, Joe F. Colvin enjoys taking members of Congress on frequent trips to France and Japan — both heavily dependent on nuclear power — and to Nevada, where nuclear waste is likely to be stored.

The trips, Colvin said, help lawmakers and their staffs see the potential benefits of nuclear power for themselves. "It's reality," he said, "not perception."

Colvin, 58, the president and chief operating officer of the Nuclear Energy Institute, has coordinated a campaign to reshape the image of nuclear energy in ways that are aggressive, yet not intimidating. The institute's Web site, for example, includes statistics boasting about such issues as improvements in reactor design — but it also has a "Science Club" for children, with animated graphics describing various aspects of "the nuclear world."

On Capitol Hill, Colvin has operated in a friendly yet focused fashion. He has built solid relationships with Republicans such as Senate Energy and Natural Resources Committee Chairman Frank H. Murkowski of Alaska.

However, Colvin said he also has sought to engage nuclear critics such as Rep. Edward J. Markey, D-Mass. A self-described optimist, Colvin even holds out hope of winning over members of Nevada's congressional delegation, who have bitterly opposed storing high-level waste at Yucca Mountain, 100 miles northwest of Las Vegas.

"We don't write anybody [in Congress] off," he said. "Everybody is important — every state."

Colvin took the helm of the institute in 1996 after two years as its executive vice president. An Oklahoma-born engineer, he spent 21 years in the Navy's nuclear submarine program. "It was a mandatory requirement that every officer except the supply officer had to be nuclear-trained," he said.

Contributions from the Nuclear Industry

Lawmakers with the largest contributions from the nuclear industry in the last two election cycles serve on the House Armed Services, Commerce (now Energy and Commerce) or Appropriations committees.

COMPANIES	1997-2000
General Atomics	$749,593
Nuclear Energy Institute	231,210
CBS Corp. (Westinghouse Electric)	197,600
Mirant Corp. (formerly Southern Co.)	132,500
Yankee Atomic Electric Co.	27,521
Vermont Yankee Nuclear Power Corp.	17,750
U.S. Enrichment Corp.	5,400
STP Nuclear Operating Co.	1,000
BNFL Nuclear Services Inc.	750

RECIPIENTS	1997-2000
Rep. John P. Murtha, D-Pa.	$28,000
Rep. Joe Knollenberg, R-Mich.	27,153
Rep. John M. Spratt, Jr., D-S.C.	25,998
Rep. Lindsey Graham, R-S.C.	25,497
Rep Jerry Lewis, R-Calif.	21,500
Rep. Floyd D. Spence, R-S.C.	21,500
Rep. Peter J. Visclosky, D-Ind.	20,498
Rep. Bob Filner, D-Calif.	20,000
Rep. Joe Skeen, R-N.M.	20,000
Rep. Ken Calvert, R-Calif.	19,000
Rep. Duncan Hunter, R-Calif.	18,750
Sen. Rick Santorum, R-Pa.	18,000
Sen. Frank H. Murkowski, R-Alaska	16,499
Rep. Joe L. Barton, R-Texas	14,249
Rep. Chet Edwards, D-Texas	14,000

Domenici is confident that at least some provisions of his legislation will become law this year. He said he might use his chairmanship of the Appropriations subcommittee to fund some of his proposals in the fiscal 2002 energy and water spending bill without waiting for a broader package to clear the House and Senate.

"This is the right time to put nuclear energy legislation before the Senate and the Congress," he said. "I would hope that we could eventually get an authorization bill. If that becomes impossible, I will seek any venue I can." ◆

Senate Democrats Will Turn Up Heat On Bush to Deliver Proposals For Reducing Global Warming

President Bush got a cool reception over his global warming position when he met with European allies in Sweden on June 14, and Democrats are planning to make Congress an even less hospitable setting.

Senate Democrats plan a series of steps — from holding hearings on specific legislation to adding policy riders to appropriations bills — that they hope will increase the pressure on Bush to offer concrete proposals to reduce greenhouse gases through mandatory reduction of emissions. The gases are believed to be a major contributor to rising temperatures worldwide.

"There's little doubt that we're going to address the issue," Majority Leader Tom Daschle, D-S.D., said June 14.

Bush said before his trip that he would push for a number of proposals to combat warming — including more research into climate change and technologies that could affect it. He also reiterated his opposition to the 1997 Kyoto Protocol, saying it was "fatally flawed in fundamental ways."

The agreement, which called on the United States to reduce emissions of greenhouse gases 7 percent below 1990 levels by 2012, was never ratified by the Senate. (*Background, 2001 CQ Weekly, p. 724; 1997 Almanac, p. 4-13*)

"Climate change is not isolated to Europe or to America. It is a global effect," Swedish Prime Minister Goeran Persson said at a news conference with Bush and other heads of state in Goteberg, Sweden. "If you are in favor of or against the Kyoto protocol, you have to take action."

"We agreed to create new channels of cooperation on this important topic," Bush said after the news conference. "We don't agree on the Kyoto treaty, but we do agree that climate change is a serious issue."

Bush said he objects to the Kyoto pact in part because developing nations are exempt. "The goals were not realis-

tic. But that doesn't mean we cannot continue to work together," he said.

Bush and a Cabinet-level task force studying the issue emphasized that a June 6 National Academy of Sciences report requested by the White House found some scientific uncertainty on the causes and possible effects of global warming. The report also said that warming "could well have serious adverse societal and economic impacts by the end of this century." (*2001 CQ Weekly, p. 1378*)

Democrats see Bush's environmental policies — which include abandoning a pledge to regulate carbon dioxide emissions and delaying tougher standards on arsenic levels in drinking water — as a major political liability for Republicans.

"I don't think there's any doubt that science has now demonstrated without equivocation, without question, that actions must be taken to alleviate the problems of global warming and [carbon dioxide] emissions in particular," Daschle said June 12. "The only way that's going to happen is if we invoke mandatory controls."

Possible Committee Action

Now that they control several key committees, a number of Senate Democrats plan to call hearings — and possibly move legislation — this summer on global warming.

For example, Joseph I. Lieberman, D-Conn., chairman of the Governmental Affairs Committee, is likely to bring up a global warming bill (S 1008) by top Senate appropriators Robert C. Byrd, D-W.Va., and Ted Stevens, R-Alaska.

Their bill would authorize nearly $5 billion over 10 years to create new federal centers to study global warming and propose solutions. (*2001 CQ Weekly, p. 1378*)

Lieberman also may use his position as chairman of the Environment and Public Works Subcommittee on Clean Air, Wetlands, Private Property and Nuclear Safety to move a measure (S

556) he is cosponsoring with James M. Jeffords, I-Vt., that would regulate emissions of four major gases believed to contribute to global warming.

Bush has proposed regulating three of the gases — nitrogen oxide, sulfur dioxide and mercury— but not carbon dioxide, which is believed to be one of the main contributors to warming. (*2001 CQ Weekly, p. 607*)

John Kerry, D-Mass., an ally of environmental groups, presides over the Commerce, Science and Transportation Subcommittee on Oceans and Fisheries and said he hopes to hold hearings "soon" on climate change.

Energy and Natural Resources Committee Chairman Jeff Bingaman, D-N.M., has been trying to find common ground with Republicans on Bush's energy plan. (*2001 CQ Weekly, p. 1369*)

However, Bingaman said he "was disappointed [Bush] didn't commit the administration to concrete steps to reduce greenhouse gases."

Administration officials say more studies are needed. "There's still some science that is unclear," EPA administrator Christine Todd Whitman told reporters June 12. "As we move forward and decide on actions that we need to take, it would be helpful to have real science behind what those levels should be."

Whitman also urged Congress to enact parts of the administration's energy plan that could reduce greenhouse gases. And she said the task force is "looking at the multi-emissions bill."

Bush's three-pollutant policy faces challenges from the left and the right. Jeffords and Democrats want to move the four-pollutant measure. But conservatives say no legislation that would further regulate the coal industry and other fossil fuel producers is needed.

"Until we have the science in place, I don't think there's much chance for that [bill]," said Sen. Larry E. Craig, R-Idaho, who convened a private June 8 briefing of scientists, lawmakers and White House officials on the issue. ◆

Moderate Democrats Hold Key To Bush's Anti-Missile Program

President must overcome senators' skepticism, Russian rigidity about ending ABM pact

When President Bush sits down with Russian President Vladimir V. Putin in Ljubljana, Slovenia, on June 16 for their first summit, moderate Democrats back home in Congress will be watching closely. They hold the key to Bush's ambitious plan to build a national anti-missile defense system, but they worry that it could jeopardize the 1972 treaty limiting anti-ballistic missile (ABM) systems.

Putin has warned that if the United States abrogates the ABM treaty, Russia will abandon all other arms reduction agreements. U.S. allies and most congressional Democrats fear that would lead to a new nuclear arms race.

The Bush team contends that if Putin is convinced the United States is determined to deploy an anti-missile system, he will collaborate in crafting a new strategic framework, either by modifying the ABM pact or by replacing it with some other agreement.

Defense Secretary Donald H. Rumsfeld adopted such a hard line during a meeting of NATO defense ministers in Brussels on June 7-8. "Deploying missile defenses capable of protecting the U.S., friends and allies will eventually require moving beyond the ABM Treaty," Rumsfeld said.

But the administration's campaign to show that anti-missile defense is inevitabile may be hindered by moderate Democrats who insist they are open to the merits of missile defense but do not want to deploy a system that has not been rigorously tested or that would entail abrogating the ABM Treaty.

Senate Intelligence Committee Chairman Bob Graham, D-Fla., for instance, called the ABM Treaty "one of the foundation stones of our national security."

"We should look at ways of revising it," Graham said, "but getting rid of it would not be smart."

Bush's challenge is to break a cycle of opposition in which Senate skeptics reinforce Putin's refusal to give ground on the treaty and vice versa.

Conservative activists insist that missile defense is a winning political issue and that Bush can line up Democrats, particularly those from states he carried, by taking the issue to the country.

While Bush has not ruled that out, he has been taking a more conciliatory approach, trying to ease the concerns of wavering lawmakers by emphasizing his determination to consult with Russia and nervous U.S. allies in Europe about how to craft a new security relationship with Russia that would replace or substantially amend the ABM Treaty. (*Bush speech excerpts, p. 114*)

Bush reinforced that conciliatory approach June 6, announcing that he would reopen negotiations with North Korea on its weapons programs and proliferation.

Those talks, which the Clinton administration had said were making substantial progress, were suspended soon after Bush took office. White House officials said at the time that they wanted evidence that North Korea was serious.

The new collaborative approach toward Russia appeals to key Democrats such as Sen. Bill Nelson of Florida, a member of both the Foreign Relations and Armed Services Committees. "Russia needs us, and we need the Russians," said Nelson. "We need to be partners to stabilize the world and end nuclear proliferation."

Quick Contents

President Bush is trying to convince Russian leaders that he will build an anti-missile system whether or not they agree to rewrite or replace the 1972 ABM treaty. Congress is unlikely to go along with such a tough approach and would not support abrogating the treaty.

Rumsfeld walks through rain past Ukrainian soldiers during a visit to Kiev on June 5. He later told NATO ministers that Bush would build missile defenses no matter what.

Non-Proliferation Programs Could Get Boost From Democrats

Democrats hope to use their control of the Senate to substantially increase spending for "Nunn-Lugar" non-proliferation programs in Russia, rather than reducing them as President Bush has proposed.

However, they will have to overcome criticism by some lawmakers that the programs either do not work well enough or spend much of their money in the United States.

The programs — which have developed from legislation (PL 102-228) that former Senate Armed Services Committee Chairman Sam Nunn, D-Ga. (1972-97) and Richard G. Lugar, R-Ind., wrote in 1991 — help Russia safeguard and destroy nuclear, chemical and biological weapons and find alternative work for former Soviet weapons scientists.

During his presidential campaign, Bush called for increased spending on these programs.

But in his fiscal 2002 budget request, Bush proposed $100 million in cuts in Energy Department non-proliferation programs that were initiated by Nunn, Lugar and Sen. Pete V. Domenici of New Mexico, ranking Republican on the Energy and Water Development Appropriations Subcommittee.

Bush's request for $774 million for the Energy Department activities is almost half the $1.3 billion President Bill Clinton was preparing to seek in fiscal 2002, according to Rose Gottemoeller, who headed Energy Department non-proliferation programs for the Clinton administration.

The Bush administration also is reviewing Nunn-Lugar programs at the State and Defense departments, though the president largely spared those from budget cuts.

New Senate Armed Services Committee Chairman Carl Levin, D-Mich., and Foreign Relations Committee Chairman Joseph R. Biden Jr., D-Del., have criticized the proposed Energy Department cuts, saying increased funding for the pro-grams would be more important than building a national missile defense system, as Bush has proposed.

"The proliferation of weapons of mass destruction or fissile material in the hands of people who would use them remains the greatest threat to our security," Levin said in a May 11 speech at the National Defense University. "Keep in mind that Russia has enough plutonium and highly enriched uranium for some 60,000-80,000 nuclear weapons — a proliferation nightmare waiting to become a reality if we do not work hard with Russia to reduce that threat."

Levin and Biden have urged Congress to endorse the outlines of a bipartisan report commissioned by the Energy Department and written by former Senate Majority Leader Howard H. Baker Jr., R-Tenn. (1967-85), now Bush's ambassador to Japan, and former White House counsel Lloyd Cutler, a Democrat. Baker and Cutler called for spending $30 billion over the next eight to 10 years to secure Russian nuclear and other dangerous material in Russia, saying it was "the most urgent unmet national security threat to the United States today."

Jobs for Scientists

Yet proponents face a substantial challenge in winning more money for the Nunn-Lugar programs.

Some lawmakers are skeptical of the effectiveness of the programs and Russia's commitment to them. Others prefer programs that eliminate Russian hardware but are leery of those designed to find jobs for Russian weapons scientists.

Energy Secretary Spencer Abraham told the House Energy and Water Development Appropriations Subcommittee May 2 that some of the largest cuts Bush proposed are in programs that, intentionally or not, spend much of their money in the United States, not Russia.

For example, Bush proposed cutting the Nuclear Cities Initiative from $26.6 million in the current fiscal year to $6.6 million in fiscal 2002. The program aims to create civilian jobs for weapons scientists in cities closed to outsiders during the Soviet years.

The General Accounting Office reported in May that about 70 percent of the program's budget was spent at U.S. laboratories. Similar complaints have been lodged in the past against another program designed to keep Russian scientists from selling their expertise abroad. (*1999 CQ Weekly, p. 839*)

The Bush administration has asked for less money than Clinton was planning to request to implement a U.S.-Russian agreement for disposal of weapons-grade plutonium because, Abraham said, the financially strapped Russians were not going to spend similar amounts of money reducing their stockpile.

Logical Ways

Still, Domenici, Lugar and other supporters of the Nunn-Lugar programs have expressed confidence that Congress will restore the money Bush was to cut from the Energy Department programs, noting that in the past, lawmakers have generally supported Nunn-Lugar.

"This will seem a logical way of working with the Russians constructively to destroy something that threatens us," Lugar said.

But some Republicans grumble that the programs use precious defense dollars for foreign aid and indirectly subsidize Russia's military budget.

And Lugar and other supporters acknowledge that a major threat to the programs is the ad hoc way in which they have developed since the end of the Cold War. He and Biden have supported legislation (S 673) by Sen. Chuck Hagel, R-Neb., to create a coordinating committee.

The domestic politics will come to a head when Bush asks Congress to fund specific programs that would violate the ABM Treaty. Thus far, he has kept all his options open, saying that Rumsfeld is reviewing various options for the type of anti-missile network he will ask Congress to fund.

But Pentagon Comptroller Dov Zakheim told reporters May 31 that the fiscal 2002 Pentagon budget amendment Bush is expected to send Congress within a few weeks would include money to jump-start the missile defense effort.

Until Bush proposes a specific program, the cost is guesswork. But skeptics insist the kind of system he has hinted at could cost $100 billion, or double the $50 billion price tag estimated for Clinton's more modest national missile defense plan.

Defense contractors reportedly have briefed top Pentagon officials on specific proposals to field a very limited defense by 2004, even before the system has been fully tested. That approach almost surely would face tough going with centrists such as Democrat Evan Bayh of Indiana.

"We need to be for a missile defense that will protect America," Bayh said in an interview, "but that means it needs to work."

By conceding the potential value of missile defense but insisting that any system be thoroughly tested, the centrists may be framing a key issue of this year's debate: The ABM Treaty prohibits testing of all but a narrowly defined type of weapon. If Russia does not quickly agree to changes that would give the Pentagon more leeway to test some of the weapons Bush wants to consider, will Senate Democrats block those tests in order to avoid violating the treaty?

Rogues and the Treaty

Unlike President Ronald Reagan's 1983 proposal for a national anti-missile shield — the plan critics derided as "star wars" — that would have been intended to fend off thousands of Soviet warheads, Bush wants a more modest system that could knock down a limited number of missiles that a rogue regime might launch.

The administration has warned that such countries would not have to actually fire a missile: The threat alone could blackmail the United States into not coming to the aid of an ally that

was being invaded, for instance.

"We intend for this missile defense capability to be directed at . . . handfuls, not hundreds [of attacking warheads]," a senior defense official told reporters June 7. "This is not something that is intended to undermine in any fashion the security of Russia. We know that, the Russians know that, and the Russians know that we know that."

Russian leaders, however, have argued that such a limited system could easily be upgraded to a more extensive system if U.S.-Russian relations deteriorated.

Even President Bill Clinton's plan for deploying a small number of interceptor missiles in Alaska to deal with a missile launched from North Korea would require a substantial revision of the ABM Treaty, which bans any national defense. The Bush administration's plan to consider using Navy ships to protect U.S. territory would require additional changes, since the treaty bans all mobile anti-missile weapons. (*2001 CQ Weekly, p. 1024*)

Grudging Agreement

Although congressional Democrats went along with Clinton's plan, many did so grudgingly, sharing the concern of arms control activists that it might lead to a new arms race.

"The arms race concern of a generation ago has gone away," Senate Foreign Relations Committee Chairman Joseph R. Biden Jr., D-Del., said in a May 10 speech. "But the concern about nuclear instability is no longer just a U.S.-Soviet matter. Today it is a global issue."

In 1998, Senate Democrats blocked debate on an essentially symbolic bill offered by Thad Cochran, R-Miss., declaring it national policy to deploy a nationwide missile defense as soon as technologically feasible. The climate changed after the November 1998 election, when Bayh and other newcomers joined centrist Democrats like Joseph I. Lieberman of Connecticut and Mary L. Landrieu of Louisiana in insisting that the party could not just flatly oppose missile defense.

The Cochran bill was subsequently enacted. (*1999 Almanac, p. 9-36*)

The outlook is different now that Congress faces a Republican president who says he will propose a program that would "go beyond" the ABM

Treaty. After Bush reaffirmed his commitment to missile defense in a May 1 speech, top Senate Democrats vowed to fight him if he meant to unilaterally abandon the treaty.

Conservative missile defense activists have mapped two lines of attack on the ABM Treaty.

Some legal experts, including Douglas J. Feith, Bush's nominee to be undersecretary of Defense for policy, argue that the treaty simply ceased to exist with the dissolution in 1991 of the Soviet Union. Levin and other Senate Armed Services Committee Democrats grilled Feith on his analysis — and on its implications for other agreements with the former Soviet Union — during a June 5 confirmation hearing. Feith's view is shared by some top congressional Republicans, such as Sen. Jesse Helms of North Carolina, ranking member on the Foreign Relations Committee.

Other treaty opponents have urged Bush simply to exercise the provision of the treaty that allows either party to withdraw on six months' notice. While the legal case is not crystal clear, it appears that Bush would have the constitutional authority to withdraw without seeking congressional approval.

However, Bush would need Congress to fund any anti-missile system. In that case, he would need to round up enough of those Democrats not unalterably opposed to missile defense for a filibuster-proof 60-vote majority.

If Bush is intent on trying to deploy some type of missile defense as quickly as possible, the easiest option would be to dust off Clinton's plan for a land-based system in Alaska that would use a new radar to be built on the Aleutian island of Shemya.

Building the radar would violate the ABM Treaty, although there was a range of legal opinions within the Clinton administration as to how far work could proceed before the treaty would be unequivocally breached. In any case, the Aleutian weather is so bad that construction could take place only during summer months.

Last September, Clinton put the project on hold, citing unsuccessful tests of the anti-missile interceptor.

The Washington Post reported June 8 that one option before the Pentagon is to step up the tempo of test flights for the interceptor missile and then deploy a handful of them in Alaska by March 2004 without waiting for the new radar.

Initially, the interceptors could be guided by upgrading existing early-warning radars, which are less well suited for the job than the so-called "X-band" radar planned for Shemya.

Other than the land-based system in Alaska, there are few missile defense options that could be fielded any time soon.

Frank J. Gaffney Jr., a leading missile defense advocate who is president of the Center for Security Policy, says the Clinton administration denied support to other anti-missile programs. "You really did see the Clinton team sow salt in the ground," Gaffney said in an interview.

As a near-term expedient for dealing with the possibility of a missile attack from North Korea, Gaffney has proposed that the Navy station two Aegis cruisers near Korea in hopes that they could shoot down a long-range missile immediately after launch, before it had gained too much speed.

The ships' anti-missile capability could be upgraded later, he says.

Maneuvering in the Middle

None of those near-term options meet the demands of Democrats for thorough testing and a transitional agreement with Russia.

Gaffney and other missile defense advocates contend that Bush could win congressional approval by appealing to the public. The passage of the Cochran bill, they say, showed that Democrats were unwilling to appear to be opposed to missile defense.

"The reason they voted in favor of it was because they believed there were some non-trivial political risks associated with continuing to reject . . . missile defense," Gaffney says.

But opponents of missile defense have strong arguments, including the fear of a new arms race if Russia particularly does not concur in changes to the ABM Treaty. A worldwide arms race could leave the United States more vulnerable that it is now.

Particularly in light of the checkered test history of various anti-missile programs, critics would hammer at any proposal to cut corners on a rigorous testing program for the sake of early deployment.

By that same token, Democrats would be less well positioned to object to a proposal for rigorous testing that would violate the tight restrictions of the ABM Treaty.

Bush's Policy Evolution

President Bush has softened his approach to missile defense and the 1972 Anti-Ballistic Missile (ABM) Treaty since taking office. Following are excerpts from a campaign speech on the subject and a more recent address.

Sept. 23, 1999, speech at The Citadel in South Carolina:

"At the earliest possible date, my administration will deploy antiballistic missile systems, both theater and national, to guard against attack and blackmail.

"To make this possible, we will offer Russia the necessary amendments to the Anti-Ballistic Missile Treaty, an artifact of Cold War confrontation. Both sides know that we live in a different world from 1972, when that treaty was signed. If Russia refuses the changes we propose, we will give prompt notice, under the provisions of the treaty, that we can no longer be a party to it. I will have a solemn obligation to protect the American people and our allies, not to protect arms control agreements signed almost 30 years ago."

May 1, 2001, speech at the National Defense University:

"We need a new framework that allows us to build missile defenses to counter the different threats of today's world. To do so, we must move beyond the constraints of the 30-year-old ABM Treaty. This treaty does not recognize the present or point us to the future. It enshrines the past. No treaty that prevents us from addressing today's threats, that prohibits us from pursuing promising technology to defend ourselves, our friends and our allies is in our interests or in the interests of world peace. . . . "

"When ready, and working with Congress, we will deploy missile defenses to strengthen global security and stability. . . .

"Russia and the United States should work together to develop a new foundation for world peace and security in the 21st century. We should leave behind the constraints of an ABM Treaty that perpetuates a relationship based on distrust and mutual vulnerability. This treaty ignores the fundamental breakthroughs in technology during the last 30 years. It prohibits us from exploring all options for defending against the threats that face us, our allies and other countries.

"That's why we should work together to replace this treaty with a new framework that reflects a clear and clean break from the past, and especially from the adversarial legacy of the Cold War.

"This new cooperative relationship should look to the future, not to the past. It should be reassuring, rather than threatening. It should be premised on openness, mutual confidence and real opportunities for cooperation, including the area of missile defense.

"It should allow us to share information so that each nation can improve its early warning capability and its capability to defend its people and territory. And perhaps one day, we can even cooperate in a joint defense. . . .

"We may have areas of difference with Russia, but we are not — and must not be — strategic adversaries. Russia and America both face new threats to security. Together, we can address today's threats and pursue today's opportunities. We can explore technologies that have the potential to make us all safer."

"If you put money in for more testing, on what grounds would [they] say, 'Take it out?' " asks Peter Huessy, a missile defense proponent with the National Defense University Foundation.

Indeed, in recent interviews both Levin and Biden insisted that a rigorous testing process should precede any deployment decision.

Biden, in particular, has contended that the ABM treaty would not preclude widespread tests of various options. "What does the ABM treaty stop us from doing now?" Biden said. "We can do all the testing we need to do now." ◆

Appendix

The Legislative Process in Brief

Note: Parliamentary terms used below are defined in the glossary.

Introduction of Bills

A House member (including the resident commissioner of Puerto Rico and non-voting delegates of the District of Columbia, Guam, the Virgin Islands and American Samoa) may introduce any one of several types of bills and resolutions by handing it to the clerk of the House or placing it in a box called the hopper. A senator first gains recognition of the presiding officer to announce the introduction of a bill. If objection is offered by any senator, the introduction of the bill is postponed until the following day.

As the next step in either the House or Senate, the bill is numbered, referred to the appropriate committee, labeled with the sponsor's name and sent to the Government Printing Office so that copies can be made for subsequent study and action. Senate bills may be jointly sponsored and carry several senators' names. Until 1978, the House limited the number of members who could cosponsor any one bill; the ceiling was eliminated at the beginning of the 96th Congress. A bill written in the executive branch and proposed as an administration measure usually is introduced by the chairman of the congressional committee that has jurisdiction.

Bills — Prefixed with HR in the House, S in the Senate, followed by a number. Used as the form for most legislation, whether general or special, public or private.

Joint Resolutions — Designated H J Res or S J Res. Subject to the same procedure as bills, with the exception of a joint resolution proposing an amendment to the Constitution. The latter must be approved by two-thirds of both houses and is thereupon sent directly to the administrator of general services for submission to the states for ratification instead of being presented to the president for his approval.

Concurrent Resolutions — Designated H Con Res or S Con Res. Used for matters affecting the operations of both houses. These resolutions do not become law.

Resolutions — Designated H Res or S Res. Used for a matter concerning the operation of either house alone and adopted only by the chamber in which it originates.

Committee Action

With few exceptions, bills are referred to the appropriate standing committees. The job of referral formally is the responsibility of the Speaker of the House and the presiding officer of the Senate, but this task usually is carried out on their behalf by the parliamentarians of the House and Senate. Precedent, statute and the jurisdictional mandates of the committees as set forth in the rules of the House and Senate determine which committees receive what kinds of bills. An exception is the referral of private bills, which are sent to whatever committee is designated by their sponsors. Bills are technically considered "read for the first time" when referred to House committees.

When a bill reaches a committee it is placed on the committee's calendar. At that time the bill comes under the sharpest congressional focus. Its chances for passage are quickly determined — and the great majority of bills falls by the legislative roadside. Failure of a committee to act on a bill is equivalent to killing it; the measure can be withdrawn from the committee's purview only by a discharge petition signed by a majority of the House membership on House bills, or by adoption of a special resolution in the Senate. Discharge attempts rarely succeed.

The first committee action taken on a bill usually is a request for comment on it by interested agencies of the government. The committee chairman may assign the bill to a subcommittee for study and hearings, or it may be considered by the full committee. Hearings may be public, closed (executive session) or both. A subcommittee, after considering a bill, reports to the full committee its recommendations for action and any proposed amendments.

The full committee then votes on its recommendation to the House or Senate. This procedure is called "ordering a bill reported." Occasionally a committee may order a bill reported unfavorably; most of the time a report, submitted by the chairman of the committee to the House or Senate, calls for favorable action on the measure since the committee can effectively "kill" a bill by simply failing to take any action.

After the bill is reported, the committee chairman instructs the staff to prepare a written report. The report describes the purposes and scope of the bill, explains the committee revisions, notes proposed changes in existing law and, usually, includes the views of the executive branch agencies consulted. Often committee members opposing a measure issue dissenting minority statements that are included in the report.

Usually, the committee "marks up" or proposes amendments to the bill. If they are substantial and the measure is complicated, the committee may order a "clean bill" introduced, which will embody the proposed amendments. The original bill then is put aside and the clean bill, with a new number, is reported to the floor.

The chamber must approve, alter or reject the committee amendments before the bill itself can be put to a vote.

Floor Action

After a bill is reported back to the house where it originated, it is placed on the calendar.

There are five legislative calendars in the House, issued in one cumulative calendar titled *Calendars of the United States House of Representatives and History of Legislation*. The House

How a Bill Becomes a Law

This graphic shows the most typical way in which proposed legislation is enacted into law. There are more complicated, as well as simpler, routes, and most bills never become law. The process is illustrated with two hypothetical bills, House bill No. 1 (HR 1) and Senate bill No. 2 (S 2). Bills must be passed by both houses in identical form before they can be sent to the president. The path of HR 1 is traced by a gray line, that of S 2 by a black line. In practice, most bills begin as similar proposals in both houses.

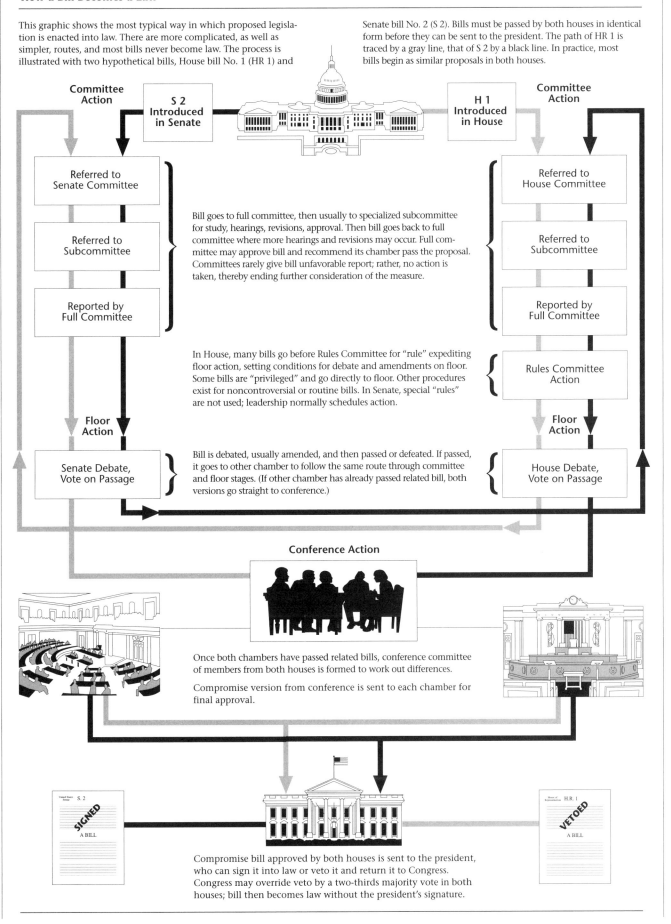

Committee Action

S 2 Introduced in Senate

H 1 Introduced in House

Committee Action

Referred to Senate Committee

Referred to Subcommittee

Reported by Full Committee

Referred to House Committee

Referred to Subcommittee

Reported by Full Committee

Bill goes to full committee, then usually to specialized subcommittee for study, hearings, revisions, approval. Then bill goes back to full committee where more hearings and revisions may occur. Full committee may approve bill and recommend its chamber pass the proposal. Committees rarely give bill unfavorable report; rather, no action is taken, thereby ending further consideration of the measure.

In House, many bills go before Rules Committee for "rule" expediting floor action, setting conditions for debate and amendments on floor. Some bills are "privileged" and go directly to floor. Other procedures exist for noncontroversial or routine bills. In Senate, special "rules" are not used; leadership normally schedules action.

Rules Committee Action

Floor Action

Floor Action

Senate Debate, Vote on Passage

House Debate, Vote on Passage

Bill is debated, usually amended, and then passed or defeated. If passed, it goes to other chamber to follow the same route through committee and floor stages. (If other chamber has already passed related bill, both versions go straight to conference.)

Conference Action

Once both chambers have passed related bills, conference committee of members from both houses is formed to work out differences.

Compromise version from conference is sent to each chamber for final approval.

United States Senate **S 2**
~~SIGNED~~
A BILL

House of Representatives **H.R. 1**
~~VETOED~~
A BILL

Compromise bill approved by both houses is sent to the president, who can sign it into law or veto it and return it to Congress. Congress may override veto by a two-thirds majority vote in both houses; bill then becomes law without the president's signature.

calendars are:

The Union Calendar to which are referred bills raising revenues, general appropriations bills and any measures directly or indirectly appropriating money or property. It is the Calendar of the Committee of the Whole House on the State of the Union.

The House Calendar to which are referred bills of public character not raising revenue or appropriating money.

The Corrections Calendar to which are referred bills to repeal rules and regulations deemed excessive or unnecessary when the Corrections Calendar is called the second and fourth Tuesday of each month. (Instituted in the 104th Congress to replace the seldom-used Consent Calendar.) A three-fifths majority is required for passage.

The Private Calendar to which are referred bills for relief in the nature of claims against the United States or private immigration bills that are passed without debate when the Private Calendar is called the first and third Tuesdays of each month.

The Discharge Calendar to which are referred motions to discharge committees when the necessary signatures are signed to a discharge petition.

There is only one legislative calendar in the Senate and one "executive calendar" for treaties and nominations submitted to the Senate. When the Senate Calendar is called, each senator is limited to five minutes' debate on each bill.

Debate. A bill is brought to debate by varying procedures. If a routine measure, it may await the call of the calendar. If it is urgent or important, it can be taken up in the Senate either by unanimous consent or by a majority vote. The majority leader, in consultation with the minority leader and others, schedules the bills that will be taken up for debate.

In the House, precedence is granted if a special rule is obtained from the Rules Committee. A request for a special rule usually is made by the chairman of the committee that favorably reported the bill, supported by the bill's sponsor and other committee members. The request, considered by the Rules Committee in the same fashion that other committees consider legislative measures, is in the form of a resolution providing for immediate consideration of the bill. The Rules Committee reports the resolution to the House where it is debated and voted on in the same fashion as regular bills. If the Rules Committee fails to report a rule requested by a committee, there are several ways to bring the bill to the House floor — under suspension of the rules, on Calendar Wednesday or by a discharge motion.

The resolutions providing special rules are important because they specify how long the bill may be debated and whether it may be amended from the floor. If floor amendments are banned, the bill is considered under a "closed rule," which permits only members of the committee that first reported the measure to the House to alter its language, subject to chamber acceptance.

When a bill is debated under an "open rule," amendments may be offered from the floor. Committee amendments always are taken up first but may be changed, as may all amendments up to the second degree; that is, an amendment to an amendment to an amendment is not in order.

Duration of debate in the House depends on whether the bill is under discussion by the House proper or before the House when it is sitting as the Committee of the Whole House on the State of the Union. In the former, the amount of time for debate either is determined by special rule or is allocated with an hour for each member if the measure is under consideration without a rule. In the Committee of the Whole the amount of time agreed on for general debate is equally divided between proponents and opponents. At the end of general discussion, the bill is read section by section for amendment. Debate on an amendment is limited to five minutes for each side; this is called the "five-minute rule." In practice, amendments regularly are debated more than ten minutes, with members gaining the floor by offering pro forma amendments or obtaining unanimous consent to speak longer than five minutes.

Senate debate usually is unlimited. It can be halted only by unanimous consent by "cloture," which requires a three-fifths majority of the entire Senate except for proposed changes in the Senate rules. The latter requires a two-thirds vote.

The House considers almost all important bills within a parliamentary framework known as the Committee of the Whole. It is not a committee as the word usually is understood; it is the full House meeting under another name for the purpose of speeding action on legislation. Technically, the House sits as the Committee of the Whole when it considers any tax measure or bill dealing with public appropriations. It also can resolve itself into the Committee of the Whole if a member moves to do so and the motion is carried. The Speaker appoints a member to serve as the chairman. The rules of the House permit the Committee of the Whole to meet when a quorum of 100 members is present on the floor and to amend and act on bills, within certain time limitations. When the Committee of the Whole has acted, it "rises," the Speaker returns as the presiding officer of the House and the member appointed chairman of the Committee of the Whole reports the action of the committee and its recommendations. The Committee of the Whole cannot pass a bill; instead it reports the measure to the full House with whatever changes it has approved. The full House then may pass or reject the bill — or, on occasion, recommit the bill to committee. Amendments adopted in the Committee of the Whole may be put to a second vote in the full House.

Votes. Voting on bills may occur repeatedly before they are finally approved or rejected. The House votes on the rule for the bill and on various amendments to the bill. Voting on amendments often is a more illuminating test of a bill's support than is the final tally. Sometimes members approve final passage of bills after vigorously supporting amendments that, if adopted, would have scuttled the legislation.

The Senate has three different methods of voting: an untabulated voice vote, a standing vote (called a division) and a recorded roll call to which members answer "yea" or "nay" when their names are called. The House also employs voice and standing votes, but since January 1973 yeas and nays have been recorded by an electronic voting device, eliminating the need for time-consuming roll calls.

Another method of voting, used in the House only, is the teller vote. Traditionally, members filed up the center aisle past counters; only vote totals were announced. Since 1971, one-fifth of a quorum can demand that the votes of individual members be recorded, thereby forcing them to take a public position on amendments to key bills. Electronic voting now is commonly used for this purpose.

After amendments to a bill have been voted upon, a vote may be taken on a motion to recommit the bill to committee. If carried, this vote removes the bill from the chamber's calendar and is usually a death blow to the bill. If the motion is unsuccessful, the bill then is "read for the third time." An actual reading usually is dispensed with. Until 1965, an opponent of a bill could delay this move by objecting and asking for a full reading of an engrossed (certified in final form) copy of the bill. After the "third reading," the vote on final passage is taken.

Examples of Legislative Documents

The final vote may be followed by a motion to reconsider, and this motion may be followed by a move to lay the motion on the table. Usually, those voting for the bill's passage vote for the tabling motion, thus safeguarding the final passage action. With that, the bill has been formally passed by the chamber. While a motion to reconsider a Senate vote is pending on a bill, the measure cannot be sent to the House.

Action in Second House

After a bill is passed it is sent to the other chamber. This body may then take one of several steps. It may pass the bill as is — accepting the other chamber's language. It may send the bill to committee for scrutiny or alteration, or reject the entire bill, advising the other house of its actions. Or it simply may ignore the bill submitted while it continues work on its own version of the proposed legislation. Frequently, one chamber may approve a version of a bill that is greatly at variance with the version already passed by the other house, and then substitute its contents for the language of the other, retaining only the latter's bill number.

A provision of the Legislative Reorganization Act of 1970 permits a separate House vote on any non-germane amendment added by the Senate to a House-passed bill and requires a majority vote to retain the amendment. Previously the House was forced to act on the bill as a whole; the only way to defeat the non-germane amendment was to reject the entire bill.

Often the second chamber makes only minor changes. If these are readily agreed to by the other house, the bill then is routed to the president. However, if the opposite chamber significantly alters the bill submitted to it, the measure usually is "sent to conference." The chamber that has possession of the "papers" (engrossed bill, engrossed amendments, messages of transmittal) requests a conference and the other chamber must agree to it. If the second house does not agree, the bill dies.

Conference, Final Action

Conference. A conference works out conficting House and Senate versions of a legislative bill. The conferees usually are senior members appointed by the presiding officers of the two houses, from the committees that managed the bills. Under this arrangement the conferees of one house have the duty of trying to maintain their chamber's position in the face of amending actions by the conferees (also referred to as "managers") of the other house.

The number of conferees from each chamber may vary, the range usually being from three to nine members in each group, depending upon the length or complexity of the bill involved. There may be five representatives and three senators on the conference committee, or the reverse. But a majority vote controls the action of each group so that a large representation does not give one chamber a voting advantage over the other chamber's conferees.

Theoretically, conferees are not allowed to write new legislation in reconciling the two versions before them, but this curb sometimes is bypassed. Many bills have been put into acceptable compromise form only after new language was provided by the conferees. The 1970 Reorganization Act attempted to tighten restrictions on conferees by forbidding them to introduce any language on a topic that neither chamber sent to conference or to modify any topic beyond the scope of the different House and Senate versions.

Frequently the ironing out of difficulties takes days or even weeks. Conferences on involved appropriations bills sometimes are particularly drawn out.

As a conference proceeds, conferees reconcile differences between the versions, but generally they grant concessions only insofar as they remain sure that the chamber they represent will accept the compromises. Occasionally, uncertainty over how either house will react, or the positive refusal of a chamber to back down on a disputed amendment, results in an impasse, and the bills die in conference even though each was approved by its sponsoring chamber.

Conferees sometimes go back to their respective chambers for further instructions, when they report certain portions in disagreement. Then the chamber concerned can either "recede and concur" in the amendment of the other house or "insist on its amendment."

When the conferees have reached agreement, they prepare a conference report embodying their recommendations (compromises). The report, in document form, must be submitted to each house.

The conference report must be approved by each house. Consequently, approval of the report is approval of the compromise bill. In the order of voting on conference reports, the chamber which asked for a conference yields to the other chamber the opportunity to vote first.

Final Steps. After a bill has been passed by both the House and Senate in identical form, all of the original papers are sent to the enrolling clerk of the chamber in which the bill originated. He then prepares an enrolled bill, which is printed on parchment paper. When this bill has been certified as correct by the secretary of the Senate or the clerk of the House, depending on which chamber originated the bill, it is signed first (no matter whether it originated in the Senate or House) by the Speaker of the House and then by the president of the Senate. It is next sent to the White House to await action.

If the president approves the bill, he signs it, dates it and usually writes the word "approved" on the document. If he does not sign it within 10 days (Sundays excepted) and Congress is in session, the bill becomes law without his signature.

However, should Congress adjourn before the 10 days expire, and the president has failed to sign the measure, it does not become law. This procedure is called the pocket veto.

A president vetoes a bill by refusing to sign it and, before the 10-day period expires, returning it to Congress with a message stating his reasons. The message is sent to the chamber that originated the bill. If no action is taken on the message, the bill dies. Congress, however, can attempt to override the president's veto and enact the bill, "the objections of the president to the contrary notwithstanding." Overriding a veto requires a two-thirds vote of those present, who must number a quorum and vote by roll call.

Debate can precede this vote, with motions permitted to lay the message on the table, postpone action on it or refer it to committee. If the president's veto is overridden by a two-thirds vote in both houses, the bill becomes law. Otherwise it is dead.

When bills are passed finally and signed, or passed over a veto, they are given law numbers in numerical order as they become law. There are two series of numbers, one for public and one for private laws, starting at the number "1" for each two-year term of Congress. They are then identified by law number and by Congress — for example, Private Law 21, 97th Congress; Public Law 250, 97th Congress (or PL 97–250).

The Budget Process in Brief

Through the budget process, the president and Congress decide how much to spend and tax during the upcoming fiscal year. More specifically, they decide how much to spend on each activity, ensure that the government spends no more and spends it only for that activity, and report on that spending at the end of each budget cycle.

The President's Budget

The law requires that, by the first Monday in February, the president submit to Congress his proposed federal budget for the next fiscal year, which begins on October 1. In order to accomplish this, the president establishes general budget and fiscal policy guidelines. Based on these guidelines, executive branch agencies make requests for funds and submit them to the White House's Office of Management and Budget (OMB) nearly a year prior to the start of a new fiscal year. The OMB, receiving direction from the president and administration official, reviews the agencies' requests and develops a detailed budget by December. From December to January the OMB prepares the budget documents, so that the president can deliver it to Congress in February.

The president's budget is the executive branch's plan for the next year — but it is just a proposal. After receiving it, Congress has its own budget process to follow from February to October. Only after Congress passes the required spending bills — and the president signs them — has the government created its actual budget.

Action in Congress

Congress first must pass a "budget resolution" — a framework within which the members of Congress will make their decisions about spending and taxes. It includes targets for total spending, total revenues, and the deficit, and allocations within the spending target for the two types of spending — discretionary and mandatory.

Discretionary spending, which currently accounts for about 33 percent of all federal spending, is what the president and Congress must decide to spend for the next year through the thirteen annual appropriations bills. It includes money for such activities as the FBI and the Coast Guard, for housing and education, for NASA and highway and bridge construction, and for defense and foreign aid.

Mandatory spending, which currently accounts for 67 percent of all spending, is authorized by laws that have already been passed. It includes entitlement spending — such as for Social Security, Medicare, veterans' benefits, and food stamps — through which individuals receive benefits because they are eligible based on their age, income, or other criteria. It also includes interest on the national debt, which the government pays to individuals and institutions that hold Treasury bonds and other government securities. The only way the president

and Congress can change the spending on entitlement and other mandatory programs is if they change the laws that authorized the programs.

Currently, the law imposes a limit or "cap" through 1998 on total annual discretionary spending. Within the cap, however, the president and Congress can, and often do, change the spending levels from year to year for the thousands of individual federal programs.

In addition, the law requires that legislation that would raise mandatory spending or lower revenues — compared to existing law — be offset by spending cuts or revenue increases. This requirement, called "pay-as-you-go" is designed to prevent new legislation from increasing the deficit.

Once Congress passes the budget resolution, it turns its attention to passing the thirteen annual appropriations bills and, if it chooses, "authorizing" bills to change the laws governing mandatory spending and revenues.

Congress begins by examining the president's budget in detail. Scores of committees and subcommittees hold hearings on proposals under their jurisdiction. The House and Senate Armed Services Authorizing Committees, and the Defense and Military Construction Subcommittees of the Appropriations Committees, for instance, hold hearings on the president's defense budget. The White House budget director, cabinet officers, and other administration officials work with Congress as it accepts some of the president's proposals, rejects others, and changes still others. Congress can change funding levels, eliminate programs, or add programs not requested by the president. It can add or eliminate taxes and other sources of revenue, or make other changes that affect the amount of revenue collected. Congressional rules require that these committees and subcommittees take actions that reflect the congressional budget resolution.

The president's budget, the budget resolution, and the appropriations or authorizing bills measure spending in two ways — "budget authority" and "outlays." Budget authority is what the law authorizes the federal government to spend for certain programs, projects, or activities. What the government actually spends in a particular year, however, is an outlay. For example, when the government decides to build a space exploration system, the president and Congress may agree to appropriate $1 billion in budget authority. But the space system may take ten years to build. Thus, the government may spend $100 million in outlays in the first year to begin construction and the remaining $900 million during the next nine years as the construction continues.

Congress must provide budget authority before the federal agencies can obligate the government to make outlays. When Congress fails to complete action on one or more of the regular annual appropriations bills before the fiscal year begins on October 1, budget authority may be made on a temporary basis through continuing resolutions. Continuing resolutions make budget authority available for limited periods of time, generally at rates related through some formula to the rate provided in the previous year's appropriation.

Monitoring the Budget

Once Congress passes and the president signs the federal appropriations bills or authorizing laws for the fiscal year, the government monitors the budget through (1) agency program managers and budget officials, including the Inspectors General, who report only to the agency head; (2) the Office of Management and Budget; (3) congressional committees; and (4) the General Accounting Office, an auditing arm of Congress.

This oversight is designed to (1) ensure that agencies comply with legal limits on spending, and that they use budget authority only for the purposes intended; (2) see that programs are operating consistently with legal requirements and existing policy; and (3) ensure that programs are well managed and achieving the intended results.

The president may withhold appropriated amounts from obligation only under certain limited circumstances — to provide for contingencies, to achieve savings made possible through changes in requirements or greater efficiency of operations, or as otherwise provided by law. The Impoundment Control Act of 1974 specifies the procedures that must be followed if funds are withheld. Congress can also cancel previous authorized budget authority by passing a rescissions bill — but it also must be signed by the president.

Glossary of Congressional Terms

Absolute Majority—A vote requiring approval by a majority of all members of a house rather than a majority of members present and voting. Also referred to as constitutional majority.

Act—(1) A bill passed in identical form by both houses of Congress and signed into law by the president or enacted over his veto. A bill also becomes an act without the president's signature if he does not return it to Congress within 10 days (Sundays excepted) and if Congress has not adjourned within that period. (2) Also, the technical term for a bill passed by at least one house and engrossed.

Adjourn for More Than Three Days—Under Article I, Section 5, of the Constitution, neither house may adjourn for more than three days without the approval of the other. The necessary approval is given in a concurrent resolution and agreed to by both houses, which may permit one or both to take such an adjournment.

Adjournment Sine Die—Final adjournment of an annual or two-year session of Congress; literally, adjournment without a day. The two houses must agree to a privileged concurrent resolution for such an adjournment. A sine die adjournment precludes Congress from meeting again until the next constitutionally fixed date of a session (January 3 of the following year) unless Congress determines otherwise by law or the president calls it into special session. Article II, Section 3, of the Constitution authorizes the president to adjourn both houses until such time as he thinks proper when the two houses cannot agree to a time of adjournment, but no president has ever exercised this authority.

Adjournment to a Day (and Time) Certain—An adjournment that fixes the next date and time of meeting for one or both houses. It does not end an annual session of Congress.

Advice and Consent—The Senate's constitutional role in consenting to or rejecting the president's nominations to executive branch and judicial offices and the treaties he submits. Confirmation of nominees requires a simple majority vote of the senators present and voting. Treaties must be approved by a two-thirds majority of senators present and voting.

Amendment—A formal proposal to alter the text of a bill, resolution, amendment, motion, treaty, or some other text. Technically, it is a motion. An amendment may strike out (eliminate) part of a text, insert new text, or strike out and insert—that is, replace all or part of the text with new text. The texts of amendments considered on the floor are printed in full in the *Congressional Record*.

Amendment in the Nature of a Substitute—Usually, an amendment to replace the entire text of a measure. It strikes out everything after the enacting clause and inserts a version that may be somewhat, substantially, or entirely different. When a committee adopts extensive amendments to a measure, it often incorporates them into such an amendment. Occasionally, the term is applied to an amendment that replaces a major portion of a measure's text.

Annual Authorization—Legislation that authorizes appropriations for a single fiscal year and usually for a specific amount. Under the rules of the authorization-appropriation process, an annually authorized agency or program must be reauthorized each year if it is to receive appropriations for that year. Sometimes Congress fails to enact the reauthorization but nevertheless provides appropriations to continue the program, circumventing the rules by one means or another.

Appeal—A member's formal challenge of a ruling or decision by the presiding officer. On appeal, a house or a committee may overturn the ruling by majority vote. The right of appeal ensures the body against arbitrary control by the chair. Appeals are rarely made in the House and are even more rarely successful. Rulings are more frequently appealed in the Senate and occasionally overturned, in part because its presiding officer is not the majority party's leader, as in the House.

Apportionment—The action, after each decennial census, of allocating the number of members in the House of Representatives to each state. By law, the total number of House members (not counting delegates and a resident commissioner) is fixed at 435. The number allotted to each state is based approximately on its proportion of the nation's total population. Since the Constitution guarantees each state one representative no matter how small its population, exact proportional distribution is virtually impossible. The mathematical formula currently used to determine the apportionment is called the Method of Equal Proportions. (*See Method of Equal Proportions.*)

Appropriation—(1) Legislative language that permits a federal agency to incur obligations and make payments from the Treasury for specified purposes, usually during a specified period of time. (2) The specific amount of money made available by such language. The Constitution prohibits payments from the Treasury except "in Consequence of Appropriations made by Law." With some exceptions, the rules of both houses forbid consideration of appropriations for purposes that are unauthorized in law or of appropriation amounts larger than those authorized in law. The House of Representatives claims the exclusive right to originate appropriation bills—a claim the Senate denies in theory but accepts in practice.

Authorization—(1) A statutory provision that establishes or continues a federal agency, activity or program for a fixed or indefinite period of time. It may also establish policies and restrictions and deal with organizational and administrative matters. (2) A statutory provision that authorizes appropriations for an agency, activity, or program. The appropriations may be authorized for one year, several years, or an indefinite period of time, and the authorization may be for a specific amount of money or an indefinite amount ("such sums as may be necessary"). Authorizations of specific amounts are construed as ceilings on the amounts that subsequently may be appropriated in an appropriation bill, but not as minimums; either house may appropriate lesser amounts or nothing at all.

Backdoor Spending Authority—Authority to incur obligations that evades the normal congressional appropriations process because it is provided in legislation other than appropriation acts. The most common forms are borrowing authority, contract authority, and entitlement authority.

Baseline—A projection of the levels of federal spending, revenues, and the resulting budgetary surpluses or deficits for the upcoming and subsequent fiscal years, taking into account laws enacted to date and assuming no new policy decisions. It provides a benchmark for measuring the budgetary effects of proposed changes in federal revenues or spending, assuming certain economic conditions.

Bill—The term for the chief vehicle Congress uses for enacting laws. Bills that originate in the House of Representatives are designated as H.R., those in the Senate as S., followed by a number assigned in the order in which they are introduced during a two-year Congress. A bill becomes a law if passed in identical language by both houses and signed by the president, or passed over his veto, or if the president fails to sign it within 10 days after he has received it while Congress is in session.

Bills and Resolutions Introduced—Members formally present measures to their respective houses by delivering them to a clerk in the chamber when their house is in session. Both houses permit any number of members to join in introducing a bill or resolution. The first member listed on the measure is the sponsor; the other members listed are its cosponsors.

Bills and Resolutions Referred—After a bill or resolution is introduced, it is normally sent to one or more committees that have jurisdiction over its subject, as defined by House and Senate rules and precedents. A Senate measure is usually referred to the committee with jurisdiction over the predominant subject of its text, but it may be sent to two or more committees by unanimous consent or on a motion offered jointly by the majority and minority leaders. In the House, a rule requires the Speaker to refer a measure to the committee that has primary jurisdiction. The Speaker is also authorized to refer measures sequentially to additional committees.

Borrowing Authority—Statutory authority permitting a federal agency, such as the Export-Import Bank, to borrow money from the public or the Treasury to finance its operations. It is a form of backdoor spending. To bring such spending under the control of the congressional appropriation process, the Congressional Budget Act requires that new borrowing authori-

ty shall be effective only to the extent and in such amounts as are provided in appropriations acts.

Budget—A detailed statement of actual or anticipated revenues and expenditures during an accounting period. For the national government, the period is the federal fiscal year (October 1–September 30). The budget usually refers to the president's budget submission to Congress early each calendar year. The president's budget estimates federal government income and spending for the upcoming fiscal year and contains detailed recommendations for appropriation, revenue, and other legislation. Congress is not required to accept or even vote directly on the president's proposals, and it often revises the president's budget extensively. (*See Fiscal Year.*)

Budget Act—Common name for the Congressional Budget and Impoundment Control Act of 1974, which established the basic procedures of the current congressional budget process; created the House and Senate Budget committees; and enacted procedures for reconciliation, deferrals, and rescissions. (*See Budget Process, Deferral, Impoundment, Reconciliation, Rescission. See also Gramm-Rudman-Hollings Act of 1985.*)

Budget and Accounting Act of 1921—The law that, for the first time, authorized the president to submit to Congress an annual budget for the entire federal government. Prior to the act, most federal agencies sent their budget requests to the appropriate congressional committees without review by the president.

Budget Authority—Generally, the amount of money that may be spent or obligated by a government agency or for a government program or activity. Technically, it is statutory authority to enter into obligations that normally result in outlays. The main forms of budget authority are appropriations, borrowing authority, and contract authority. It also includes authority to obligate and expend the proceeds of offsetting receipts and collections. Congress may make budget authority available for only one year, several years, or an indefinite period, and it may specify definite or indefinite amounts.

Budget Process—(1) In Congress, the procedural system it uses (a) to approve an annual concurrent resolution on the budget that sets goals for aggregate and functional categories of federal expenditures, revenues, and the surplus or deficit for an upcoming fiscal year; and (b) to implement those goals in spending, revenue, and, if necessary, reconciliation and debt-limit legislation. (2) In the executive branch, the process of formulating the president's annual budget, submitting it to Congress, defending it before congressional committees, implementing subsequent budget-related legislation, impounding or sequestering expenditures as permitted by law, auditing and evaluating programs, and compiling final budget data. The Budget and Accounting Act of 1921 and the Congressional Budget and Impoundment Control Act of 1974 established the basic elements of the current budget process. Major revisions were enacted in the Gramm-Rudman-Hollings Act of 1985 and the Budget Enforcement Act of 1990.

Budget Resolution—A concurrent resolution in which Congress establishes or revises its version of the federal budget's broad financial features for the upcoming fiscal year and several additional fiscal years. Like other concurrent resolutions, it does not have the force of law, but it provides the framework within which Congress subsequently considers revenue, spending, and other budget-implementing legislation. The framework consists of two basic elements: (1) aggregate budget amounts (total revenues, new budget authority, outlays, loan obligations and loan guarantee commitments, deficit or surplus, and debt limit); and (2) subdivisions of the relevant aggregate amounts among the functional categories of the budget. Although it does not allocate funds to specific programs or accounts, the budget committees' reports accompanying the resolution often discuss the major program assumptions underlying its functional amounts. Unlike those amounts, however, the assumptions are not binding on Congress.

By Request—A designation indicating that a member has introduced a measure on behalf of the president, an executive agency, or a private individual or organization. Members often introduce such measures as a courtesy because neither the president nor any person other than a member of Congress can do so. The term, which appears next to the sponsor's name, implies that the member who introduced the measure does not necessarily endorse it. A House rule dealing with by-request introductions dates from 1888, but the practice goes back to the earliest history of Congress.

Calendar—A list of measures or other matters (most of them favorably reported by committees) that are eligible for floor consideration. The House has five calendars; the Senate has two. A place on a calendar does not guarantee consideration. Each house decides which measures and matters it will take up, when, and in what order, in accordance with its rules and practices.

Calendar Wednesday—A House procedure that on Wednesdays permits its committees to bring up for floor consideration nonprivileged measures they have reported. The procedure is so cumbersome and susceptible to dilatory tactics, however, that committees rarely use it.

Call of the Calendar—Senate bills that are not brought up for debate by a motion, unanimous consent, or a unanimous consent agreement are brought before the Senate for action when the calendar listing them is "called." Bills must be called in the order listed. Measures considered by this method usually are noncontroversial, and debate on the bill and any proposed amendments is limited to a total of five minutes for each senator.

Caucus—(1) A common term for the official organization of each party in each house. (2) The official title of the organization of House Democrats. House and Senate Republicans and Senate Democrats call their organizations "conferences." (3) A term for an informal group of members who share legislative interests, such as the Black Caucus, Hispanic Caucus, and Children's Caucus.

Censure—The strongest formal condemnation of a member for misconduct short of expulsion. A house usually adopts a resolution of censure to express its condemnation, after which the presiding officer reads its rebuke aloud to the member in the presence of his colleagues.

Chamber—The Capitol room in which a house of Congress normally holds its sessions. The chamber of the House of Representatives, officially called the Hall of the House, is consider-

ably larger than that of the Senate because it must accommodate 435 representatives, four delegates, and one resident commissioner. Unlike the Senate chamber, members have no desks or assigned seats. In both chambers, the floor slopes downward to the well in front of the presiding officer's raised desk. A chamber is often referred to as "the floor," as when members are said to be on or going to the floor. Those expressions usually imply that the member's house is in session.

Christmas Tree Bill—Jargon for a bill adorned with amendments, many of them unrelated to the bill's subject, that provide benefits for interest groups, specific states, congressional districts, companies, and individuals.

Classes of Senators—A class consists of the 33 or 34 senators elected to a six-year term in the same general election. Since the terms of approximately one-third of the senators expire every two years, there are three classes.

Clean Bill—After a House committee extensively amends a bill, it often assembles its amendments and what is left of the bill into a new measure that one or more of its members introduces as a "clean bill." The revised measure is assigned a new number.

Clerk of the House—An officer of the House of Representatives responsible principally for administrative support of the legislative process in the House. The clerk is invariably the candidate of the majority party.

Cloture—A Senate procedure that limits further consideration of a pending proposal to 30 hours in order to end a filibuster. Sixteen senators must first sign and submit a cloture motion to the presiding officer. One hour after the Senate meets on the second calendar day thereafter, the chair puts the motion to a yea-and-nay vote following a live quorum call. If three-fifths of all senators (60 if there are no vacancies) vote for the motion, the Senate must take final action on the cloture proposal by the end of the 30 hours of consideration and may consider no other business until it takes that action. Cloture on a proposal to amend the Senate's standing rules requires approval by two-thirds of the senators present and voting.

Code of Official Conduct—A House rule that bans certain actions by House members, officers, and employees; requires them to conduct themselves in ways that "reflect creditably" on the House; and orders them to adhere to the spirit and the letter of House rules and those of its committees. The code's provisions govern the receipt of outside compensation, gifts, and honoraria, and the use of campaign funds; prohibit members from using their clerk-hire allowance to pay anyone who does not perform duties commensurate with that pay; forbids discrimination in members' hiring or treatment of employees on the grounds of race, color, religion, sex, handicap, age, or national origin; orders members convicted of a crime who might be punished by imprisonment of two or more years not to participate in committee business or vote on the floor until exonerated or reelected; and restricts employees' contact with federal agencies on matters in which they have a significant financial interest. The Senate's rules contain some similar prohibitions.

College of Cardinals—A popular term for the subcommittee chairmen of the appropriations committees, reflecting their influence over appropriation measures. The chairmen of the full appropriations committees are sometimes referred to as popes.

Committee—A panel of members elected or appointed to perform some service or function for its parent body. Congress has four types of committees: standing, special or select, joint, and, in the House, a Committee of the Whole.

Committees conduct investigations, make studies, issue reports and recommendations, and, in the case of standing committees, review and prepare measures on their assigned subjects for action by their respective houses. Most committees divide their work among several subcommittees. With rare exceptions, the majority party in a house holds a majority of the seats on its committees, and their chairmen are also from that party.

Committee of the Whole—Common name of the Committee of the Whole House on the State of the Union, a committee consisting of all members of the House of Representatives. Measures from the union calendar must be considered in the Committee of the Whole before the House officially completes action on them; the committee often considers other major bills as well. A quorum of the committee is 100, and it meets in the House chamber under a chairman appointed by the Speaker. Procedures in the Committee of the Whole expedite consideration of legislation because of its smaller quorum requirement, its ban on certain motions, and its five-minute rule for debate on amendments. Those procedures usually permit more members to offer amendments and participate in the debate on a measure than is normally possible. The Senate no longer uses a Committee of the Whole.

Committee Veto—A procedure that requires an executive department or agency to submit certain proposed policies, programs, or action to designated committees for review before implementing them. Before 1983, when the Supreme Court declared that a legislative veto is unconstitutional, these provisions permitted committees to veto the proposals. They no longer do so, and the term is now something of a misnomer. Nevertheless, agencies usually take the pragmatic approach of trying to reach a consensus with the committees before carrying out their proposals, especially when an appropriations committee is involved.

Concurrent Resolution—A resolution that requires approval by both houses but is not sent to the president for his signature and therefore cannot have the force of law. Concurrent resolutions deal with the prerogatives or internal affairs of Congress as a whole. Designated H. Con. Res. in the House and S. Con. Res. in the Senate, they are numbered consecutively in each house in their order of introduction during a two-year Congress.

Conference—(1) A formal meeting or series of meetings between members representing each house to reconcile House and Senate differences on a measure (occasionally several measures). Since one house cannot require the other to agree to its proposals, the conference usually reaches agreement by compromise. When a conference completes action on a measure, or as much action as appears possible, it sends its recommendations to both houses in the form of a conference report, accompanied by an explanatory statement. (2) The official title of the organization of all Democrats or Republicans in the Senate and of all Republicans in the House of Representatives. (*See Party Caucus.*)

Confirmations—(*See Nomination.*)

Congress—(1) The national legislature of the United States, consisting of the House of Representatives and the Senate. (2) The national legislature in office during a two-year period. Congresses are numbered sequentially; thus, the 1st Congress of 1789–1791 and the 102d Congress of 1991–1993. Before 1935, the two-year period began on the first Monday in December of odd-numbered years. Since then it has extended from January of an odd-numbered year through noon on January 3 of the next odd-numbered year. A Congress usually holds two annual sessions, but some have had three sessions and the 67th Congress had four. When a Congress expires, measures die if they have not yet been enacted.

Congressional Record—The daily, printed, and substantially verbatim account of proceedings in both the House and Senate chambers. Extraneous materials submitted by members appear in a section titled "Extensions of Remarks." A "Daily Digest" appendix contains highlights of the day's floor and committee action plus a list of committee meetings and floor agendas for the next day's session.

Although the official reporters of each house take down every word spoken during the proceedings, members are permitted to edit and "revise and extend" their remarks before they are printed. In the Senate section, all speeches, articles, and other material submitted by senators but not actually spoken or read on the floor are set off by large black dots, called bullets. However, bullets do not appear when a senator reads part of a speech and inserts the rest. In the House section, undelivered speeches and materials are printed in a distinctive typeface. The term "permanent *Record*" refers to the bound volumes of the daily *Record*s of an entire session of Congress.

Congressional Terms of Office—A term normally begins on January 3 of the year following a general election and runs two years for representatives and six years for senators. A representative chosen in a special election to fill a vacancy is sworn in for the remainder of his predecessor's term. An individual appointed to fill a Senate vacancy usually serves until the next general election or until the end of the predecessor's term, whichever comes first. Some states, however, require their governors to call a special election to fill a Senate vacancy shortly after an appointment has been made.

Continuing Resolution (CR)—A joint resolution that provides funds to continue the operation of federal agencies and programs at the beginning of a new fiscal year if their annual appropriation bills have not yet been enacted; also called continuing appropriations.

Contract Authority—Statutory authority permitting an agency to enter into contracts or incur other obligations even though it has not received an appropriation to pay for them. Congress must eventually fund them because the government is legally liable for such payments. The Congressional Budget Act of 1974 requires that new contract authority may not be used unless provided for in advance by an appropriation act, but it permits a few exceptions.

Controllable Expenditures—Federal spending that is permitted but not mandated by existing authorization law and therefore may be adjusted by congressional action in appropriation bills. *(See Appropriation.)*

Correcting Recorded Votes—The rules of both houses prohibit members from changing their votes after a vote result has been announced. Nevertheless, the Senate permits its members to withdraw or change their votes, by unanimous consent, immediately after the announcement. In rare instances, senators have been granted unanimous consent to change their votes several days or weeks after the announcement.

Votes tallied by the electronic voting system in the House may not be changed. But when a vote actually given is not recorded during an oral call of the roll, a member may demand a correction as a matter of right. On all other alleged errors in a recorded vote, the Speaker determines whether the circumstances justify a change. Occasionally, members merely announce that they were incorrectly recorded; announcements can occur hours, days, or even months after the vote and appear in the *Congressional Record.*

Corrections Calendar—Members of the House may place on this calendar bills reported favorably from committee that repeal rules and regulations considered excessive or unnecessary. Bills on the Corrections Calendar normally are called on the second and fourth Tuesday of each month at the discretion of the Speaker in consultation with the minority leader. A bill must be on the calendar for at least three legislative days before it can be brought up for floor consideration. Once on the floor, a bill is subject to one hour of debate equally divided between the chairman and ranking member of the committee of jurisdiction. A vote may be called on whether to recommit the bill to committee with or without instructions. To pass, a three-fifths majority, or 261 votes if all House members vote, is required.

Cosponsor—A member who has joined one or more other members to sponsor a measure. *(See Bills and Resolutions Introduced.)*

Current Services Estimates—Executive branch estimates of the anticipated costs of federal programs and operations for the next and future fiscal years at existing levels of service and assuming no new initiatives or changes in existing law. The president submits these estimates to Congress with his annual budget and includes an explanation of the underlying economic and policy assumptions on which they are based, such as anticipated rates of inflation, real economic growth, and unemployment, plus program caseloads and pay increases.

Custody of the Papers—Possession of an engrossed measure and certain related basic documents that the two houses produce as they try to resolve their differences over the measure.

Dance of the Swans and the Ducks—A whimsical description of the gestures some members use in connection with a request for a recorded vote, especially in the House. When a member wants his colleagues to stand in support of the request, he moves his hands and arms in a gentle upward motion resembling the beginning flight of a graceful swan. When he wants his colleagues to remain seated in order to avoid such a vote, he moves his hands and arms in a vigorous downward motion resembling a diving duck.

Dean—Within a state's delegation in the House of Representatives, the member with the longest continuous service.

Debt Limit—The maximum amount of outstanding federal public debt permitted by law. The limit (or ceiling) covers virtually all debt incurred by the government except agency debt. Each congressional budget resolution sets forth the new debt limit that may be required under its provisions.

Deferral—An impoundment of funds for a specific period of time that may not extend beyond the fiscal year in which it is proposed. Under the Impoundment Control Act of 1974, the president must notify Congress that he is deferring the spending or obligation of funds provided by law for a project or activity. Congress can disapprove the deferral by legislation.

Deficit—The amount by which the government's outlays exceed its budget receipts for a given fiscal year. Both the president's budget and the annual congressional budget resolution provide estimates of the deficit or surplus for the upcoming and several future fiscal years.

Degrees of Amendment—Designations that indicate the relationships of amendments to the text of a measure and to each other. In general, an amendment offered directly to the text of a measure is an amendment in the first degree, and an amendment to that amendment is an amendment in the second degree. Both houses normally prohibit amendments in the third degree—that is, an amendment to an amendment to an amendment.

Dilatory Tactics—Procedural actions intended to delay or prevent action by a house or a committee. They include, among others, offering numerous motions, demanding quorum calls and recorded votes at every opportunity, making numerous points of order and parliamentary inquiries, and speaking as long as the applicable rules permit. The Senate's rules permit a battery of dilatory tactics, especially lengthy speeches, except under cloture. In the House, possible dilatory tactics are more limited. Speeches are always subject to time limits and debate-ending motions. Moreover, a House rule instructs the Speaker not to entertain dilatory motions and lets the Speaker decide whether a motion is dilatory. However, the Speaker may not override the constitutional right of a member to demand the yeas and nays, and in practice usually waits for a point of order before exercising that authority. *(See Cloture.)*

Discharge a Committee—Remove a measure from a committee to which it has been referred in order to make it available for floor consideration. Noncontroversial measures are often discharged by unanimous consent. However, because congressional committees have no obligation to report measures referred to them, each house has procedures to extract controversial measures from recalcitrant committees. Six discharge procedures are available in the House of Representatives. The Senate uses a motion to discharge, which is usually converted into a discharge resolution.

Discharge Calendar—The House calendar to which motions to discharge committees are referred when they have the required number of signatures (218) and are awaiting floor action.

Discharge Petition—(*See Discharge a Committee.*)

Discharge Resolution—In the Senate, a special motion that any senator may introduce to relieve a committee from consideration of a bill before it. The resolution can be called up for Senate approval or disapproval in the same manner as any other Senate business. (*House procedure, see Discharge a Committee.*)

Division Vote—A vote in which the chair first counts those in favor of a proposition and then those opposed to it, with no record made of how each member votes. In the Senate, the chair may count raised hands or ask senators to stand, whereas the House requires members to stand; hence, often called a standing vote. Committees in both houses ordinarily use a show of hands. A division usually occurs after a voice vote and may be demanded by any member or ordered by the chair if there is any doubt about the outcome of the voice vote. The demand for a division can also come before a voice vote. In the Senate, the demand must come before the result of a voice vote is announced. It may be made after a voice vote announcement in the House, but only if no intervening business has transpired and only if the member was standing and seeking recognition at the time of the announcement. A demand for the yeas and nays or, in the House, for a recorded vote, takes precedence over a division vote.

Enacting Clause—The opening language of each bill, beginning "Be it enacted by the Senate and House of Representatives of the United States of America in Congress assembled..." This language gives legal force to measures approved by Congress and signed by the president or enacted over his veto. A successful motion to strike it from a bill kills the entire measure.

Engrossed Bill—The official copy of a bill or joint resolution as passed by one chamber, including the text as amended by floor action, and certified by the clerk of the House or the secretary of the Senate (as appropriate). Amendments by one house to a measure or amendments of the other also are engrossed. House engrossed documents are printed on blue paper; the Senate's are printed on white paper.

Enrolled Bill—The final official copy of a bill or joint resolution passed in identical form by both houses. An enrolled bill is printed on parchment. After it is certified by the chief officer of the house in which it originated and signed by the House Speaker and the Senate president pro tempore, the measure is sent to the president for his signature.

Entitlement Program—A federal program under which individuals, businesses, or units of government that meet the requirements or qualifications established by law are entitled to receive certain payments if they seek such payments. Major examples include Social Security, Medicare, Medicaid, unemployment insurance, and military and federal civilian pensions. Congress cannot control their expenditures by refusing to appropriate the sums necessary to fund them because the government is legally obligated to pay eligible recipients the amounts to which the law entitles them.

Executive Calendar—The Senate's calendar for committee reports on its executive business, namely treaties and nominations. The calendar numbers indicate the order in which items were referred to the calendar but have no bearing on when or if the Senate will consider them. The Senate, by motion or unanimous consent, resolves itself into executive session to consider them.

Executive Document—A document, usually a treaty, sent by the president to the Senate for approval. It is referred to a committee in the same manner as other measures. Resolutions to ratify treaties have their own "treaty document" numbers. For example, the first treaty submitted in the 106th Congress would be "Treaty Doc 106-1."

Executive Order—A unilateral proclamation by the president that has a policy-making or legislative impact. Members of Congress have challenged some executive orders on the grounds that they usurped the authority of the legislative branch. Although the Supreme Court has ruled that a particular order exceeded the president's authority, it has upheld others as falling within the president's general constitutional powers.

Executive Privilege—The assertion that presidents have the right to withhold certain information from Congress. Presidents have based their claim on: (1) the constitutional separation of powers; (2) the need for secrecy in military and diplomatic affairs; (3) the need to protect individuals from unfavorable publicity; (4) the need to safeguard the confidential exchange of ideas in the executive branch; and (5) the need to protect individuals who provide confidential advice to the president.

Executive Session—A meeting of a Senate or House committee (or occasionally of either chamber) that only its members may attend. Witnesses regularly appear at committee meetings in executive session — for example, Defense Department officials during presentations of classified defense information. Other members of Congress may be invited, but the public and press are not to attend.

Expenditures—The actual spending of money as distinguished from the appropriation of funds. Expenditures are made by the disbursing officers of the administration; appropriations are made only by Congress. The two are rarely identical in any fiscal year. In addition to some current budget authority, expenditures may represent budget authority made available one, two, or more years earlier.

Expulsion—A member's removal from office by a two-thirds vote of his house; the super majority is required by the Constitution. It is the most severe and most rarely used sanction a house can invoke against a member. Although the Constitution provides no explicit grounds for expulsion, the courts have ruled that it may be applied only for misconduct during a member's term of office, not for conduct before the member's election. Generally, neither house will consider expulsion of a member convicted of a crime until the judicial processes have been exhausted. At that stage, members sometimes resign rather than face expulsion. In 1977 the House adopted a rule urging members convicted of certain crimes to voluntarily abstain from voting or participating in other legislative business.

Federal Debt—The total amount of monies borrowed and not yet repaid by the federal government. Federal debt consists of public debt and agency debt. Public debt is the portion of the federal debt borrowed by the Treasury or the Federal Financing Bank directly from the public or from another federal fund or account. For example, the Treasury regularly borrows money from the Social Security trust fund. Public debt accounts for about 99 percent of the federal debt. Agency debt refers to the debt incurred by federal agencies like the Export-Import Bank, but excluding the Treasury and the Federal Financing Bank, which are authorized by law to borrow funds from the public or from another government fund or account.

Filibuster—The use of obstructive and time-consuming parliamentary tactics by one member or a minority of members to delay, modify, or defeat proposed legislation or rules changes. Filibusters are also sometimes used to delay urgently needed measures in order to force the body to accept other legislation. The Senate's rules permitting unlimited debate and the extraordinary majority it requires to impose cloture make filibustering particularly effective in that chamber. Under the stricter rules of the House, filibusters in that body are short-lived and therefore ineffective and rarely attempted

Fiscal Year—The federal government's annual accounting period. It begins October 1 and ends on the following September 30. A fiscal year is designated by the calendar year in which it ends and is often referred to as FY. Thus, fiscal year 1999 began October 1, 1998, ended September 30, 1999, and is called FY99. In theory, Congress is supposed to complete action on all budgetary measures applying to a fiscal year before that year begins. It rarely does so.

Five-Minute Rule—In its most common usage, a House rule that limits debate on an amendment offered in Committee of the Whole to five minutes for its sponsor and five minutes for an opponent. In practice, the committee routinely permits longer debate by two devices: the offering of pro forma amendments, each debatable for five minutes, and unanimous consent for a member to speak longer than five minutes. Also a House rule that limits a committee member to five minutes when questioning a witness at a hearing until each member has had an opportunity to question that witness.

Floor Manager—A majority party member responsible for guiding a measure through its floor consideration in a house and for devising the political and procedural strategies that might be required to get the measure passed. The presiding officer gives the floor manager priority recognition to debate, offer amendments, oppose amendments, and make crucial procedural motions.

Frank—Informally, a member's legal right to send official mail postage free under his or her signature; often called the franking privilege. Technically, it is the autographic or facsimile signature used on envelopes instead of stamps that permits members and certain congressional officers to send their official mail free of charge. The franking privilege has been authorized by law since the first Congress, except for a few months in 1873. Congress reimburses the U.S. Postal Service for the franked mail it handles.

Function or Functional Category—A broad category of national need and spending of budgetary significance. A category provides an accounting method for allocating and keeping track of budgetary resources and expenditures for that function because it includes all budget accounts related to the functions subject or purpose such as agriculture, administration of justice,

commerce and housing and energy. Functions do not necessarily correspond with appropriations acts or with the budgets of individual agencies.

Germane—Basically, on the same subject as the matter under consideration. A House rule requires that all amendments be germane. In the Senate, only amendments proposed to general appropriation bills and budget resolutions or under cloture must be germane. Germaneness rules can be evaded by suspension of the rules in both houses, by unanimous consent agreements in the Senate, and by special rules from the Rules Committee in the House.

Gerrymandering—The manipulation of legislative district boundaries to benefit a particular party, politician, or minority group. The term originated in 1812 when the Massachusetts legislature redrew the lines of state legislative districts to favor the party of Gov. Elbridge Gerry, and some critics said one district looked like a salamander.

Gramm-Rudman-Hollings Act of 1985—Common name for the Balanced Budget and Emergency Deficit Control Act of 1985, which established new budget procedures intended to balance the federal budget by fiscal year 1991. The timetable subsequently was extended and then deleted. The act's chief sponsors were senators Phil Gramm (R-Texas), Warren Rudman (R-N.H.), and Ernest Hollings (D-S.C.).

Grandfather Clause—A provision in a measure, law, or rule that exempts an individual, entity, or a defined category of individuals or entities from complying with a new policy or restriction. For example, a bill that would raise taxes on persons who reach the age of 65 after a certain date inherently grandfathers out those who are 65 before that date. Similarly, a Senate rule limiting senators to two major committee assignments also grandfathers some senators who were sitting on a third major committee prior to a specified date.

Grants-in-Aid—Payments by the federal government to state and local governments to help provide for assistance programs or public services.

Hearing—Committee or subcommittee meetings to receive testimony from witnesses on proposed legislation during investigations or for oversight purposes. Relatively few bills are important enough to justify formal hearings. Witnesses often include experts, government officials, spokespersons for interested groups, officials of the General Accounting Office, and members of Congress. Also, the printed transcripts of hearings.

Hold—A senator's request that his or her party leaders delay floor consideration of certain legislation or presidential nominations. The majority leader usually honors a hold for a reasonable period of time, especially if its purpose is to assure the senator that the matter will not be called up during his or her absence or to give the senator time to gather necessary information.

Hold-Harmless Clause—In legislation providing a new formula for allocating federal funds, a clause to ensure that recipients of those funds do not receive less in a future year than they did in the current year if the new formula would result in a reduction for them. Similar to a grandfather clause, it has been used most frequently to soften the impact of sudden reductions in federal grants. (*See Grandfather Clause.*)

Hopper—A box on the clerk's desk in the House chamber into which members deposit bills and resolutions to introduce them. In House jargon, to drop a bill in the hopper is to introduce it.

Hour Rule—(1) A House rule that permits members, when recognized, to hold the floor in debate for no more than one hour each. The majority party member customarily yields one-half the time to a minority member. Although the hour rule applies to general debate in Committee of the Whole as well as in the House, special rules routinely vary the length of time for such debate and its control to fit the circumstances of particular measures.

House—The House of Representatives, as distinct from the Senate, although each body is a "house" of Congress.

House as in Committee of the Whole—A hybrid combination of procedures from the general rules of the House and from the rules of the Committee of the Whole, sometimes used to expedite consideration of a measure on the floor.

House Calendar—The calendar reserved for all public bills and resolutions that do not raise revenue or directly or indirectly appropriate money or property when they are favorably reported by House committees.

House Manual—A commonly used title for the handbook of the rules of the House of Representatives, published in each Congress. Its official title is *Constitution, Jefferson's Manual, and Rules of the House of Representatives.*

House of Representatives—The house of Congress in which states are represented roughly in proportion to their populations, but every state is guaranteed at least one representative. By law, the number of voting representatives is fixed at 435. Four delegates and one resident commissioner also serve in the House; they may vote in their committees but not on the House floor. Although the House and Senate have equal legislative power, the Constitution gives the House sole authority to originate revenue measures. The House also claims the right to originate appropriation measures, a claim the Senate disputes in theory but concedes in practice. The House has the sole power to impeach, and it elects the president when no candidate has received a majority of the electoral votes. It is sometimes referred to as the lower body.

Immunity—(1) Members' constitutional protection from lawsuits and arrest in connection with their legislative duties. They may not be tried for libel or slander for anything they say on the floor of a house or in committee. Nor may they be arrested while attending sessions of their houses or when traveling to or from sessions of Congress, except when charged with treason, a felony, or a breach of the peace. (2) In the case of a witness before a committee, a grant of protection from prosecution based on that person's testimony to the committee. It is used to compel witnesses to testify who would otherwise refuse to do so on the constitutional ground of possible self-incrimination. Under such a grant, none of a witness testimony may be used against him or her in a court proceeding except in a prosecution for perjury or for giving a false statement to Congress.

Impeachment—The first step to remove the president, vice president, or other federal civil officers from office and to disqualify them from any future federal office "of honor, Trust or Profit." An impeachment is a formal charge of treason, bribery, or "other high Crimes and Misdemeanors." The House has the sole power of impeachment and the Senate the sole power of trying the charges and convicting. The House impeaches by a simple majority vote; conviction requires a two-thirds vote of all senators present.

Impoundment—An executive branch action or inaction that delays or withholds the expenditure or obligation of budget authority provided by law. The Impoundment Control Act of 1974 classifies impoundments as either deferrals or rescissions, requires the president to notify Congress about all such actions, and gives Congress authority to approve or reject them. The Constitution is unclear on whether a president may refuse to spend appropriated money, but Congress usually expects the president to spend at least enough to achieve the purposes for which the money was provided whether or not he agrees with those purposes.

Joint Committee—A committee composed of members selected from each house. The functions of most joint committees involve investigation, research, or oversight of agencies closely related to Congress. Permanent joint committees, created by statute, are sometimes called standing joint committees. Once quite numerous, only four joint committees remained as of 1997: Joint Economic, Joint Taxation, Joint Library, and Joint Printing. No joint committee has authority to report legislation.

Joint Resolution—A legislative measure that Congress uses for purposes other than general legislation. Like a bill, it has the force of law when passed by both houses and either approved by the president or passed over the president's veto. Unlike a bill, a joint resolution enacted into law is not called an act; it retains its original title.

Most often, joint resolutions deal with such relatively limited matters as the correction of errors in existing law, continuing appropriations, a single appropriation, or the establishment of permanent joint committees. Unlike bills, however, joint resolutions also are used to propose constitutional amendments; these do not require the president's signature and become effective only when ratified by three-fourths of the states. The House designates joint resolutions as H.J. Res., the Senate as S.J. Res. Each house numbers its joint resolutions consecutively in the order of introduction during a two-year Congress.

Journal—The official record of House or Senate actions, including every motion offered, every vote cast, amendments agreed to, quorum calls, and so forth. Unlike the *Congressional Record,* it does not provide reports of speeches, debates, statements, and the like. The Constitution requires each house to maintain a *Journal* and to publish it periodically.

King of the Mountain (or Hill) Rule—(*See Queen of the Hill Rule.*)

Lame Duck—Jargon for a member who has not been reelected, or did not seek reelection, and is serving the balance of his or her term.

Lame Duck Session—A session of a Congress held after the election for the succeeding Congress, so-called after the lame duck members still serving.

Law—An act of Congress that has been signed by the president, passed over the president's veto, or allowed to become law without the president's signature.

Legislative Day—The day that begins when a house meets after an adjournment and ends when it next adjourns. Because the House of Representatives normally adjourns at the end of a daily session, its legislative and calendar days usually coincide. The Senate, however, frequently recesses at the end of a daily session, and its legislative day may extend over several calendar days, weeks, or months. Among other uses, this technicality permits the Senate to save time by circumventing its morning hour, a procedure required at the beginning of every legislative day

Legislative Veto—A procedure, declared unconstitutional in 1983, that allowed Congress or one of its houses to nullify certain actions of the president, executive branch agencies, or independent agencies. Sometimes called congressional vetoes or congressional disapprovals. Following the Supreme Court's 1983 decision, Congress amended several legislative veto statutes to require enactment of joint resolutions, which are subject to presidential veto, for nullifying executive branch actions.

Live Pair—A voluntary and informal agreement between two members on opposite sides of an issue under which the member who is present for a recorded vote withholds or withdraws his or her vote because the other member is absent.

Loan Guarantee—A statutory commitment by the federal government to pay part or all of a loans principal and interest to a lender or the holder of a security in case the borrower defaults.

Lobby—To try to persuade members of Congress to propose, pass, modify, or defeat proposed legislation or to change or repeal existing laws. A lobbyist attempts to promote his or her own preferences or those of a group, organization, or industry. Originally the term referred to persons frequenting the lobbies or corridors of legislative chambers in order to speak to lawmakers. In a general sense, lobbying includes not only direct contact with members but also indirect attempts to influence them, such as writing to them or persuading others to write or visit them, attempting to mold public opinion toward a desired legislative goal by various means, and contributing or arranging for contributions to members election campaigns. The right to lobby stems from the First Amendment to the Constitution, which bans laws that abridge the right of the people to petition the government for a redress of grievances.

Logrolling—Jargon for a legislative tactic or bargaining strategy in which members try to build support for their legislation by promising to support legislation desired by other members or by accepting amendments they hope will induce their colleagues to vote for their bill.

Mace—The symbol of the office of the House sergeant at arms. Under the direction of the Speaker, the sergeant at arms is responsible for preserving order on the House floor by holding up the mace in front of an unruly member, or by carrying the mace up and down the aisles to quell boisterous behavior. When the House is in session, the mace sits on a pedestal at the Speaker's right; when the House is in Committee of the Whole, it is moved to a lower pedestal. The mace is 46 inches high and consists of 13 ebony rods bound in silver and topped by a silver globe with a silver eagle, wings outstretched, perched on it.

Majority Leader—The majority party's chief floor spokesman, elected by that party's caucus—sometimes called floor leader. In the Senate, the majority leader also develops the party's political and procedural strategy, usually in collaboration with other party officials and committee chairmen. He negotiates the Senates agenda and committee ratios with the minority leader and usually calls up measures for floor action. The chamber traditionally concedes to the majority leader the right to determine the days on which it will meet and the hours at which it will convene and adjourn. In the House, the majority leader is the Speaker's deputy and heir apparent. He helps plan the floor agenda and the party's legislative strategy and often speaks for the party leadership in debate.

Majority Whip—In effect, the assistant majority leader, in either the House or Senate. His job is to help marshal majority forces in support of party strategy and legislation.

Manual—The official handbook in each house prescribing in detail its organization, procedures, and operations.

Marking Up a Bill—Going through the contents of a piece of legislation in committee or subcommittee to, for example, consider its provisions in large and small portions, act on amendments to provisions and proposed revisions to the language, and insert new sections and phraseology. If the bill is extensively amended, the committee's version may be introduced as a separate bill, with a new number, before being considered by the full House or Senate. (*See Clean Bill.*)

Method of Equal Proportions—The mathematical formula used since 1950 to determine how the 435 seats in the House of Representatives should be distributed among the 50 states in the apportionment following each decennial census. It minimizes as much as possible the proportional difference between the average district population in any two states. Because the Constitution guarantees each state at least one representative, 50 seats are automatically apportioned. The formula calculates priority numbers for each state, assigns the first of the 385 remaining seats to the state with the highest priority number, the second to the state with the next highest number, and so on until all seats are distributed. (*See Apportionment.*)

Midterm Election—The general election for members of Congress that occurs in November of the second year in a presidential term.

Minority Leader—The minority party's leader and chief floor spokesman, elected by the party caucus; sometimes called minority floor leader. With the assistance of other party officials and the ranking minority members of committees, the minority leader devises the party's political and procedural strategy.

Minority Whip—Performs duties of whip for the minority party. (*See also Majority Whip.*)

Minority Staff—Employees who assist the minority party members of a committee. Most committees hire separate majority and minority party staffs, but they also may hire nonpartisan staff.

Motion—A formal proposal for a procedural action, such as to consider, to amend, to lay on the table, to reconsider, to recess, or to adjourn. It has been estimated that at least 85 motions are possible under various circumstances in the House of Representatives, somewhat fewer in the Senate. Not all motions are created equal; some are privileged or preferential and enjoy priority over others. And some motions are debatable, amendable or divisible, while others are not.

Nomination—A proposed presidential appointment to a federal office submitted to the Senate for confirmation. Approval is by majority vote. The Constitution explicitly requires confirmation for ambassadors, consuls, public Ministers (department heads), and Supreme Court justices. By law, other federal judges, all military promotions of officers, and many high-level civilian officials must be confirmed.

Oath of Office—Upon taking office, members of Congress must swear or affirm that they will "support and defend the Constitution . . . against all enemies, foreign and domestic," that they will "bear true faith and allegiance" to the Constitution, that they take the obligation "freely, without any mental reservation or purpose of evasion," and that they will "well and faithfully discharge the duties" of their office. The oath is required by the Constitution; the wording is prescribed by a statute. All House members must take the oath at the beginning of each new Congress.

Obligations—Orders placed, contracts awarded, services received, and similar transactions during a given period that will require payments during the same or future period. Such amounts include outlays for which obligations had not been previously recorded and reflect adjustments for differences between obligations previously recorded and actual outlays to liquidate those obligations.

Omnibus Bill—A measure that combines the provisions of several disparate subjects into a single and often lengthy bill.

One-Minute Speeches—Addresses by House members at the beginning of a legislative day. The speeches may cover any subject but are limited to one minute's duration.

Order of Business (House)—The sequence of events during the meeting of the House on a new legislative day prescribed by a House rule; also called the general order of business. The sequence consists of (1) the chaplain's prayer; (2) approval of the *Journal*; (3) pledge of allegiance (4) correction of the reference of public bills; (5) disposal of business on the Speaker's table; (6) unfinished business; (7) the morning hour call of committees and consideration of their bills (largely obsolete); (8) motions to go into Committee of the Whole; and (9) orders of the day (also obsolete). In practice, on days specified in the rules, the items of business that follow approval of the *Journal* are supplanted in part by the special order of business (for example, the corrections, discharge, or private calendars or motions to suspend the rules) and on any day by other privileged business (for example, general appropriation bills and special rules)

or measures made in order by special rules. By this combination of an order of business with privileged interruptions, the House gives precedence to certain categories of important legislation, brings to the floor other major legislation from its calendars in any order it chooses, and provides expeditious processing for minor and noncontroversial measures.

Order of Business (Senate)—The sequence of events at the beginning of a new legislative day prescribed by Senate rules. The sequence consists of (1) the chaplain's prayer; (2) *Journal* reading and correction; (3) morning business in the morning hour; (4) call of the calendar during the morning hour; and (5) unfinished business.

Outlays—Amounts of government spending. They consist of payments, usually by check or in cash, to liquidate obligations incurred in prior fiscal years as well as in the current year, including the net lending of funds under budget authority. In federal budget accounting, net outlays are calculated by subtracting the amounts of refunds and various kinds of reimbursements to the government from actual spending.

Override a Veto—Congressional enactment of a measure over the president's veto. A veto override requires a recorded two-thirds vote of those voting in each house, a quorum being present. Because the president must return the vetoed measure to its house of origin, that house votes first, but neither house is required to attempt an override, whether immediately or at all. If an override attempt fails in the house of origin, the veto stands and the measure dies.

Oversight—Congressional review of the way in which federal agencies implement laws to ensure that they are carrying out the intent of Congress and to inquire into the efficiency of the implementation and the effectiveness of the law. The Legislative Reorganization Act of 1946 defined oversight as the function of exercising continuous watchfulness over the execution of the laws by the executive branch.

Pairing—A procedure that permits two or three members to enter into voluntary arrangements that offset their votes so that one or more of the members can be absent without changing the result. The names of paired members and their positions on the vote (except on general pairs) appear in the *Congressional Record*. Members can be paired on one vote or on a series of votes.

Parliamentarian—The official advisor to the presiding officer in each house on questions of procedure. The parliamentarian and his assistants also answer procedural questions from members and congressional staff, refer measures to committees on behalf of the presiding officer, and maintain compilations of the precedents. The House parliamentarian revises the House Manual at the beginning of every Congress and usually reviews special rules before the Rules Committee reports them to the House. Either a parliamentarian or an assistant is always present and near the podium during sessions of each house.

Party Caucus—Generic term for each party's official organization in each house. Only House Democrats officially call their organization a caucus. House and Senate Republicans and Senate Democrats call their organizations conferences. The party caucuses elect their leaders, approve committee assignments and chairmanships (or ranking minority members, if the party is in the minority), establish party committees and study groups, and discuss party and legislative policies. On rare occasions, they have stripped members of committee seniority or expelled them from the caucus for party disloyalty.

Petition—A request or plea sent to one or both chambers from an organization or private citizens' group asking support of particular legislation or favorable consideration of a matter not yet receiving congressional attention. Petitions are referred to appropriate committees.

Pocket Veto—The indirect veto of a bill as a result of the president withholding approval of it until after Congress has adjourned sine die. A bill the president does not sign, but does not formally veto while Congress is in session, automatically becomes a law 10 days (excluding Sundays) after it is received. But if Congress adjourns its annual session during that 10-day period, the measure dies even if the president does not formally veto it.

Point of Order—A parliamentary term used in committee and on the floor to object to an alleged violation of a rule and to demand that the chair enforce the rule. The point of order immediately halts the proceedings until the chair decides whether the contention is valid.

Pork or Pork Barrel Legislation—Pejorative terms for federal appropriations, bills, or policies that provide funds to benefit a legislator's district or state, with the implication that the legislator presses for enactment of such benefits to ingratiate himself or herself with constituents rather than on the basis of an impartial, objective assessment of need or merit.

The terms are often applied to such benefits as new parks, post offices, dams, canals, bridges, roads, water projects, sewage treatment plants, and public works of any kind, as well as demonstration projects, research grants, and relocation of government facilities. Funds released by the president for various kinds of benefits or government contracts approved by him allegedly for political purposes are also sometimes referred to as pork.

Postcloture Filibuster—A filibuster conducted after the Senate invokes cloture. It employs an array of procedural tactics rather than lengthy speeches to delay final action. The Senate curtailed the postcloture filibusters effectiveness by closing a variety of loopholes in the cloture rule in 1979 and 1986.

President of the Senate—The vice president of the United States in his constitutional role as presiding officer of the Senate. The Constitution permits the vice president to cast a vote in the Senate only to break a tie, but he is not required to do so.

President Pro Tempore—Under the Constitution, an officer elected by the Senate to preside over it during the absence of the vice president of the United States. Often referred to as the "pro tem," he is usually the majority party senator with the longest continuous service in the chamber and also, by virtue of his seniority, a committee chairman. When attending to committee and other duties, the president pro tempore appoints other senators to preside.

Previous Question—A nondebatable motion which, when agreed to by majority vote, usually cuts off further debate, prevents the offering of additional amendments, and brings the pending matter to an immediate vote. It is a major debate-limiting device in the House; it is not permitted in Committee of the Whole or in the Senate.

Printed Amendment—A House rule guarantees five minutes of floor debate in support and five minutes in opposition, and no other debate time, on amendments printed in the Congressional Record at least one day prior to the amendment's consideration in the Committee of the Whole. In the Senate, although amendments may be submitted for printing, they have no parliamentary standing or status. An amendment submitted for printing in the Senate, however, may be called up by any senator.

Private Bill—A bill that applies to one or more specified persons, corporations, institutions, or other entities, usually to grant relief when no other legal remedy is available to them. Many private bills deal with claims against the federal government, immigration and naturalization cases, and land titles.

Private Calendar—Commonly used title for a calendar in the House reserved for private bills and resolutions favorably reported by committees. The private calendar is officially called the Calendar of the Committee of the Whole House.

Privilege—An attribute of a motion, measure, report, question, or proposition that gives it priority status for consideration. Privileged motions and motions to bring up privileged questions are not debatable.

Privileged Questions—The order in which bills, motions, and other legislative measures are considered by Congress is governed by strict priorities. A motion to table, for instance, is more privileged than a motion to recommit. Thus, a motion to recommit can be superseded by a motion to table, and a vote would be forced on the latter motion only. A motion to adjourn, however, takes precedence over a tabling motion and thus is considered of the "highest privilege." (*See also Questions of Privilege.*)

Pro Forma Amendment—In the House, an amendment that ostensibly proposes to change a measure or another amendment by moving "to strike the last word" or "to strike the requisite number of words." A member offers it not to make any actual change in the measure or amendment but only to obtain time for debate.

Proxy Voting—The practice of permitting a member to cast the vote of an absent colleague in addition to his own vote. Proxy voting is prohibited on the floors of the House and Senate, but the Senate permits its committees to authorize proxy voting, and most do. In 1995, House rules were changed to prohibit proxy voting in committee.

Public Law—A public bill or joint resolution enacted into law. It is cited by the letters P.L. followed by a hyphenated number. The digits before the hyphen indicate the number of the Congress in which it was enacted; the digits after the hyphen indicate its position in the numerical sequence of public measures that became law during that Congress. For example, the

Budget Enforcement Act of 1990 became P.L. 101-508 because it was the 508th measure in that sequence for the 101st Congress. *(See also Private Bill.)*

Queen of the Hill Rule—A special rule from the House Rules Committee that permits votes on a series of amendments, especially complete substitutes for a measure, in a specified order, but directs that the amendment receiving the greatest number of votes shall be the winning one. This kind of rule permits the House to vote directly on a variety of alternatives to a measure. In doing so, it sets aside the precedent that once an amendment has been adopted, no further amendments may be offered to the text it has amended. Under an earlier practice, the Rules Committee reported "king of the hill" rules under which there also could be votes on a series of amendments, again in a specified order. If more than one of the amendments was adopted under this kind of rule, it was the last amendment to receive a majority vote that was considered as having been finally adopted, whether or not it had received the greatest number of votes.

Questions of Privilege—These are matters affecting members of Congress individually or collectively. Matters affecting the rights, safety, dignity, and integrity of proceedings of the House or Senate as a whole are questions of privilege in both chambers.

Questions involving individual members are called questions of "personal privilege." A member rising to ask a question of personal privilege is given precedence over almost all other proceedings. An annotation in the House rules points out that the privilege rests primarily on the Constitution, which gives a member a conditional immunity from arrest and an unconditional freedom to speak in the House. *(See also Privileged Questions.)*

Quorum—The minimum number of members required to be present for the transaction of business. Under the Constitution, a quorum in each house is a majority of its members: 218 in the House and 51 in the Senate when there are no vacancies. By House rule, a quorum in Committee of the Whole is 100. In practice, both houses usually assume a quorum is present even if it is not, unless a member makes a point of no quorum in the House or suggests the absence of a quorum in the Senate. Consequently, each house transacts much of its business, and even passes bills, when only a few members are present.

For House and Senate committees, chamber rules allow a minimum quorum of one-third of a committee's members to conduct most types of business.

Ramseyer Rule—A House rule that requires a committee's report on a bill or joint resolution to show the changes the measure, and any committee amendments to it, would make in existing law.

Readings of Bills—Traditional parliamentary procedure required bills to be read three times before they were passed. This custom is of little modern significance. Normally a bill is considered to have its first reading when it is introduced and printed, by title, in the *Congressional Record*. In the House, its second reading comes when floor consideration begins. (This is the most likely point at which there is an actual reading of the bill, if there is any.) The second reading in the Senate is supposed to occur on the legislative day after the measure is introduced, but before it is referred to committee. The third reading (again, usually by title) takes place when floor action has been completed on amendments.

Reapportionment—*(See Apportionment.)*

Recess—(1) A temporary interruption or suspension of a meeting of a chamber or committee. Unlike an adjournment, a recess does not end a legislative day. Because the Senate often recesses from one calendar day to another, its legislative day may extend over several calendar days, weeks, or even months. (2) A period of adjournment for more than three days to a day certain, especially over a holiday or in August during odd-numbered years.

Recognition—The power of recognition of a member is lodged in the Speaker of the House and the presiding officer of the Senate. The presiding officer names the member who will speak first when two or more members simultaneously request recognition.

Recommit—To send a measure back to the committee that reported it; sometimes called a straight motion to recommit to distinguish it from a motion to recommit with instructions. A successful motion to recommit kills the measure unless it is accompanied by instructions.

Reconciliation—A procedure for changing existing revenue and spending laws to bring total federal revenues and spending within the limits established in a budget resolution. Congress has applied reconciliation chiefly to revenues and mandatory spending programs, especially entitlements. Discretionary spending is controlled through annual appropriation bills.

Reconsider a Vote—A motion to reconsider the vote by which an action was taken has, until it is disposed of, the effect of putting the action in abeyance. In the Senate, the motion can be made only by a member who voted on the prevailing side of the original question or by a member who did not vote at all. In the House, it can be made only by a member on the prevailing side.

A common practice in the Senate after close votes on an issue is a motion to reconsider, followed by a motion to table the motion to reconsider. On this motion to table, senators vote as they voted on the original question, which allows the motion to table to prevail, assuming there are no switches. The matter then is finally closed and further motions to reconsider are not entertained. In the House, as a routine precaution, a motion to reconsider usually is made every time a measure is passed. Such a motion almost always is tabled immediately, thus shutting off the possibility of future reconsideration, except by unanimous consent.

Motions to reconsider must be entered in the Senate within the next two days of actual session after the original vote has been taken. In the House they must be entered either on the same day or on the next succeeding day the House is in session.

Recorded Vote—(1) Generally, any vote in which members are recorded by name for or against a measure; also called a record vote or roll-call vote. The only recorded vote in the Senate is a vote by the yeas and nays and is commonly called a roll-call vote. (2) Technically, a recorded vote is one demanded in the House of Representatives and supported by at least one-fifth of a quorum (44 members) in the House sitting as the House or at least 25 members in Committee of the Whole.

Report—(1) As a verb, a committee is said to report when it submits a measure or other document to its parent chamber. (2) A clerk is said to report when he or she reads a measure's title, text, or the text of an amendment to the body at the direction of the chair. (3) As a noun, a committee document that accompanies a reported measure. It describes the measure, the committee's views on it, its costs, and the changes it proposes to make in existing law; it also includes certain impact statements. (4) A committee document submitted to its parent chamber that describes the results of an investigation or other study or provides information the committee is required to provide by rule or law.

Reprimand—A formal condemnation of a member for misbehavior, considered a milder reproof than censure. The House of Representatives first used it in 1976. The Senate first used itin 1991. (*See also Censure, Code of Official Conduct, Expulsion.*)

Rescission—A provision of law that repeals previously enacted budget authority in whole or in part. Under the Impoundment Control Act of 1974, the president can impound such funds by sending a message to Congress requesting one or more rescissions and the reasons for doing so. If Congress does not pass a rescission bill for the programs requested by the president within 45 days of continuous session after receiving the message, the president must make the funds available for obligation and expenditure. If the president does not, the comptroller general of the United States is authorized to bring suit to compel the release of those funds. A rescission bill may rescind all, part, or none of an amount proposed by the president, and may rescind funds the president has not impounded.

Resolution—(1) A simple resolution; that is, a nonlegislative measure effective only in the house in which it is proposed and not requiring concurrence by the other chamber or approval by the president. Simple resolutions are designated H. Res. in the House and S. Res. in the Senate. Simple resolutions express nonbinding opinions on policies or issues or deal with the internal affairs or prerogatives of a house. (2) Any type of resolution: simple, concurrent, or joint. (*See Concurrent Resolution, Joint Resolution.*)

Revise and Extend One's Remarks—A unanimous consent request to publish in the *Congressional Record* a statement a member did not deliver on the floor, a longer statement than the one made on the floor, or miscellaneous extraneous material.

Rider—Congressional slang for an amendment unrelated or extraneous to the subject matter of the measure to which it is attached. Riders often contain proposals that are less likely to become law on their own merits as separate bills, either because of opposition in the committee of jurisdiction, resistance in the other house, or the probability of a presidential veto. Riders are more common in the Senate.

Rule—(1) A permanent regulation that a house adopts to govern its conduct of business, its procedures, its internal organization, behavior of its members, regulation of its facilities, duties of an officer, or some other subject it chooses to govern in that form. (2) In the House, a privileged simple resolution reported by the Rules Committee that provides methods and conditions for floor consideration of a measure or, rarely, several measures.

Secretary of the Senate—The chief administrative and budgetary officer of the Senate. The secretary manages a wide range of functions that support the operation of the Senate as an organization as well as those functions necessary to its legislative process, including recordkeeping, document management, certifications, housekeeping services, administration of oaths, and lobbyist registrations.

Select or Special Committee—A committee established by a resolution in either house for a special purpose and, usually, for a limited time. Most select and special committees are assigned specific investigations or studies, but are not authorized to report measures to their chambers.

Senate—The house of Congress in which each state is represented by two senators; each senator has one vote. Article V of the Constitution declares that "No State, without its Consent, shall be deprived of its equal Suffrage in the Senate." The Constitution also gives the Senate equal legislative power with the House of Representatives. Although the Senate is prohibited from originating revenue measures, and as a matter of practice it does not originate appropriation measures, it can amend both. Only the Senate can give or withhold consent to treaties and nominations from the president. It also acts as a court to try impeachments by the House and elects the vice president when no candidate receives a majority of the electoral votes. It is often referred to as "the upper body," but not by members of the House.

Senate Manual—The handbook of the Senate's standing rules and orders and the laws and other regulations that apply to the Senate, usually published once each Congress.

Senatorial Courtesy—The Senate's practice of declining to confirm a presidential nominee for an office in the state of a senator of the president's party unless that senator approves.

Sequestration—A procedure for canceling budgetary resources that is, money available for obligation or spending to enforce budget limitations established in law. Sequestered funds are no longer available for obligation or expenditure.

Sine Die—(*See Adjournment Sine Die.*)

Slip Law—The first official publication of a measure that has become law. It is published separately in unbound, single-sheet form or pamphlet form. A slip law usually is available two or three days after the date of the law's enactment.

Speaker—The presiding officer of the House of Representatives and the leader of its majority party. The Speaker is selected by the majority party and formally elected by the House at the beginning of each Congress. Although the Constitution does not require the Speaker to be a member of the House, in fact, all Speakers have been members.

Special Session—A session of Congress convened by the president, under his constitutional authority, after Congress has adjourned sine die at the end of a regular session. (*See Adjournment Sine Die.*)

Spending Authority—The technical term for backdoor spending. The Congressional Budget Act of 1974 defines it as borrowing authority, contract authority, and entitlement authority for which appropriation acts do not provide budget authority in advance. Under the Budget Act, legislation that provides new spending authority may not be considered unless it provides that the authority shall be effective only to the extent or in such amounts as provided in an appropriation act.

Sponsor—The principal proponent and introducer of a measure or an amendment.

Standing Committee—A permanent committee established by a House or Senate standing rule or standing order. The rule also describes the subject areas on which the committee may report bills and resolutions and conduct oversight. Most introduced measures must be referred to one or more standing committees according to their jurisdictions.

Standing Vote—An alternative and informal term for a division vote, during which members in favor of a proposal and then members opposed stand and are counted by the chair. (*See Division Vote.*)

Star Print—A reprint of a bill, resolution, amendment, or committee report correcting technical or substantive errors in a previous printing; so called because of the small black star that appears on the front page or cover.

Statutes at Large—A chronological arrangement of the laws enacted in each session of Congress. Though indexed, the laws are not arranged by subject matter nor is there an indication of how they affect or change previously enacted laws. The volumes are numbered by Congress, and the laws are cited by their volume and page number. The Gramm-Rudman-Hollings Act, for example, appears as 99 Stat. 1037.

Strike from the *Record*—Expunge objectionable remarks from the *Congressional Record,* after a member's words have been taken down on a point of order.

Strike Out the Last Word—A motion whereby a House member is entitled to speak for five minutes on an amendment then being debated by the chamber. A member gains recognition from the chair by moving to "strike out the last word" of the amendment or section of the bill under consideration. The motion is proforma, requires no vote, and does not change the amendment being debated.

Substitute—A motion, amendment, or entire bill introduced in place of the pending legislative business. Passage of a substitute measure kills the original measure by supplanting it. The substitute also may be amended. (*See also Amendment in the Nature of a Substitute.*)

Sunshine Rules—Rules requiring open committee hearings and business meetings, including markup sessions, in both houses, and also open conference committee meetings. However, all may be closed under certain circumstances and using certain procedures required by the rules.

Super Majority—A term sometimes used for a vote on a matter that requires approval by more than a simple majority of those members present and voting; also referred to as extraordinary majority.

Supplemental Appropriation Bill—A measure providing appropriations for use in the current fiscal year, in addition to those already provided in annual general appropriation bills. Supplemental appropriations are often for unforeseen emergencies.

Suspension of the Rules (House)—An expeditious procedure for passing relatively noncontroversial or emergency measures by a two-thirds vote of those members voting, a quorum being present.

Suspension of the Rules (Senate)—A procedure to set aside one or more of the Senate's rules; it is used infrequently, and then most often to suspend the rule banning legislative amendments to appropriation bills.

Table a Bill—Motions to table, or to "lay on the table," are used to block or kill amendments or other parliamentary questions. When approved, a tabling motion is considered the final disposition of that issue. One of the most widely used parliamentary procedures, the motion to table is not debatable, and adoption requires a simple majority vote.

In the Senate, however, different language sometimes is used. The motion may be worded to let a bill "lie on the table," perhaps for subsequent "picking up." This motion is more flexible, keeping the bill pending for later action, if desired. Tabling motions on amendments are effective debate-ending devices in the Senate.

Teller Vote—A voting procedure, formerly used in the House, in which members cast their votes by passing through the center aisle to be counted, but not recorded by name, by a member from each party appointed by the chair. The House deleted the procedure from its rules in 1993, but during floor discussion of the deletion a leading member stated that a teller vote would still be available in the event of a breakdown of the electronic voting system.

Treaty—A formal document containing an agreement between two or more sovereign nations. The Constitution authorizes the president to make treaties, but he must submit them to the Senate for its approval by a two-thirds vote of the senators present. Under the Senate's rules, that vote actually occurs on a resolution of ratification. Although the Constitution does not give the House a direct role in approving treaties, that body has sometimes insisted that a revenue treaty is an invasion of its prerogatives. In any case, the House may significantly affect the application of a treaty by its equal role in enacting legislation to implement the treaty.

Trust Funds—Special accounts in the Treasury that receive earmarked taxes or other kinds of revenue collections, such as user fees, and from which payments are made for special purposes or to recipients who meet the requirements of the trust funds as established by law. Of the more than 150 federal government trust funds, several finance major entitlement programs, such as Social Security, Medicare, and retired federal employees' pensions. Others fund infrastructure construction and improvements, such as highways and airports.

Unanimous Consent—Without an objection by any member. A unanimous consent request asks permission, explicitly or implicitly, to set aside one or more rules. Both houses and their committees frequently use such requests to expedite their proceedings.

Unanimous Consent Agreement—A device used in the Senate to expedite legislation. Much of the Senate's legislative business, dealing with both minor and controversial issues, is conducted through unanimous consent or unanimous consent agreements. On major legislation, such agreements usually are printed and transmitted to all senators in advance of floor debate. Once agreed to, they are binding on all members unless the Senate, by unanimous consent, agrees to modify them. An agreement may list the order in which various bills are to be considered, specify the length of time bills and contested amendments are to be debated and when they are to be voted upon, and, frequently, require that all amendments introduced be germane to the bill under consideration. In this regard, unanimous consent agreements are similar to the "rules" issued by the House Rules Committee for bills pending in the House.

Unfunded Mandate—Generally, any provision in federal law or regulation that imposes a duty or obligation on a state or local government or private sector entity without providing the necessary funds to comply. The Unfunded Mandates Reform Act of 1995 amended the Congressional Budget Act of 1974 to provide a mechanism for the control of new unfunded mandates.

Union Calendar—A calendar of the House of Representatives for bills and resolutions favorably reported by committees that raise revenue or directly or indirectly appropriate money or property. In addition to appropriation bills, measures that authorize expenditures are also placed on this calendar. The calendar's full title is the Calendar of the Committee of the Whole House on the State of the Union.

U.S. Code—Popular title for the *United States Code: Containing the General and Permanent Laws of the United States in Force on. . . .* It is a consolidation and partial codification of the general and permanent laws of the United States arranged by subject under 50 titles. The first six titles deal with general or political subjects, the other 44 with subjects ranging from agriculture to war, alphabetically arranged. A supplement is published after each session of Congress, and the entire Code is revised every six years.

Veto—The president's disapproval of a legislative measure passed by Congress. He returns the measure to the house in which it originated without his signature but with a veto message stating his objections to it. When Congress is in session, the president must veto a bill within 10 days, excluding Sundays, after he has received it; otherwise it becomes law without his signature. The 10-day clock begins to run at midnight following his receipt of the bill. (*See also Committee Veto, Item Veto, Override a Veto, Pocket Veto.*)

Voice Vote—A method of voting in which members who favor a question answer aye in chorus, after which those opposed answer no in chorus, and the chair decides which position prevails.

War Powers Resolution of 1973—An act that requires the president "in every possible instance" to consult Congress before he commits U.S. forces to ongoing or imminent hostilities. If he commits them to a combat situation without congressional consultation, he must notify Congress within 48 hours. Unless Congress declares war or otherwise authorizes the operation to continue, the forces must be withdrawn within 60 or 90 days, depending on certain conditions. No president has ever acknowledged the constitutionality of the resolution.

Whip—The majority or minority party member in each house who acts as assistant leader, helps plan and marshal support for party strategies, encourages party discipline, and advises his leader on how his colleagues intend to vote on the floor. In the Senate, the Republican whip's official title is assistant leader.

Without Objection—Used in lieu of a vote on noncontroversial motions, amendments, or bills that may be passed in either the House or Senate if no member voices an objection.

Yeas and Nays—A vote in which members usually respond "aye" or "no" (despite the official title of the vote) on a question when their names are called in alphabetical order. The Constitution requires the yeas and nays when a demand for it is supported by one-fifth of the members present, and it also requires an automatic yea-and-nay vote on overriding a veto. Senate precedents require the support of at least one-fifth of a quorum, a minimum of 11 members with the present membership of 100.

Yielding—When a member has been recognized to speak, no other member may speak unless he or she obtains permission from the member recognized. This permission is called yielding and usually is requested in the form, "Will the gentleman yield to me?" While this activity occasionally is seen in the Senate, the Senate has no rule or practice to parcel out time.

Constitution of the United States

We the People of the United States, in Order to form a more perfect Union, establish Justice, insure domestic Tranquility, provide for the common defence, promote the general Welfare, and secure the Blessings of Liberty to ourselves and our Posterity, do ordain and establish this Constitution for the United States of America.

ARTICLE I

Section 1. All legislative Powers herein granted shall be vested in a Congress of the United States, which shall consist of a Senate and House of Representatives.

Section 2. The House of Representatives shall be composed of Members chosen every second Year by the People of the several States, and the Electors in each State shall have the Qualifications requisite for Electors of the most numerous Branch of the State Legislature.

No Person shall be a Representative who shall not have attained to the age of twenty five Years, and been seven Years a Citizen of the United States, and who shall not, when elected, be an Inhabitant of that State in which he shall be chosen.

[Representatives and direct Taxes shall be apportioned among the several States which may be included within this Union, according to their respective Numbers, which shall be determined by adding to the whole Number of free Persons, including those bound to Service for a Term of Years, and excluding Indians not taxed, three fifths of all other Persons.][1] The actual Enumeration shall be made within three Years after the first Meeting of the Congress of the United States, and within every subsequent Term of ten Years, in such Manner as they shall by Law direct. The Number of Representatives shall not exceed one for every thirty Thousand, but each State shall have at Least one Representative; and until such enumeration shall be made, the State of New Hampshire shall be entitled to chuse three, Massachusetts eight, Rhode-Island and Providence Plantations one, Connecticut five, New-York six, New Jersey four, Pennsylvania eight, Delaware one, Maryland six, Virginia ten, North Carolina five, South Carolina five, and Georgia three.

When vacancies happen in the Representation from any State, the Executive Authority thereof shall issue Writs of Election to fill such Vacancies.

The House of Representatives shall chuse their Speaker and other Officers; and shall have the sole Power of Impeachment.

Section 3. The Senate of the United States shall be composed of two Senators from each State, [chosen by the Legislature thereof,][2] for six Years; and each Senator shall have one Vote.

Immediately after they shall be assembled in Consequence of the first Election, they shall be divided as equally as may be into three Classes. The Seats of the Senators of the first Class shall be vacated at the Expiration of the second Year, of the second Class at the Expiration of the fourth Year, and of the third Class at the Expiration of the sixth Year, so that one third may be chosen every second Year; [and if Vacancies happen by Resignation, or otherwise, during the Recess of the Legislature of any State, the Executive thereof may make temporary Appointments until the next Meeting of the Legislature, which shall then fill such Vacancies.][3]

No Person shall be a Senator who shall not have attained to the Age of thirty Years, and been nine Years a Citizen of the United States, and who shall not, when elected, be an Inhabitant of that State for which he shall be chosen.

The Vice President of the United States shall be President of the Senate, but shall have no Vote, unless they be equally divided.

The Senate shall chuse their other Officers, and also a President pro tempore, in the Absence of the Vice President, or when he shall exercise the Office of President of the United States.

The Senate shall have the sole Power to try all Impeachments. When sitting for that Purpose, they shall be on Oath or Affirmation. When the President of the United States is tried, the Chief Justice shall preside: And no Person shall be convicted without the Concurrence of two thirds of the Members present.

Judgment in Cases of Impeachment shall not extend further than to removal from Office, and disqualification to hold and enjoy any Office of honor, Trust or Profit under the United States: but the Party convicted shall nevertheless be liable and subject to Indictment, Trial, Judgment and Punishment, according to Law.

Section 4. The Times, Places and Manner of holding Elections for Senators and Representatives, shall be prescribed in each State by the Legislature thereof; but the Congress may at any time by Law make or alter such Regulations, except as to the Places of chusing Senators.

The Congress shall assemble at least once in every Year, and such Meeting shall [be on the first Monday in December],[4] unless they shall by Law appoint a different Day.

Section 5. Each House shall be the Judge of the Elections, Returns and Qualifications of its own Members, and a Majority of each shall constitute a Quorum to do Business; but a smaller Number may adjourn from day to day, and may be authorized to compel the Attendance of absent Members, in such Manner, and under such Penalties as each House may provide.

Each House may determine the Rules of its Proceedings, punish its Members for disorderly Behaviour, and, with the Concurrence of two thirds, expel a Member.

Each House shall keep a Journal of its Proceedings, and from time to time publish the same, excepting such Parts as may in their Judgment require Secrecy; and the Yeas and Nays of the Members of either House on any question shall, at the Desire of one fifth of those Present, be entered on the Journal.

Neither House, during the Session of Congress, shall, without the Consent of the other, adjourn for more than three days, nor to any other Place than that in which the two Houses shall be sitting.

Section 6. The Senators and Representatives shall receive a Compensation for their Services, to be ascertained by Law, and paid out of the Treasury of the United States. They shall in all Cases, except Treason, Felony and Breach of the Peace, be privileged from Arrest during their Attendance at the Session of their respective Houses, and in going to and returning from the same; and for any Speech or Debate in either House, they shall not be questioned in any other Place.

No Senator or Representative shall, during the Time for which he was elected, be appointed to any civil Office under the Authority of the United States, which shall have been created, or the Emoluments whereof shall have been encreased during such time; and no Person holding any Office under the United States, shall be a Member of either House during his Continuance in Office.

Section 7. All Bills for raising Revenue shall originate in the House of Representatives; but the Senate may propose or concur with Amendments as on other Bills.

Every Bill which shall have passed the House of Representatives and the Senate, shall, before it become a Law, be presented to the President of the United States; If he approve he shall sign it, but if not he shall return it, with his Objections to that House in which it shall have originated, who shall enter the Objections at large on their Journal, and proceed to reconsider it. If after such Reconsideration two thirds of that House shall agree to pass the Bill, it shall be sent, together with the Objections, to the other House, by which it shall likewise be reconsidered, and if approved by two thirds of that House, it shall become a Law. But in all such Cases the Votes of both Houses shall be determined by yeas and Nays, and the Names of the Persons voting for and against the Bill shall be entered on the Journal of each House respectively. If any Bill shall not be returned by the President within ten Days (Sundays excepted) after it shall have been presented to him, the Same shall be a Law, in like Manner as if he had signed it, unless the Congress by their Adjournment prevent its Return, in which Case it shall not be a Law.

Every Order, Resolution, or Vote to which the Concurrence of the Senate and House of Representatives may be necessary (except on a question of Adjournment) shall be presented to the President of the United States; and before the Same shall take Effect, shall be approved by him, or being disapproved by him, shall be repassed by two thirds of the Senate and House of Representatives, according to the Rules and Limitations prescribed in the Case of a Bill.

Section 8. The Congress shall have Power To lay and collect Taxes, Duties, Imposts and Excises, to pay the Debts and provide for the common Defence and general Welfare of the United States; but all Duties, Imposts and Excises shall be uniform throughout the United States;

To borrow Money on the credit of the United States;

To regulate Commerce with foreign Nations, and among the several States, and with the Indian Tribes;

To establish an uniform Rule of Naturalization, and uniform Laws on the subject of Bankruptcies throughout the United States;

To coin Money, regulate the Value thereof, and of foreign Coin, and fix the Standard of Weights and Measures;

To provide for the Punishment of counterfeiting the Securities and current Coin of the United States;

To establish Post Offices and post Roads;

To promote the Progress of Science and useful Arts, by securing for limited Times to Authors and Inventors the exclusive Right to their respective Writings and Discoveries;

To constitute Tribunals inferior to the supreme Court;

To define and punish Piracies and Felonies committed on the high Seas, and Offences against the Law of Nations;

To declare War, grant Letters of Marque and Reprisal, and make Rules concerning Captures on Land and Water;

To raise and support Armies, but no Appropriation of Money to that Use shall be for a longer Term than two Years;

To provide and maintain a Navy;

To make Rules for the Government and Regulation of the land and naval Forces;

To provide for calling forth the Militia to execute the Laws of the Union, suppress Insurrections and repel Invasions;

To provide for organizing, arming, and disciplining, the Militia, and for governing such Part of them as may be employed in the Service of the United States, reserving to the States respectively, the Appointment of the Officers, and the Authority of training the Militia according to the discipline prescribed by Congress;

To exercise exclusive Legislation in all Cases whatsoever, over such District (not exceeding ten Miles square) as may, by Cession of particular States, and the Acceptance of Congress, become the Seat of the Government of the United States, and to exercise like Authority over all Places purchased by the Consent of the Legislature of the State in which the Same shall be, for the Erection of Forts, Magazines, Arsenals, dock-Yards, and other needful Buildings; — And

To make all Laws which shall be necessary and proper for carrying into Execution the foregoing Powers, and all other Powers vested by this Constitution in the Government of the United States, or in any Department or Officer thereof.

Section 9. The Migration or Importation of such Persons as any of the States now existing shall think proper to admit, shall not be prohibited by the Congress prior to the Year one thousand eight hundred and eight, but a Tax or duty may be imposed on such Importation, not exceeding ten dollars for each Person.

The Privilege of the Writ of Habeas Corpus shall not be suspended, unless when in Cases of Rebellion or Invasion the public Safety may require it.

No Bill of Attainder or ex post facto Law shall be passed.

No Capitation, or other direct, Tax shall be laid, unless in Proportion to the Census or Enumeration herein before directed to be taken.[5]

No Tax or Duty shall be laid on Articles exported from any State.

No Preference shall be given by any Regulation of Commerce or Revenue to the Ports of one State over those of another; nor shall Vessels bound to, or from, one State, be obliged to enter, clear, or pay Duties in another.

No Money shall be drawn from the Treasury, but in Consequence of Appropriations made by Law; and a regular Statement and Account of the Receipts and Expenditures of all public Money shall be published from time to time.

No Title of Nobility shall be granted by the United States: And no Person holding any Office of Profit or Trust under them, shall, without the Consent of the Congress, accept of any present, Emolument, Office, or Title, of any kind whatever, from any King, Prince, or foreign State.

Section 10. No State shall enter into any Treaty, Alliance, or Confederation; grant Letters of Marque and Reprisal; coin Money; emit Bills of Credit; make any Thing but gold and silver Coin a Tender in Payment of Debts; pass any Bill of Attainder, ex post facto Law, or Law impairing the Obligation of Contracts, or grant any Title of Nobility.

No State shall, without the Consent of the Congress, **lay** any Imposts or Duties on Imports or Exports, except what may be absolutely necessary for executing it's inspection Laws: and the net Produce of all Duties and Imposts, laid by any State on Imports or Exports, shall be for the Use of the Treasury of the United States; and all such Laws shall be subject to the Revision and Controul of the Congress.

No State shall, without the Consent of Congress, lay any Duty of Tonnage, keep Troops, or Ships of War in time of Peace, enter into any Agreement or Compact with another State, or with a foreign Power, or engage in War, unless actually invaded, or in such imminent Danger as will not admit of delay.

ARTICLE II

Section 1. The executive Power shall be vested in a President of the United States of America. He shall hold his Office during the Term of four Years, and, together with the Vice President, chosen for the same Term, be elected, as follows

Each State shall appoint, in such Manner as the Legislature thereof may direct, a Number of Electors, equal to the whole Number of Senators and Representatives to which the State may be entitled in the Congress: but no Senator or Representative, or Person holding an Office of Trust or Profit under the United States, shall be appointed an Elector.

[The Electors shall meet in their respective States, and vote by Ballot for two Persons, of whom one at least shall not be an Inhabitant of the same State with themselves. And they shall make a List of all the Persons voted for, and of the Number of Votes for each; which List they shall sign and certify, and transmit sealed to the Seat of the Government of the United States, directed to the President of the Senate. The President of the Senate shall, in the Presence of the Senate and House of Representatives, open all the Certificates, and the Votes shall then be counted. The Person having the greatest Number of Votes shall be the President, if such Number be a Majority of the whole Number of Electors appointed; and if there be more than one who have such Majority, and have an equal Number of Votes, then the House of Representatives shall immediately chuse by Ballot one of them for President; and if no Person have a Majority, then from the five highest on the list the said House shall in like Manner chuse the President. But in chusing the President, the Votes shall be taken by States, the Representation from each State having one Vote; A quorum for this Purpose shall consist of a Member or Members from two thirds of the States, and a Majority of all the States shall be necessary to a Choice. In every Case, after the Choice of the President, the Person having the greatest Number of Votes of the Electors shall be the Vice President. But if there should remain two or more who have equal Votes, the Senate shall chuse from them by Ballot the Vice President.][6]

The Congress may determine the Time of chusing the Electors, and the Day on which they shall give their Votes; which Day shall be the same throughout the United States.

No Person except a natural born Citizen, or a Citizen of the United States, at the time of the Adoption of this Constitution, shall be eligible to the Office of President; neither shall any Person be eligible to that Office who shall not have attained to the Age of thirty five Years, and been fourteen Years a Resident within the United States.

In Case of the Removal of the President from Office, or of his Death, Resignation, or Inability to discharge the Powers and Duties of the said Office,[7] the Same shall devolve on the Vice President, and the Congress may by Law provide for the Case of Removal, Death, Resignation or Inability, both of the President and Vice President, declaring what Officer shall then act as President, and such Officer shall act accordingly, until the Disability be removed, or a President shall be elected.

The President shall, at stated Times, receive for his Services, a Compensation, which shall neither be encreased nor diminished during the Period for which he shall have been elected, and he shall not receive within that Period any other Emolument from the United States, or any of them.

Before he enter on the Execution of his Office, he shall take the following Oath or Affirmation: — "I do solemnly swear (or affirm) that I will faithfully execute the Office of President of the United States, and will to the best of my Ability, preserve, protect and defend the Constitution of the United States."

Section 2. The President shall be Commander in Chief of the Army and Navy of the United States, and of the Militia of the several States, when called into the actual Service of the United States; he may require the Opinion, in writing, of the principal Officer in each of the executive Departments, upon any Subject relating to the Duties of their respective Offices, and he shall have Power to grant Reprieves and Pardons for Offences against the United States, except in Cases of Impeachment.

He shall have Power, by and with the Advice and Consent of the Senate, to make Treaties, provided two thirds of the Senators present concur; and he shall nominate, and by and with the Advice and Consent of the Senate, shall appoint Ambassadors, other public Ministers and Consuls, Judges of the supreme Court, and all other Officers of the United States, whose Appointments are not herein otherwise provided for, and which shall be established by Law: but the Congress may by Law vest the Appointment of such inferior Officers, as they think proper, in the President alone, in the Courts of Law, or in the Heads of Departments.

The President shall have Power to fill up all Vacancies that may happen during the Recess of the Senate, by granting Commissions which shall expire at the End of their next Session.

Section 3. He shall from time to time give to the Congress Information of the State of the Union, and recommend to their Consideration such Measures as he shall judge necessary and expedient; he may, on extraordinary Occasions, convene both Houses, or either of them, and in Case of Disagreement between them, with Respect to the Time of Adjournment, he may adjourn them to such Time as he shall think proper; he shall receive Ambassadors and other public Ministers; he shall take Care that the Laws be faithfully executed, and shall Commission all the Officers of the United States.

Section 4. The President, Vice President and all civil Officers of the United States, shall be removed from Office on Impeachment for, and Conviction of, Treason, Bribery, or other high Crimes and Misdemeanors.

ARTICLE III

Section 1. The judicial Power of the United States, shall be vested in one supreme Court, and in such inferior Courts as the Congress may from time to time ordain and establish. The Judges, both of the supreme and inferior Courts, shall hold their

Offices during good Behaviour, and shall, at stated Times, receive for their Services, a Compensation, which shall not be diminished during their Continuance in Office.

Section 2. The judicial Power shall extend to all Cases, in Law and Equity, arising under this Constitution, the Laws of the United States, and Treaties made, or which shall be made, under their Authority; — to all Cases affecting Ambassadors, other public Ministers and Consuls; — to all Cases of admiralty and maritime Jurisdiction; — to Controversies to which the United States shall be a Party; — to Controversies between two or more States; — between a State and Citizens of another State;[8] — between Citizens of different States; — between Citizens of the same State claiming Lands under Grants of different States, and between a State, or the Citizens thereof, and foreign States, Citizens or Subjects.

In all Cases affecting Ambassadors, other public Ministers and Consuls, and those in which a State shall be Party, the supreme Court shall have original Jurisdiction. In all the other Cases before mentioned, the supreme Court shall have appellate Jurisdiction, both as to Law and Fact, with such Exceptions, and under such Regulations as the Congress shall make.

The Trial of all Crimes, except in Cases of Impeachment, shall be by Jury; and such Trial shall be held in the State where the said Crimes shall have been committed; but when not committed within any State, the Trial shall be at such Place or Places as the Congress may by Law have directed.

Section 3. Treason against the United States, shall consist only in levying War against them, or in adhering to their Enemies, giving them Aid and Comfort. No Person shall be convicted of Treason unless on the Testimony of two Witnesses to the same overt Act, or on Confession in open Court.

The Congress shall have Power to declare the Punishment of Treason, but no Attainder of Treason shall work Corruption of Blood, or Forfeiture except during the Life of the Person attainted.

ARTICLE IV

Section 1. Full Faith and Credit shall be given in each State to the public Acts, Records, and judicial Proceedings of every other State. And the Congress may by general Laws prescribe the Manner in which such Acts, Records and Proceedings shall be proved, and the Effect thereof.

Section 2. The Citizens of each State shall be entitled to all Privileges and Immunities of Citizens in the several States.

A Person charged in any State with Treason, Felony, or other Crime, who shall flee from Justice, and be found in another State, shall on Demand of the executive Authority of the State from which he fled, be delivered up, to be removed to the State having Jurisdiction of the Crime.

[No Person held to Service or Labour in one State, under the Laws thereof, escaping into another, shall, in Consequence of any Law or Regulation therein, be discharged from such Service or Labour, but shall be delivered up on Claim of the Party to whom such Service or Labour may be due.][9]

Section 3. New States may be admitted by the Congress into this Union; but no new State shall be formed or erected within the Jurisdiction of any other State; nor any State be formed by the Junction of two or more States, or Parts of States, without the Consent of the Legislatures of the States concerned as well as of the Congress.

The Congress shall have Power to dispose of and make all needful Rules and Regulations respecting the Territory or other Property belonging to the United States; and nothing in this Constitution shall be so construed as to Prejudice any Claims of the United States, or of any particular State.

Section 4. The United States shall guarantee to every State in this Union a Republican Form of Government, and shall protect each of them against Invasion; and on Application of the Legislature, or of the Executive (when the Legislature cannot be convened) against domestic Violence.

ARTICLE V

The Congress, whenever two thirds of both Houses shall deem it necessary, shall propose Amendments to this Constitution, or, on the Application of the Legislatures of two thirds of the several States, shall call a Convention for proposing Amendments, which, in either Case, shall be valid to all Intents and Purposes, as Part of this Constitution, when ratified by the Legislatures of three fourths of the several States, or by Conventions in three fourths thereof, as the one or the other Mode of Ratification may be proposed by the Congress; Provided [that no Amendment which may be made prior to the Year One thousand eight hundred and eight shall in any Manner affect the first and fourth Clauses in the Ninth Section of the first Article; and][10] that no State, without its Consent, shall be deprived of its equal Suffrage in the Senate.

ARTICLE VI

All Debts contracted and Engagements entered into, before the Adoption of this Constitution, shall be as valid against the United States under this Constitution, as under the Confederation.

This Constitution, and the Laws of the United States which shall be made in Pursuance thereof; and all Treaties made, or which shall be made, under the Authority of the United States, shall be the supreme Law of the Land; and the Judges in every State shall be bound thereby, any Thing in the Constitution or Laws of any State to the Contrary notwithstanding.

The Senators and Representatives before mentioned, and the Members of the several State Legislatures, and all executive and judicial Officers, both of the United States and of the several States, shall be bound by Oath or Affirmation, to support this Constitution; but no religious Test shall ever be required as a Qualification to any Office or public Trust under the United States.

ARTICLE VII

The Ratification of the Conventions of nine States, shall be sufficient for the Establishment of this Constitution between the States so ratifying the Same.

Done in Convention by the Unanimous Consent of the States present the Seventeenth Day of September in the Year of our Lord one thousand seven hundred and Eighty seven and of the Independence of the United States of America the Twelfth. IN WITNESS whereof We have hereunto subscribed our Names,

George Washington,
President and
deputy from Virginia.

New Hampshire:	John Langdon
	Nicholas Gilman.
Massachusetts:	Nathaniel Gorham,
	Rufus King.
Connecticut:	William Samuel Johnson,
	Roger Sherman.

New York:	Alexander Hamilton.
New Jersey:	William Livingston,
	David Brearley,
	William Paterson,
	Jonathan Dayton.
Pennsylvania:	Benjamin Franklin,
	Thomas Mifflin,
	Robert Morris,
	George Clymer,
	Thomas FitzSimons,
	Jared Ingersoll,
	James Wilson,
	Gouverneur Morris.
Delaware:	George Read,
	Gunning Bedford Jr.,
	John Dickinson,
	Richard Bassett,
	Jacob Broom.
Maryland:	James McHenry,
	Daniel of St. Thomas Jenifer,
	Daniel Carroll.
Virginia:	John Blair,
	James Madison Jr.
North Carolina:	William Blount,
	Richard Dobbs Spaight,
	Hugh Williamson.
South Carolina:	John Rutledge,
	Charles Cotesworth Pinckney,
	Charles Pinckney,
	Pierce Butler.
Georgia:	William Few,
	Abraham Baldwin.

[The language of the original Constitution, not including the Amendments, was adopted by a convention of the states on September 17, 1787, and was subsequently ratified by the states on the following dates: Delaware, December 7, 1787; Pennsylvania, December 12, 1787; New Jersey, December 18, 1787; Georgia, January 2, 1788; Connecticut, January 9, 1788; Massachusetts, February 6, 1788; Maryland, April 28, 1788; South Carolina, May 23, 1788; New Hampshire, June 21, 1788.

Ratification was completed on June 21, 1788.

The Constitution subsequently was ratified by Virginia, June 25, 1788; New York, July 26, 1788; North Carolina, November 21, 1789; Rhode Island, May 29, 1790; and Vermont, January 10, 1791.]

Amendments

Amendment I

(First ten amendments ratified December 15, 1791.)

Congress shall make no law respecting an establishment of religion, or prohibiting the free exercise thereof; or abridging the freedom of speech, or of the press; or the right of the people peaceably to assemble, and to petition the Government for a redress of grievances.

Amendment II

A well regulated Militia, being necessary to the security of a free State, the right of the people to keep and bear Arms, shall not be infringed.

Amendment III

No Soldier shall, in time of peace be quartered in any house, without the consent of the Owner, nor in time of war, but in a manner to be prescribed by law.

Amendment IV

The right of the people to be secure in their persons, houses, papers, and effects, against unreasonable searches and seizures, shall not be violated, and no Warrants shall issue, but upon probable cause, supported by Oath or affirmation, and particularly describing the place to be searched, and the persons or things to be seized.

Amendment V

No person shall be held to answer for a capital, or otherwise infamous crime, unless on a presentment or indictment of a Grand Jury, except in cases arising in the land or naval forces, or in the Militia, when in actual service in time of War or public danger; nor shall any person be subject for the same offence to be twice put in jeopardy of life or limb; nor shall be compelled in any criminal case to be a witness against himself, nor be deprived of life, liberty, or property, without due process of law; nor shall private property be taken for public use, without just compensation.

Amendment VI

In all criminal prosecutions, the accused shall enjoy the right to a speedy and public trial, by an impartial jury of the State and district wherein the crime shall have been committed, which district shall have been previously ascertained by law, and to be informed of the nature and cause of the accusation; to be confronted with the witnesses against him; to have compulsory process for obtaining witnesses in his favor, and to have the Assistance of Counsel for his defence.

Amendment VII

In Suits at common law, where the value in controversy shall exceed twenty dollars, the right of trial by jury shall be preserved, and no fact tried by a jury, shall be otherwise re-examined in any Court of the United States, than according to the rules of the common law.

Amendment VIII

Excessive bail shall not be required, nor excessive fines imposed, nor cruel and unusual punishments inflicted.

Amendment IX

The enumeration in the Constitution, of certain rights, shall not be construed to deny or disparage others retained by the people.

Amendment X

The powers not delegated to the United States by the Constitution, nor prohibited by it to the States, are reserved to the States respectively, or to the people.

Amendment XI (Ratified February 7, 1795)

The Judicial power of the United States shall not be construed to extend to any suit in law or equity, commenced or prosecuted against one of the United States by Citizens of another State, or by Citizens or Subjects of any Foreign State.

Amendment XII (Ratified June 15, 1804)

The Electors shall meet in their respective states and vote by ballot for President and Vice-President, one of whom, at least, shall not be an inhabitant of the same state with themselves; they shall name in their ballots the person voted for as President, and in distinct ballots the person voted for as Vice-President, and they shall make distinct lists of all persons voted for as President, and of all persons voted for as Vice-President, and of the number of votes for each, which lists they shall sign and certify, and transmit sealed to the seat of the government of the United States, directed to the President of the Senate; — The President of the Senate shall, in the presence of the Senate and House of Representatives, open all the certificates and the votes shall then be counted; — The person having the greatest number of votes for President, shall be the President, if such number be a majority of the whole number of Electors appointed; and if no person have such majority, then from the persons having the highest numbers not exceeding three on the list of those voted for as President, the House of Representatives shall choose immediately, by ballot, the President. But in choosing the President, the votes shall be taken by states, the representation from each state having one vote; a quorum for this purpose shall consist of a member or members from two-thirds of the states, and a majority of all the states shall be necessary to a choice. [And if the House of Representatives shall not choose a President whenever the right of choice shall devolve upon them, before the fourth day of March next following, then the Vice-President shall act as President, as in the case of the death or other constitutional disability of the President. —][11] The person having the greatest number of votes as Vice-President, shall be the Vice-President, if such number be a majority of the whole number of Electors appointed, and if no person have a majority, then from the two highest numbers on the list, the Senate shall choose the Vice-President; a quorum for the purpose shall consist of two-thirds of the whole number of Senators, and a majority of the whole number shall be necessary to a choice. But no person constitutionally ineligible to the office of President shall be eligible to that of Vice-President of the United States.

Amendment XIII (Ratified December 6, 1865)

Section 1. Neither slavery nor involuntary servitude, except as a punishment for crime whereof the party shall have been duly convicted, shall exist within the United States, or any place subject to their jurisdiction.

Section 2. Congress shall have power to enforce this article by appropriate legislation.

Amendment XIV (Ratified July 9, 1868)

Section 1. All persons born or naturalized in the United States, and subject to the jurisdiction thereof, are citizens of the United States and of the State wherein they reside. No State shall make or enforce any law which shall abridge the privileges or immunities of citizens of the United States; nor shall any State deprive any person of life, liberty, or property, without due process of law; nor deny to any person within its jurisdiction the equal protection of the laws.

Section 2. Representatives shall be apportioned among the several States according to their respective numbers, counting the whole number of persons in each State, excluding Indians not taxed. But when the right to vote at any election for the choice of electors for President and Vice President of the United States, Representatives in Congress, the Executive and Judicial officers of a State, or the members of the Legislature thereof, is denied to any of the male inhabitants of such State, being

twenty-one years of age,[12] and citizens of the United States, or in any way abridged, except for participation in rebellion, or other crime, the basis of representation therein shall be reduced in the proportion which the number of such male citizens shall bear to the whole number of male citizens twenty-one years of age in such State.

Section 3. No person shall be a Senator or Representative in Congress, or elector of President and Vice President, or hold any office, civil or military, under the United States, or under any State, who, having previously taken an oath, as a member of Congress, or as an officer of the United States, or as a member of any State legislature, or as an executive or judicial officer of any State, to support the Constitution of the United States, shall have engaged in insurrection or rebellion against the same, or given aid or comfort to the enemies thereof. But Congress may by a vote of two-thirds of each House, remove such disability.

Section 4. The validity of the public debt of the United States, authorized by law, including debts incurred for payment of pensions and bounties for services in suppressing insurrection or rebellion, shall not be questioned. But neither the United States nor any State shall assume or pay any debt or obligation incurred in aid of insurrection or rebellion against the United States, or any claim for the loss or emancipation of any slave; but all such debts, obligations and claims shall be held illegal and void.

Section 5. The Congress shall have power to enforce, by appropriate legislation, the provisions of this article.

Amendment XV (Ratified February 3, 1870)

Section 1. The right of citizens of the United States to vote shall not be denied or abridged by the United States or by any State on account of race, color, or previous condition of servitude.

Section 2. The Congress shall have power to enforce this article by appropriate legislation.

Amendment XVI (Ratified February 3, 1913)

The Congress shall have power to lay and collect taxes on incomes, from whatever source derived, without apportionment among the several States, and without regard to any census or enumeration.

Amendment XVII (Ratified April 8, 1913)

The Senate of the United States shall be composed of two Senators from each State, elected by the people thereof, for six years; and each Senator shall have one vote. The electors in each State shall have the qualifications requisite for electors of the most numerous branch of the State legislatures.

When vacancies happen in the representation of any State in the Senate, the executive authority of such State shall issue writs of election to fill such vacancies: *Provided,* That the legislature of any State may empower the executive thereof to make temporary appointments until the people fill the vacancies by election as the legislature may direct.

This amendment shall not be so construed as to affect the election or term of any Senator chosen before it becomes valid as part of the Constitution.

Amendment XVIII (Ratified January 16, 1919)[13]

Section 1. After one year from the ratification of this article the manufacture, sale, or transportation of intoxicating liquors within, the importation thereof into, or the exportation thereof from the United States and all territory subject to the jurisdiction thereof for beverage purposes is hereby prohibited.

Section 2. The Congress and the several States shall have concurrent power to enforce this article by appropriate legislation.

Section 3. This article shall be inoperative unless it shall have been ratified as an amendment to the Constitution by the legislatures of the several States, as provided in the Constitution, within seven years from the date of the submission hereof to the States by the Congress.

Amendment XIX (Ratified August 18, 1920)

The right of citizens of the United States to vote shall not be denied or abridged by the United States or by any State on account of sex.

Congress shall have power to enforce this article by appropriate legislation.

Amendment XX (Ratified January 23, 1933)

Section 1. The terms of the President and Vice President shall end at noon on the 20th day of January, and the terms of Senators and Representatives at noon on the 3d day of January, of the years in which such terms would have ended if this article had not been ratified; and the terms of their successors shall then begin.

Section 2. The Congress shall assemble at least once in every year, and such meeting shall begin at noon on the 3d day of January, unless they shall by law appoint a different day.

Section 3.[14] If, at the time fixed for the beginning of the term of the President, the President elect shall have died, the Vice President elect shall become President. If a President shall not have been chosen before the time fixed for the beginning of his term, or if the President elect shall have failed to qualify, then the Vice President elect shall act as President until a President shall have qualified; and the Congress may by law provide for the case wherein neither a President elect nor a Vice President elect shall have qualified, declaring who shall then act as President, or the manner in which one who is to act shall be selected, and such person shall act accordingly until a President or Vice President shall have qualified.

Section 4. The Congress may by law provide for the case of the death of any of the persons from whom the House of Representatives may choose a President whenever the right of choice shall have devolved upon them, and for the case of the death of any of the persons from whom the Senate may choose a Vice President whenever the right of choice shall have devolved upon them.

Section 5. Sections 1 and 2 shall take effect on the 15th day of October following the ratification of this article.

Section 6. This article shall be inoperative unless it shall have been ratified as an amendment to the Constitution by the legislatures of three-fourths of the several States within seven years from the date of its submission.

Amendment XXI (Ratified December 5, 1933)

Section 1. The eighteenth article of amendment to the Constitution of the United States is hereby repealed.

Section 2. The transportation or importation into any State, Territory, or possession of the United States for delivery or use therein of intoxicating liquors, in violation of the laws thereof, is hereby prohibited.

Section 3. This article shall be inoperative unless it shall have been ratified as an amendment to the Constitution by

conventions in the several States, as provided in the Constitution, within seven years from the date of the submission hereof to the States by the Congress.

Amendment XXII (Ratified February 27, 1951)

Section 1. No person shall be elected to the office of the President more than twice, and no person who has held the office of President, or acted as President, for more than two years of a term to which some other person was elected President shall be elected to the office of the President more than once. But this Article shall not apply to any person holding the office of President when this Article was proposed by the Congress, and shall not prevent any person who may be holding the office of President, or acting as President, during the term within which this Article become operative from holding the office of President or acting as President during the remainder of such term.

Section 2. This article shall be inoperative unless it shall have been ratified as an amendment to the Constitution by the legislatures of three-fourths of the several States within seven years from the date of its submission to the States by the Congress.

Amendment XXIII (Ratified March 29, 1961)

Section 1. The District constituting the seat of Government of the United States shall appoint in such manner as the Congress may direct:

A number of electors of President and Vice President equal to the whole number of Senators and Representatives in Congress to which the District would be entitled if it were a State, but in no event more than the least populous State; they shall be in addition to those appointed by the States, but they shall be considered, for the purposes of the election of President and Vice President, to be electors appointed by a State; and they shall meet in the District and perform such duties as provided by the twelfth article of amendment.

Section 2. The Congress shall have power to enforce this article by appropriate legislation.

Amendment XXIV (Ratified January 23, 1964)

Section 1. The right of citizens of the United States to vote in any primary or other election for President or Vice President, for electors for President or Vice President, or for Senator or Representative in Congress, shall not be denied or abridged by the United States or any State by reason of failure to pay any poll tax or other tax.

Section 2. The Congress shall have power to enforce this article by appropriate legislation.

Amendment XXV (Ratified February 10, 1967)

Section 1. In case of the removal of the President from office or of his death or resignation, the Vice President shall become President.

Section 2. Whenever there is a vacancy in the office of the Vice President, the President shall nominate a Vice President who shall take office upon confirmation by a majority vote of both Houses of Congress.

Section 3. Whenever the President transmits to the President pro tempore of the Senate and the Speaker of the House of Representatives his written declaration that he is unable to discharge the powers and duties of his office, and until he transmits to them a written declaration to the contrary, such powers and duties shall be discharged by the Vice President as Acting President.

Section 4. Whenever the Vice President and a majority of either the principal officers of the executive departments or of such other body as Congress may by law provide, transmit to the President pro tempore of the Senate and the Speaker of the House of Representatives their written declaration that the President is unable to discharge the powers and duties of his office, the Vice President shall immediately assume the powers and duties of the office as Acting President.

Thereafter, when the President transmits to the President pro tempore of the Senate and the Speaker of the House of Representatives his written declaration that no inability exists, he shall resume the powers and duties of his office unless the Vice President and a majority of either the principal officers of the executive department or of such other body as Congress may by law provide, transmit within four days to the President pro tempore of the Senate and the Speaker of the House of Representatives their written declaration that the President is unable to discharge the powers and duties of his office. Thereupon Congress shall decide the issue, assembling within forty-eight hours for that purpose if not in session. If the Congress, within twenty-one days after receipt of the latter written declaration, or, if Congress is not in session, within twenty-one days after Congress is required to assemble, determines by two-thirds vote of both Houses that the President is unable to discharge the powers and duties of his office, the Vice President shall continue to discharge the same as Acting President; otherwise, the President shall resume the powers and duties of his office.

Amendment XXVI (Ratified July 1, 1971)

Section 1. The right of citizens of the United States, who are eighteen years of age or older, to vote shall not be denied or abridged by the United States or by any State on account of age.

Section 2. The Congress shall have power to enforce this article by appropriate legislation.

Amendment XXVII (Ratified May 7, 1992)

No law varying the compensation for the services of the Senators and Representatives shall take effect, until an election of Representatives shall have intervened.

Notes

1. The part in brackets was changed by section 2 of the Fourteenth Amendment.
2. The part in brackets was changed by the first paragraph of the Seventeenth Amendment.
3. The part in brackets was changed by the second paragraph of the Seventeenth Amendment.
4. The part in brackets was changed by section 2 of the Twentieth Amendment.
5. The Sixteenth Amendment gave Congress the power to tax incomes.
6. The material in brackets has been superseded by the Twelfth Amendment.
7. This provision has been affected by the Twenty-fifth Amendment.
8. These clauses were affected by the Eleventh Amendment.
9. This paragraph has been superseded by the Thirteenth Amendment.
10. Obsolete.
11. The part in brackets has been superseded by section 3 of the Twentieth Amendment.
12. See the Nineteenth and Twenty-sixth Amendments.
13. This Amendment was repealed by section 1 of the Twenty-first Amendment.
14. See the Twenty-fifth Amendment.

SOURCE: U.S. Congress, House, Committee on the Judiciary, *The Constitution of the United States of America, as Amended*, 100th Cong., 1st sess., 1987, H Doc 100-94.

Congressional Information on the Internet

A huge array of congressional information is available for free at Internet sites operated by the federal government, colleges and universities, and commercial firms. The sites offer the full text of bills introduced in the House and Senate, voting records, campaign finance information, transcripts of selected congressional hearings, investigative reports, and much more.

THOMAS

The most important site for congressional information is THOMAS (*http://thomas.loc.gov*), which is named for Thomas Jefferson and operated by the Library of Congress. THOMAS's highlight is its databases containing the full text of all bills introduced in Congress since 1989, the full text of the *Congressional Record* since 1989, and the status and summary information for all bills introduced since 1973.

THOMAS also offers special links to bills that have received or are expected to receive floor action during the current week and newsworthy bills that are pending or that have recently been approved. Finally, THOMAS has selected committee reports, answers to frequently asked questions about accessing congressional information, publications titled *How Our Laws Are Made* and *Enactment of a Law*, and links to lots of other congressional Web sites.

House of Representatives

The U.S. House of Representatives site (*http://www.house.gov*) offers the schedule of bills, resolutions, and other legislative issues the House will consider in the current week. It also has updates about current proceedings on the House floor and a list of the next day's meeting of House committees. Other highlights include a database that helps users identify their representative, a directory of House members and committees, the House ethics manual, links to Web pages maintained by House members and committees, a calendar of congressional primary dates and candidate-filing deadlines for ballot access, the full text of all amendments to the Constitution that have been ratified and those that have been proposed but not ratified, and lots of information about Washington, D.C., for visitors.

Another key House site is The Office of the Clerk On-line Information Center (*http://clerkweb.house.gov*), which has records of all roll-call votes taken since 1990. The votes are recorded by bill, so it is a lengthy process to compile a particular representative's voting record. The site also has lists of committee assignments, a telephone directory for members and committees, mailing label templates for members and committees, rules of the current Congress, election statistics from 1920 to the present, biographies of Speakers of the House, biographies of women who have served since 1917, and a virtual tour of the House Chamber.

One of the more interesting House sites is operated by the Subcommittee on Rules and Organization of the House

Committee on Rules (*http://www.house.gov/rules/crs_reports. htm*). Its highlight is dozens of Congressional Research Service reports about the legislative process. Some of the available titles include *Legislative Research in Congressional Offices: A Primer, How to Follow Current Federal Legislation and Regulations, Investigative Oversight: An Introduction to the Law, Practice, and Procedure of Congressional Inquiry*, and *Presidential Vetoes 1789– Present: A Summary Overview*.

A final House site is the Internet Law Library (*http://uscode. house.gov*). This site has a searchable version of the U.S. Code, which contains the text of public laws enacted by Congress, and a tutorial for searching the Code. There also is a huge collection of links to other Internet sites that provide state and territorial laws, laws of other nations, and treaties and international laws.

Senate

At least in the Internet world, the Senate is not as active as the House. Its main Web site (*http://www.senate.gov*) has records of all roll-call votes taken since 1989 (arranged by bill), brief descriptions of all bills and joint resolutions introduced in the Senate during the past week, and a calendar of upcoming committee hearings. The site also provides the standing rules of the Senate, a directory of senators and their committee assignments, lists of nominations that the president has submitted to the Senate for approval, links to Web pages operated by senators and committees, and a virtual tour of the Senate.

Information about the membership, jurisdiction, and rules of each congressional committee is available at the U.S. Government Printing Office site (*http://www.access.gpo.gov/congress/ index.html*). It also has transcripts of selected congressional hearings, the full text of selected House and Senate reports, and the House and Senate rules manuals.

General Reference

The U.S. General Accounting Office, the investigative arm of Congress, operates a site (*http://www.gao.gov*) that provides the full text of its reports from 1996 to the present. The reports cover a wide range of topics: aviation safety, combating terrorism, counternarcotics efforts in Mexico, defense contracting, electronic warfare, food assistance programs, Gulf War illness, health insurance, illegal aliens, information technology, long-term care, mass transit, Medicare, military readiness, money laundering, national parks, nuclear waste, organ donation, student loan defaults, and the year 2000 computing crisis, among others.

The GAO Daybook is an excellent current awareness tool. This electronic mailing list distributes a daily list of reports and testimony released by the GAO. Subscriptions are available by sending an E-mail message to *majordomo@www.gao.gov*, and in the message area typing "subscribe daybook" (without the quotation marks).

Current budget and economic projections are provided at the Congressional Budget Office Web site (*http://www.cbo.gov*). The site also has reports about the economic and budget outlook for the next decade, the president's budget proposals, federal civilian employment, Social Security privatization, tax reform, water use conflicts in the West, marriage and the federal income tax, and the role of foreign aid in development, among other topics. Other highlights include monthly budget updates, historical budget data, cost estimates for bills reported by congressional committees, and transcripts of congressional testimony by CBO officials.

Campaign Finance

Several Internet sites provide detailed campaign finance data for congressional elections. The official site is operated by the Federal Election Commission (*http://www.fec.gov*), which regulates political spending. The site's highlight is its database of campaign reports filed from May 1996 to the present by House and presidential candidates, political action committees, and political party committees. Senate reports are not included because they are filed with the Secretary of the Senate. The reports in the FEC's database are scanned images of paper reports filed with the commission.

The FEC site also has summary financial data for House and Senate candidates in the current election cycle, abstracts of court decisions pertaining to federal election law from 1976 to 1997, a graph showing the number of political action committees in existence each year from 1974 to the present, and a directory of national and state agencies that are responsible for releasing information about campaign financing, candidates on the ballot, election results, lobbying, and other issues. Another useful feature is a collection of brochures about federal election law, public funding of presidential elections, the ban on contributions by foreign nationals, independent expenditures supporting or opposing a candidate for federal office, contribution limits, filing a complaint, researching public records at the FEC, and other topics. Finally, the site provides the FEC's legislative

recommendations, its annual report, a report about its first twenty years in existence, the FEC's monthly newsletter, several reports about voter registration, election results for the most recent presidential and congressional elections, and campaign guides for corporations and labor organizations, congressional candidates and committees, political party committees, and nonconnected committees.

The best online source for campaign finance data is FECInfo (*http://www.tray.com/fecinfo*), which is operated by former Federal Election Commission employee Tony Raymond. FECInfo's searchable databases provide extensive itemized information about receipts and expenditures by federal candidates and political action committees from 1980 to the present. The data, which are obtained from the FEC, are quite detailed. For example, for candidates contributions can be searched by Zip Code. The site also has data on soft money contributions, lists of the top political action committees in various categories, lists of the top contributors from each state, and much more.

Another interesting site is Campaign Finance Data on the Internet (*http://www1.soc.american.edu/campfin*), which is operated by the American University School of Communication. It provides electronic files from the FEC that have been reformatted in .dbf format so they can be used in database programs such as Paradox, Access, and FoxPro. The files contain data on PAC, committee, and individual contributions to individual congressional candidates.

More campaign finance data is available from the Center for Responsive Politics (*http://www.opensecrets.org*), a public interest organization. The center provides a list of all "soft money" donations to political parties of $100,000 or more in the current election cycle and data about "leadership" political action committees associated with individual politicians. Other databases at the site provide information about travel expenses that House members received from private sources for attending meetings and other events, activities of registered federal lobbyists, and activities of foreign agents who are registered in the United States.

Index